Counter-Terrorist Financing Law and Policy

Since the 9/11 attacks the world has witnessed the creation of both domestic and international legal instruments designed to disrupt and interdict the financial activities of terrorists. This book analyses the counter-terrorist financing law (CTF), policy and practice at the national level, focusing on Turkey. The work examines the limits and capabilities of CTF efforts on terrorism threats and determines the effectiveness of CTF efforts in Turkey, a country which has a pivotal role in terms of countering terrorism regionally and internationally.

The Turkish case study is supported by an empirical study involving 37 semi-structured interviews with CTF practitioners and law enforcement experts with different affiliations and backgrounds. The findings illustrate that Turkey's CTF system has not obtained an adequate level of effectiveness as a result of lack of proper implementation of its policy in the bureaucratic, legal and operational spheres. It is evident that the administrative and legal systems in Turkey are established according to the 'one-size-fits-all' international CTF standards and thus are compliant with the international CTF benchmarks, yet the interviews reveal significant challenges at the implementation level including lack of training and financial security, heavy handed bureaucracy, inadequate coordination and communication between international and national levels.

This book will be an invaluable resource for academics, students and policy makers working in the areas of financial crime and terrorism.

Bürke Uğur Başaranel, Gendarmerie and Coast Guard Academy, Ankara, TURKEY.

Umut Türkşen, Coventry Law School and Centre for Financial and Corporate Integrity, Coventry University, UK.

The Law of Financial Crime
Series Editor: Nicholas Ryder

Available titles in this series include:

Fighting Financial Crime in the Global Economic Crisis
Nicholas Ryder, Umut Türkşen and Sabine Hassler

The Financial War on Terror
A Review of Counter-Terrorist Financing Strategies Since 2001
Nicholas Ryder

The Financial Crisis and White Collar Crime – Legislative and Policy Responses
A Critical Assessment
Edited by Nicholas Ryder, Jon Tucker and Umut Türkşen

Countering Economic Crime
A Comparative Analysis
Axel Palmer

The Global Anti-Corruption Regime
The Case of Papua New Guinea
Hannah Harris

Financial Crime and Corporate Misconduct
A Critical Evaluation of Fraud Legislation
Edited by Chris Monaghan and Nicola Monaghan

Corporate Liability for Insider Trading
Juliette Overland

Corruption in the Global Era
Causes, Sources and Forms of Manifestation
Lorenzo Pasculli and Nicholas Ryder

For more information about this series, please visit: www.routledge.com/The-Law-of-Financial-Crime/book-series/FINCRIME

Counter-Terrorist Financing Law and Policy

An analysis of Turkey

Bürke Uğur Başaranel and
Umut Türkşen

Routledge
Taylor & Francis Group
LONDON AND NEW YORK

First published 2019
by Routledge

2 Park Square, Milton Park, Abingdon, Oxfordshire OX14 4RN
52 Vanderbilt Avenue, New York, NY 10017

Routledge is an imprint of the Taylor & Francis Group, an informa business

First issued in paperback 2020

British Library Cataloguing-in-Publication Data
A catalogue record for this book is available from the British Library

Library of Congress Cataloging-in-Publication Data
A catalog record for this book has been requested

ISBN: 978-1-138-59263-6 (hbk)
ISBN: 978-0-367-67097-9 (pbk)

Typeset in Galliard
by Apex CoVantage, LLC

Contents

Acknowledgements

This book could not have been possible without the generous support of Swansea University and Coventry University.

Umut would like to thank his wife, Jo, and his children, Melike, Evren and Kyra, for having the patience with him for taking on yet another book project.

Bürke would like to thank his wife, Selma, their daughter, Serap Naida, and his sister, Pelin, for their unwavering support and love during the writing of this book.

We dedicate this book to all the victims of terrorism.

Figures

Abbreviations

AEDPA:	Antiterrorism and Effective Death Penalty Act
AKP:	Justice and Development Party
AML:	Anti-Money Laundering
ARA:	Armenian Revolutionary Army
ARF:	Armenian Revolutionary Federation
ASALA:	Armenian Secret Army for the Liberation of Armenia
ATM:	Automatic Teller Machine
BDP:	Peace and Democracy Party
BSA:	Bank Secrecy Act
CDD:	Customer Due Diligence
CHP:	Republican People's Party
CIA:	Central Intelligence Agency
COE:	Council of Europe
CT:	Counter-Terrorism
CTF:	Counter-Terrorist Financing
CTC:	Counter Terrorism Committee
C-TED:	Counter-Terrorism Executive Directorate
CTRs:	Currency Transaction Reports
DEA:	Drug Enforcement Agency
DHKP/C:	Revolutionary People's Liberation Party/Front
ELF:	Earth Liberation Front
ETA:	Basque Fatherland and Liberty
EU:	European Union
FARC:	Revolutionary Armed Forces of Colombia
FATF:	Financial Action Task Force
FBI:	Federal Bureau of Investigation
FETO/PSS:	Fetullahist Terrorist Organisation/Parallel State Structure
FinCEN:	Financial Crimes Enforcement Network
FIU:	Financial Intelligence Unit
FSRBs:	FATF-Style Regional Bodies
IBDA-C:	Great Eastern Islamic Raiders' Front
ICSFT:	International Convention for the Suppression of the Financing of Terrorism

IED: Improvised Explosive Device
IEEPA: International Emergency Economic Powers Act
IHH: Turkish Foundation for Human Rights and Freedoms and Humanitarian Relief
IMF: International Monetary Fund
IRA: Irish Republican Army
IRS: Financial Institution Regulators and Internal Revenue Service
IS: Islamic State
ISIS: The 'so-called' Islamic State of Iraq and Syria
IVTS: Informal Value Transfer Systems
JCAG: Justice Commandos of the Armenian Genocide
KDGM: Turkish Undersecretariat of Public Order and Security
KYC: Know Your Customer
LTTE: Liberation Tigers of Tamil Eelam
MASAK: Turkish Financial Crimes Investigation Board
MFA: Turkish Ministry of Foreign Affairs
MHP: Nationalist Movement Party
MIT: Turkish National Intelligence Agency
MLA: Mutual Legal Assistance
MLKP: Marxist Leninist Communist Party
MMOGs: Massively Multi Player Online Games
MSBs: Money Sending Businesses
NATO: North Atlantic Treaty Organization
NCCT: Non-Cooperative Countries and Territories
NGO: Non-Governmental Organisation
NSC: National Security Council of Turkey
NORAID: Irish Northern Aid Committee
OECD: Organisation for Economic Cooperation and Development
OFAC: Office of Foreign Assets Control
PATRIOT: Providing Appropriate Tools Required to Intercept and Obstruct Terrorism
PIRA: Provisional Irish Republican Army
PKK: Kurdistan Workers' Party
PLO: Palestinian Liberation Organisation
PYD: Democratic Union Party
SARs: Suspicious Activity Reports
SDGTs: Specially Designated Global Terrorists
START: National Consortium for the Study of Terrorism and Responses to Terrorism
STRs: Suspicious Transaction Reports
SWIFT: Society for Worldwide Interbank Financial Telecommunication
TAK: Kurdistan Freedom Falcons
TCC: Turkish Criminal Code
TCO: Transnational Criminal Organisation
TE-SAT: EU Terrorism Situation and Trend Report

TFTP: Terrorist Financing Tracking Program
TKP/ML: Turkish Communist Party/Marxist-Leninist
TPAO: Turkish Petroleum Corporation
TÜPRAŞ: Turkish Petroleum Refineries Corporation
UN: United Nations
UNODC: United Nations Office on Drugs and Crime
UNSC: United Nations Security Council
UNSCR: United Nations Security Council Resolution
US: United States of America
UYAP: National Judiciary Informatics System
WB: World Bank
WODC: Netherlands Ministry of Justice Research and Document Centre
YPG: People's Protection Units

1 Introduction

1.1 Background

Looking from a retrospective lens there are many milestones where history was shaped by key events such as breaking up of the Roman Empire, the invention of nuclear weapons and fall of the Berlin Wall. The infamous date of 11 September 2001 is also one of these critical turning points in the history not only for the people of the United States of America but also the rest of the world (The Guardian, 2002). In the wake of this horrendous incident, before starting to conduct a kinetic 'War on Terror', the US government started to wage a financial war against the terrorists and their sponsors. For many, this type of struggle against terrorism was rather new with all its implications and impact globally.

While this targeting of financing of terrorism is thought to be a new and novel approach, in reality it was not. Since the 1970s, in addition to the West German counter-terrorism efforts against the Baader-Meinhof Gang or Red Army Faction (RAF), the UK government has conducted significant counter-terrorism policies and strategies against terrorist groups by targeting their financial sources coming from the Republican and Loyalists organisations such as the Irish Republican Army (IRA), the Provisional IRA (PIRA), the Ulster Defence Force (UDF) and the Ulster Volunteer Force (UVF) (Adams, 1986; Horgan & Taylor, 1999, 2003; Silke, 1998, 2000). Moreover, the legal instruments produced by the United Nations (UN) such as the International Convention for the Suppression of the Financing of Terrorism (1999) (the Convention),[1] and series of Security Council Resolutions including the UN Security Council Resolution 1267 (1999) for Al Qaeda and Taliban and after the attacks on 9/11, the UN Security Council Resolution 1373 (2001) can be grouped as the first initiatives at the international sphere.

What made this new financial counter-terrorism approach stand out was its swift global expansion and transformation, and the main claim regarding pledges for addressing terrorist organisations and their structures using the analogy of

1 Ryder asserts that the "International Convention was *heavily* influenced by the al-Qaeda terrorist attacks on the US embassies in Nairobi and Dar es Salaam on August 13, 1998 . . ." (Ryder, 2015, p. 6).

"[m]oney is the lifeblood of terrorist operations" (Bush, 2001b). The increasing amount of the frozen assets and the number of people and entities blacklisted because of CTF processes increased both at the national level in the US and further afield internationally (Ryder & Turksen, 2013). It should be noted that prior to the attacks of 9/11 there were only four signatories to the Convention. After 9/11, this number increased significantly. At the time of writing this book, there were 188 parties and 132 signatories to the International Convention (UN Treaty Collections, 2017).

The binding UN Security Council Resolutions (in particular Resolution 1373) have become a pivotal authority and a reference point for regional and national CTF measures (United Nations, 2016). Resolution 1373 contains four key CTF provisions.[2] Firstly, it requires states to thwart and control the financing of terrorism. Secondly, it criminalises the collection of terrorist funds in states' territories. Thirdly, it allows for freezing of the funds, financial assets and economic resources of people who commit or try to commit acts of terrorism. Finally, it prohibits any national within the states' territories to provide funds, financial assets or economic resources to people who seek to commit acts of terrorism.

According to this 'new' type of counter-terrorism strategy, countering terrorist financing is designed to fulfil four main objectives.

- Prevention of terrorist acts, or disrupting their activities or mitigating the effects of terrorism;
- Deterrence of people supporting terrorists by creating awareness or training those who might provide support wittingly or unwittingly;
- Gathering intelligence on terrorist networks or post- or pre-terrorist attacks; and
- Protecting political advantage to gain the trust and support of the public and show them that suitable actions are being taken by the authorities against terrorists (Eckert & Biersteker, 2010).

Although there is no available data to confirm to what extent the first three of these objectives were achieved successfully other than the untested claims of the officials (Builta & Heller, 2011), the last objective might be said to have been utilised by governments effectively. In order to convince the public about such achievements, official figures relating to designated names and frozen assets were also published. For example, the high level of designations and asset freezing conducted by the Department of Treasury was published by the Bush administration on a monthly basis (Roth, Greenburg, & Wille, 2004, p. 79).

2 The scope and remit of UN Security Council Resolution 1373 has been amended by UN Security Council Resolutions 1390, 1456 and 1566 respectively. This series of measures has criminalised the financing of terrorism, compelled nation states to tackle terrorist financing, legitimised the freezing of terrorist assets and travel bans on suspects and put in place a sanctions regime.

It is evident that the assistance and the support of the US for this new type of fight against terrorism has propelled the issue to a multilateral level. In other words, the unilateral US based CTF measures[3] were exported to the multilateral international environment through the assistance of the UN in general and the UN Counter-Terrorism Committee in particular as well as other key international organisations such as the Financial Action Task Force (FATF), the International Monetary Foundation (IMF) and the World Bank (WB). Applying this new international strategy and regime, which are mainly converted from the existing anti-money laundering applications, a novel set of rules, standards, tasks and serious costs have been introduced for the public and private sectors to comply with. Furthermore, as will be explained in Chapter 3, various mechanisms and incentives have been used in order to motivate and/or coerce states and members of the financial sector to fully adopt international CTF standards. Biersteker and Eckert (2008b) and Passas (2006b) approach this issue from a critical standpoint, noting that this new "one for all" application of the AML converted CTF regime both in the US and the international milieu caused many grievances in terms of human and privacy rights. Moreover, it has brought an undeniably high cost for private financial sector compliance (Geiger, 2007; de Goede, 2012; McCulloch & Pickering, 2005; LexisNexis, 2016; and Ryder & Turksen, 2009). As de Goede (2012) argues, the untested application of blacklisting or designations; asset freezing; sanctions on non-profit organisations and alternative value transfer systems; racial and religious profiling; and non-legal financial surveillance applications created an environment in which security and financial domains conflate, and the daily lives of people become a part of security and speculation.

On the other hand, the proponents of this new type of financial warfare argue that "[m]oney is their [terrorists'] enabler, but it's also their Achilles' heel" (Zarate, 2013, p. 2). While the recent individual terrorist acts may not require substantial amounts of money[4] and resources or require sophisticated levels of preparation (e.g. a telephone call to a racing event claiming that there is a bomb in one of the parked vehicles would cost pennies or a rental car to commit violent attacks on people would cost less than a hundred US dollars), terrorist organisations, networks and individuals therein require substantial financial support and funds for their activities before and after their terrorist acts. While some of the terrorist funding is created via organised criminal activities (*inter alia*, robbery,

3 The initial US Presidential Executive Order 13224 following the 9/11 attacks allowed the Department of Treasury to freeze the funds of Osama bin Laden, members of al Qaeda and the Taliban (Exec. Order No. 13,224, 66 Fed. Reg. 49,079 (Sept. 23, 2001)). This was soon followed by the USA Patriot Act 2001, Title III of which was entitled, 'The International Money Laundering Abatement and Anti-Terrorist Financing Act 2001'. Title III is divided into three sections or subtitles. The first is entitled 'International Counter Money Laundering'; the second is Bank Secrecy Act Amendments and Related Improvements'; and the third 'Currency Crimes and Protection' (USA Patriot Act 2001, Pub. L. No. 107–56, § 311–377).

4 See Ryder (2018), presenting a critical account of the cost of recent terrorist attacks.

drug trafficking, extortion, kidnapping, looting and selling of historical artefacts in the black market), a number of more recent terrorist organisations (e.g. ISIS) possess quasi-state like attributes and act in a state like fashion in order to finance their activities.

For example, ISIS receives gifts and zakat;[5] collects taxes; sells electricity, gas and oil; runs internet cafes; and controls border crossings and other amenities (Cohen, 2014). It is well known that many of these financing activities take place across borders. Another source of funding can be charitable donations (U.S. Department of Treasury, 2017): fundraisers operating in more permissive jurisdictions in the Middle East solicit donations ultimately destined for terrorist groups (Cohen, 2014a). It has been reported that these networks as well as numerous non-profit organisations use couriers, wire transfers, hawalas and exchange houses to move those funds to Syria, often to extremists (Cohen, 2014a).

Given these realities, the main logic behind combating the financial sources of terrorism is based on the postulation that every terrorist organisation needs financial resources, and without transferable assets they cannot survive and sustain their operations. Therefore, it is supposed that if this weakness could be exploited, then terrorist organisations would be eliminated. Although, at least in theory, this idea sounds good and at the first glance seems easily implementable, from a practical point of view it is almost impossible to realise it in the current conditions. In the following chapter, it will be illustrated that the terrorists have plenty of financial sources and various methods for collecting, using, moving and storing currencies and other valuable assets by exploiting every possible opportunity available to them. Another untested assumption faced by this new CTF regime is the compatibility and complementary nature of AML measures, which are mainly designed for preventing and detecting proceeds of crimes generated by transnational/organised crime syndicates whose main motivations are based on mostly financial gains. Furthermore, another challenge and area of uncertainty is the lack of commonly accepted or academically confirmed findings on the efficacy of the current international and domestic level of CTF regimes. As Levi (2010, p. 662) noted, "[c]urrently, it remains largely a matter of faith in assertions by those in authority rather than on published evidence that anti-terror financial intelligence efforts have some impact beyond the immediate operational outcomes". In other words, it is only an untested assumption that the current CTF regime and related applications work effectively and produce desired outcomes against terrorist threats. Therefore, all of these issues emerge as critical questions, which need to be scrutinised through detailed and evidence-based research and critical inquiry.

Although huge amounts of investment and financial support have been given by states and the private sector for establishing, adopting and implementing CTF

5 Zakat is one of the Five Pillars of Islam which requires, according to some interpretations, a Muslim to pay 1/40 (2.5%) of his/her wealth and income annually for charitable and religious purposes.

systems, determining the extent to which the existing CTF system can be used for addressing terrorist financing remains a significant knowledge gap in the field of counter-terrorism studies. In this respect, conceiving the capabilities and limitations of CTF in specific contexts and jurisdictions can be useful for developing and amending counter approaches designed against the terrorism threat. Such a systematic inquiry also provides the opportunity for policy makers and other officials to calibrate the accuracy and improve the strength of CTF enforcement measures. If particular policies and practices were found not to be effective, these could inform other jurisdictions and would save states and financial sectors wasting efforts and resources and avoid unwanted side effects in terms of violation of human rights and privacy.

Within this context, the book aims to contribute to the understanding of both the nature of terrorist financing and the counter-terrorist financing activities. Firstly, the analysis in this book reveals that having all the main international legal instruments and related CTF institutions in place at the national level does not guarantee that an overall CTF system will be implemented effectively or produce the desired results at an operational level.

Secondly, as observed in the case of the Republic of Turkey, states which did not have previous experience in counter-terrorist financing and the necessary financial security bureaucracy could face difficulties in undertaking CTF focused law enforcement capabilities. Building such a capacity requires a training process which needs time and long-term investment. The multifaceted and multidisciplinary nature of CTF forces responsible actors and key stakeholders into developing an interagency working environment and specialisation on the key elements of terrorist financing and counter measures at an institutional level. Staff working on CTF related missions and operations need to possess a complex combination of expertise and experience including counter-terrorism policing methods, intelligence gathering, forensic accountancy and criminal justice rather than a monolithic background which ignores critical enablers and capabilities.

Thirdly, as will be seen in the case of Turkey and in light of the interviews conducted with experts from different law enforcement backgrounds, adopting a CTF regime which is designed and directed against the threats from a Western interpretation of the issue might not always be compatible with the target countries' interests and the unique security threats they encounter. In other words, a 'one for all' approach can fail to address unique conditions that exist at the national level thus may yield limited or different results. For instance, narrow interpretation of and approach to CTF purely focusing on religiously motivated terrorism automatically excludes other types of terrorist threats. The majority of UNSC Resolutions in the context of countering terrorism concentrate on the domains of financial activities of terrorists and terrorist organisations, and the recent official reports and legal provisions at the national level (e.g. in the US and the UK) mainly target religiously inspired terrorist groups such as Al Qaeda, Al Nusra, and more recently the so-called ISIS. These organisations and individuals are all part of radical the Islamic movement which targets Western countries and their interests by intimidation and terrorist acts all over the world. That is why countries such as the US, the UK, Australia and members of the European Union which represent the Western bloc support and spearhead the international CTF measures target these religiously inspired terrorist organisations globally (Turksen, 2010). However, it should be noted (as it was also mentioned during the interviews we conducted) that there are not many terrorist organisations named or targeted financially other than religiously inspired terrorist organisations such as Al Qaeda, Hezbollah, Boko Haram or the so-called ISIS. This situation inevitably creates difficulties for states which face different forms of terrorist threat and thus have different priorities to address and accordingly adopt unique approaches in terms of targeting the financial activities of these terrorist groups. Consequently, finding a common understanding in terms of tested and effective CTF measures has emerged as a critical point.

Arguably (as outlined above), the UN Resolution 1373 (2001) seems to cover this gap by its over-encompassing yet vague provisions. However, it can be argued that this resolution is more like a reminder or a user manual, owing to its neutral character which does not designate any terrorist groups or entities, unlike preceding UN Resolutions. It is worth noting that the UNSC Resolutions which are created under Chapter 7 of the UN Charter are legally binding on the UN member states, and the UNSC CTC is tasked with monitoring the compliance of the member states with these UNSC Resolutions. However, in practice, UN Resolution 1373 (2001) does not have any enforcement mechanism or weight for addressing other types of terrorist threats. Owing to the lack of a universal definition of terrorism in this Resolution or in any other international legal instrument and the fact that there are no designated terrorist organisations listed therein, it is hard to decide what is terrorism and who is a terrorist and who shall be targeted according to this Resolution at the international level. Without having an accurate or a unified definition of terrorism, each country has a different approach and conflicting decisions on what constitutes terrorism and the appropriate methods to counter it and punish its perpetrators. Unsurprisingly, the contentious nature of the act of defining terrorism or determining and naming terrorist organisations and persons plays a negative role in countering financing of terrorism both at policy and operational levels.

As the case of Turkey clearly illustrates, even though Turkey has faced both national and international terrorist threats over the last five decades and been conducting dense counter-terrorism campaigns against different types of terrorist organisations since the 1970s, it did not incorporate any explicit CTF measures in its counter-terrorism policy and strategy. Furthermore, the current international CTF regime is not successful at meeting the interests of individual states owing to the costs of implementation and at times because of the blanket approach therein. Subsequently, states choose the simplest and/or cheapest course of action and superficial application of the CTF regime, rather than embracing the spirit of countering the financing of terrorism. As is demonstrated by our analysis in Chapter 5, even though the newly enacted CTF legislation (Law on Prevention of Financing of Terrorism, 2013) of Turkey is in compliance with the international CTF regime in general, the important features of its legal instruments, such as asset freezing provisions, cannot even be applied to terrorist organisations domestically owing to national legal concerns. Such a trend indicates that the main concern of the individual states might be fulfilling the recommended requirements on their face value rather than imbedding CTF as an integral part of their counter-terrorism strategy. This might also mean that the vital importance and the role played by the CTF applications for countering terrorism, as mainly evaluated uncritically by Western authorities and international organisations, are not shared and perceived similarly at the national/state level. In other words, CTF might be seen as a burden for these countries.

Another important argument we put forward is that cooperation at both the domestic and international levels is critical for conducting an effective CTF. This applies to both internal/domestic terrorist threats and international terrorism. Although the internal cooperation and coordination problems might be similar for many countries (Council on Foreign Relations, 2011),[6] this research indicates that bureaucratic structure and the bureaucratic positions of institutions can be significant for improving the coordination and cooperation. Structures and designs can be changed and should be adapted according to the specific conditions of the country, terrorist organisations and social, cultural, economic and political situations. However, having an interagency type organisation could be of key importance for creating the right environment for cooperation and coordination between all the responsible units. Moreover, it should be pointed out that there are difficulties arising from the tension between the private financial sector and law enforcement and government officials due to the sensitive and classified nature of the information in terms of financial activities of terrorist groups and terror suspects. As examined in Chapter 3 and the case of Turkey, CTF has mainly revolved around high security issues which are very difficult for intelligence and security institutions to share with the private sector. Yet the private sector needs this kind of sensitive information in order to render a big chunk of financial data into more accurate and well selected CTF related financial data and reporting, which can be more efficient and useful for the intelligence and security agencies' efforts. Obviously, there is a paradox here, and as one of the CTF experts rightly notes in Chapter 5, this is an 'asymmetric information problem' which needs to be solved by the practitioners from the private and public sectors.

Regarding CTF cooperation at the international level, the case of Turkey illustrates that although there are many designated or blacklisted terrorist organisations as well as numerous soft (e.g. FATF Recommendations, 2012c) and hard (e.g. UNSC Resolutions) international legal instruments, the international cooperation – in real terms – has not reached the desired level. It has been

6 The Council on Foreign Relations (2011) indicated that the current international counterterrorism regime has three main weaknesses. Firstly, lack of a universal agreement over what constitutes terrorism. Secondly, multilateral cooperation and action in compliance and enforcement of existing CTF instruments. Thirdly, although counter-radicalisation and de-radicalisation initiatives have gained some attention over the last five years, progress is lacking, particularly in states with limited resources and expertise.

observed that states might be ignorant or indifferent about certain terrorist organisations, even about those that exist, generate funds and operate within their borders, or even worse, about those that are designated in their own terrorist lists, as long as they do not pose a direct serious threat to them. This insincerity is a very critical issue which hampers the seriousness of the efforts of the states for collective action against terrorist financing.[7] It can be asserted that even if a state has an exemplary CTF legal system, without sincere collective multilateral cooperation and coordination there will be no ultimate success against terrorists as the terrorist assets are generated in several jurisdictions and move across several borders before being utilised.

Since the first CTF measures have been implemented in Turkey pursuant to the amendments to the Turkish Anti-Terror Laws in 2006, terrorist organisations, especially PKK, have not experienced any serious financial shortage or an inability to sustain operational activities. Consequently, it is not possible to declare that the CTF regime in Turkey, which incorporates international CTF standards into its statutes, has had the desired efficacy. In the confines of the case of Turkey, it has not been possible to determine with certainty whether this failure is caused by the incompetence of the practitioners and institutional deficiencies, or the inadequacy of the overall impact of CTF efforts in the face of a terrorist organisation which has high capacity and sophisticated financing avenues.

In this book four different but interrelated explanations for the inadequacy of Turkey's current CTF system are examined in Chapter 5. The analysis shows that firstly, having all the legislative and related CTF institutions in place at the national level does not guarantee an effective CTF system. Secondly, states such as Turkey, with limited CTF experience, struggle to implement CTF, and therefore training is needed. Thirdly, in light of the unique conditions and security threats in Turkey, the 'Western' interpretation and priority – namely 'war against Islamist terrorism' – are not necessarily compatible with Turkey's main security concerns. Finally, states are essentially adopting the CTF regime on paper without critical evaluation of whether such measures fit operation and enforcement capabilities. Although the first three explanations are important and examined thoroughly, it can be highlighted that the level of CTF training at the individual and institutional level is the cardinal component of the CTF system of Turkey in terms of increasing the levels of implementation and effectiveness. In tandem with having the right legal regime (efficacy of the CTF measures) in a given jurisdiction, for an effective CTF system and implementation in practice, fit for purpose training is essential because in order to counter the financing of terrorism there must be competent and well-trained CTF practitioners, who can apply and

7 For example, in context of the terrorist attacks by the PKK (Kurdistan Workers' Party) in Turkey over the last 40 years, it is evident that there has been foreign support for the PKK terrorists – or at least a refusal to cooperate against them. This has become a major factor for Turkey in countering this terrorist threat (which is estimated to cost Turkey $8 billion annually) and led to 10,284 deaths and 16,198 injuries between 1984 and 1998 (Criss & Çetiner, 2000).

enforce the law effectively. For Turkey's current CTF system this is not the case, because CTF related tasks are all novel applications for most of the practitioners whose respective competencies are not at a desired level.

From a micro perspective, it can be asserted that the efficacy of the CTF measures and the competency of the CTF practitioners determine the effectiveness of the CTF efforts. Moreover, countering the financial activities of terrorists is a broad issue which encapsulates practitioners from very different backgrounds; thus training again emerges as a key component for establishing cooperation among CTF personnel and coordination of CTF efforts. As examined in Chapter 5, the level of competency of and cooperation between Turkish CTF practitioners from different backgrounds, such as financial intelligence, law enforcement, accountancy and auditing, intelligence agencies, legal institutions, the financial sector and banks, are low. For Turkey, combining the diverse efforts of its CTF practitioners is one of the key problems. Therefore, organising joint CTF trainings can play a vital role in helping CTF practitioners to 'speak the same language' and understand each other's requirements and struggles far better, although their backgrounds, institutions, terminologies and working environments differ. It can be argued that by increasing the level of CTF practitioners' knowledge, experience and competency on the issue, the effectiveness of the CTF system in Turkey can be improved. Undoubtedly, the accumulation of this knowledge and experience needs time.

From a macro perspective, training is also key for creating a robust CTF awareness, which has direct correlation with the success of the CTF system. It can be noted that the importance of the CTF issues can be understood by educating people and increasing their awareness through qualified CTF training programmes beyond law enforcement agencies, designed for both the public and private sectors. It is obvious that an effective CTF system requires a holistic approach as well as support and understanding among the CTF practitioners, ordinary citizens, the private financial sector and policy makers, whereas without having CTF awareness they cannot become a part of the solution. As many interviewees stated, training levels of practitioners who are responsible for conducting CTF related tasks are inadequate, and Turkey is in the infancy of the learning process. Having said that, it should be also noted that there have been a number of initiatives to increase the level of training and competency at the individual and institutional levels, and there is a general and genuine willingness to tackle the financing of terrorism and improve the CTF regime therein. However, it will take time and significant investment for Turkey to reach the desired level of CTF standards.

1.2 The focus of the book

Any terrorist or other types of organised criminal structures needs human and financial resources. The absence of one or both would definitely have a detrimental effect on that organisation. The current international CTF measures are being promoted and implemented with the assumption that they are useful for addressing and diminishing terrorist financing, therefore, countering terrorism. Yet the efficacy of the current international counter-terrorist financing regime in a national context has been given scant attention. This book aims to fill this gap.

Turkey and its current CTF system and its applications have been chosen as the subject areas of inquiry in this book because Turkey, logistically and politically, sits in a unique position bridging Asia and Europe as the only Muslim country that is a member of NATO.[8] This unique strategic position and proximity to some of the biggest and deadliest conflicts in the region give Turkey an important role in countering terrorist financing. Consequently, in harmony with the above objectives, the main research question which this book aims to answer is: what is the efficacy of the CTF system in Turkey? The aim of asking this question is to examine how Turkey is dealing with its terrorist threat using the CTF system both on the domestic and international levels. Secondly, if Turkey's CTF system is deemed fit for purpose, then what are the key performance indicators? In other words, what are the determining factors for success and effectiveness or failure of the CTF applications? Identifying the main reasons behind any success or failure of the CTF regime may provide useful insights for evaluating and improving CTF systems elsewhere. Thirdly, in line with the previous question, we pose the following question: What are the challenges encountered by Turkey in terms of its CTF system and its operation? This question focuses on the main problems faced at individual, institutional, national and international levels of CTF implementation and practice, such as competency of CTF experts and staff, adequacy of legal system, bureaucratic hierarchy, diplomatic relations, international coordination and cooperation.

1.3 Scope and approach of this book

There are many different types of research on terrorism and countering terrorism which focus on and analyse terrorism in different contexts (*inter alia*, terrorist ideologies; epistemological, ontological and ethical considerations of counter-terrorism; international counter-terrorist policing policy; conflict, security and justice; aviation terrorism and security; maritime terrorism; critical infrastructure protection; cyberterrorism; terrorism and human rights) (Ranstrop, 2007). In this regard, this book approaches the issue from the perspective of countering the financing of terrorism. More specifically the focal point of this study is to find out the level of efficacy and aptness of existing CTF systems from a national perspective. This research can be seen as a first step in understanding and analysing CTF systems around the world because the increase in detailed case studies is likely to pave the way for regional and multilateral comparative studies in the future.

As is the case with most critical studies involving security in general and national security and counter-terrorism in particular, research for this book

8 NATO pursues its own Euro-Atlantic counter-terrorism strategy which is informed by international rules and agreements (NATO, 2017).

encountered the common problems of the scarcity of sources and existing empirical research on operational data. Although there are some academic sources on counter-terrorist financing in Turkey, they mainly focus on issues such as the types of financial sources of terrorist organisations, and CTF related legislations from descriptive and doctrinal perspectives (e.g. Akin, 2009; Aydınonat, 2012; Aykın & Sözmen, 2009; Çakmak & Altunok, 2009; Özgenç, 2013; Yenidünya & Değirmenci, 2008; Yıldırım, 2012, 2013) rather than presenting an elaborate analysis based on empirical evidence. Correspondingly, in addition to the lack of academic publications and secondary resources, owing to the sensitivity and the classified nature of the CTF information, it was not possible to access and use some of official primary data and documents in this research. Thus, all the sources used here are non-classified open sources.

In order to present a consistent flow, this research looks at the genesis of CTF in Turkey; yet the focus is the interval from 11 September 2001 to present day. From a temporal perspective, the time range covers the dates when the international and collective CTF regime and its national ramifications had begun to be established and felt by many nations. In particular, the development of the US's 'financial war on terrorism' before the 'War on Terror' began, the transformation of international CTF efforts and organisations and last but not least Turkey's CTF activities in terms of legal and institutional domains are within this limited period.

Understanding and critical assessment of the adequacy of the existing efforts for the prevention of financing of terrorism and the feasibility of the international CTF policy in practice in the context of individual states are important for the integrity, success and sustainability of such efforts. Within the above-mentioned limits, this book aims to reveal the extent to which the existing CTF system in Turkey is fit for purpose and successful in addressing Turkey's determined objectives and various terrorist financing threats. Another important dimension this research examines is the extent to which the international CTF regime that was established after 2001 by converting AML applications (mainly put forward by the UN and FATF) fits and meets the security demands of national priorities. The evaluation of efforts against terrorist financing by taking into account both international and national constraints is envisaged to provide useful insights for designing a more successful counter-terrorism response which take into account contextual and local, social, political, legal and cultural factors.

Given the main goal and the research questions we address, this research follows 'constructionism' as an ontological standpoint.[9] As a result, this book adopts what is known in legal research as a 'socio-legal – law in action' methodology. Looking from ontological and socio-legal perspectives, our analysis incorporates personal views and the social interactions of the CTF practitioners and experts who are not only end user stakeholders but also experienced and have knowledge

9 The constructionist school of thought asserts that "social phenomena and their meanings are continually being accomplished by social actors" (Bryman, 2015, p. 29).

from their respective professional and operational backgrounds which they produce through their personal interactions and reflections in this field. One of the novel aims of this research is to identify and incorporate such insights from CTF practitioners' perspective regarding the efficacy of the CTF regime in which they operate.

Correspondingly, from an epistemological framework, this study fits into interpretivism which is based on the idea that "[. . .] a strategy is required to respect the differences between people and the objects of the natural scientists and therefore requires the social scientist to grasp the subjective meaning of social action" (Bryman, 2015, p. 26). For the purposes of this book, the personal views, experiences and stories collected through interviews with the CTF practitioners are vitally important in order to understand the efficacy of the policy of countering terrorist financing and its effectiveness. First-hand knowledge and experience acquired through these actors (qualitative research) will provide a significant contribution to understanding the difference between the theory of CTF and the practical application in the real world.

Subsequently, our analysis incorporates the findings from a total of 23 semi-structured interview questions designed to evaluate the efficacy and success of the CTF system in Turkey.[10] In this regard, 35 semi-structured interviews were conducted with 37 CTF practitioners and experts from different institutions and backgrounds[11] *inter alia*, law enforcement agencies, security forces, legal authorities, the Financial Intelligence Unit, the Customs Office, the private financial sector, scholars (most of whom have a professional background in counter-terrorism and intelligence), the Ministry of Foreign Affairs and the Turkey-EU Delegation.

As will be detailed in Chapter 4, Turkey has been targeted by different types of terrorist organisations and terrorism waves for many years. In other words, Turkey has been fighting against nearly all kinds of terrorism: leftist, separatist, religious, domestic, state-sponsored and international, and therefore it should be accepted that Turkey has a significant amount of counter-terrorism experience which has been accumulated from years of failures and successes. However, it is rather surprising to see that the CTF practices in Turkey are new and have limited application in comparison to counter-terrorism instruments found in other countries. The process of compliance with the new international CTF regime and incorporation of these amendments into the Turkish legal system was not easy. Furthermore, during this period the Financial Action Task Force, which is a quasi-official international organisation, criticised and ultimately threatened to suspend the membership of Turkey as a country with strategic Anti-Money Laundering/Counter-Terrorist Financing (AML/CFT) deficiencies. Following this, Turkey enacted its new CTF legislation on 16 February 2013 to address FATF's criticisms and prevent the suspension of its FATF membership. Although FATF continued to hold Turkey in the category of 'high risk and other monitored

10 For the questions, please see Appendix A.

11 For a detailed list of interviewees, please see Appendix B.

jurisdictions' for a while, Turkey has managed to address most of the issues and deficiencies which the FATF had identified. However, the impact and efficacy of these changes on Turkish CTF efforts have not been examined. Accordingly, studying Turkey's counter-terrorist financing regime is important in order to understand whether the FATF recommendations have improved Turkey's efforts against terrorist financing or not.

Another factor is that the geographic and geopolitical location of Turkey increases the importance of its CTF measures. Turkey is located between the Middle East and Europe as a bridge where many terrorist organisations such as the PKK, Al Qaeda, and ISIS operate. Moreover, two of its neighbouring countries, Syria and Iraq, cannot control their internal security and have become safe havens for terrorists due to the continuing serious civil wars and conflicts in these regions. In other words, Turkey is at the centre of many of the conflicts in the region. In this regard, examining a country where terrorism and financing of terrorism activities were hardly to be expected or very limited would not provide useful conditions for evaluating the efficacy and success of the existing CTF system. However, Turkey has the necessary conditions in order to assess the efficacy of the international CTF regime and its implementation in a national context.

1.4 Structure of the book

This book comprises of six chapters. The first chapter, after a brief explanation of the focus, scope and approaches of the study, indicates the gap in the field of terrorist financing research. Consequently, in this chapter, the main research questions are presented. As part of this chapter the theoretical framework of the research, ontological and epistemological stands of the study and related methodologies are briefly explained.

In Chapter 2 the concept of financing terrorism and related literature are reviewed. In addition, the theoretical approaches, which examine organisational and decision-making features of terrorist financing, are examined. Moreover, the financial resources and methods regarding raising, transferring, storing, layering and integration methods applied by terrorist organisations and their online activities are explained. In other words, before addressing CTF activities, the concept of terrorist financing as one of the main phenomena of this research is scrutinised in light of the existing literature.

Chapter 3 examines counter-terrorist financing efforts and systems. In this regard, the US-based CTF system and the rise of the international CTF regime are looked at from legal, administrative and implementation perspectives. Subsequently, the international CTF regime and its capabilities and applications are analysed from a historical perspective, taking into account the CTF developments in the US in order to expose the links between the two. The significant CTF methods, such as designations, asset freezing, financial intelligence and investigations, are also discussed critically. Using secondary sources and official documents, reports and legal instruments, this chapter clarifies the genesis of this new international CTF regime, its national and international applications, the existing tool box for CTF and the critique provided by academia.

Chapter 4 can be considered as the introduction to the analytical section of this book. In this part of the study, before starting the analysis of the CTF regime in Turkey, the nature and types of the terrorism threats faced by Turkey over 40 years are presented. In this regard, various factions of terrorist movements such as the leftist, separatist and religiously motivated terrorist organisations including DHKP-C, PKK and Hezbollah and their financial and operational activities are outlined. The aim of this chapter is to provide a prelude for the case of Turkey and the dimension of the terrorist threats faced therein.

Chapter 5 provides the main empirical analysis. The data used here was mainly collected from the field via interviews conducted with CTF practitioners, experts from different backgrounds. In this regard, the place and importance of the CTF applications in the long-lived counter-terrorism practices of Turkey have been investigated from a chronological perspective. After explaining the establishment of the CTF system in Turkey, the efficacy of the legal and institutional domains is discussed. The level of implementation and the obstacles facing CTF practices are scrutinised in terms of capacity, training, technology, coordination and cooperation and international relations perspectives. Lastly, the overall impact and success of the CTF system are analysed. In summary, this chapter answers the main research question of whether the CTF system is effective in Turkey from the viewpoints of the CTF practitioners and experts who have spent time in the field of counter-terrorism and synthesises the findings of the analysis with the relevant literature.

In Chapter 6, the findings of the study are restated and summarised. The findings of the study and related theoretical implications are commented on. Following this part, policy-related recommendations are suggested in terms of having a better CTF system in Turkey. Lastly, possible future research and related questions in terms of terrorist financing are offered for the policy makers and prospective researchers who desire to contribute to this field in the near future.

2 Financing of terrorism

2.1 Introduction

After the multiple terror attacks of 9/11 which killed 2,977 people, the terminology in the lexicon of subversive and anti-terrorist studies and literature has been extended to include the terms 'financing of terrorism' and 'terrorist financing'. These terms now appear in both the academic and non-academic literature and have found acceptance in discourse both domestically and internationally. Moreover, there are real world applications against them. Thus, the main aim of this chapter is to deconstruct the concept of terrorist financing and its components and grab its implications. By presenting different theoretical approaches, this chapter examines the importance of the financial aspects of terrorism and its dynamics. In this regard, we demonstrate that it is hard to address all funding activities of terrorists because of the abundance of available sources and opportunities.

Critical understanding of terrorist financing is not largely based on empirical research but on general assumptions and anecdotes which can be deceptive or misleading for policy makers (Myres, 2012). The post–Cold War period with its globalised markets and opportunities provides a plethora of financial sources and methods for terrorist organisations to support and sustain their activities (Romaniuk, 2014). While the main tendency for understanding terrorist financing focuses on its sources, the social, cultural, economic, political and geographical effects and interactions should also be taken into account from a multidimensional perspective. Firstly, the chapter provides the definition of 'terrorist financing' and explains its importance for terrorist organisations. Secondly, terrorist financing is examined from a theoretical perspective, and different funding models are examined so as to understand terrorists' financial activities. Lastly, the current financial sources and methods utilised by terrorist organisations and illicit financial transfer methods are explained.

Before we consider what terrorist financing is, it is important to understand the overarching concept of 'terrorism' in order to appreciate where the 'financing of terrorism' concept is placed. In any event, this is an important starting point for any critical discussion on terrorism and related subjects, because the concept and definition of 'terrorism' and 'terrorist' have serious influence on the states' actions and policies and individuals affected by them. Although there are many different definitions found in domestic and international domains, it should be noted that there is no commonly accepted definition of 'terrorism' at either the international or domestic level (Turksen, 2010, p. 80).

2.2 Understanding terrorism and financing of terrorism

It is hard to define terrorism owing to differing expectations, interests, perspectives and political subjectivity of states and institutions both at the domestic and the international domains. It should be noted that states and the international organisations have their own definitions of terrorism which are tailored according to their specific roles. These different definitions and altered interpretations regarding what can be called an act of terrorism and who is perpetrator of terrorism lead us to the conclusion of the classic school of thought 'one man's terrorist is another man's freedom fighter' (Ganor, 2002) as the best explanation of the current situation. Inevitably the lack of a commonly accepted definition of terrorism has consequences in the real world in terms of countering terrorism and terrorist financing. Simply put, the level of cooperation and coordination between states in terms of countering terrorism and its financial sphere are hampered because reaching an agreement on the limits and framework of terrorism and terrorists is still speculative and ambiguous for many. Similarly, Ridley and Alexander (2011, p. 39) note that:

> The lack of a comprehensive definition of terrorism, even in the late 1990s, hindered both strategic analysis and formulation and enactment of anti-terrorist financing legislation. In response to 9/11, there was an opportunity to promulgate a unified definition as a basis when international governments, law enforcement and regulatory agencies were focussed against a threat that had apparently assumed proportions hitherto unknown and unforeseen. However, paradoxically, the 9/11 crisis necessitated such a focus. The frenzy of international interface was the very reason why no such legal definition was forthcoming.

Moreover, the level of cooperation and coordination for countering terrorist financing at the international level is analysed in Chapter 5, wherein we point out that not having a clear definition and understanding of terrorism among the actors of the international community is one of the important factors which impacts the efficacy of the CTF system at the international and domestic levels. In Turkey, terrorism is described in the Anti-Terrorism Law (1991) Article 1 as:

> Terrorism is any kind of act done by one or more persons belonging to an organization with the aim of changing the characteristics of the Republic as specified in the Constitution, its political, legal, social, secular and economic

system, damaging the indivisible unity of the State with its territory and nation, endangering the existence of the Turkish State and Republic, weakening or destroying or seizing the authority of the State, eliminating fundamental rights and freedoms, or damaging the internal and external security of the State, public order or general health by means of pressure, force and violence, terror, intimidation, oppression or threat.

(Translated from Turkish by MASAK, 2014).

In the UK, the definition of terrorism is provided by the Terrorism Act 2000, Section 1 as:

1 In this Act "terrorism" means the **use or threat of action** where –

(a) the action falls within subsection (2),
(b) the use or threat is designed to **influence the government** [or an **international governmental organisation**] or to **intimidate the public** or a section of the public, and
(c) the use or threat is made for the purpose of **advancing** a **political, religious [racial] or ideological cause**.

2 Action falls within this subsection if it –

(a) involves serious violence against a person,
(b) involves serious damage to property,
(c) endangers a person's life, other than that of the person committing the action,
(d) creates a serious risk to the health or safety of the public or a section of the public, or
(e) is designed seriously to interfere with or seriously to disrupt an electronic system.

3 The use or threat of action falling within subsection (2) which involves the use of firearms or explosives is terrorism whether or not subsection (1)(b) is satisfied.

4 In this section –

(a) "action" **includes action outside the United Kingdom**,
(b) a reference to any person or to property is a reference to any person, or to property, **wherever situated**,
(c) a reference to the public includes a reference to the **public of a country other than the United Kingdom**, and
(d) "the government" means the government of the United Kingdom, of a Part of the United Kingdom **or of a country other than the United Kingdom**.

5 In this Act a reference to action taken for the purposes of terrorism includes a reference to action taken for the benefit of a proscribed organisation.

In the US, the definition of terrorism can be found in 18 US Code § 2331 which provides that:

1 The term "international terrorism" means activities that

(A) involve **violent acts or acts dangerous to human life** that are a violation of the criminal laws of the United States or of any State, or that would be a criminal violation if committed within the jurisdiction of the United States or of any State;
(B) appear to be intended

(i) to **intimidate or coerce a civilian population**;
(ii) to **influence the policy of a government** by intimidation or coercion; or
(iii) to affect the conduct of a government by **mass destruction, assassination, or kidnapping**; and

(C) Occur primarily outside the territorial jurisdiction of the United States, or transcend national boundaries in terms of the means by which they are accomplished, the persons they appear intended to intimidate or coerce, or the locale in which their perpetrators operate or seek asylum.

NATO (2016), on the other hand, defines terrorism as "the unlawful use or threatened use of force or violence, instilling fear and terror, against individuals or property in an attempt to coerce or intimidate governments or societies, or to gain control over a population, to achieve political, religious or ideological objectives".

Having considered these four different definitions, the main differences between them can be summarised as follows:[1]

After this brief comparative explanation of the concept and definitions of terrorism, the following section begins by exploring what the term financing of terrorism means, what terrorists need financing for and how they provide their financial requirements.

2.2.1 *What is financing of terrorism?*

'Terrorist resourcing' which is a broader concept includes the financing of terrorism. This term can be defined as the acquisition and supervision of all required goods for terrorist groups (Myres, 2012). Vittori classifies these needs into three categories: money or other readily liquid assets; tangible goods, such as life's necessities, personnel, and items needed to conduct attacks; and, intangible goods such as operational space, security, intelligence, and some level of training and expertise (2009, pp. 444–445).

1 Our thanks go to Dr Ben Stanford (Coventry University) for the initial idea for this comparative table.

Table 2.1 Concepts and Definitions of Terrorism

	United Kingdom	*United States of America*	*Republic of Turkey*	*NATO*
Action	Use or threat of violence/ damage/ danger to life/ interference with electronic systems.	Violent acts or acts dangerous to human life that violate US criminal laws, or that would be criminal violations if committed within the jurisdiction of the United States or of any State.	Any kind of act by means of pressure, force and violence, terror, intimidation, oppression or threat.	The unlawful use or threatened use of force or violence and instilling fear and terror against individuals or property.
Target	Influence the government or an international organisation **OR** Intimidate the public.	Influence the policy of a government by intimidation or coercion **OR** Intimidate or coerce a civilian population **OR** Affect the conduct of a government by mass destruction, assassination, or kidnapping.	Change the characteristics of the Republic as specified in the Constitution, its political, legal, social, secular and economic system; damage the indivisible unity of the State with its territory and nation; endanger the existence of the Turkish State and Republic; weaken or destroy or seize the authority of the state; eliminate fundamental rights and freedoms or damage the internal and external security of the State, public order or general health.	To coerce or intimidate governments or societies, or to gain control over a population to achieve political, religious or ideological objectives.
Motive	On political, religious, racial or ideological grounds.	N/A	N/A	N/A

As with other institutions and groups, terrorist organisations need sources of finance to survive and pursue their ideological, religious and separatist goals (Bures, 2010, p. 418; Myres, 2012, p. 693; Rudner, 2006, p. 32). Simply, one of the mostly accepted assumptions is that terrorism requires money, and it will be difficult and nearly impossible for terrorist groups to sustain their organisation and undertake their violent activities without it (Freeman, 2011, p. 461; Levitt & Jacobson, 2008, p. 67).

Raphaeli describes money as an "engine" of terrorism (2003, p. 60). Correspondingly, Tofangsaz (2012, p. 399) describes the financing of terrorism as a processing of funds in order to support and make easier conducting terrorist operations. Generally, the financing of terrorism can be classified into three categories:

1 efforts for raising and collecting funds;
2 activities of moving and transferring gathered funds; and
3 keeping the money until it is needed (Vittori, 2011, p. 26).

Referring to this classification, Myres (2012, p. 693) suggests a definition of 'terrorist financing' or 'financing of terrorism' from a different perspective as "the dedicated pursuit of adequate capitalisation within a market of violence, wherein terrorist organisations seek to extract resources and funding from the social, political and economic environment in which they operate". Therefore, as a part of terrorist resourcing processes, all these definitions of the terrorist financing concept similarly comprise raising, storing, managing and distributing money and financial means for the use of terrorist organisations.

Article 2 of the International Convention for the Suppression of the Financing of Terrorism (CTF Convention) (1999) states that a person commits the criminal offence of terrorist financing "if that person by any means, directly or indirectly, unlawfully and wilfully, provides or collects funds with the intention that they should be used or in the knowledge that they are to be used, in full or in part, in order to carry out:

(a) An act which constitutes an offence within the scope of and as defined in one of the treaties listed in the annex; or
(b) Any other act intended to cause death or serious bodily injury to a civilian, or to any other person not taking an active part in the hostilities in a situation of armed conflict, when the purpose of such act, by its nature or context, is to intimidate a population, or to compel a government or an international organization to do or to abstain from doing any act".

Clunan (2006, p. 574) aptly observed that before "the terrorist bombings of the US embassies in Tanzania and Kenya [. . .] the issue of terrorist financing was handled almost entirely as a problem of state sponsors of terrorism, or money laundering and criminal finance by non-state actors". Thus, other means of financing and actors (e.g. donations, quasi-state taxation, sale of energy products etc.) were omitted.

The guidance provided by the World Bank defines terrorist financing as "the financial support, in any form, of terrorism or of those who encourage, plan, or engage in it" (Schott, 2006, p. I-1). This general approach to terrorist financing is also found in the definition provided by the International Monetary Fund (IMF) which defines it as "the solicitation, collection or provision of funds" with the intention of using them "to support terrorist acts or organizations"(International Monetary Fund, 2018).

It is also important to note that prior to 9/11 and the subsequent UN Security Resolutions, only four states had signed and ratified the CTF Convention, 1999 (O'Neill, 2012, p. 31). The latest report on the number of signatories indicates a stark difference whereby 188 states have ratified the CTF Convention (UN Treaty Collections, 2017). Even though there were legal responses by the UN following terrorist attacks before 9/11 (e.g. the attacks by Al Qaeda on US embassies in Nairobi and Dar es Salaam in 1998),[2] these were not supported by the international community to the same degree. Both UNSC Resolution 1267 and 1373 were adopted unanimously at the Security Council. However, the latter, which was adopted after 9/11, instigated almost a universal support for the Convention. Complementing the general spirit of the CTF Convention, UNSC Resolution 1373 (2001) puts forward a number of substantive CTF provisions which stipulate that all states shall:

- prevent and suppress the financing of terrorist acts;
- criminalise generation and collection of funds for terrorism;
- freeze without delay funds and other financial assets or economic resources of persons supporting and/or engaged in terrorism;
- take necessary steps to prevent terrorism;
- deny safe haven to those who finance terrorism;
- ensure those engaged in financing of terrorism are brought to justice; and
- assist each other in criminal investigations and proceedings in CTF.

Subsequently there were 34 further UNSC Resolutions addressing financing terrorism; the most recent one (at the time of writing this book) was UNSC Resolution 2368 in 2017.[3]

2.2.2 *Expenses of terrorist organisations*

Even though conducting a terrorist attack may need small amounts of money, running a terrorist organisation for a special purpose requires considerable

2 Following these attacks, the UN Security Council issued Resolution 1267 (1999), which generated a sanctions regime that applied to persons and/or entities that were associated with the Taliban, Osama bin Laden and Al Qaeda. The list of these entities and the summary narratives of the rationale for listing them under the sanctions regime are available at www.un.org/sc/suborg/en/sanctions/1267/aq_sanctions_list/summaries.

3 UNSC Resolution 2368 (2017), recalling previous resolutions 1267 (1999), 1333 (2000), 1363 (2001), 1373 (2001), 1390 (2002), 1452 (2002), 1455 (2003), 1526 (2004), 1566 (2004), 1617 (2005), 1624 (2005), 1699 (2006), 1730 (2006), 1735 (2006), 1822 (2008), 1904 (2009), 1988 (2011), 1989 (2011), 2083 (2012), 2133 (2014), 2161 (2014), 2170 (2014), 2178 (2014), 2195 (2014), 2199 (2015), 2214 (2015), 2249 (2015), 2253 (2015), 2309 (2016), 2322 (2016), 2331 (2016), 2341 (2017), 2347 (2017), 2354 (2017).

financial resources (Freeman, 2011, p. 462) and operational capacity. Financial assets needed for activities such as training, logistic support, travel, safe houses, propaganda, reconnaissance, social and political activities, evading detection and communication make it clear that running a terrorist organisation is much costlier than conducting a single attack at a given time and place (Acharya, 2009, p. 288; Rudner, 2006, pp. 37–42).

According to Lemieux and Prates (2011, p. 369) every type of terrorism requires "short term (operational)"[4] and "sustaining (strategic)"[5] forms of funding for waging its campaigns. In this regard terrorist organisations could use the money they have for the purposes of command and control; training (Acharya, 2009, pp. 288–289; Rudner, 2006, p. 38); providing safe haven (Acharya, 2009, pp. 289–290) or safe houses (Rudner, 2006, p. 40); recruitment, propaganda (Acharya, 2009, p. 290), and travel (Rudner, 2006, p. 37) and technology (Roth & Sever, 2007, p. 911) related expenses; communication (Rudner, 2006, p. 39); and conducting terrorist attacks (Acharya, 2009, pp. 290–292). These financing needs are not exhaustive and can change according to particular terrorist organisations' structure, preferred methods and future requirements.

2.2.3 Theoretical approaches to financing terrorism

It generally appears that the public acts of violence caused by terrorism have captured the attention of social science researchers more than the financing of terrorism which maintains and enables such crimes. Some researchers such as Vittori (2009, 2011), Wittig (2009, 2011), Geltzer (2011), Freeman (2011, 2012), and Levitt (2003) have produced important studies, which created a school of thought by fixing attention on terrorist group autonomy, typological concerns and critical sociological and economic aspects therein. However, similar to the studies conducted on terrorism, it could be said that terrorist financing related analysis has mostly been created without referencing systematic theoretical frameworks and depends mainly on "anecdotes" and immature debates which examine the aptness of special policy decisions (Myres, 2012, p. 693; Silke, 2004). According to Reuter and Truman (2004, p. 8) a significant number of counter measures against the financing of terrorism have been used for years which depend on untested assumptions. In this context, it could be asserted that to understand the dynamics of terrorist financing and forming counter solutions, qualitative and quantitative empirical and theoretical research should be conducted utilising

4 Short-term sources generally are exploited by operational financing which reflects a means to an end funding such as low profile activities, restricted competence (Ehrenfeld, 2003, as cited in Lemieux & Prates, 2011, p. 369). Operational financing is an essential task oriented process and requires unsophisticated financing for de-centralised cell type units. Generally, legal and illegal sources are used for operatives financing.

5 Secondly, strategic financing supports long-term activities of more organised and structured terrorist activities such as recruitment, propaganda and sustainment of their constituency (Lemieux & Prates, 2011, p. 369).

mainly primary data from the field. Otherwise the existing literature will not be enough to explain many aspects of these phenomena.

In this framework, Wittig (2009, p. 145) finds the current perception and approaches to the financing of terrorism as malign and ineffective because the wrong questions are asked by officials, policy makers and scholars to understand this problem. Instead of these incorrect questions such as "who finances and how do they do it", Wittig argues that the attention should be turned to "how financial activity influences terrorist behaviour and what such activity tells us about the place terrorists truly occupy in today's global system". While the former question looks for what terrorist financing shows about terrorist organisations and "[. . .] in essence focuses on the instrumentality of financial activity to terrorist actors", the latter, in terms of terrorist financing activities, demonstrates the relationship between society and terrorists therein. In other words, asking this question takes into account social, political, economic, cultural, normative and cognitive factors and their interaction with each other that constitute terrorist financing (Wittig, 2009, pp. 149–150). Asking these "right questions", Wittig does not follow the classical understanding; rather he opens a new perspective in order to understand the social links and instrumental forms of terrorist financing. It is accepted that this approach presents a wider perspective for grasping the dynamics of terrorist financing and allows for a better analysis of the measures to counter it.

Furthermore, Myres (2012, p. 693) suggests a "micro-theory" of financing of terrorism dealing with socials/sociological, economic, political and military subjects with a strong theoretical concept which is underpinned by two main points:

a) [. . .] demand for organised political violence on the one hand (by states and/or sub-national actors); and
b) a supply of financial and materiel sources that turn the demand into actuality".

According to this theory the financial success depends on a terrorist group's organisational structure and capability for launching a specialised financing position and "high levels of organisational learning". Myres (2012, p. 694) also notes that terrorists make their financial decisions in light of their organisational degree of perceiving the accessible opportunities available, the degree of ability to generate financial gains from these available chances effectively and the degree of the utilisation of these funds economically and strategically to develop and sustain their organisation (Myres, 2012, p. 694). Thus, the level of organisational sophistication and learning ability are important factors for terrorists.

Role specialisation

Even though the majority of counter-terrorism studies analyse the "organisation" from the perspective of differences between "hierarchical" and "network" organisations (Crenshaw, 1987), approaching this subject from the financial dimension can discover other essential features of 'organisation'. According to Myres (2012, p. 694), there is a strong and direct relationship between the planning, execution and management of financial operation functions and the organisational structure the learning of the terrorist groups. As Adams (1987, as cited in Myres, 2012, p. 694) notes, "[i]t is always the case that [for] any terrorist organisation to survive [it] needs to develop a more sophisticated financial apparatus than the common image" adding that "[t]o survive, terrorist groups need to cross an economic divide that separates those who live a hand-to-mouth existence from those who can actually plan ahead. All those groups which have come and gone in the last twenty years have failed to cross that divide". The financial success and sustainability also seem to be directly linked to the survival of terrorist organisations.

Similarly, Vittori (2009, p. 445), Horgan and Taylor (1997, p. 3) and Kiser (2005, p. 30) note that if contemporary large-scale terrorist organisations, which have advanced organisational structures, want to survive, they must have "functional differentiation" and recruit members who specialise in certain skills such as financing of bomb making. Furthermore, Lemieux and Prates (2011, p. 370) note that "the structural complexity [coordination], sophisticated management [communication] and the scope of activity [specialisation]" determine the nature of terrorist financing, needs of operational capability and sustainability of terrorist organisations. Without having a specialised section for financing, terrorist groups are faced with serious problems such as corruption and nepotism, which can cause very severe damage to their organisations (Acharya, 2009, p. 293).

In light of these arguments, it can be asserted that successful and effective terrorist organisations possess specialised financial operations because these kinds of bureaucratic diversifications help meet the requirements of complex and multidimensional activities such as finding suitable sources and raising funds for operational activities.[6] Inevitably, "terrorist group[s] that do not develop a finance role specialisation open themselves to increased risks of mission failure, either as a result of counterterrorism efforts or in relation to internal splintering" (Myres, 2012, p. 697). In other words, it can be said that without developing an advanced and specialised financial system, terrorist groups are likely to have decreased organisational flexibility, which has a direct relation to their sustainability in the face of counter-terrorist measures.

Funding models for terrorist financing

Gupta (2005, pp. 28–29) and most of the other experts agree that money is the "life blood" of terrorist organisations. Terrorists need significant amounts of money for the above-mentioned reasons, and there are a number of funding methods available ranging from state sponsorship to donations, from criminal activities to legal businesses for terrorist organisations to raise money (Freeman, 2011). Besides counting the number of financial sources of terrorist organisations, it is also

6 Hezbollah and Provisional Irish Republican Army (PIRA) can be given as suitable examples for financial specialisation and organisational design which provide these two groups diverse financial sources and successful political gains (Myres, 2012, p. 696).

important to answer the question of why terrorist groups have different financing sources. For instance, why do some terrorist groups mainly depend on drug trafficking while others use donations and charities or organising social campaigns; what kind of factors affect terrorist organisations decision-making process when choosing these funding methods (Freeman, 2011, p. 461; Myres, 2012, p. 697)?

In order to answer this question Freeman (2011) develops a theoretical approach, helps explain the advantages and disadvantages of all financial sources for terrorist groups. Freeman uses six key criteria for measuring the advantages and disadvantages of four main terrorist financing sources:

1 State sponsorship;
2 Illegal activities;
3 Legal activities; and
4 Popular support (charity and donations).

These sources are further assessed by six key criteria, namely quantity, legitimacy, security, reliability, control and simplicity (Freeman, 2011, pp. 461–462).[7]

Freeman (2011) suggests that there is no perfect funding source or mixture of sources; all have some pros and cons. It can be supposed that decision makers in terrorist organisations rationally evaluate these key criteria and make trade-offs in the

7 The first criterion is quantity. Briefly, terrorist organisations want as much money as possible because with more money, terrorist groups can conduct more effective and complex terrorist attacks, provide social services and be more secure against counter-measures (Freeman, 2011, p. 463). The second is legitimacy, which is required by terrorists to prolong their longevity. The legitimacy level of their goals or ideology determines the amount of support from their constituency. If they have illegitimate aims, they are more likely to have limited support in all means (Freeman, 2011, p. 463). The third criterion is security, which has a vital importance for terrorists in basic terms. It is undoubtedly true that as underground structures terrorist organisations must operate secretly to be minimally affected by the counter-terrorist efforts of law enforcement or military forces of states. Thus, it is important for terrorists to select suitable financial sources to circumvent the cycle of intelligence units. (Williams, 2008, pp. 145–146). Reliability is another important factor for terrorist organisation decision making. Reliability of sources of funding can be described as whether the funds coming from these sources are stable and expected. Demography and geography are two factors that have direct impacts on the reliability of sources. For raising consistent revenues from reliable sources, terrorists should locate their position geographically near or around these sources. (Freeman, 2011, p. 464). Control is a further key criterion for terrorist groups. A terrorist group's control on its members and operational agenda can be increased or decreased according to the selection of different funding sources. Some of these sponsors such as states and individual donors can try to control terrorist organisations, which mainly terrorists are reluctant to, using the power of their money. (Freeman, 2011, p. 464). The last key criterion is simplicity. Freeman (2011, p. 464) claims that similar to other types of organisations terrorist groups prefer simple methods of financing themselves. Simple methods need simple abilities and simple processes, and there will be fewer costs compared with other methods. Petty crimes, such as theft or extortion, need fewer skills than cyber-crimes or drug trafficking. Moreover, terrorists who have regular external support are less likely to allocate much effort to financing activities than other groups.

process of selecting the right financing source for their organisation. In this context, the main accepted assumption is that terrorist organisations are rational actors.[8]

Nationalism-privatisation relationship

Moreover, Geltzer (2011) notes that a trade-off between nationalism (state sponsorship) and privatisation (autonomy) determines the financing method of terrorist organisations. In this analogy, nationalisation defines state sponsorship, and privatisation resembles autonomous financing activities which terrorist groups use for raising money. In this context, Geltzer (2011) claims that terrorists make their decisions according to a cost-benefit assessment in terms of nationalism and privatisation. According to this approach, if a terrorist group is looking for a constituency for the first time where it will not be a problem sharing its agenda with others, it is more likely that this group will use nationalised financing which will help it establish its constituency. In contrast, if the terrorist organisation has a well-established and robust constituency with a well-defined agenda, then choosing privatised financing will allow terrorists to act more freely as their constituency will not be their first priority anymore (Geltzer, 2011, p. 163).

While Myres (2012) and Geltzer (2011) accept the idea that terrorist organisations often have options which could be selected by them, in reality, this may not be the case because the conditions they operate in are influenced by local factors which compel terrorist organisations to turn to specific funding options. At the same time, it should be noted again that deeming all choices made by terrorists to be rational might be misleading, due to the fact that it is not possible to determine how rational they are with the existing limited data available on this topic.

Effects of terrorist organisational models

A terrorist group's organisational model and structure have considerable influence on the financial decision-making process of terrorists. In this context Geltzer (2011, p. 146) and Vittori (2011) have made similar observations which have aptly identified the interaction between a terrorist organisation's financial support base and the group's idea of autonomy to follow their agenda:

> The more "investors" [be they states, private donors, other terrorist groups, or charities], there are, the less control any one donor has over the group, and the more autonomy the latter will retain. [. . .] Therefore, a group with one or very few resourcing avenues will find itself beholden to them.
>
> (Vittori, 2011, p. 4).

8 It is worth noting that the presumption of terrorist groups acting rationally can be misleading as terrorist organisations might not always be rational actors and tend to make pragmatic, emotional and/or rush decisions.

In addition to the influence of organisational mechanisms on financial decision making, understanding the factors which affect the lifespan of terrorist organisations allows policy makers and scholars to measure the effectiveness and success of their counter-terrorism methods and efforts. In this context Vittori (2009) has examined the survival of the terrorist organisation's relationship with its autonomy and capability levels. Autonomy was defined by Vittori (2009) as the organisations' freedom from the effects of donors, investors or the states which sponsor them; and capability is defined as the level of the organisations' ability to conduct operational activities and cause violence.

Terrorist groups are classified as low-, medium- and high-level autonomy organisations. With 'Low Autonomy Groups', one or very small number of donors control the sources and the operations of the terrorist organisation. 'Medium Autonomy Groups' consist of two sub-categories: the first is 'franchise'. This type of group has a small number of external donors who control significant numbers of sources whereas terrorist organisations also have a significant number of sources from their own internal assets. In this situation, the external donor such as a state or other terrorist organisation has control over a terrorist group, but not completely. In the second category, a terrorist group can have sources from 'numerous small donors' such as diaspora funding. In 'High Autonomy Groups', there is no control mechanism from outside of the organisation. In addition, a significant amount of resources are collected from highly diversified internal sources. High level autonomy groups may emerge from two environments. One is a very small group, which is a cell or several cells in a terrorist organisation that are operational and self-sourcing. Eco-terrorist organisations can be given as an example. In the second case, the terrorist group has diversified external and internal sources wherein no single sponsor or donor has any control over them (Vittori, 2009, p. 448).

Vittori (2009) also observes that terrorist organisations classified as having moderate- to high-level autonomy and capabilities can exist longer than other terrorist organisations. In other words, it appears that a terrorist organisation's lifetime has a positive correlation with its financial autonomy and operational sophistication (Vittori, 2009). According to Hoffman (2006, p. 242), the financial assistance provided by sympathisers and constituencies and the level of sustenance have a direct effect on the lifetime of terrorist organisations. Moreover, Hoffman (2006, p. 242) suggests that religious or nationalist/separatist terrorist groups mostly have support from their root communities which facilitate their survival capacity. In contrast to Hoffman's (2006) claims, Vittori's (2009) empirical research about the longevity of terrorist organisations according to their autonomy and capability level clearly shows that all types of terrorist organisations such as separatist, religious and political groups have at least a 30 percent probability of surviving in their first year. It appears that the stated goals and purposes of these terrorist organisations do not affect their lifespan. In this regard Vittori's (2009) research provides important findings for developing counter measures.

Centralisation of resources and operations

Zelinsky and Shubik (2009, p. 328) propose a new typology for terrorist organisations which compares them with business firms and analyses them according to their 'centrality level' of 'operation' and 'funding' for designing more effective strategies against terrorist financing. They build their framework around two axes: centralisation of sources and centralisation of operations in which they use centralisation as a metric in this model. In light of this perspective, Zelinsky and Shubik (2009, pp. 327–329) suggest four different business firm typology models: 'hierarchy', 'venture capital', 'franchise', and 'brand' models.[9]

In short, Zelinsky and Shubik (2009) believe that this new organisational typology provides a clear understanding of organisational structures of terrorist organisations revealing their similarities to business firms and corporations. It could be debated how suitable it is to compare the profit oriented nature of business with ideologically motivated terrorist organisations. However, as this study provides analysis of weak and strong points of terrorist organisations, it could provide important insights into designing an effective counter-terrorist policy.

In international business, one of the main debates is the comparative advantages and disadvantages of nationalisation and privatisation of resources for economic organisations. Geltzer (2011, pp. 145–146) uses this debate as a conceptual framework to explain terrorist financing from nationalisation and privatisation dimensions. He claims that the funding of terrorist organisations has

9 The first model is 'hierarchy' which is the most centralised operations and funding model. The command and control structures are very strong and strict in this type of organisation. These structures can conduct long-term and expansive projects, but they need large amounts of money to sustain the activities. The leadership controls the attacks and financing. Hezbollah and the IRA (Irish Republican Army) can be given as examples (Zelinsky & Shubik, 2009, p. 329). 'Venture capital' is the second model where a terrorist organisation has decentralised operations and centralised sources. Due to lack of operational centrality, these groups cannot run large-scale installations such as camps. Additionally, they do not have the ability to make long-term plans, and therefore cannot sustain this type of attack. However, their resources are controlled by a central point. Al Qaeda, for instance, employed this model from 1990 to September 2001 (Zelinsky & Shubik, 2009, p. 329). The third model, called 'franchise' groups, has centralised operations with decentralised resources in contrast to the 'venture capital' model. Financial decentralisation prevents this type of organisation from conducting large-scale operations because leadership does not have the capability to fund these activities. However, these organisations can make long-term plans; they can conduct protracted operations (Zelinsky & Shubik, 2009, p. 329). The last model is called the 'brand' model. In this type of organisational model both resources and operations are conducted in a decentralised way. They mainly depend on ideological self-identification and ad hoc alliances between their loosely established units. These organisations are the hardest one for infiltration by security forces because they share a common ideology and brand name, whereas they do not have any link with the other cells. This is also a very small organisational structure; thus, it is difficult for them make long-term plans and attacks. However, this type of structures may continue its existence even when many compounds of organisation are eliminated (Zelinsky & Shubik, 2009, p. 330). The Earth Liberation Front (ELF) can be given as an example for this model (Joosse, 2007).

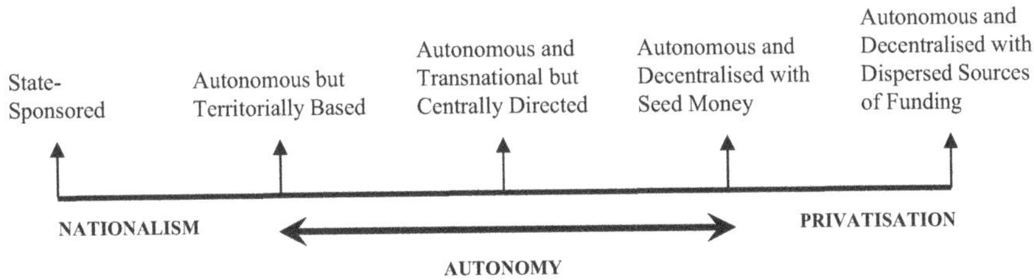

Figure 2.1 Nationalisation-Privatisation Spectrum (Geltzer, 2011)

transformed and created five different financing models for terrorist groups from state sponsorship to autonomous activity. These five financing models are "state-sponsored; autonomous but territorially based; autonomous and transnational but centrally directed; autonomous and decentralised with seed money; autonomous and decentralised with dispersed sources of funding" (Figure 2.1) (Geltzer, 2011, pp. 145–146).[10]

Geltzer concludes that the cost-benefit analysis of nationalisation (state sponsorship) has a direct relation with the group's constituency and shows that privatisation (autonomous activity) has a strong effect on a terrorist organisation's agenda. In other words, nationalisation increases a terrorist organisation's public

10 The first financing model is state-sponsored; states are financially supporting terrorist organisations for their own interests (Geltzer, 2011). The second is the "autonomous but territorially based" model. This model moves forward from state sponsorship to a more autonomous position. In this model a terrorist group resembles the main characteristics of a state and strongly controls a territory which can provide it protection (Napoleoni, 2005, as cited in Geltzer, 2011, p. 147). In the beginning, these groups might depend on state funds, but later they start to raise their own money. Consequently, as long as a terrorist organisation controls a specific territory and provides state like services to its constituency, it is more likely that they will secure their activities even though states do not fund them (Geltzer, 2011, p. 147) For example, the Islamic State controls and operates in Iraq and Syria. The third model, "autonomous and transnational but centrally directed terrorist funding", has a transnational nature but is managed from a central command point. They do not need any state or territory to control. However, rising, moving, and distributing of funds is undertaken by a central hierarchy. Al Qaeda's 9/11 attack was funded utilising this central model. Another model is "autonomous and decentralised with seed money". In this model cell units of terrorist organisations which are autonomous are funded centrally only in the beginning. Afterwards these cell units must sustain and raise their own money using this first seed money: for example, by opening shops and other business branches. The Bali attacks, which were conducted by the Jemaah Islamiyah terrorist organisation in 2002, for instance, were funded with this model. The final model is the "autonomous and decentralised with dispersed sources of funding" model, which encompasses the highest degree of autonomy for terrorist financing. In this model, the main terrorist group presents a wider framework for cell units and provides support for specific attacks, whereas other arrangements such as raising money are done before an attack; these are all responsibilities of cell units. In other words, terrorist cells are highly autonomous to fund themselves.

support while privatisation augments a terrorist group's agenda, and terrorist groups select their financing model according to their nationalisation and privatisation trade-off (Geltzer, 2011, pp. 145–146).

Furthermore, Acharya (2009, p. 286) explains how terrorists' organisational structures are affected by the evolution of terrorist financing. In this regard, it is claimed that military and financial counter measures undertaken against terrorist organisations cause them to lose their strength and operational capabilities. In other words, although before the 9/11 attacks terrorist organisations were more integrated and had highly capable structures, in the post 9/11 era, with the introduction of counter-terrorism measures, they have operated via more decentralised groups and networks. Subsequently, these loosely connected groups started to supply themselves in the absence of central leadership and financial sources. Such transformation has been experienced as a survival response to the dangers of a hierarchical organisation structure (Acharya, 2009).

However, such generalisation may not be applicable to all terrorist organisations. For example, while it is possible to observe this transformation in the context of Al Qaeda and its affiliated organisations, this theory does not explain other terrorist organisations, such as the PKK (Kurdistan Workers Party) which has sustained its financing structure despite thickening counter-terrorism measures. In light of the data available to date, it is not possible to determine the exact impact of counter-terrorism measures on the financial models. However, it should be noted that the financial transformation of terrorist organisations started at the end of Cold War rather than post 9/11.

According to Acharya (2009) terrorist groups are more resilient in this new decentralised structure. These smaller units have started to raise their own financial sources using various methods within their local region in which they do not have to store money or transfer it to other places unlike centralised structures. Acharya also contends that this change in financing models has impacted the operational and financial capabilities of terrorist organisations. These self-funded autonomous structures have started to make their operational decisions as well as their financial decisions. In these circumstances, such autonomous structures may not find large amounts of revenue, which directly limits their operational capacity.

However, the form of the attacks has become smaller and less costly which is more suitable for locally operated cell structures. After this transformation, terrorists first need a small amount of money for conducting their attacks which are difficult to detect and prevent. Secondly, these more decentralised and loosely connected cells have started to raise money locally which protects them against security forces; thirdly terrorists have learned how to use their limited money more efficiently and effectively (Acharya, 2009, pp. 285–286).

2.3 Funding sources for terrorist financing

In the previous section, criteria for terrorist organisations' financial decisions and related funding models are explained. Here, different types of funding sources for terrorist financing will be examined. Although funding models and conditions can be different, it is important to understand the source dimension of terrorist financing. Where and how terrorist organisations generate money and how they move and store it are vital as to their security and their capability to conduct operations (Barrett, 2012, p. 722). In addition, it is important to inquire about other possible sources of terrorism financing as there is a virtually infinite range of sources and activities (including state sponsorship of robbery, international organised crime, kidnapping for ransom, extortion of wealthy businessmen, charity organisations etc.) which can be used for terrorist financing (Freeman, 2011, p. 462). Danziger (2012, p. 213) quotes from the FATF Paper that terrorist funding can be characterised in many forms and classified in broad groupings which are identified as: self-funding activities, funds/proceeds from criminal activities, legitimate funds passing through the banking system, and alternative remittance systems (e.g. hawala).

Tofangsaz (2012, p. 399) emphasises that terrorist groups' aims, organisational structures and forms have a degree of influence on terrorist financing and the sources which can derive from legal and illegal activities. Accordingly, such financial sources are divided into two groups. The first one is "Financial Support" which comprises donations, constituency solicitations and funds coming from states, organisations and individuals. The second one is "Revenue Generating Activities" which comprise funds that are raised through criminal and illegal activities (Tofangsaz, 2012, pp. 399–400).

Furthermore, as Myres (2012, p. 699) points out, investment in terrorist organisations can take two different forms. The first one is "voluntarily invested capital" which consists of investments from states, sub-state organisations and individuals. Many terrorist groups demand such investment because this can enhance their capabilities and offer a degree of state protection (Geltzer, 2011, pp. 151–153). The second investment type is "appropriated or stimulated investment", and this type of money stream is gained from legitimate, illegitimate and rent-seeking fundraising activities.

Freeman (2011, p. 465), on the other hand, classifies financing sources of terrorism into four categories: "state sponsorship, legal activities, illegal activities and popular support". In this context, Myres (2012) puts forward an investor type spectrum, which generally classifies investors into three groups: "Autonomous \ Independent Individual Investors" (Diaspora Based Individual Donors), "Project Committed Investors" (Charitable Societies, Individuals and Religious Establishments), "High Risk \ High Yield Investors" (States, Terrorist Organisations) according to the expectation and risk categories of investors (see Figure 2.2).

Even though there are several financing sources and typologies which use different names for the same sources, this monograph adopts a combination of different approaches. Thus, Geltzer's (2011) classification which divides terrorist financing sources into two main groups (state sponsorship and autonomous financing activities) according to their autonomy level is used in this section of our analysis. Furthermore, autonomous financing activities may be sub-divided into two groups: legal activities and illegal activities which can include the movement

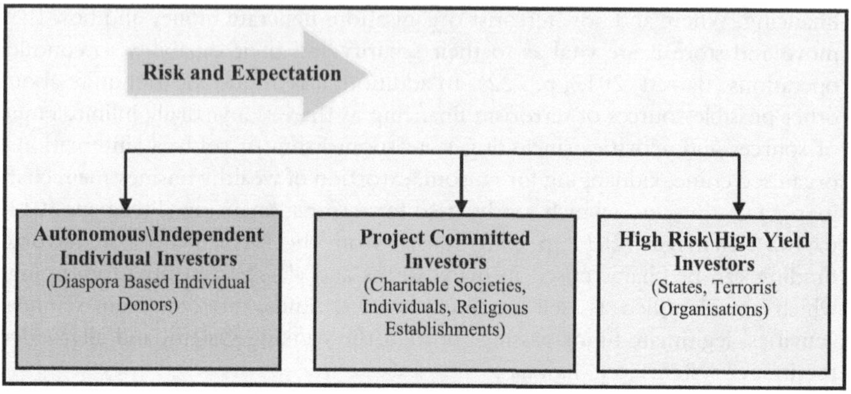

Figure 2.2 Investor Type Spectrum (Myres, 2012)

or transferring methods of terrorist funds and internet based financing activities. These are also examined below.

2.3.1 State sponsorship

One of the main sources of terrorism financing is state sponsorship (Freeman, 2011, p. 465). It is widely accepted by most counter-terrorism experts that a state sponsor is a country that wilfully, knowingly and intentionally provides direct support for terrorist groups (Winer, 2008, p. 114). Such states often have specific aims for their investment. Myres inferring from Byman (2005), as cited in Myres, 2012, p. 701), summarises possible investment principles and goals of state sponsors of terrorism:

- "using the terrorist group to meet geostrategic goals against an adversary state;
- promoting a particular ideological perspective or to advance the vision of norm entrepreneurs at the expense of an 'other'; and/or
- assisting members of a common identity group or 'kin' who are perceived as suffering oppression vis-à-vis other groups".

In addition, for some states, supporting and sponsoring terrorist activities have other drivers and aims. These can include improving regional influence and effectiveness, destabilising other countries, supporting opposition movements, and assisting regime change.

Passas (2007, p. 24) emphasises that state sponsorships of terrorism has diminished in recent years. Especially in the Cold War era state sponsorship was more common around the world. For instance, it is claimed that Marxist and communist groups were supported mainly by the Soviet Union. On the other hand, the United States of America was also funding and using terrorist organisations such as the Contras in Nicaragua (Adams, 1986, pp. 73–75). Adams (1986, p. 64) also alleged that some of the Arab states such as Libya provided around $100 million in financial assistance annually to many terrorist groups, including the Red Brigades, the IRA, the ETA (Basque Fatherland and Liberty), the Japanese Red Army and the Baader-Meinhof gang, Tupamaros in Uruguay and Moros in Philippines. It cannot be denied that states covertly support terrorist organisations. However, in comparison to the past, Cold War period, it is true that the numbers and the size of state sponsored terrorism is lower.

From the perspective of terrorist organisations, state sponsorship presents many advantages. Such funding is often simple, stable, secure and large in quantity for groups who have state sponsorship (Freeman, 2011). In addition, state sponsored groups can focus on other activities rather than funding. Moreover, the state provides terrorist groups protection against law enforcement agencies and state authorities (Geltzer, 2011). Vittori (2009, p. 462) observes that terrorist groups which are state sponsored can operate and sustain their activities longer.

On the other hand, state sponsorship can have negative side effects for terrorist organisations in terms of control and independence (Freeman, 2011). This kind of sponsorship can limit their freedom; thus they may become a servant of the state (Geltzer, 2011), because the state can use its financial support to direct and control the group's operations (Freeman, 2011). The terrorist organisation may be forced to conduct activities which it would not undertake otherwise (Freeman, 2011). Another point is that the state regime and the terrorist group's existence and future direction may depend on and affect each other. International sanctions and other measures on the sponsor state directly affect the terrorist organisation. Furthermore, the sponsor state or its policies may change which may then eliminate terrorist organisations (Freeman, 2011). Lastly, state sponsorship can be easily targeted by counter-terrorist efforts, and in some cases, sponsor states can cut the financing, which will decrease the lifetime of terrorist groups, for their own interests (Geltzer, 2011, pp. 151–155).[11]

Adams (1986, p. 80) advocates the view that the state sponsor has a critical role at the initial foundation of a terrorist group. Nevertheless, when this establishment is completed, then successful a terrorist organisation follows more independent ways progressively. In brief, terrorist organisations have been transforming their funding strategies from state sponsorship to using autonomous financing sources which is discussed below.

2.3.2 Autonomous financing

It is acknowledged that terrorist groups have learned that state sponsorship is not reliable, and if they want to survive, they must gain their own money and assets

11 For instance, after the Soviet Union dissolved in the 1990s, many Marxist terrorist groups lost their financial support, and following international pressure, Libya shifted its policies and cut its funding to terrorists (Freeman, 2011, p. 466).

(Adams, 1986, p. 80). It is also claimed that the diminution of financial sources from state sponsorship, especially after the Cold War, coerced terrorist establishments to discover new and different financing activities and sources (Hutchinson & O'Malley, 2007, p. 1095). Lemieux and Prates (2011, p. 371) remark that terrorist groups need to attain entrepreneurship skills to prop up their funding function, as well as understanding and meeting the requirements of their constituencies. Levitt and Jacobson (2008, p. 67) note that terrorist finance has rapidly changed over the last decades owing to the terrorist groups' compulsion to avoid security forces and the utilisation of new emerging technological opportunities through which terrorist organisations can raise funds autonomously from legal sources such as humanitarian and business organisations as well as illegal sources such as drug and human trafficking, arms trading, all kinds of smuggling and robbery crimes (Clunan, 2006, p. 570).

Autonomous financing has costs and benefits for terrorist groups. From the autonomous financing perspective, independent privatised financing provides terrorist groups much more freedom to form their organisational and operational decisions. Rudner (2006, p. 42) emphasises that "self-financing is also consistent with, and supports, the decentralisation and localisation of terrorist networks and sub-networks". These groups can move independently, and some terrorist organisations such as those with a strong financial system like Al Qaeda can take the role of states and provide support to other terrorist groups. In addition, the success of a terrorist organisation increases its financial budget. Due to their independent nature, these groups are not affected by the changes made in states' regimes. Using various autonomous financing sources, which are distributed around the globe dispersedly, decreases the effectiveness of counter measures and provides terrorists protection. This type of sourcing also eliminates the difficulty and risk of transferring money, if cell units are able to collect and generate their own money (Geltzer, 2011, pp. 155–158).

Autonomous financing has some disadvantages too. The reliability and stability of funding is not so predictable in autonomous financing, and generally this type of financing depends on the terrorist group's popularity, abilities for raising fund in a counter-terrorism environment, competition between rival groups and the situation of financial sources. Moreover, in these kinds of activities, terrorist groups have to communicate with and contact the outside world, which creates a weakness against intelligence and security units. Moreover, legitimacy of funding (those deriving from criminal activities in particular) can result in loss of general support of communities (Geltzer, 2011, pp. 158–160). Even though, autonomous financing sources have pros and cons, they are continuously utilised by terrorists.

Legal activities

Private donations, quasi-legitimate businesses, charities, religious organisations and front organisations are used mainly in this type of funding (Rudner, 2010, p. 702).

LEGAL BUSINESSES

Terrorist organisations employ the licit business sector to raise and distribute their funds effectively (Lemieux & Prates, 2011; Navias, 2002, p. 69). Another point is that terrorist organisations can raise and keep their money in legal economic systems by money laundering methods utilising these companies (Croissant & Barlow, 2007, p. 138).[12]

Moreover, financing by legal activities and sources is especially secure for terrorist organisations. It is not easy for security forces to detect financing of terrorist organisations through legal businesses. At the same time, funding via legal activities has certain disadvantages. Firstly, from law enforcement and counter-terrorism perspectives, these legitimate businesses can be used as an entrance door to the terrorist organisation's network and communications. Secondly, running legal businesses is not simple; as a result, terrorist organisations dealing with legal activities should have advanced business skills and provide information to establish businesses and use financial services offered by various sectors (e.g. banks). Thirdly, terrorist groups can end up generating lower amounts of financing from legal businesses than criminal enterprises (Freeman, 2011, pp. 469–470).

Regardless of their respective purposes, terrorist organisations exist within various forms of business sectors and run them with their professionalised skills. Furthermore, these legal businesses open the doors of legal and less monitored normal economic life; thus, terrorist groups can enjoy the benefits of their vague exploitation and integration.

SOURCES OF POPULAR SUPPORT (CHARITIES/NGOS, DIASPORA GROUPS, INDIVIDUAL DONATIONS)

It is generally agreed that a great number of terrorist entities depend on their sympathisers and constituencies for funding (Freeman, 2011, p. 470). According to Winer (2008, p. 115) charities provide four main advantages for terrorists: attracting many unwitting and witting donors, increasing public support, protecting against government intervention and the ability to operate in conflict areas with the cover of charitable purpose.

12 For example, Al Qaeda and its cells have run numerous licit businesses such as peanut farms, honey trading companies, tanneries, furniture companies, construction companies, fishing businesses and manufacturing companies (Basile, 2004, p. 172; Burke, 2003, p. 145); ETA has its own furniture stores in France (Alexander, 2004, p. 51); the Provisional IRA (PIRA) and the Loyalists in Northern Ireland have used a broad range of legitimate businesses from running night clubs and pubs to gaming machines and from taxi services to security firms for their financing (Adams, 1986, p. 7; Silke, 1998) and Al Qaeda affiliated Jemaah Islamiyah from Southeast Asia allegedly operates vehicle repair firms, computer software marketing and medical supplies trading companies (Rudner, 2006, p. 45); LTTE (Liberation Tigers of Tamil Eelam) also is alleged to have owned commercial maritime shipping companies, ocean liners, jewellery stores and restaurants for their funding (Hafeez, 2009).

It is claimed that charitable donations are one of the most significant fundraising sources for terrorist organisations (Freeman, 2011, p. 470; Lemieux & Prates, 2011, p. 371). In addition, Rudner (2006, p. 42, 2010, p. 703) alleges that funds generated from deviation of grants and donations constitute the largest substantial amount of resources for terrorist organisations. It is clear that donations and charities can be used for raising funds; however, there is not any available data substantiating Rudner's (2006) claim. Charities by providing humanitarian assistance and services attract significant public support and are accepted as sacred and valuable. Consequently, this general perception can be easily exploited by terrorist organisations, and large donations can be diverted from charity organisations into their coffers without attracting the attention of security forces (Rudner, 2006; U.S. Department of Treasury, 2005). By using charities, terrorist groups can create a positive image in their community, which increases public support and the collection of grants from both witting and unwitting donors. Therefore, this social support makes it difficult to intervene and prevent exploitation of charities by security forces (Rudner, 2006, 2010). By establishing front charities, terrorists can disguise the identity of their donors and collect funds (which are often tax free) from legitimate donors and illegitimate ones (Rudner, 2006, p. 43). Raphaeli (2003, p. 62) claims that charities can be used for raising funds and also as a means to channel the money to different locations clandestinely.

However, as Clunan (2006, p. 570) notes, charities which provide humanitarian relief services and financial assistance to places hit by war and conflicts may not be aware that some of their funds go to terrorists. A blanket stigmatisation, prohibition and closure of such charities by states can create drastic consequences for the well-being of people who are in need of serious humanitarian assistance (Passas, 2006a; de Goede, 2012). Secondly, if these charities are closed, it opens the possibility that other illegitimate charities may step in and accept donations which are then transferred to terrorists.

Donations from wealthy donors and sympathisers, front organisations or ethno-cultural diasporas are another source for terrorist entities (Rudner, 2006, p. 43). In addition, terrorist organisations can establish front organisations under the name of a developmental or aid NGO which sustain mainly public infrastructure such as schools, religious places, health clinics and welfare centres (Rudner, 2010) which can be used by terrorist groups to gain public support and raise funds.

In addition to diaspora communities where terrorists can raise funds (Freeman, 2011),[13] individual donors also support terrorist entities by paying donations and membership fees directly. These benefactors may directly give their money to

13 Diaspora based individual donors can be given as an example in this category such as donors of the US based Irish Northern Aid Committee (NORAID), who were providing 50 percent of the revenue of PIRA in 1970s (Freeman, 2011, p. 470; Myres, 2012, p. 700). In addition LTTE was raising around \$7 to \$22 million annually from the Tamil Diaspora in Canada (Freeman, 2011, p. 470).

organisations or a network to meet requirements of operatives and other members such as travel, training and living expenses (Rudner, 2006). In this context, mainly wealthy individuals and businessmen supply money of their own will but sometimes they can be threatened and coerced to give money (Roberge, 2007, p. 198; Rudner, 2010, p. 705).

It can be concluded that popular support and public based funding activities have some benefits and costs for terrorist organisations. Firstly, these sources demonstrate the legitimacy of the terrorist organisation under the guise of charitable activities. Secondly, through charity, popular support is simple and easier to acquire. Similar to the state sponsored terrorism funding model, all the terrorist organisation has to do is to wait for the donations to come to their coffers. Thirdly, these sources are reliable for terrorist organisations, and they present a geographical flexibility to terrorists' financing (Freeman, 2011, p. 470).[14]

On the other hand, terrorists may lose some control in order not to undermine popular support and satisfy their constituencies' demands; thus, terrorist leaderships may act differently than the predetermined, original plans. Secondly, the attractiveness of this popular support may lead to the emergence of new groups who want to stick to the original and fundamental ideology.[15] A third disadvantage is that the general economic conditions and capacity of the charitable outfit and its members directly impacts the terrorist budget (Freeman, 2011, p. 470).

On the whole terrorist organisations find advanced instruments and covert structures to exploit and use legitimate economic activities for their cause. They can appear as a legitimate and ordinary business such as a restaurant, a well-designed pub or a charity purported to be providing regular service or humanitarian aid. This makes identification of terrorist funding a great challenge for law enforcement agencies.

Illegal activities

In addition to state sponsorship and pseudo-legal financing sources, illegal activities are another important fundraising method for terrorists. It is widely accepted that especially in the 1990s, as a result of eroding state funding, proceeds of crime have become favourable for terrorist organisations. In addition, Freeman (2011, p. 466) opines that the constraining, controlling and unstable nature of state sponsorship has pushed terrorist organisations to seek financial sources from illegal activities. In this period, weak regulation of financial systems, porous borders and advanced money laundering mechanisms also facilitated criminal activities with the purpose of raising funds for terrorism (Croissant & Barlow, 2007,

14 Charities can go everywhere in the world and collect money for terrorists in the name of humanitarian or disaster assistance efforts.

15 For example, when the IRA accepted a ceasefire and engaged in political dialogue rather than paramilitary activities, the Real IRA emerged.

p. 135; Dishman, 2001, p. 43). Myres (2012, p. 703) argues that when legitimate financial sources of terrorists decrease or become inaccessible, then terrorist groups are likely to gravitate towards criminal markets. Correspondingly, Hutchinson and O'Malley (2007, p. 1095) suggest that especially after the 9/11 attacks the more robust legal environment with its focus on terrorists' money supply may have forced terrorists to conduct criminal activities. However, Tupman (2009, p. 194) claims that, "the 'War on Terrorism', by making more activities illegal, may be creating new areas of global economic activity" to emerge (for the purposes of terrorist finance).

Using illegal sources for funding terrorist organisations comes with certain risks and benefits. Firstly, terrorist organisations can raise large amounts of liquid funds from illegal activities (e.g. the sale of drugs), and these activities can provide quick income for terrorists (Freeman, 2011). However, these activities may lead to unstable money flows compared to regular income from a legal business activity (Myres, 2012). Secondly, these activities dent the authority of the state because terrorists demonstrate that the government cannot control its territory or protect its population against these crimes (Freeman, 2011). Moreover, the image and integrity of a terrorist organisation and the popular support they have, because of the values behind which they stand, could be damaged because of committing criminal activities such as drug trafficking (Myres, 2012).[16] Thirdly, conducting some these criminal activities can be relatively easy (Freeman, 2011),[17] but terrorist organisations have to appoint and train extra personnel for these specific tasks. Another point is that in the criminal milieu, terrorist organisations have to deal with numerous challenges such as cooperation with other criminal syndicates through facilitators who can cooperate with police or embezzle funds destined for the terrorist organisation (Myres, 2012, p. 703; Shapiro, 2007; Shapiro & Siegel, 2007). Moreover, gaining large amounts of money through criminal activities can cause corruption and power struggles among terrorists (Freeman, 2011). In addition to the security risks, dealing with criminal activities bears internal organisational risks; for example, with the financial wealth created by crime, terrorists could leave their ideological and religious goals and motivation, thus become becoming 'common' criminals.

Terrorist entities can raise a large amount of money from illegal activities such as extortion, protection money, taxes, kidnapping and ransom, theft, smuggling, petty crime and counterfeiting goods (Freeman, 2011, p. 466) which are suitable for conventional money laundering (Clunan, 2006, p. 570). Myres (2012, p. 703) emphasises that the dynamic and adaptable nature of terrorists'

16 For example, Islam prohibits the sale and use of drugs, alcohol and other narcotic substances. Thus, if a religiously motivated terrorist organization which claims to defend Islamic values is found to be engaged in trading such goods, then the general support for it may diminish.

17 Robbing a bank or extortion, for instance, do not require complex and advanced skills and training.

decision-making mechanism enables them choose to enter particular criminal markets if they believe they can attain a profitable position which will generate funds.[18]

Some terrorist organisations are known to demand that people pay their so-called "revolution taxes". For example, Shining Path (Sendero Lumineso), Revolutionary Armed Forces of Colombia (FARC) and ETA use this method for financing. In addition, "extortion" is a popular method used by terrorists to raise funds especially from wealthy businessmen. According to Silke (1998, p. 349), loyalist groups in Northern Ireland mainly used extortion for raising funds.

Kidnapping officials and wealthy business owners and keeping them for ransom are used effectively to generate revenue and provide publicity to terrorist organisations.[19] It is believed that kidnapping is one of the most profitable sources for terrorists (Picarelli & Shelley, 2007, p. 44). Terrorist groups can also raise large amounts of money from bank robberies and stealing valuable items, such as gold, silver, precious stones, artefacts and antiquities.

Drug trafficking has been accepted as the largest source of income for terrorist and criminal organisations (Hutchinson & O'Malley, 2007). The relationship between terrorism and drug trafficking has been called "narco-terrorism".[20] FARC, PKK, Shining Path and the Afghan Taliban are well-known organisations which conduct drug related financing activities. Even though some terrorist organisations engage in the growing and selling of drugs, it is claimed that generally terrorist organisations prefer to take part in the distribution and shipment phases of drug traffic. Moreover, terrorists can provide protection to drug dealers in return for sharing the profit with them (Freeman, 2011).

Human trafficking and smuggling have become profitable for criminals and terrorists since the 1990s (Hutchinson & O'Malley, 2007).[21] Terrorists smuggle almost everything such as drugs, arms, humans, cigarettes, cash, diamonds and animals for their funding (Freeman, 2011). For example, the IRA raised $2 million per annum from exports of pigs openly bought from the Republic of Ireland and sold in Northern Ireland whereby they were also able claim export subsidy (£8 per pig) to smuggle the same pigs back to Ireland again and repeat this activity.

18 For example, it was reported that the Madrid train bombings were financed by drug trafficking, robberies and automatic teller machine (ATM) frauds in 2004. Another example is the 2002 Bali bombings which were funded by gold stolen from jewellery stores (Rudner, 2006, p. 44; Winer, 2008, p. 115).

19 For example, in the Philippines, the Al Qaeda affiliated Abu Sayyaf and Moro Islamic Liberation Front have kidnapped foreign tourists and aid workers for ransom (Sanderson, 2004; Anderson, 1998, as cited in Hutchinson & O'Malley, 2007, p. 1097).

20 This term was first coined by Peruvian President Fernando Belaunde Terry in 1982 to refer to the attacks on the agents of drug law enforcement agencies (Thomas, 2009, pp. 1885–1886).

21 For example, it was reported that PKK smuggle people from Iraq to Europe for around 2000–3000 Euros per person (Freeman, 2011).

Besides such complex and organised cross-border criminal activities, terrorist organisations can raise funds from small-scale crimes. These crimes can include manufacturing fake credit cards, credit card fraud and stealing passports from tourists and selling them (Freeman, 2011). Furthermore, it is reported that terrorists generate revenue from pirated and counterfeit goods such as clothing, compact discs, perfume, videos and currencies (Freeman, 2011; Raphaeli, 2003) which traditionally attract lower punishments in criminal courts.

Understanding the dynamics of criminal funding and terrorism

As can be seen above, terrorist organisations engage in a range of criminal activities to raise funds. In this context Hutchinson and O'Malley (2007, p. 1098) suggest that the organisational capacity and needs of terrorist organisations determine the types of criminal activities they choose. These criminal activities and terrorist organisations are classified under two basic categories: 'ephemeral-sporadic' and 'organised-enduring' (Hutchinson & O'Malley, 2007). Ephemeral-sporadic groups are terrorist organisations which commit more simple and basic types of 'sporadic' crimes such as such as kidnapping, extortion and robbery/thievery and do not need large amounts of money for attacks. Organised enduring terrorist organisations on the other hand have high-level skills, capacity and networks for crimes such as drug trafficking, arms trade, human smuggling and counterfeit goods and currencies.

With the diminishing of state sponsored terrorism especially after the Cold War period, terrorists turned to organised crime to generate income. Subsequently, the differences between terrorist and transnational criminal organisations (TCO) have become vague (Picarelli, 2012, p. 181) and difficult to identify. Terrorists have learned advanced techniques from criminals such as how to smuggle and transhipment and distribution of drugs and other illegal commodities, money laundering and communication systems. On the other hand, criminals have gained advanced information related to military training and being provided access to more sophisticated weapon technologies (Eccarius-Kelly, 2012, p. 239) and operational knowhow. It is claimed that terrorist and criminal organisations have developed a unique exchange system whereby drugs, arms and valuable metals and stones (known as the "triangular informal currency system") are used instead of cash (Lemieux & Prates, 2011, p. 373). Arguably, these assets are much more difficult to trace and can be exchanged with ease anywhere in the world.

It can be argued that terrorist organisations and TCOs may cooperate to advance their aims and interests by improving their 'in house' capabilities. However, rather than long-term strategic partnerships, they may forge short-term partnerships for on-the-spot activities (Dishman, 2001). On the other hand, Picarelli (2012) suggests that terrorist organisations and TCOs have transformed and resembled each other: hence the difficulty in distinguishing them. As a result of these long-term partnerships, they have created hybrid organisations, as opposed to the idea of short-term relationships put forward by Dishman (2001).

Furthermore, according to Dishman (2005), the information age has caused a transformation of the hierarchical structures of various organisations and firms. More importantly, the effective efforts and success of the law enforcement agencies forced these criminal and terrorist organisations to change their traditional hierarchical structure to a new network based organisational structure consisting of smaller autonomous cells, which provides more resilience and secrecy to these organisations to survive.

As a result of the dynamics of this transformation, with altered aims and activities, terrorist organisations might evolve into totally different organisations then originally envisaged (Cronin, 2009, pp. 146–153). In other words, they can transform into profit-seeking organisations instead of pursuing political, ideological and religious goals. Rosenthal (2008) sees "for-profit terrorists" as a new type of terrorist structure, which has the ability to use features of terrorists and criminals at the same time for their own interests instead of advancing their ideology.

According to Rosenthal (2008) there are three catalysts for this evolution or adaptation from a purely ideological to a for-profit terrorist organisation. The first is the elimination of terrorist leadership structure. The second factor is political change which can damage the ideological beliefs of terrorists. Thirdly, opportunities for great financial revenues, which can change the minds and motivation of terrorists whereby they may become more interested in profits than pursuing their original organisational aims (Freeman, 2011). It can be asserted that converting terrorist organisations into criminal entities may weaken them ideologically and facilitate the process of tackling them.

Money laundering

If there is a large amount of income from criminal activity, the group involved in it must find a way to keep and control these assets without drawing any attention to themselves (Irwin, Choo, & Liu, 2012a). Criminal organisations and terrorists use money-laundering techniques for their financial purposes.[22] Although terrorists and criminals both benefit from the money-laundering process, in practice they have some subtle differences. Irwin et al. (2012a) observe that money launderers and terrorism financers appear to have different preferences for placement, layering and integration techniques.

Although terrorism financers use channels similar to those of money launderers, they do not tend to utilise as many or complex placement, layering and integration techniques. Rather, they prefer to use fewer techniques, which maintain high levels of anonymity and appear safe. Sums of monies involved in money laundering and terrorism financing vary significantly. It is emphasised

22 According to the Australian Institute of Criminology the definition of money laundering is "[. . .] the process by which the proceeds of crime are put through a series of transactions, which disguise their illicit origins, and make them appear to have come from a legitimate source" (Graycar & Grabosky, 1996. as cited in A. S. Irwin, Choo, & Liu, 2012b, p. 322).

that the terrorist organisations launder significantly smaller amounts of money than criminals (Irwin et al., 2012a, pp. 105–106). This might be a result of terrorist financing operations including smaller amounts of money, and it can be suggested that terrorists operate with a goal directed approach rather than a profit seeking one.

While some suggest that the financing of terrorism and money laundering are related and/or integrated concepts, Clunan (2006) claims that terrorist finance is different from money laundering. Correspondingly, Roberge (2007) emphasises that, even though money laundering and financing of terrorism have some similarities, they are very different concepts essentially. Money laundering serves criminals, whose aim is just profits, as a tool to conceal their gains and make them look legitimate. On the other hand, the financing of terrorism supports terrorist organisations to sustain and achieve their ideological aims.

It is known that terrorists can raise funds by both legal and illegal activities for future terrorist activities and attacks. In these circumstances, the crime of financing terrorism has a preparatory nature referring to future (Tofangsaz, 2012). In short, even though terrorist financing and money laundering have some similarities, different motivations (profit seeking and political goals) and the availability of legal sources for terrorist financing make the essential distinction between them.

Internet based sources

Like any other organisation, a terrorist organisation uses the internet for various purposes including for financing its activities (Weimann, 2006, p. 134), publicizing its ideology and recruitment. The anonymity, the speed and the broad range of communication abilities provided by the internet are used by terrorists for their financing, recruitment and propaganda activities effectively. The internet also provides terrorists a cross border and global reach, timely efficiency and a certain degree of secrecy (Jacobson, 2010, p. 353). In addition, the internet can be used by terrorist organisations as an effective and attractive tool for raising, transferring and laundering funds. In the last two decades, the increasing internet usage by the public and the lack of suitable legislation have caused criminals and terrorists to replace their activities on this platform (Bensted, 2012). It is claimed that especially after the 9/11 attacks terrorist organisations have increased their utilisation of the internet (Jacobson, 2010). In this context terrorists generally raise funds from direct solicitations through websites and e-mail correspondence, using legitimate sources such as charities and banks as fronts, cybercrime activities, credit card fraud and identity theft via the internet (Bensted, 2012). For example, Al Qaeda and ISIS are known to use websites, internet based chat rooms and forums to solicit and raise funds, for recruitment and for publicity.

Direct solicitation of donations via the internet is a primary method for terrorist fundraising. Terrorist entities use websites, chat rooms and targeted e-mails to collect money from their sympathisers (Hinnen, 2004; Lewis, 2005). According to Thomas (2003), terrorists analyse internet users' demographic information and select suitable people to send e-mails asking for donations.

Another internet based source is infiltrating charities and NGOs to mask their financing activities and transfer funds from these charities for terrorist goals. In this case, it is not easy to distinguish the source of money. In addition, online charities can be established as front organisations all around the world by terrorists whereby they can evade national laws (Bensted, 2012; Jacobson, 2010, pp. 355–356).

The advantages and the efficiency provided by online banking systems make them preferable to terrorist organisations for their revenue generating activities. Moreover, terrorists using online banking systems, which provide the ability to transfer small amounts of money, can bypass banking reporting systems and make it difficult for officials to trace online funds (Bensted, 2012). Anonymity and no face interaction make online banking advantageous for terrorist entities (Hinnen, 2004).

Cyber laundering and credit card fraud, which often take place in multiple jurisdictions, are also popular methods for terrorist financing which are difficult for law enforcement agencies to counter. Laundering money via the internet is relatively easy and untraceable due to the global and anonymous nature of the internet (Baldwin, 2004). Further, it is even more difficult to detect the online activities of terrorists who use informal value transfer systems as a result of lack of records and identity information (Bensted, 2012). E-commerce and auction sites are also used by terrorist groups to raise money (Tibbetts, 2002). In addition, using credit card fraud and identity theft, terrorists can access bank accounts and bypass bank reporting systems (Baldwin, 2004). Terrorists are known to raise money and reach personal identity information using fraudulent company websites (Hinnen, 2004).

Moreover, digital technology offers new opportunities for transferring money. Internet based tools for transferring money such as PayPal and mobile phones can be used to channel funds called 'M-payments' which are very popular in African states because of their weak financial control and monitoring systems (Jacobson, 2010). Furthermore, in recent years online gambling sites (Jacobson, 2010) and 'Massively Multi Player Online Games' (MMOGs) such as "Second Life" and "World of Warcraft" have been used by both criminals and terrorists for money laundering and terrorist financing purposes (Irwin et al., 2012a). It has also been reported that virtual/cryptocurrencies such Bitcoin and Ethereum are likely to be used by terrorist organisations because of the anonymity and ease of use they provide (Goldman et al., 2017, p. 2).

2.4 Movement of money and assets (channelling funds)

Financing of terrorism not only covers activities related to raising funds, but also includes the transfer of raised money and other assets to cells, operatives and individuals. Terrorist organisations use different means for transferring funds to various units and persons within the organisation (Rudner, 2006).

2.4.1 Informal Value Transfer Systems (IVTS)

IVTS operate outside the formal banking system, and they have crucial importance for developing countries and diaspora communities (Rudner, 2010). In many parts of the world, these systems serve the people and countries which cannot access and/or meet the expense of formal financial systems. Furthermore, these services are useful for cash-based economies where the formal banking system is not developed as is the case in Somalia (Danziger, 2012). The policy makers of developing countries, who understand that international money transfers have vital importance for their countries' future, try to decrease the costs of transactions using technology and increasing the speed and convenience of these kinds of transfers (Passas, 2006a). These financial systems are generally used in countries in the Middle East, Africa and South Asia for both commercial and non-commercial transfers and payments (Rudner, 2010). Terrorist organisations and their supporters may use 'Informal Value Transfer Systems' (IVTS) because of the secrecy they provide (Rudner, 2006). Even though these transfer methods employ the same rules, they have different names in different geographical areas (Passas, 2006a).[23]

IVTS can be characterised with trust, mutuality of interests and self-regulatory arrangements, which protect customers from their losses without requiring the same level of due diligence standards found in formal banking regimes. Additionally, these informal transfer systems are more reliable, cheap, convenient and competitive than banks and other financial enterprises. Moreover, in some cases it has been found that formal banking systems were exploiting immigrant workers with extra high costs and lower exchange rates than those provided by IVTS. These IVTS provide liquidity at crisis times and assist developing countries better than foreign investments (Passas, 2006a). In fact, the hawala system works as an informal global network of individuals who transfer money for their customers such as wiring services.[24]

Raphaeli (2003) notes that these informal systems do not leave any paper trail behind, and the records of all transactions are not detailed enough for further investigations from the terrorist financing perspective. According to Basile (2004, pp. 175–176), these informal systems are used by both legitimate people

23 "Hawala" denotes "transfer" in Arabic, which in the context of money transfer, means a movement of money through a private, complex and global network of agents. Its root goes back to the Indian subcontinent, and with immigration, it has grown in its use in other parts of the world. For instance, in South Asia the same transfer method is called "Hundi"; "Fei ch'ien" is the Chinese version; and in Filipino, they call it "Padala". It can be said that they are all IVTS in terms of their functions but have different names (Passas, 2006a).

24 In this system, dealers do not make any money transaction between each other. Instead, the first dealer calls or use other types of communication systems to instruct the second dealer about the amount of money and the information about the recipient of that money. Then the second dealer pays the money to the correct recipient. This money transfer itself is not accounted for, as the dealers hold their balances. Later they can adjust the balance with a single money transfer or precious stones and other methods (Basile, 2004).

and terrorists to channel their money without detection by the global banking system and keeping any records. Basile (2004) also emphasises that unregulated legitimate IVTS are open to terrorist organisations' exploitation. In other words, lack of regulation and paper trail make IVTS an attractive transfer method for terrorist organisations.

Moreover, it is also difficult to expose the loose network structure of these systems which mostly consist of familial or tribal relationships (Croissant & Barlow, 2007). However, de Goede (2003, 2012) rightly criticises the unfairly built discourses regarding IVTS and how the IVTS are stigmatised as evil terrorist tools by several scholars (e.g. Ganguly, 2001; Weiner & Johnston, 2001; Navias, 2002; Greenberg, Wechsler, & Wolosky, 2002; Kochan, 2005). Moreover, as Passas (2006a) notes, there is a real risk that criminals can exploit these informal systems, and they can be regarded as problems for states' monetary policies. However, numerous investigations have revealed that terrorists (including those who were behind the 9/11 and Madrid attacks) did not use any informal value transfer systems but instead, made use of formal channels such as banks, credit cards and electronic transfers in the US and the UK (Passas, 2006a). In addition, according to a report by a Dutch authority, there was no evidence to suggest that IVTS were used by terrorists inside the US and Europe (Passas, 2005, p. 37). However, after 9/11 attacks the US policy makers and law enforcement agencies in particular have targeted hawala and increased their efforts to regulate IVTS because they believe that they are used by terrorists (Passas, 2006a).

2.4.2 Formal banking systems

It is known that the preferred medium for laundering illicit funds and terrorist finance is formal financial institutions, and both non-terrorist criminals and terrorists use professionals to help hide, disguise and/or transfer their illicit gains (Turksen, 2018, p. 332). Underlying reasons for this trend are the expertise, experience, efficiency and relatively low cost of the services which the formal financial sector offers. It is not surprising that terrorist organisations use international formal banking systems and other financial services for channelling and laundering their funds. Terrorist groups navigate these regimes with adroit skills. For example, they transfer small amounts of money in order not to trigger any suspicion or red flags by banks and law enforcement agencies.

It has been claimed that certain terrorist organisations exploit the Islamic banking network for transferring and laundering money (Raphaeli, 2003).[25] The Islamic banking network operates in the formal financial system with the required banking licences and is informed by Islamic (Sharia) law, which bans interest. These profits are used internally or donated to charities. Basile (2004) claims

25 The Islamic banking network is a global system, which has strong links with third world countries, tax havens and developed countries such as the United Kingdom and the United States.

that the transfers sent from Islamic correspondent banks to Western banks are checked with less scrutiny, and this weakness is exploited by terrorist organisations. In addition, Ridley and Alexander (2011) emphasise that Islamic banking has weak points in the context of illicit money transfers, and the regulatory framework, management and financial services they provide can be different in various jurisdictions. Having said that, the US and the European banks and financial entities have the same problems as Islamic banks (de Goede, 2003)[26] and do not always follow unified benchmarks for auditing, due diligence and reporting. It is important to note that terrorists used the US and other Western financial institutions to hold, transfer and utilise their money. They also deposited their money from overseas to US bank accounts using wire transfers, cash and traveller checks and ATM and credit card transactions in the US (Winer, 2008). Terrorist organisations find and exploit the weak points of financial systems and combine different financial systems in harmony to serve their goals.

2.4.3 *Other transfer methods*

In addition to IVTS and formal banking systems, terrorist organisations use other money transfer methods such as cash couriers, money mules, trade based transactions and trading of precious stones.

Firstly, terrorist groups generally use cash couriers as another transfer method. These couriers can move with cash, gemstones and other valuable assets. In order to conceal their identities, they use fraudulent passports and other identity documents (Rudner, 2006). In tandem with the increase in recording, reporting and safeguarding measures in formal financial transactions, the use of cash couriers between borders has also increased. The cash courier system is common especially in the Middle East because of porous border conditions and the cash-based culture, unlike the Western-based credit card economy (Raphaeli, 2003), which presents an additional challenge for CTF practice.

Secondly, trade based transactions can be exploited for transferring large amounts of money and funds (Rudner, 2006 and Passas, 2006a). These types of transactions involve high value which can be easily converted to liquid assets which can be exchanged locally for cash such as export transactions of honey in the Middle East (Rudner, 2006).

Thirdly, gemstones, gold and diamonds possess portable and untraceable value, and these precious stones and metals can be used as a transfer method by terrorist organisations (Rudner, 2006). The detailed field study on the usage of diamonds by Passas and Jones (2006, p. 1) found that there is conflicting and inconclusive evidence concerning terrorist groups and diamonds trade. This might indicate that the findings from the field can be contradictory and misleading. As Rudner

26 For example, Al Qaeda used Western banks and formal money transfer systems such as "France's Credit Lyonnais, Germany's Commerzbank" to move its money around the world (de Goede, 2003).

(2006) claims, it is possible for terrorists to use diamonds and other precious stones; however, the research by Passas and Jones (2006) provides compelling evidence for further study pertaining to this aspect of terrorist financing.

2.5 Conclusion

In this chapter the subject of the financing of terrorism has been discussed from the terrorist organisations' perspective which reveals that generation and management of financial assets are essential for the operational capabilities and sustainability of terrorist organisations. In addition, the chapter offers numerous theoretical approaches to terrorist financing as well as organisational and structural differences amongst them. The main sources of terrorist financing have been critically analysed, and the pros and cons of different terrorist financing options and methods have been identified. Lastly, money-transferring methods of terrorist organisations have been described, and the practical application of terrorist financing has been examined from a sub-national organisational level. We can conclude that terrorists can raise funds from diverse and flexible resources. Additionally, the number of these methods and sources for terrorists is only limited by their creativity. These methods also evolve in tandem with law and policy changes as well as the socio-economic environment in which terrorists operate. Consequently, countering and disrupting terrorists' financial activities and sources are difficult tasks in such conditions.

In the next chapter the current situation of counter-terrorist financing will be analysed.

3 Countering terrorist financing

3.1 Introduction

In this chapter, we approach the subject of CTF from a law enforcement position. Therefore, various CTF efforts and measures are examined.

In the first section of this chapter, CTF efforts in the US will be assessed by considering the legal system, law enforcement units, intelligence agencies and private financial institutions therein. This focus mainly drives from the fact that after the 9/11 terrorist attacks, the US government has spearheaded counter-terrorism efforts both domestically and internationally (e.g. at the United Nations (UN) Security Council and the FATF) and influenced the evolution of CTF practices. Thus, analysing the US CTF strategy and regime can provide an understanding of the subject and the drivers behind regional (e.g. EU) and international CTF law and practice.

In the second part of this chapter, CTF measures at the international level will be assessed. This section will mainly concentrate on the UN efforts, conventions and resolutions related to the financing of terrorism. In this context, the UN's 1999 'Convention for Suppression of the Financing of Terrorism' and the relevant UN Security Council Resolutions and mechanisms will be discussed to explain the role of the UN in creating a new security environment. The next section will focus on international CTF efforts from regional and international organisations' perspective. The efforts and the organisational approaches of different international actors such as the European Union (EU), the Financial Action Task Force (FATF), the Egmont Group, the International Monetary Fund (IMF), and the World Bank (WB) will be illustrated.

After this, the current CTF strategies and measures will be discussed. Moreover, the inclusion of private financial institutions such as banks and money sending businesses (MSBs) into the CTF framework as well as their responsibilities will be explained. Under this banner, blacklisting, asset freezing, financial intelligence/investigation methods and more importantly the effectiveness of these mechanisms will be commented on. In particular, the adaptation of Anti-Money Laundering (AML) techniques as CTF measures and their suitability will be critically analysed, and the question of how to measure the effectiveness of CTF methods will be addressed.

3.2 National CTF efforts

Even though financing of terrorism was identified as an important enabler for terrorist organisations prior to 9/11, the US and other governments did not prioritise terrorist financing until after the 9/11 attacks in 2001. Shortly after these attacks, CTF became a strategic priority for most Western governments, and CTF measures were put in place swiftly (Passas, 2006b, p. 281). The US and the other countries' efforts have concentrated on specific measures such as designating, freezing the assets of suspected people and entities and collecting financial intelligence. Moreover, as a leading actor, the US government has made numerous legislative, structural and organisational transformations to combat this threat more effectively (Levitt & Jacobson, 2008, p. 67).

3.2.1 The US CTF system: Pre-9/11

Before the 9/11 attacks there was limited public curiosity about financing of terrorism. Additionally, there were very few regulatory mechanisms addressing this problem, and the CTF practice was confined to a small number of experts' knowledge (Eckert, 2008, p. 209). Until the mid-1980s anti-drug strategies were the focal point of the US government, whereas around 1990 the term 'financing of terrorism' started to appear following numerous terrorist attacks against the US institutions (Levi, 2010, p. 651). Until the attacks on US embassies in Tanzania and Kenya in 1998, terrorist financing was perceived as a problem which was confined to state-sponsorship of terrorism, money laundering or money from criminal activity (Clunan, 2006, p. 574). Thus, during that time the CTF strategies focused mainly on compelling states to cut off their support for terrorist organisations and suppressing criminal organisations which aided them (Winer, 2008, p. 114). Another prominent aspect of this period was that US executives concentrated on anti-money laundering measures (Shetterly, 2005, p. 332), and especially during 1980s and 1990s legislative efforts targeted illicit money transferring via formal banking system (Bensted, 2012, p. 238).

It seems that the US did not make an orchestrated and decisive effort against financing of terrorism (Clunan, 2006, p. 583) as can be evidenced by the 9/11 Commission Report (2004) and the 9/11 Commission Monograph on Terrorist Financing Staff Report (Roth et al., 2004). These reports highlight several weaknesses in the US CTF regime including non-integrated data collection, misperceptions related to information exchange between responsible agencies, organisational barriers, turf wars and lack of attention by the US government and Congress.

Donohue (2008, pp. 147–148) points out the three main legal instruments established for investigative and regulatory measures for CTF prior to 9/11. The first one is the International Emergency Economic Powers Act (IEEPA) (1977), the second legislative instrument is the Antiterrorism and Effective Death Penalty

Act (AEDPA) (1996), and the third regime consisted of statutes related to drug trafficking and AML prior to the 9/11 attacks.[1]

Clunan (2006, p. 586) notes that the IEEPA (1977) was the most powerful legal tool dealing with terrorist financing prior to the 9/11 terrorist attacks.[2] During the 1990s, the US executive office created a list of "Prohibited Persons and Specially Designated Terrorists" to ban their financial transactions under the IEEPA (Donohue, 2008, p. 148). Owing to the fact that this statute is mainly about foreign policy and national security subjects, its provisions and application were subjected to less judicial review (Cuellar, 2003, pp. 360–361). The initial application of this act concentrated on nation-states such as Libya, Cuba (Donohue, 2008, p. 148), Iran and Sudan (Clunan, 2006, p. 586 and Eckert, 2008, p. 212).[3] However, in the 1990s, the US executive started to use IEEPA (1977) against non-state actors such as Palestinian terrorist organisations and drug trafficking cartels such as the Colombian Cali Cartel (Donohue, 2008, p. 148). It can be seen that during the Cold War period, the US CTF policy and law mainly concentrated on threats in the context of state-sponsored terrorism which then evolved to focus on non-state threats.

After the Oklahoma terrorist attacks in 1995,[4] the US Congress enacted AEDPA (1996), legislation for addressing foreign threats. With this statute, "State Sponsors of Terrorism" and "Designated Foreign Terrorist Organisations" lists were created to apply financial constraints on these organisations (Donohue, 2008, p. 149).[5] The third stream of legislative authority emerged as a product of anti-money laundering efforts (mostly concentrating on drug related money

1 These statutes are the Bank Secrecy Act (BSA) (1970), the Anti-Drug Abuse Act (1988), the Housing and Community Development Act (1992), and the Money Laundering and Financial Crimes Strategy Act (1998).

2 According to this statute if the president announces a national emergency in the face of an extraordinary and unusual threat against the US, then IEEPA (1977) provides him/her a wide range of economic regulation and authority (Donohue, 2008, p. 148). In these circumstances, the president can use these broad powers to designate individuals and entities as a security threat, freeze their assets and block their transactions and trades. Consequently, according to this legislation, under general presidential wartime or national emergency powers, the Office of Foreign Assets Control (OFAC), under the Treasury Department, identifies designated individuals and organisations and issues an order for their accounts to be frozen or blocked (Clunan, 2006, p. 586). OFAC's task is to undertake sanctions against foreign states whose policies are contrary to the US foreign policy interests and security (Eckert, 2008, p. 211).

3 The Clinton administration used this act against drug traffickers and groups who threatened the Middle East Peace Process in a novel way; however, only after 1998 embassy bombings were the Taliban, Osama Bin Laden and Al Qaeda put on a Specially Designated Terrorists list under the IEEPA (1977) (Clunan, 2006, p. 586).

4 The Oklahoma attacks were domestic and conducted by an ex-Army soldier and security guard named Timothy McVeigh (FBI, 2018).

5 Additionally, this statute gives permission for civil suits against foreign states or their agencies or instruments, which either conduct or provide support for terrorist organisations or attacks. Thus providing "material support" become a criminal offence not only in the US territory but also outside the US (Bantekas, 2003, p. 328).

laundering) (Donohue, 2008, p. 151). These new anti-money laundering provisions criminalised undertaking transactions to further or disguise proceeds of criminal activity (Cuellar, 2003, p. 338). The main objective was to create a paper trail for detecting and tracking abuses of tax and criminal laws.[6] Prior to the 9/11 attacks, it is evident that there was no broad approach to pursuing terrorist financing, and this subject was not highly prioritised by the US authorities.

The Clinton administration started to re-conceptualise terrorism throughout the 1990s to a new paradigm which encompassed threats from non-state sources of terrorism and its financing rather than traditional enemy states of the Cold War era (Clunan, 2006, p. 587). According to Clunan (2006, p. 587) and the 9/11 Commission Report (2004, pp. 102–107), by the end of the Clinton administration, the US executive recognised terrorists as non-state actors and their financial activities as a serious security problem. Nonetheless, the White House was too slow to recognise this fact. Thus, it failed to develop a coordinated counterterrorism strategy during this period (Clunan, 2006, p. 587).[7] The negative consequences of this limited understanding of terrorist financing was observed in the post-9/11 period.

3.2.2 The US CTF system: post-9/11

The events of 9/11 dramatically changed the counter-terrorism and security environment in the US, and terrorist financing has become a vanguard issue on the political agenda (Roberge, 2007, p. 196). In this period the US has developed many counter measures against terrorism (Ridley & Alexander, 2011, p. 41). Consequently, within a very short time, responsible federal agencies came together and started to work to reveal the financial roots of the attacks. As a result, new units were formed, and an agreement to work in interagency style cooperation was reached (Clunan, 2006, p. 588). Eckert (2008, p. 214) acknowledges that existing powers and applications, terrorist designations and asset freezing mechanisms, which had been neglected by policy makers, were brought to the centre of the Bush administration's "war against terrorism". Similarly, policy makers in the US tried to address the question of terrorist financing by utilising

6 According to Donohue (2008) three statutes come to the forefront in this stream: the Bank Secrecy Act (BSA) (1970), the Anti-Drug Abuse Act (1988) and the Housing and Community Development Act (1992).

7 According to Clunan (2006, p. 588), the new administration of George W. Bush started its term without understanding the importance of the non-state security threats which were supposed to be learned during the Clinton government period. They chose rather to focus on state based threats. The Bush administration, also, had not focused on the financial activities and assets of Al Qaeda and the Taliban initially (Levi, 2010, p. 654). Moreover, Weiner and Johnston (2001) note that prior to the 9/11 terrorist attacks the Bush administration did not have any desire to compel anti-money laundering laws for international banks and other financial institutions. Even the UN 1999 Convention for the Suppression of the Financing of the Terrorism had not been ratified by the US during this time (Passas, 2006b, p. 281).

pre-existing anti-money laundering measures (Roberge, 2007, p. 196). Subsequently, without any comprehensive critical examination and not knowing if or how they might fit with the money laundering measures, CTF measures were enacted under the AML regime in haste.

After the attacks, within a two-week period, one of the initial and immediate responses was the announcement of Executive Order 13224 by the Bush administration under the authority of then International Emergency Economic Powers Act, 2001 (Eckert, 2008, p. 214; Bush, 2001a).[8] Consequently, the authority of Treasury Department has been increased due to the importance of its role in enforcing this Executive Order. Thus, the US Treasury expanded its capability for designating individuals and entities as terrorists, targeting their financial activities, freezing their assets and preventing their access to the international financial system (Eckert, 2008, p. 214). Notably, the Treasury Department's Office of Foreign Assets Control (OFAC) took on the task of tracking the assets of Bin Laden and Al Qaeda (Clunan, 2006, p. 592). Donohue (2008, p. 166) claims that Executive Order 13224 (Bush, 2001a), in which Bush's (2001b) famous 'Rose Garden speech' was referred to as a "draconian" initiative, exchanged criminal law standards with an intelligence norm.[9] Firstly, with this Executive Order (Bush, 2001a), a list of 'Specially Designated Global Terrorists' (SDGTs), initially consisting of 27 individuals and organisations, was formed (Eckert, 2008, p. 214). These persons and entities were assumed to be directly or indirectly connected to Al Qaeda and its affiliated groups, and therefore their assets were frozen

8 This Executive Order (Bush, 2001a) basically provides the US government with the authority to designate and block the assets of foreign individuals and institutions who are suspected of having relationships with any act of terrorism. Shortly, this regulation enabled blacklisting and asset-freezing mechanism powers for the US administration (Bush, 2001a; Ridley & Alexander, 2011, p. 41).

9 Consequently, the Al Barakaat case can be given as a prominent example of the negative effects of wrong CTF implementation. Al Barakaat was a financial organization which filled the commercial banking gap after the banking system in Somalia had collapsed. Al Barakaat was providing especially Somalian expatriate workers and other Somali citizens hawala services along with other Islamic banking and internet services. With Operation Green Quest, on 7 November, 2001, the Bush administration blocked the assets of 62 organisation and individuals including Somalia-based Al Barakaat. At that time Al Barakaat was accused of providing financial and communication services to terrorists in 40 different countries. At that moment, Al Barakaat was the only banking institution, employer and internet service provider for war-torn Somalia. Therefore, closing Al Barakaat negatively affected the Somalia diaspora in the US who sent their money to their impoverished families who lived in refugee camps. In brief, the action against Al Barakaat affected the Somalian population, for whom the remittances were vital (de Goede, 2003). Four and a half years later Al Barakaat was not convicted of having links with terrorism whereas it was convicted of remitting money without a licence (Passas, 2006a). Passas (2006a) rightly argues that, even though the 9/11 terrorists used formal banking systems and Western banks there was no any enforcement effort against them. However, although Al Barakaat did not have any proved links with terrorism, it was destroyed by the US CTF measures against the hawala system. It is concluded that this message undermines the current efforts against terrorist financing and affects public perception and sensations in a negative way.

(Amicelle & Favarel-Garrigues, 2012, p. 107). With this Executive Order, US citizens were also prohibited from trading, money transferring or any financial relationship with suspected Al Qaeda or Bin Laden related individuals and institutions (Eckert, 2008, p. 214).[10] Notably, if any foreign bank or financial institution fails to give information to the US government, they face the risk of having their assets and fund transfers frozen within the United States (Donohue, 2008, p. 166). In the beginning, SDGT's list was being revised in every four weeks, and at the end of 2001, 158 individuals and entities were designated by the US (Amicelle & Favarel-Garrigues, 2012, p. 107; Eckert, 2008, p. 214).

The main objectives of Executive Order 13224 were "to follow the money as a trail to terrorists and to freeze the money to disrupt their actions" (Bush, 2001a; Eckert, 2008, p. 214). Nonetheless, according to Donohue (2008, p. 166) and Amicelle and Favarel-Garrigues (2012, p. 108). Executive Order 13224 mainly focused on "stopping the money flow to al Qaeda and convincing the public that something is being done". Equally important is de Goede's (2012, p. 36) interpretation, wherein she provides a different perspective and assesses Executive Order 13224 as "the paradigm shift toward the proactive pursuit of terrorism suspects".

With this Presidential Order the 'war on terrorist financing' was globalised in two ways. Firstly, the other countries were compelled to comply with this order as President Bush (2001b) warned explicitly: "If you do business with the terrorists, if you support or sponsor them, you will not do business with the United States of America".[11] Secondly, from the terrorist organisations' perspective, the application of the law was extended. Even though in the beginning only Al Qaeda and Taliban related individuals and entities were targeted by this regulation, the US administration has expanded the mandate of Executive Order 13224. Therefore, not only Al Qaeda and Taliban but also other organisations such as Hamas, Hezbollah, the FARC and Real IRA were added into the list (Eckert, 2008, pp. 214, 215). Consequently, the Executive Order's scope and content became globalised.

10 If, for instance, an organisation or individual has not stopped their commercial activities with the listed individuals or entities, they could easily be placed on the same designation list, and their assets might be blocked. Moreover, merely having association with the listed ones, without providing any material support, can be sufficient for the US to freeze their assets. In addition, the Executive Order (Bush, 2001a) prohibits anyone from managing the blocked assets; it also prohibits any US entity to try to circumvent prohibitions and prohibits providing money to the listed individuals or entities for humanitarian purposes.

11 In the continuum of this speech Paul O'Neill (Bush, 2001b) supported this message robustly by saying, "[w]ith the signing of this executive order, we have the President's explicit directive to block the U.S. assets of any domestic or foreign financial institution that refuses to cooperate with us in blocking assets of terrorist organizations. This order is a notice to financial institutions around the world, if you have any involvement in the financing of the al Qaeda organization, you have two choices: cooperate in this fight, or we will freeze your U.S. assets; we will punish you for providing the resources that make these evil acts possible."

Another important change in the legislative arena was the approval of the "Uniting and Strengthening America by Providing Appropriate Tools Required to Intercept and Obstruct Terrorism Act (PATRIOT Act)" (2001), which was signed on 26 October 2001 by President Bush (Shetterly, 2005, p. 332). The PATRIOT Act took the central place in the US CTF efforts, providing law enforcement and financial regulators special powers and instruments in terms of combatting money laundering and confiscating terrorist properties (Navias, 2007, p. 173). Weiss (2009, p. 30) points out that due to the fact that legal sources for terrorist finance were used more frequently than illegal ones, it was challenging to produce any effective and concrete results in terms of CTF under the umbrella of AML provisions (which concentrate on the laundering of proceeds of criminal/illegal assets). Therefore, the US PATRIOT Act (2001) was introduced with a view to addressing this shortcoming. Eckert (2008, p. 216) claims that this act increased the effectiveness of existing anti-money laundering measures for establishing a CTF framework.[12] Similarly, as Clunan (2006, p. 592) points out this act improved the US government's regulatory powers against money laundering and financial crimes.

According to Donohue (2008, pp. 160–164), the PATRIOT Act instigated significant changes in four important areas. Firstly, it broadened the executive power under the IEEPA (1977) and introduced more advanced and wider investigative powers that the already existing ones (Danziger, 2012, p. 216).[13]

Secondly and more importantly, this act strengthened the state's regulatory regime by increasing the powers of the state (Donohue, 2008, p. 161)[14] and creating a compulsory reporting regime for key sectors (banks, accountancy firms, etc.).

12 Title III of the PATRIOT Act, which is also known as the 'International Money Laundering Abatement and Anti-Terrorist Financing Act of 2001', focuses on the subject and introduces new measures. Especially with Title III, existing money laundering statutes such as the 'Bank Secrecy Act (1970)', the 'Currency and Foreign Transaction Reporting Act', the 'Money Laundering Control Act (1986)', the 'Annunzio-Wilie Anti-Money Laundering Act [also known as the Housing and Community Development Act] (1992)', the 'Money Laundering Suppression Act (1994)' and the 'Money Laundering and the Financial Crimes Act (1998)' were revised, and their focus was shifted from mere criminal acts to terrorist financing (Smith, 2007, p. 155; Weiss, 2009, pp. 28–32). Additionally, the 'International Emergency Economic Powers Act (IEEPA)' was also revised under Title III of PATRIOT Act. Thus the Secretary of the Treasury gained similar special powers which IEEPA (1977) already had related to financing of terrorism (Trafton, 2007, p. 492).

13 Three important amendments were made to the IEEPA (1977) with this act. It gives the US executive an opportunity to submit confidential evidence in camera and *ex parte* in trials. Additionally, the state gained the power of blocking assets during investigations. According to this statute there was also no requirement for any solid relationship between the violence and the assets frozen, and similarly there was no proportion for seized assets regarding the crime committed (Donohue, 2008, p. 161).

14 Improved information collection powers and due diligence obligations were brought by this act, and financial institutions especially were required to identify the beneficial owners of the bank accounts, They were also required to make it harder for money launderers to disguise their identities.

Creating a transparent financial system was the objective of the US government (Danziger, 2012, p. 216), thus 'Know Your Customer (KYC)' and wire transfer regulations which were strongly rejected by the financial sector in the past came into effect by this act (Clunan, 2006, p. 592).[15] The financial institutions such as banks, savings associations, credit unions, brokers-dealers and mutual funds are required to increase their customer identification processes. Therefore, with this information, linking different accounts with different entities and individuals became much easier for law enforcement and intelligence agencies. Furthermore, the PATRIOT Act (2001) required everyone who received $10,000 or more from a commercial or business activity to file Suspicious Activity Reports (SARs) to the Department of Treasury. Non-financial businesses are also required to file 'Currency Transaction Reports' (CTRs) to the Financial Crimes Enforcement Network (FinCEN), and with this statute the registration and regulation of unlicensed money-transferring businesses became mandatory. Thirdly, the forfeiture powers were expanded, and new predicate offences in terms of freezing and forfeiting assets were introduced.[16] In addition, with this act, the burden of proof against any confiscation or freezing of any property became the individual's responsibility (Donohue, 2008, p. 163).[17] Lastly, the PATRIOT Act provided wider extraterritorial powers whereby the US judicial authority could reach to foreign persons, foreign banks or other foreign institutions for dealing with money laundering and terrorist financing activities (Donohue, 2008, pp. 163–164).

In addition to these important changes, the US PATRIOT Act made exchanging financial information much easier among law enforcement, regulators, intelligence agencies and financial institutions. FinCEN has been authorised to share information with banks regarding money laundering and terrorist financing (Eckert, 2008, p. 217). Furthermore, to prevent the flight of assets and to avoid allowing suspects to engage in any harmful activity or transactions, the OFAC was given the authority to block and freeze assets and transfers of any suspect entities and individuals before any formal designation took place (Eckert, 2008, p. 217). It is claimed that the OFAC worked very hard to add the names of individuals and entities, which were provided by the Central Intelligence Agency (CIA), to the designation list at the initial stage.

Under the Title III of the US PATRIOT Act (2001), the Bank Secrecy Act (BSA), 1970 requirements were extended by including MSBs and all financial entities; counter measures were allowed against jurisdictions and institutions

15 According to this regulation financial institutions have to collect personal information about their customers, such as their correct full name, date of birth and social security or passport numbers, and they have to keep the data for five years.

16 Conspicuously, the aims of these new measures were to prevent corrupt foreign officials from exploiting the US financial system and to prevent illegal money remission, business and bulk cash smuggling of more than $10,000 within the internal borders.

17 Thus, those who have been accused and whose assets have been forfeited have to find a way to explain why the state should not confiscate their assets (Donohue, 2008).

which failed to take suitable actions to prevent money laundering activity, correspondent accounts of certain financial entities were forbidden, information exchange activity was expanded and financial institutions were required to be more elaborate on customer identification (Eckert, 2008, p. 216). With the enactment of the US PATRIOT Act the systemic problems and weaknesses of the financial system, which in the past enabled organisations such as Al Qaeda, to wage attacks and sustain its organisation successfully, were addressed to a certain degree.

From an organisational restructuring perspective, some of the government institutions were reorganised (Ridley & Alexander, 2011, p. 44). Intelligence and law enforcement agencies conceiving the significance of the threat have created new specialised units led by personnel with substantial experience in CTF, which concentrate on the terrorist financing problem as a unique phenomenon and treat it more seriously and professionally. With the assistance of new legislative environment, many legal barriers such as information exchange between different agencies, difficulties regarding reaching financial records and reliable evidence, controlling foreign banks and regulating money remitters, which complicated financial investigations, were removed. Therefore, an expanded active interagency mechanism was founded among various organisations for combatting terrorist financing (Roth et al., 2004).[18]

Maintaining integration and cooperation between law enforcement agencies is a difficult task. Freeman (2012) states that redundancy, inadequate cooperation, coordination and weak information exchange between CTF agencies are some of the key shortcomings of the US CTF effort. He points out that there are many organisations with CTF duties such as the Treasury, the State Department, the Federal Bureau of Investigation (FBI), the CIA, the Departments of Defense and Homeland Security and the Drug Enforcement Agency (DEA), and this kind of a multi-headed structure makes CTF coordination and cooperation more complicated.

Interviews conducted with officials from the US CTF organisations reveal that while the US has adequate legal powers and motivation, it is difficult to build a capacity for collective action among the agencies (Clunan, 2006, p. 589). Additionally, it has been argued that instead of joining their collective struggle against the financial activities of terrorists, the US CTF agencies have chosen to follow

18 The US CTF mechanism consists of many departments and agencies *inter alia*: the Offices of Department of Treasury are OFAC, FinCEN, the Financial Institution Regulators and the Internal Revenue Service (IRS); the Departments of Homeland Security and Justice are the Bureau of Customs and Border Protection (CBP), the Bureau of Immigration and Customs Enforcement (ICE), the US Secret Service, the Federal Bureau of Investigation (FBI) and under the FBI structure, theTerrorist Financing Operations Section (TFOS), the Bureau of Alcohol, Tobacco, Firearms and Explosives (ATF) and the Drug Enforcement Agency (DEA); and within the Department of State the Office of the Coordinator for Counterterrorism (S/CT) and within S/CT is the Counterterrorism Finance and Designation Unit; the Department of Justice and the Central Intelligence Agency (CIA) (Weiss, 2009).

their bureaucratic agendas. Even though the initial motivation between government organisations was welcome, this cooperation was not good enough in practice, and most importantly, bureaucratic politics weakened the effectiveness of the whole strategy. Further, a number of significant bureaucratic challenges were experienced between government agencies after terrorist attacks (Clunan, 2006, pp. 589–591).[19]

In the background of these turf battles, the real debate was about the selection of the most effective CTF strategy which the US should apply. The first strategy consists of designating and detaining terrorists with their affiliates, freezing and blocking their properties and building a legislative, administrative and regulatory structure to make designations and asset freezing legal. The second strategy can be called 'follow the money' or intelligence led strategy, which focuses on collecting, analysing and sharing financial intelligence for tracking terrorists and preventing their future attacks and advanced regulation of formal and informal financial sectors.

The selection of a particular strategy seems to depend on the position and the defined interests of the agency involved (Welch, 1992, p. 118). Accordingly, the Department of Treasury and the Department of Justice, which have financial regulatory, AML and law enforcement mandates, are most likely to choose the designation and asset freezing strategy (Clunan, 2006, p. 591) which they believe is highly public; thus these designations can help in arresting terrorists. Besides, freezing assets can be measured easily; this criterion can be utilised to illustrate the success of the agency and the government against terrorism. It has been claimed that if proper evidentiary standards are used, this strategy can be appropriate for the prosecutorial and investigative organisations (Clunan, 2006).

In contrast, the intelligence led strategy becomes preferable for the intelligence community such as the CIA, the FBI and FinCEN, because such an approach enables these agencies to track, capture and/or terminate terrorists and provides needed information to profile these terrorists and their networks. In addition, for the foreign affairs agencies, the disguised nature of this strategy can be utilised in their secret communications or diplomatic exchanges with other countries (away from public knowledge and scrutiny). Additionally, the financial sector also prefers an intelligence led strategy because this can lessen the government's robust regulation of their activities and reporting duties whereby sharing the customers' financial information would be less transparent. While these strategies are not mutually exclusive, giving more weight to one of them can significantly disrupt the other's effectiveness. As resources are scarce, both strategies create a tendency among agencies towards keeping information for themselves in order to protect their privileges and operational relevance, instead of sharing it with others (Clunan, 2006, pp. 591–592).

19 For instance, the bureaucratic battles between the Treasury and the CIA or between the US Customs and the FBI can be given as noteworthy examples in this context (Clunan, 2006).

Empirical evidence by the academia (Clunan, 2006) as well as the Terrorist Financing Staff Monograph (Roth et al., 2004, p. 79) reveal that right after the 9/11 terrorist attacks, despite the fact that both strategies were being applied by the Bush administration, the 'designations and asset freezing' strategy was the preferred method during that period. Especially with the adaptation of Executive Order 13224 (Bush, 2001a) and the US PATRIOT Act 2001, the positions of the Department of Treasury and its related sub-units such as OFAC were emboldened. In a short space of time, this led to many individuals and organisations being designated as terrorists, and their assets were frozen by the OFAC without appropriate evidence (Clunan, 2006, pp. 592–593). As Roth, *et al* put it (2004, p. 79):

> The post-9/11 period at OFAC was "chaos." The goal set at the policy levels of the White House and Treasury was to conduct a public and aggressive series of designations to show the world community and our allies that the United States was serious about pursuing the financial targets. It entailed a major designation every four weeks, accompanied by derivative designations throughout the month. As a result, Treasury officials acknowledged that some of the evidentiary foundations for the early designations were quite weak.

Clearly, the White House, the Secretary of the Treasury and the Attorney General, advocated these efforts. Nonetheless, from a legal perspective, these high-profile designations were significantly problematic and controversial; the amount of frozen assets was exaggerated (Clunan, 2006, p. 593), and the sweeping nature of the designation (without proper evidence and due process) resulted in an international outcry and significant pressure from US allies, especially in cases involving their citizens. Subsequently, the US was compelled to de-list some of the individuals and entities in August 2002 (Roth et al., 2004, pp. 84–86). At that time, the CIA concluded that designation was not effective on terrorists because they were able to circumvent these measures by moving their assets to non-designated individuals or entities. That is also why the CIA strongly insisted on the intelligence led or 'follow the money' strategy (Clunan, 2006, p. 593). After these initial inadequacies within the designation and asset freezing strategies and having had the opportunity to assess the difficulties that the Treasury had in tracking small amounts of money, providing robust evidence for prosecution and conviction of suspects, curbing the finance going to the network structures of Al Qaeda and its affiliates, the Bush administration brought in the intelligence led strategy to the forefront of its CTF efforts. The US has perceived that applying an intelligence strategy with the overall counter-terrorism efforts could provide information about the network structure of terrorist organisations, prevent their prospective attacks and interrupt their logistics systems (Roth et al., 2004, pp. 47–48). Development and employment of new tools for following the money produced apt outcomes such as the arrest of one of the most wanted Al Qaeda operatives who was alleged to have masterminded the Bali bombings in

South Asia in 2002 (Lichtblau & Risen, 2006). It can be said that the unsuccessful designation led strategy pushed the US towards adopting a more intelligence oriented approach.

In the international arena, US diplomatic efforts focused on establishing a common regime against terrorist financing. The post 9/11 period in which the international efforts by the US, particularly against Al Qaeda's financial network, indicate that the US first tried to address legal difficulties both at the international (e.g. the UN Security Council) and the domestic levels. The government also endeavoured to understand terrorist financing ***modus operandi*** as well as defining the weaknesses of its financial sectors. In order to make the war against terrorist financing a priority, the US has engaged with many international actors such as the United Nations (UN), the G7, the G8, the G20, the Financial Action Task Force (FATF), the Egmont Group and other financial and regional organisations (Shetterly, 2005, p. 339). The US especially focused its diplomatic efforts on improving the roles and leadership of the UN and FATF (Levitt & Jacobson, 2008, p. 69) in order to legitimise and strengthen its CTF strategy and the provisions therein. For example, the US undertook the co-chair position at the FATF Terrorist Financing Working Group (Shetterly, 2005) and played a pivotal role in the creation of the UN Security Council's Counter-terrorism Committee. Above all, the US has de facto externalised its CTF regime and established international terrorist financing standards and norms (Eckert, 2008, p. 217). As a result, in the weeks after the 9/11 attacks, more than 100 governments enacted legal instruments against terrorist financing and money laundering, and more than $136 million in assets were frozen globally ($36 million by the US) (Roth et al., 2004, p. 45). In addition, the US initiated condensed diplomatic and educational relationships with the other countries and financial institutions in order to improve their awareness of methods of terrorist financing and to help their capacity building by providing technical assistance, legislative drafting, developing Financial Intelligence Units (FIUs), training judges and prosecutors and providing financial supervision and training for financial investigation (Roth et al., 2004, p. 45; Shetterly, 2005, pp. 341–342).

A number of commentators claimed that despite the increasing difficulties and challenges in gathering international support and realising substantive and comprehensive results in curbing terrorist finance, these international CTF efforts by the US were a success (Levitt & Jacobson, 2008, p. 79). Basile (2004, p. 176) opines that the US counter-terrorist financing system was successful specifically against Al Qaeda domestically, yet he considers that outside the US, these measures have had limited success. According to Passas (2006b, p. 281), in the period immediately after 9/11, the US CTF measures were developed and used too hastily. Thus their application became extra-costly, unjust, counter-productive and yielded very limited positive results. Similarly, Clunan (2006, pp. 594–596) deems the US CTF regime lacking a comprehensive and coherent approach. Her interviews with CTF experts conclude that instead of establishing an international regime against terrorist financing, the US efforts have mainly concentrated on targeting individuals and entities on a tactical level. In terms of the effectiveness of its CTF practice, it is claimed that continuing terrorism threats and a wave of attacks globally demonstrate that the US efforts have had limited success (Clunan, 2006 and Passas, 2006b).

Furthermore, Clunan (2006) claims that the theoretical approach to CTF is a common 'collective action problem' for states. In this sense, many of the states benefit from disrupting terrorist organisations' financial activities, which, if not disrupted, could cause violent troubles against their authority, economy and security. While all states have a common interest in establishing international and domestic financial systems which have built-in safeguards against terrorist organisations, this comes with a cost. The costs of constraining terrorist financing are often passed on to private entities in the financial sector, as long as the costs of doing so do not surpass the benefits of attracting financial clients craving secrecy and of appeasing domestic actors (including charities, casinos, banks, money services, and civil liberty advocates) who are known to oppose government scrutiny (Clunan, 2006, p. 572). This critical stance clearly explains the main dynamics and motivation of states in adapting their CTF regimes. Therefore, it is important to examine international (multilateral) efforts and organisational structures against terrorist financing.

3.3 International CTF framework

Efforts for establishing a multilateral CTF cooperation have increased the creation of network based organisations and joint efforts for preventing terrorist financing on an international level. Correspondingly, these international measures and initiatives have brought about some significant and concrete results in national legal frameworks, the establishment and empowerment of their administrative capabilities, the application of international CTF measures and regulations and their enforcement. (Biersteker, Eckert, & Romaniuk, 2008, p. 234). It is clear that the present terrorism threat has a global character (Bures, 2010, p. 419, 2012, p. 713) which necessitates CTF strategies and measures be designed accordingly. Nevertheless, the problems pertaining to the definition of terrorism emerge as essential impediments to both academic research activities and the foundation of internationally synchronised CTF efforts. Furthermore, terrorist organisations and their structures, financing methods and decision mechanisms for these activities are changing perpetually as they are explained in the previous chapter. Cameron clarifies this situation as:

> [T]he advent of self-supporting 'nomadic terrorist network' with global or regional, rather than separatist, goals, such as al-Qaeda, has added a new dimension to the problem. A nomadic group moves between jurisdictions and operates in different jurisdictions. It can obtain its financing in one region, but carry out operations by means of active cells stationed in, or transferred to, another region.
>
> (2006, as cited in O. Bures, 2010, pp. 419–420).

In this context, Bures (2012, p. 713) reaches the conclusion that a single 'financial safe heaven' is adequate for diminishing or circumventing CTF efforts, effectiveness and success, which are firmly dependent on the weakest link in the international cooperation. Raphaeli (2003, p. 79) emphasises that a comprehensive approach which consists of repressive measures of criminal law and preventive measures has been followed to prevent terrorist financing at the international level.[20] However, Passas (2006b, p. 281) rightly points out that terrorist financing was not perceived as an important issue until the 9/11 terrorist attacks in both international and domestic platforms, whereas after this unfortunate event this entire situation has changed dramatically.[21]

Another important aspect in CTF context is the need for a multidisciplinary strategy. Gardella (2004, pp. 415–416) supports the view that addressing terrorist financing is a difficult task which requires both criminal and financial statutes and regulations which are streamlined in a multi-jurisdictional context. Therefore, international cooperation and creation of an effective regulatory framework in financial systems are essential parts of this struggle. Deficiently regulated financial systems or lack of proper implementation of regulations provide terrorist organisations opportunities for abusing such financial systems.

3.3.1 The United Nations (UN)

Even though the interest in terrorism and related subject areas such as terrorist finance, radicalisation, extremism et cetera seemed to have increased significantly after 9/11, the UN has been dealing with terrorism since 1963, when it adopted 13 conventions and numerous resolutions related to terrorism (Çakmak & Çapar, 2009, p. 172). Despite these UN backed legal instruments, it is accepted that the international legal framework against terrorism still has many shortcomings. There were no coordinated international efforts for preventing terrorism until the 9/11 attacks. Moreover, the existing solutions were inadequate for resolving this multidimensional challenge (Ward, 2003, p. 291). Similarly, the international attempts to disrupt terrorist financing were "comparatively few and ill-supported" up until 9/11 (Ridley & Alexander, 2011, p. 4150), after which the international community has started to deal with terrorist financing but faced three significant challenges: slow understanding of the requirement

20 The repressive measures contain some agreements between states for criminalisation of some offences in their legislation, exchanging information and delivering mutual legal assistance among them. Apart from that, the preventive measures consist of activities for creating a regulatory regime for the financial sector that aims to constrain the scope of the financial system, not to be exploited and abused for terrorist goals.

21 International measures as well as national ones were introduced rapidly such as ratification of the UN convention, resolutions, reporting requirements, implementation of CTF and FATF recommendations, EU directives, World Bank and IMF activities, assessment and evaluation practices and new legislations and orders for identification, freezing, seizure or confiscation of terrorist assets, which were designated.

for international cooperation, problems in defining terrorism and misperception regarding the nature and methods of financial activities of terrorist organisations.

Especially after the attacks on US Embassies in 1998, the US government, being the driving force, motivated the UN Security Council to address transnational terrorism (Oudraat, 2004, p. 30). Consequently, a series of UN Resolutions related to the Taliban and Al Qaeda have been passed by the UN Security Council (Passas, 2006a, p. 320). The UN's CTF efforts started in October 1999 with the adoption of UN Security Council Resolution (UNSCR) 1267, which targets Al Qaeda, its supporters and the Taliban regime in Afghanistan (Biersteker et al., 2008, pp. 234–235).[22] In addition, UNSCR 1267 (1999) set up a '1267 Committee' or 'Sanctions Committee' for monitoring the execution of sanctions against the Taliban and Al Qaeda in Afghanistan. With this resolution, for the first time, the UN Security Council recognised a non-state terrorist organisation as a threat to international peace and security (Clunan, 2006, p. 575). The requirement for freezing assets and blocking transactions related to Al Qaeda, relevant terrorist organisations and individuals who were listed by the UN Security Council Sanctions Committee was addressed by adopting UNSCR 1267. Additionally, with the adoption of UNSCR 1269 (1999), the term 'terrorist financing' was used specifically in a resolution not in a state-sponsorship framework (Bantekas, 2003, p. 316).

Equally important is that right after the adoption of UNSCR 1267 (1999), a French led initiative paved the way for the introduction of the International Convention for Suppression of the Financing of Terrorism (ICSFT) (1999), which establishes one of the substantial bases of countering terrorism (Bantekas, 2003, p. 323). The ICSFT (1999) establishes the main principles and the international efforts against terrorist financing (Bensted, 2012, p. 250). According to Bantekas (2003, p. 323), the main aim of this convention was to block the circulation of terrorist funds without preventing the movement of capital and the business across global markets. This convention has four main provisions (for establishing a global CTF regime) which criminalises providing or collecting funds for terrorists; prohibits the acquiring of money, assets or financial services for terrorists; obliges freezing the assets of terrorists without any delay and demands establishment of appropriate identification and reporting mechanisms for the financial sector ("The International Convention for the Suppression of the Financing of Terrorism", 1999; Rudner, 2010, p. 708).

While the initial adoption of the 1999 Convention (in terms of state signatories and ratifications) was limited and did not have the backing of the US (Ridley & Alexander, 2011, p. 41),[23] following 9/11, the US ratified this convention on

22 In this resolution, the UN Security Council demanded that the Taliban stop giving support to international terrorism and deliver Osama bin Laden to officials for his trial (Passas, 2006a, p. 320).

23 As Levi (2010, p. 652) rightly points out, despite the fact that the Convention was adopted in 1999, it only came into force in 2002 due to the fact that the Bush administration did

26 June 2002 (Passas, 2006a, p. 320), and the number of states that ratified this convention has increased significantly since (Biersteker et al., 2008, p. 235).

While it does not provide a universally agreed definition of terrorism which results in different applications of counter-terrorism legislations by states without being able to determine which acts should be named as support of terrorism, the ICSFT came up with significant novelties such as the introduction of 'due diligence' requirements for financial institutions, obligation on states to cooperate for mutual legal assistance (MLA), especially in terms of the tracing, freezing and confiscation of assets (Bantekas, 2003).

Following the ICSFT, with the adoption of the UNSCR 1333 (2000), states are required to freeze the assets of bin Laden, Al Qaeda and its associates in addition to the Taliban regime, who were added to the list formed by the UNSCR 1267 (1999) (Bures, 2012, p. 714). Passing the subsequent UNSCR 1333 (2000), the UN Security Council, for the first time, designated a non-state entity, Al Qaeda and it associates. According to Clunan (2006), the adoption of this resolution reflects the transformation of counter-terrorism strategy from targeting state sponsored terrorism to a new transnational criminal finance approach. Additionally, a monitoring team tasked for reporting to the UN Security Council was established in Pakistan and New York with the adoption of UNSCR 1363 (2001) for empowering and controlling the implementation of sanctions that were introduced with Resolutions 1267 (1999) and 1333 (2000) (Passas, 2006a, p. 320).

After the 9/11 attacks, the international stance on CTF has changed in a dramatic way (Biersteker et al., 2008, p. 236), and the international community has become more sensitive to the threat of terrorism. On 28 September 2001, the UN Security Council adopted Resolution 1373 (2001) under Chapter VII of the UN Charter, which can be identified as the first example of UN executive powers being employed to establish a permanent counter-terrorism structure (Koh, 2006, p. 82). With the adoption of this resolution the UN Security Council has introduced radical measures (Bures, 2012, p. 714) which resemble the provisions of the PATRIOT Act (2001) (Danziger, 2012, p. 215). The UNSCR 1373 (2001) requires the UN member states to: criminalise activities in terms of financing terrorism; prevent and suppress terrorist financing; freeze funds, assets or other economic entities of individuals who engaged with terrorist activities; forbid active or passive aid to terrorists; cooperate with other member states in conducting criminal investigations and exchange information regarding terrorist activities (Rudner, 2010, p. 708). Clunan (2006, p. 578) assesses this resolution as a 'mini treaty' and notes that Resolution 1373 (2001) goes beyond Resolution 1267 (1999) by not only obliging states to target Al Qaeda and the Taliban but also driving them to take actions against all terrorist organisations and their associates. This resolution was not created against a particular state or individual;

not press for it. As a result, only four states, Botswana, Sri Lanka, the United Kingdom and Uzbekistan, ratified the convention before September 2001.

rather it was formed as a more global approach that targets any individuals or groups engaged in terrorist financing. This feature of UNSCR 1371 is different than other similar UNSCRs such as 1267 (1999) and 1333 (2000), which target the Taliban and Al Qaeda and affiliated entities (Gurule, 2009, p. 30; Ridley, 2011, p. 50). Resolution 1373 (2001) has two additional important features. The first is the establishment of 'Counter Terrorism Committee' (CTC), which is responsible for monitoring the member states' compliance and implementation of the resolution.[24] The second is the *jus cogens* obligation on member states to freeze terrorist assets.

All member states are obliged to report their counter-terrorism efforts according to Resolution 1373 (2001). In addition to compliance monitoring, the CTC offers technical assistance to states. The reports sent to the CTC reveal certain challenges faced by member states. These problems can be summarised as: different understandings and implementations of key terms and provisions: for instance, rendering from a broad sense of the problem of terrorist financing to a more narrow focused issue of money laundering; some countries combat terrorism as if it is only confined to their territory or do not take any action and remain silent if their nationals are engaged in terrorist acts on the soils of other states; lack of information sharing among relevant CTF agencies; states merely focusing on judicial issues such as extradition and finally, even though many member states' capacity had been found inadequate, only a few member states seek technical assistance (Oudraat, 2004, p. 33).

While Resolution 1373 (2001) has unique and welcome features, it is not immune from certain criticism. For example, it does not define clearly what terrorism means, fails to provide criteria for listing entities and does not oblige states to provide evidence for designating individuals and/or organisations. In this process, therefore, listed groups or individuals are left without any legal redress to refute the decision for their designation. Therefore, it can be argued that although this resolution provides broad instructions and responsibilities for states, it cannot answer the questions of who will be within the scope of a terrorist organisation and how they will be targeted by it (McCulloch & Pickering, 2005, p. 476).

Similar to McCulloch and Pickering's (2005) critique, Koh (2006, pp. 95–97) perceptively identifies the lack of definition of terrorism among other problems when it comes to the implementation of Resolution 1373 (2001) at the international and the domestic levels.[25] Secondly, Koh highlights that Resolution 1373

24 The main purposes of the CTC are to monitor implementation of resolutions and to improve the capacities of member states by providing technical assistance and encouragement for states to deal with terrorism in an effective way. In contrast with the Resolution 1267 (1999) Monitoring Committee, the CTC did not create a common designation list for member states; however, the CTC took a more neutral position in order to make member states more active (Clunan, 2006, p. 578).

25 Hezbollah, for example, is designated as a terrorist organisation by the governments of Israel and the US, whereas the assessment of Lebanon is totally different, and this structure is named as a mere legitimate political organisation there.

does not contain human rights protection provisions, despite the fact that the resolution demands some limits on civil liberties. Thirdly, Koh notes that certain provisions need detailed consideration due to their incompleteness. For example, Resolution 1373 focuses merely on freezing assets and does not explain what kind of a process will be followed prior to or after terrorist assets are frozen. The combined effect of these shortcomings seems to have diminished the initial sympathy and the momentum behind Resolution 1373 by the member states.[26]

It can be observed that the CTF efforts at the international level converge on two main streams. The first one consists of UN Security Council Resolutions 1267 (1999), 1333 (2000) and additional amending resolutions which create a sanctions regime against the Taliban regime, Al Qaeda and its affiliates. The second one is the establishment of a general framework for a global counter-terrorist financing regime by the International Convention for the Suppression of Financing of Terrorism (1999) and especially UNSCR 1373 (2001) and subsequent resolutions. It appears that these two approaches shape both domestic and international responses to terrorism. While the international support (in light of the number of ratifications of the International Convention for the Suppression of Financing of Terrorism, 1999 and the implementation of UNSCR 1371) for CTF has been remarkable, the success of these has not been clear. The shock of the 9/11 attacks and the pressure related to this compelled states to adopt current AML and CTF regimes. Another detail which can be drawn from the initial development of the UN based CTF regimes is the fact that, by expanding the UNSCR 1267 list, the US has become able to sanction governments, individuals and groups. In addition, by using bilateral and regional organisations the US gained the ability to oversee and encourage compliance rather than forming a globalised international regime. This trend can be seen as externalisation of the US CTF policy via international institutions.

Equally important, Bures (2012, p. 714) claims that of the UNSCRs related to CTF, at least three of them, 1267 (1999), 1333 (2000) and 1390 (2002), represent the clear implementation of so-called 'smart (targeted) sanctions' under counter-terrorism.[27] In this context these smart sanctions have been used by

26 After second and third rounds of reports, the speed and the impetus of the process supported by CTC started to decrease. To address this problem, the UNSCR created the 'Counter-Terrorism Executive Directorate' (C-TED) in 2004 adopting Resolution 1535 (Resolution 1535 (2004), As assistance to CTC and a political mission C-TED is tasked with monitoringthe implementation of UNSCR 1373 (2001) (Biersteker, *et al.*, 2008, p. 238). Correspondingly the UNSC has reinforced the 1267 (1999) and 1333 (2000) sanctions regime by revising sanctions and adopting new resolutions since 1999 (Weiss, 2009, p. 60).

27 Since 1990, especially after the big humanitarian crisis, which occurred in Iraq as a result of comprehensive sanctions, the UNSC has started to implement the so-called 'smart' or 'targeted' sanctions, which are presumed to be more developed and refined for resolving different problems. These types of sanctions can be used for targeting individuals, businesses, a sector or a single region of a state. In addition, they can be used for different purposes such as legal prosecution of individuals, preventing massive human rights violations, enforcing peace terms and countering financing of terrorism (Biersteker, 2009, pp. 99–100).

the UN to create a 'Sanctions Committee' which proscribes people or organisations with a blacklisting mechanism to freeze their assets, impose travel bans or criminalise any attempt to provide funds or weapons. Despite the indiscriminate nature of comprehensive sanctions, targeted sanctions might be more precise and applied in small amounts and in a more flexible way. In short, the main idea for smart/targeted sanctions is not to punish all the population for the actions taken by a few (Biersteker, 2009, pp. 99–100).

Nevertheless, it is worth noting that although smart sanctions have many advantages, these sanctions can violate human rights especially in terms of CTF measures (Biersteker, 2009, p. 101). For instance, most of the designations were undertaken according to classified intelligence which was not available to other member states, and lack of due diligence became a primary reason for the EU courts to challenge the implementation of the Sanctions Committee decisions by member states.[28]

While there have been initiatives to mitigate the negative impacts of existing deficient listing, de-listing and designation processes[29] and to improve the legitimacy of the UN sanctions regime, the current CTF regime continues to be problematic: For example, there has been a decreasing number of names added to the designation list, and it has been observed that states are less eager to support and implement the UN sanctions (Gurule, 2009). Hence, Gurule (2009) has a pessimistic outlook on the UN CTF regime, wherein he opines that unless substantive efforts are taken to address the shortcomings of the CTF regime, the sanctions regime may disappear.

It is clear that the UN Security Council has established a global structure for countering terrorist financing which mainly focuses on Al Qaeda, the Taliban regime and associated members and groups' activities. Additionally, it is obvious that the UN has tried to create a global CTF regime by adopting ICSFT

28 *Kadi and Al Barakaat International Foundation v Council and Commission*, (2008) C-402/05.

29 In order to resolve problems member states adopted several resolutions. With the adoption of UNSC Resolution 1730 (2006) a manned 'Focal Point' was established to receive de-listing demands. UNSC Resolution 1735 (2006) made clear the content of statements of case and established a public release of information mechanism and improved the deficiencies related to notification of listed individuals and groups. In addition to this, UNSC Resolution 1267 Sanctions Committee started to review the names on the consolidated list, unsystematically. The improvements have been done regarding the notification process and transparency of designations by the passing of UNSC Resolution 1822 (2008) in June 2008. Furthermore, with the adoption of UNSCR Resolution 1904 (2009), listing procedures are improved, information sharing among committee members became an obligation, approval of a narrative summary of reasons for designation introduced, and committee applications are restructured for preventing indefinite holds on significant decisions. Notably, this resolution is established a new ombudsperson institution for supervising de-listing demands for 1267 list (Biersteker, 2009, pp. 111–114). Lastly, with the adoption of UNSC Resolution 1989 (2011) and 2083 (2012), the mandate of Ombudsman is extended and a systematic de-listing mechanism, which clarifies the process for designating state's requests for de-listing, are introduced by Security Council (UNSC Subsidiary Organs, 2018).

(1999) and Resolution 1373 (2001). However, the application of this regime, which offers a global movement against terrorist financing without targeting any particular organisation, has not yet become effective because of the problems and difficulties identified above. Thus, it can be concluded that although the application of the sanctions regime, in terms of setting the tone at the UN level, seems to be effective and has led to a degree of cooperation among member states, there are significant problems and difficulties related to the implementation of sanctions and designation of persons and organisations.

3.3.2 The Financial Action Task Force (FATF)

Beside the efforts of the UN and its sub-organs at addressing terrorist financing, there are also other international organisations which provide significant impetus for the design and practice of CTF policies at the multilateral level.[30] In this section, the role and contribution of FATF and its satellites, the EU, the Egmont Group, the IMF and the World Bank, are examined.

In the late 1980s an expert community for anti-money laundering issues whose focus was mainly on financial crimes in industrialised countries, began to emerge (Biersteker et al., 2008, p. 239). The majority of multilateral efforts established against money laundering and related crimes before 9/11 are used against terrorist financing acquired from criminal activities (Clunan, 2006, p. 576). In this period, a soft-law regime was created mainly by the Western states to combat financial crimes. The US with its domestic capability against financial crimes and later against terrorist financing was the main acknowledged actor of this strategy. The US's ability was underpinned by its political will to adopt and implement national financial, banking, law enforcement and anti-corruption laws domestically and give extraterritorial effect to these beyond its jurisdiction. However, at the international level, these laws were established in a fragmented way. Thus, the FATF was established at Paris Summit of the Group of 7 (G-7) countries under the guidance of the Organisation for Economic Cooperation and Development (OECD, 2013) for generating an international cooperation scaffold against money laundering (Rudner, 2010, p. 708). The foundation of FATF in 1989 against money laundering can be named as one of the first efforts at creating informal multilateral inter/trans governmental structures for combatting financial crimes.

The FATF formulates and presents best practices, which are mainly provided by the US and the UK, for dealing with financial crimes and oversees compliance degrees of states from their legislative and enforcement applications (Clunan, 2006, p. 576). In addition, the FATF has created an evaluation methodology for assessing the vulnerability of any business, institution or state to money

30 These bodies established a second parallel of CTF framework in addition to the UN's regime by re-deploying existing Anti-Money Laundering network and their officials for dealing with terrorist financing (Biersteker, *et al.*, 2008, p. 239).

laundering. Consequently, the FATF has created typologies for methods and techniques used in money laundering. These efforts and meetings have paved the way for more structured recommendations (Vlcek, 2007, p. 105). A basic framework that consists of 'Forty Recommendations on Money Laundering' was published by the FATF in 1990 and updated in 1996. (Clunan, 2006, p. 576). These recommendations were used for empowering legislative measures to authorities for tracing, assessing and confiscating laundered money or properties.

Firstly, with these recommendations the domestic regulatory system, which is required to control and report money transfers above determined limits and suspicious transactions by 'know your customer' (KYC) and customer due diligence (CDD) applications have been established. Secondly, they have created an inter-governmental regulatory regime which emboldens cooperation between states facilitating mutual legal assistance, extradition, joint investigations, general and on-request information exchanges and responding demands of foreign states for identifying, freezing, seizing and confiscating proceeds of crime (Rudner, 2010, p. 705). Notably a 'naming and shaming' campaign, 'Non-Cooperative Countries and Territories'(NCCT) initiative (Biersteker et al., 2008, p. 239), was started against countries that were uncooperative with the international efforts against money laundering in 2000. Consequently, many of these states changed their attitudes and legislations in order to be removed from that list (Clunan, 2006, p. 577). In addition to the affect it has on countries' diplomatic and public image, an FATF report informs the credit rating of a country, thus providing an additional reason to implement the FATF Recommendations.

In the wake of the 9/11 attacks, the FATF, similar to other international organisations, acted swiftly. Six weeks after the attacks, the FATF's mandate was expanded to include CTF, as a result of the Extra Plenary Session summoned in New York on 29–31 October 2001 (Ridley & Alexander, 2011, p. 41). Although subjects related to terrorist financing had been discussed by the FATF before 9/11 no substantive provision was included in its Recommendations (Biersteker et al., 2008, p. 239). Consequently, with US Treasury Secretary O'Neill's pressure to adopt new recommendations, which would support forty existing recommendations and provide guidance on identifying methods and *modus operandi* of terrorist financing were issued in the name of the 'FATF Eight Special Recommendations against Terrorist Financing' (de Goede, 2012, pp. 38–39; Ridley & Alexander, 2011, p. 41).[31] An additional ninth recommendation regarding cash couriers (FATF, 2014e) was issued by the FATF in 2004 (Bures, 2012, p. 715). Even though the FATF does not have any mandatory powers for enforcing these recommendations, they were accepted as international standards by majority of

31 These special recommendations were: "I. Ratification and implementation of UN instruments, II. Criminalising the financing of terrorism and associated money laundering, III. Freezing and confiscating terrorist assets, IV. Reporting suspicious transactions related to terrorism, V. International co-operation, VI. Alternative remittance, VII. Wire transfers, VIII. Non-profit organisations" (FATF, 2014f).

states (Bures, 2010, p. 421) which can be seen as a significant achievement for a relatively new and small international organisation.

Heng and McDonagh (2009) argue that the US national regulatory measures against terrorist financing such as the PATRIOT Act 2001 was mirrored to a certain degree by the FATF while creating its standards. It is also noted that the US continues to dominate the FATF agenda. There has been criticism of the FATF in this context because of the US role and its influence in shaping the international measures similar to the US domestic structure and forcing other states to keep records in ways that allow US law enforcement agencies to reach and use them easily (Williams, 2001, p. 142; Helleiner, 1999; Reinicke, 1998, as cited in Shields, 2005, p. 489). Correspondingly, Clunan (2006) points out that the US interference with and dominance in the FATF have resulted in the FATF prioritising the US national interests rather than creating a global CTF regime.

In conjunction with the creation of the FATF, other 'FATF-Style Regional Bodies' (FSRBs) emerged. In addition to the 37 member states of FATF, about nine FSRBs monitor and promote the implementation of FATF recommendations over 180 jurisdictions.[32] In addition, the FATF supports and encourages governments to establish Financial Intelligence Units (FIUs) devised for gathering information and producing operative intelligence about terrorist financing and money laundering (Rudner, 2010, p. 708).

While the function of the FATF for integrating existing anti-money laundering systems and institutions with counter terrorist financing is significant (Biersteker et al., 2008, p. 240), it can be claimed that the pre-existing AML regime provided the infrastructure for monitoring and developing measures against terrorist financing. Firstly, the existing institutions were operationally valuable because they provided impetus and opportunities for creating global standards for CTF framework by new recommendations, distribution of these recommendations via the FATF and FSRBs, designing mechanisms such as self-evaluations and peer reviews for improving the implementation and forming an environment for exchanging experiences and lessons. Secondly, officials and experts who operate in this network had required knowledge and perception in order to resolve problems regarding terrorist financing. However, despite the significance of FATF efforts for founding a global CTF framework, it is argued rightly that these measures remained just on paper serving only as a general policy direction for compliance of states and financial institutions rather than concentrating on practice by the end users in law enforcement (Biersteker et al., 2008, p. 241).

32 These FSRBs are the Asia/Pacific Group on Money Laundering (APG), Caribbean Financial Action Task Force (CFATF), Eurasian Group (EAG), Eastern and Southern Africa Anti-Money Laundering Group (ESAAMLG), Financial Action Task Force on Money Laundering in South America (GAFISUD), Inter-Governmental Action Group against Money Laundering in West Africa (GIABA), Middle East and North Africa Financial Action Task Force (MENAFATF), Council of Europe Committee of Experts on the Evaluation of Anti-Money Laundering Measures and the Financing of Terrorism (MONEYVAL) (FATF, 2014b).

The Forty Recommendations on AML and Nine Special Recommendations on CTF were re-formed and incorporated into a single instrument on 16 February 2012 by the FATF (Barrett, 2012, pp. 726–727; FATF, 2014e). Barrett (2012, p. 727) finds the timing for reassessment of Special Recommendations was appropriate and necessary. The significant issue emphasised with these efforts is especially necessary for states to have a 'risk based approach', which means that the efforts and sources will be directed according to the risk level of AML and CTF in a specific context and jurisdiction. According to the supporters of risk based approach, one for all application of the rules and regulations by the states which have less developed financial services and systems is likely to fail. Consequently, some states may become unenthusiastic about compliance. It is envisaged that if states can direct and concentrate their efforts on their vulnerabilities in the context of AML and CTF, and they are evaluated according to their success dealing with these risks and vulnerabilities, then they can protect their interests and counter terrorist financing more adequately (Barrett, 2012, p. 727). While the risk based approach is presented as a solution for creating synergy by fostering tailored action against terrorist finance, it is important to remember that the differentiating national interests of states might curtail the harmony and the success of this approach.

Indeed, the FATF has an important role in CTF with its recommendations, best-practice guidelines and evaluations. However, unlike the powers of UNSC, the FATF does not have any mandate or authority to enforce these measures. Nevertheless, implementation of these recommendations and guidelines across the globe indicates that the FATF possesses a degree of effective authority in bringing about compliance. De Goede (2012, pp. 47–48) explains this situation through the perspective of 'governmentality' whereby the FATF's main instrument for ensuring compliance has been its blacklisting of NCCT. The potency of blacklisting derives from the fact that when States were listed as NCCT, they could hardly operate in the international financial system as long as they remained on this list. However, in 2006 the FATF de-listed all the NCCT states, and no state has been listed since. The NCCT application was eventually replaced with a more flexible regime of determining high-risk jurisdictions. Practically, de Goede (2012, p. 47) sees the power of the FATF as mainly "extra-legal" power which operates "through education, mutual evaluation and moral suasion". Annual self-assessment and regular mutual evaluation of states, which are undertaken by the FATF, are publicised in a summarised style to the public. Notably, countries are stimulated to achieve higher scores from these assessment processes. From the perspective of the governmentality paradigm, de Goede argues that FATF does not depend on sanctions whereas employing technical standards and evaluation scores stimulates countries and financial institutions. Moreover, de Goede (2012, p. 48) finds FATF authority as a 'normalising power' which "[. . .] does not fix or prescribe the precise set of laws to be implemented but offers evolving standards of normality, best practices, and narratives of reliability that 'good' states and financial institutions will wish to adhere to" (de Goede, 2012, p. 39). It can be claimed that the FATF's authority and powers have increased significantly as a result of states' ambition towards getting higher scores from these assessments and remaining an active part of the international financial system.

It is accepted that in the pre-9/11 period, AML measures provided significant success against financial crimes. The geographical and functional expansion of this network through the FATF assisted the development of CTF cooperation between states in political and operational dimensions. The FATF's anti-money laundering experience and expertise continue to have importance for the criminal aspect of terrorist financing (Biersteker et al., 2008, p. 241). As a standard setting institution, the FATF has an important role in the international CTF campaign. Even though the FATF does not have the authority to sanction for non-compliance, it has an effective soft power arsenal (e.g. blacklisting) which induces states to adopt and comply with the regulations and standards set. Therefore, states and financial institutions in order not to be labelled as risky, which will reduce their financial activity and opportunities significantly, endeavour to adopt and implement the FATF's CTF recommendations.

3.3.3 The Egmont Group and Financial Intelligence Units (FIUs)

The Egmont Group is another informal multilateral organisation, which has important tasks and responsibilities in the international CTF regime. The Egmont Group is known as the global network of Financial Intelligence Units (FIUs), which are centralised national institutions responsible for detecting and countering money laundering and terrorist financing (Levitt & Jacobson, 2008, p. 70). The first FIUs were established in the 1990s, and they became a central point for the collection, analysis and dissemination of financial information related to money laundering (Gottselig & Underwood, 2004, p. 1). As a result, a group of FIUs gathered at a meeting at Egmont Arenberg Palace in Brussels in 1995. The Egmont Group was created to establish an informal FIUs network structure in order to increase the international cooperation against money laundering and later against terrorist financing (Egmont, 2014a). After the FATF mandate expansion in October 2001, terrorist financing became an area of responsibility for the Egmont Group. Not only with the broad recognition of international standards on terrorist financing but also states efforts at avoiding or being removed from FATF NCCT list increased the applications for becoming a member of the Egmont Group (Clunan, 2006, p. 579).

The main objective of the group is to provide an informal cooperation forum for the FIUs, whereby the abilities and effectiveness of FIUs are enhanced. This intention consists of forming a broad systemic financial intelligence sharing ability, capacity building and training activities and increased technological communication among the FIUs. It is generally accepted that the financial information sharing between FIUs is the main reason for the formation of this informal network (FinCEN, 2005).[33] Especially after conceiving the impor-

33 Presently this network consists of 155 FIUs; as the FATF recommendations encourage states to join this network, the number of member FIUs is likely to increase in the near future (Egmont, 2014a).

tance of FIUs in the fight against money laundering and terrorist financing, the IMF, WB and a number of their member states have been providing technical assistance to countries for founding and bolstering their FIUs (Gottselig & Underwood, 2004, pp. 1–2).

Although UNSCR 1373 (2001) and other international legal instruments require a reciprocal information exchange between parties and states, the effectiveness and the feasibility of implementing them may seem doubtful.[34] However, the existence of unofficial informal bodies such as FATF and the Egmont Group indicates that they have created an environment of mutual trust between states where they can share information and collaborate effectively (Bantekas, 2003, p. 330).

3.3.4 *International Monetary Fund (IMF), the World Bank (WB)*

In addition to the FATF and the Egmont Group, there are other organisations which take part in the efforts in CTF at the international level. Many of these groups had been established initially for anti-money laundering purposes and subsequently CTF was added to their agenda, these organisations cooperate with the FATF.

Both the World Bank and the IMF have significant influence on the forming of an international CTF regime. From the IMF's perspective, terrorist financing and money laundering have unpredicted macroeconomic outcomes for financial systems in terms of money demand and risks. For the WB, terrorist financing and money laundering have a devastating impact especially for developing countries (Koh, 2006, p. 169). Remarkably, the WB and the IMF activities mainly focused on developing action plans for improving efforts against terrorist financing and money laundering at the international level. The FATF recommendations were accepted as the international standards for anti-money laundering and CTF. Notably, the WB and the IMF initiated a 12-month program for evaluating the compliance of the states with the recommendations to develop a common assessment methodology in coordination with the FATF and FSRBs. Ultimately, after revising and altering the methodology which was improved and endorsed by the WB and the IMF, it has begun to be used as the common assessment methodology for measuring AML/CTF compliance (Biersteker et al., 2008, p. 241). In addition, the IMF and the WB have performed supporting functions for the international CTF/AML efforts. In this context, the IMF and the WB provide technical and lending assistance, fund research about AML/CTF typologies and organise campaigns for increasing awareness about CTF and AML (Koh, 2006, pp. 175–177). Even though the WB and the IMF publish various reports related

34 In order to overcome these caveats the Egmont Group publishes documents and reports such as 'Charter-Egmont Group of FIUs (2013)' and 'Principles of Information Exchange and Operational Guidance for FIUs (2013)' (Egmont, 2014b).

to terrorist financing, none of these reports have any mandatory requirements for the governments. The IMF and WB function is mainly centred on technical assistance; however, even though these bodies provide these supports, the initiative and incentive belong to the states whether or not to adopt these advisory provisions (Weiss, 2009, p. 62).

3.3.5 The European Union (EU)

Another leading actor against terrorist financing at the international level is the EU (Levitt & Jacobson, 2008, p. 71). After the 9/11 attacks, the EU introduced various measures and means for countering terrorism and particularly terrorist financing. Many of these instruments were created to implement the UNSC resolutions and FATF recommendations (Bures, 2010, p. 421). Consequently, the EU has adopted directives transposing the FATF recommendations regarding CTF.

Similarly, in accordance with UNSC Resolutions 1267 (1999) and 1373 (2001), blacklisting, asset freezing mechanisms and other measures were adopted by the EU (Wesseling, 2014, pp. 12–13). The EU has formed two terrorist lists, one for Al Qaeda and Taliban members, and one for the other terrorist organisations designated by the EU and its member states. All the EU member states are obliged to freeze the designated terrorist assets. To achieve this goal inter and intra state agencies have been established for directing counter terrorist financing operations, terrorist financing has been criminalised by member states, and asset freezing mechanisms have been developed within the EU. It is important to state that the EU and its member states became active members of the FATF and Egmont Group (Levitt & Jacobson, 2008, p. 71).

Responding to the UNSCR 1373 (2001) requirements, the EU drew up designated terrorist lists which classify terrorist suspects according to their citizenship as 'the EU internal' and 'the EU external'. The reason for this classification is that the EU legislation does not allow the EU to practice any of these measures against domestic terrorist suspects who are citizens of a member state. For the EU citizens, the implementation of asset freezing and other measures are undertaken by member states according to their national procedures. For the second group of individuals, the EU external terrorist suspects or terrorists, the EU is authorised to freeze their assets and to monitor terrorist lists. For transposing the obligations of UNSCR 1267 (1999) and UNSCR 1333 (2000) into the union's legislative system, the EU has chosen to adopt the consolidation list formed by the UNSC Sanctions Committee. However, in this case the EU does not have any impact on the listing and delisting processes of terrorists or related entities.

With the publication of the Strategy of Terrorist Financing in 2004, which was updated in 2008 and 2011, a new strategy of CTF was agreed to by the EU (Wesseling, 2014). This meant that a more flexible strategy was adopted for following the terrorist money and increasing the monitoring of informal money movements such as hawala, non-profit organisations and cash couriers, and for utilising financial intelligence on the security area ("The Fight against Terrorist

Financing", 2004). On this point, de Goede (2012, p. 41) opines that the EU may be more eager to act against the financial aspects of the war on terror owing to the fact that this kind of struggle is less militaristic and conceived to be "more peaceful and less controversial than the violent faces of the war on terror in Iraq and Afghanistan".

The EU has been very dynamic in freezing and regulating financial freezing mechanisms whereby CTF measures are also stipulated in the EU Action Plan on Combating Terrorism (2011) which gave rise to enhanced due diligence measures/counter measures with regards to high risk third countries, addressed risks posed by virtual currency exchange platforms and prepaid instruments, established centralised bank and payment account registers or electronic data retrieval systems, and made the access of Financial Intelligence Units to, and exchange of, information amongst them possible.

Presently the EU's financial measures against terrorism are built upon the FATF recommendations (Wesseling, 2014, p. 11). Notably, from the EU's CTF perspective one of the most significant legal instrument is the Fourth Money Laundering Directive (2015), the main goal of which is to imbed the terrorist financing and the FATF recommendations in the EU's *acquis communautaire.*[35]

35 The EU's five Money Laundering Directives, which were adopted in 1991, 2001, 2005, 2015 and 2018, have established the EU's general CTF framework. The first two directives mainly introduced anti-money laundering measures for financial and designated non-financial professional organisations and required member states to create FIUs (Bures, 2010, p. 422). The Third Directive (2005) was adopted in 2005 and started to be implemented by the member states by the end of 2007 (de Goede, 2012, pp. 40–41). However, the Third Directive (2005), as one of the wide-ranging EU regulations adopted against terrorist financing, has a wider control on the daily financial lives of EU citizens and money transfers. Consequently, this directive has brought into practice that the KYC, customer due diligence and FIUs reporting obligations within the EU. In other words, this directive has set up a large scale of private-public security cooperation (Wesseling, 2014). The Fourth AML Directive (European Union), 2005 has aimed to embolden the EU anti-money laundering framework and align the rules in the EU with the FATF recommendations. A number of entities which were not subject to the provisions of the Third Directive, such as lawyers and accountants, are all applied in this directive. Moreover, services like the trading of goods are extended by this directive. In general terms, it could be asserted that the new directive remains mostly in the same line as the last one, whereas the new one enlarges its scope to embody the latest FATF recommendations (Kartalis, 2017). The Fifth AML Directive (2018) extends the scope to virtual currency platforms and wallet providers, tax related services and traders of art; grants access to the general public to beneficial ownership information of EU based companies; makes it an obligation to consult the beneficial ownership register when performing AML due diligence; obliges member states to create a list of national public offices and functions that qualify as politically exposed (PEP); introduces strict enhanced due diligence measures for financial flows from high-risk third countries; ends the anonymity of bank and savings accounts, as well as safe deposit boxes, and creates central access mechanisms to bank account and safe deposit boxes holder information throughout the EU; makes information on real estate holders centrally available to public authorities; lowers thresholds for identifying purchasers of prepaid cards and for the use of e-money and further enhances the powers of the FIUs and facilitates cooperation and information exchange among authorities (Krais, 2018; EU Commission, 2018).

The main idea of the directive is tracking terrorist financing and provides robust reporting requirements for key enablers in the financial and legal sectors (Turksen, 2017).

It can be claimed that the EU's AML/CTF framework is a 'preventive effort'. Consequently, it has three main objectives regarding terrorist financing problem:

1 To identify clients and beneficial owners and tracking their money transfers in order to prevent possible terrorist attacks; disrupting terrorist attacks; or
2 To decrease their impacts by isolating terrorists from their financial sources or limit their access to money; and
3 To increase the trust, reputation and stability of the financial system by taking effective actions against legal and illegal sources of terrorist financing (Wesseling, 2014).

The EU's risk-based approach to AML/CTF rests on four main pillars: intelligence; awareness; training; and periodic self-evaluation. While the EU's CTF measures are not novel or different than those recommended by the FATF and those CTF measures found in many other jurisdictions (e.g. the US and Australia), what makes the EU's legal framework different is the safeguards and protection it confers to the EU citizens who may be subject to the CTF measures. The EU's legal framework not only has a robust data protection requirements for state and private sectors[36] but also enables its citizens to challenge and seek legal remedy against CTF measures directly at the supranational courts of the EU (The Court of Justice of the European Union, 2018; The European Court of Human Rights, 2018). The importance and weight of these safeguards were evidenced remarkably through the jurisprudence of these courts (Turksen, 2018) over the last two decades as well as after the disclosure of secret financial data transferring between the US and Belgium based interbank-cooperative 'Society for Worldwide Interbank Financial Telecommunication' (SWIFT) in June 2006 by the *New York Times* and *Wall Street Journal.* This disclosure started a new era between the EU and the US regarding joint CTF efforts (Lichtblau & Risen, 2006; Simpson, 2006). After the 9/11 attacks, the CIA started to use a data surveillance program clandestinely, called 'Terrorist Financing Tracking Program' (TFTP)) which later started to be directed by the US Department of Treasury's OFAC (Wesseling, 2014).[37]

Nevertheless, after the disclosure of the SWIFT scandal, US officials claimed that by using this program and the financial data therein, they reached successful results such as the arrest of one Al Qaeda operative, who was responsible for the

36 For more information, see the EU General Data Protection Regulation Portal (2018).

37 This secret financial surveillance program, TFTP, provides US intelligence and treasury officials the ability to analyse millions of banking transactions. The majority of the financial data which contains the records of bank transfers took place within the EU member state/s was transferred in mass through the SWIFT system to the TFTP program secretly (Wesseling, 2014).

2002 bombings in Bali (Lichtblau & Risen, 2006). Subsequent mutual reports on the TFTP also asserted that the programme has a value as it "has produced tens of thousands of leads and over 3,000 reports (which contain multiple TFTP leads) to counter-terrorism authorities worldwide, including over 2,100 reports to European authorities" (EU Commission, 2016). However, these cases were confined to investigations after terrorist attacks took place, thus provided very limited, if any, value for the prevention of terrorism.

These disclosures have started an intense debate within the EU Parliament and in national parliaments which resulted in rising concerns and questions regarding media responsibility, privacy of financial information and the nature of security cooperation between the US and the EU.[38] Eventually in 2010, an EU-US TFTP Agreement was signed which put in place a number of safeguards and review mechanisms which were designed to ensure security, privacy and respect of fundamental rights before any data is released to US authorities. While the EU has been willing to cooperate with the US on the CTF front, providing certain safeguards are observed, it is interesting to note that the EU deemed that an EU Terrorist Finance Tracking System (EU TFTS) is not necessary and that such a system would not be in compliance with regard to its proportionality, cost-effectiveness and respect of fundamental rights (EU Commission, 2013 (2)).

The initial opinion about this cooperative CTF model was that the TFTP would provide the necessary information to prevent terrorist attacks before they happen and assist in obtaining terrorists' identities and locations (Wesseling, 2014, p. 28 and EU Commission, 2013). However, it has become clear that the information generated from TFTP does not provide adequate data for preventing terrorist attacks; rather, it merely assists post-attack investigations.[39] In addition to the efficacy of the TFTP, the effectiveness of this program can be also challenged. For instance, in the case of the murder of Theo Van Gogh (Burke, 2004), the information produced by TFTP claims that the perpetrator, Mohammed Bouyeri, has international terrorist links; however, another report, which was prepared according to the information provided by Dutch the intelligence

38 After these revelations, some European companies allegedly raised concerns about the possibility that their private financial data were being used for commercial espionage by the US to support US companies' competence against EU firms (de Goede, 2012). While some of the governments for which the data-protection is an important issue were aggravated by this clandestine relationship, other governments, though, seem to be disturbed. However, some countries accepted this as a symbolic issue for taking a stand against the US, which especially emerged as a post-Iraq reaction against the Bush administration (Levi, 2010, p. 656).

39 Joint Reports and review exercises by the EU Commission and the US Treasury indicate that the main value of the TFTP has been in the realm of post terrorism investigations. The latest 2017 report which is titled 'Report from the Commission to the European Parliament and the Council on the Joint Review of the implementation of the Agreement between the European Union and the United States of America on the processing and transfer of passenger name records to the United States Department of Homeland Security', also confirms this (European Union Commission, 2017).

service and the court's decision, claims that the murderer does not have any international terrorist links. In this case, it may be asserted that the efficacy and effectiveness of the TFTP in the face of current terrorist threats are not clear. Furthermore, as the accuracy of the intelligence it has produced has been disputed on a number of occasions, the quality of evidence and intelligence gathering therein is in need of improvement.

Evidently, after the 9/11 terrorist attacks, the EU adopted related UNSCRs and the FATF recommendations harmoniously. In accordance with these improvements, the EU has developed its own measures and regulations, yet some of them could not be implemented in a uniform fashion owing to national constitutional, legal and political differences amongst the EU member states. Hence the EU's AML/CTF measures have always come in the form of a 'Directive' rather than a 'Regulation'.[40] Furthermore, such measures were criticised from legal, transparency, legitimacy and efficiency perspectives. This situation was argued to be a result of not only the internal differences within the EU, but also the adoption of the smart sanctions and money laundering approaches based on some unjustified postulations which do not address the terrorist threat of the EU. Thus, these approaches and CTF provisions were adopted without any critical assessment, which would take into account the applicability of these measures to the EU's terrorism issue. Although application of the smart sanctions and anti-money laundering regimes have been accepted as standards of global CTF models, the EU did not directly take any part during the process of designing them. According to Bures (2011, p. 188) these unjustified but already accepted assumptions, noted similarly by Biersteker and Eckert (2008b, pp. 4–5) as assumptions on which the CTF regime is based, can be summarised as follows: Firstly, all terrorist groups are the same, thus implementing 'one-size-fits-all' CTF regulation can be effective with all types of terrorist organisations. Secondly, terrorists may/can use mainly the formal financial institutions for transferring money. Thirdly, the regulative applications for the formal financial sector can be expanded to the operations of informal financial networks and other possible transactions methods. Lastly, hawala and other informal value transfer systems take significant part in terrorist financing, and there is an increasing interconnection between organised crime and terrorism in the developing regions of the world.

However, in light of the recent literature and empirical evidence (based on terrorist attacks and subsequent convictions) it is clear that these assumptions are increasingly inaccurate and unwarranted, especially in the case of dealing with the financing activities of home-grown terrorist cells across the EU (Bures, 2011, p. 199; EUROJUST, 2017).

40 Directives are created as to the result to be achieved and often allow a degree of discretion as to how member states achieve that.

Even though there have been impressive CTF efforts at international and regional levels whereby a majority of the states have adopted the UN, FATF and EU legal instruments in order to show their solidarity and also to avoid the high political costs of not adopting them, these efforts have been largely superficial (Clunan, 2006, p. 579). Thus, they failed to prevent and deal with the root causes of terrorism. In this drive to instil international and cooperative strategy in the CTF, unlike the EU, which is trying to set a global framework against terrorist financing, it seems that the US has shown a more focused stance on the activities of the 1267 (1999) Sanctions Committee. Using the UN platform and its legal structure via the UNSC, the US has convinced and at times coerced governments and individuals to comply with its own interests by cooperating with bilateral and regional organisations. The US has focused its effort to mobilise and form the international community to eliminate the financial activities of terrorist organisation threat, which is directed at the US, Al Qaeda and its affiliates. Moreover, the US has exported its CTF framework to the UN, the FATF and the EU platforms including practices such as asset freezing, blacklisting, suspicious activity reporting and implementation of AML measures. However, the success, efficacy and effectiveness of the implementation of these practices are yet to be answered.

It is clear that for a CTF regime to be successful against both domestic and international terrorism, a great deal of international cooperation at both the legislative and the law enforcement levels is needed, and this is not a very easy task (Bures, 2011, p. 173). Another development after the 9/11 attacks is the broadened and increased use of existing anti-money laundering cooperation on the multilateral level (Biersteker et al., 2008, p. 243) against terrorist finance. Consequently, in the section below, the international organisations and their CTF efforts are examined. This examination reveals that the different goals and interests of multiple actors and stakeholders have a decisive effect on shaping the international CTF framework.

3.4 Strategies and measures of CTF

In this part of the chapter the main CTF strategies and measures will be examined. Firstly, the main debate about the effectiveness of CTF measures will be outlined, and the adaptation of AML strategies in order to deal with terrorist financing will be discussed. Secondly, the techniques used against terrorist financing such as financial intelligence/investigation will be critiqued.

3.4.1 Effectiveness of CTF efforts

The assumed logic behind the CTF efforts is clear; if the money can be cut, the terrorists' activities can be prevented as well. It can be claimed that the CTF practices are part and parcel of counter-terrorism efforts, as the anti-money laundering framework is a part of crime reduction strategies (Bures, 2012, p. 713). According to this rationale, by limiting terrorists' resources, their attacks and impacts may be reduced or even prevented (Biersteker & Eckert, 2008b, p. 1). It is also assumed that most of the financial crimes and financing of terrorism activities leave 'financial footprints' that can be traced. Thus, following the assets and these tracks may reveal terrorist networks and their secret terrorist cells (Aufhauser, 2003, p. 3). Within these assumptions regarding CTF efforts, in the previous parts of this chapter we identified two main approaches which have been adopted at the domestic and international levels: one of them is the UN based 'Smart Sanctions Model' which consists of the application of smart sanctions and blacklisting mechanisms; the second one is the 'AML Model' which is developed and supported by the FATF and the Egmont Group. In this context, the effectiveness of these approaches and applications will be discussed.

Smart sanctions approach

It has been claimed that the effectiveness of the smart sanctions approach increased because of their shift from on-going conflicts to terrorism related subjects (Bures, 2010). Nevertheless, as was seen in the context of Afghanistan, the UN smart sanctions did not yield positive results against the Taliban and Al Qaeda (UN Monitoring Team, 2005). Moreover, it is also indicated that the existing measures such as financial and travel ban sanctions have only limited effects on transforming terrorist threats. A case in point is the home-grown terrorists (Bures, 2010, p. 427).

As Oudraat (2007, p. 343) notes, home-grown terrorists may have certain advantages such as not having any terrorist track records; they are not subject to immigration controls at the border, nor do they have to make long travels as they are citizens of the territory within which they operate, and they can realise their attacks with a small amount of money or resources. Therefore, while the smart sanctions approach may be effective as a deterrent factor against state sponsorships of terrorism, it is less effective against transnational terrorist groups such as Al Qaeda, and it can be claimed that these measures are nearly useless against individually planned and committed attacks by home-grown terrorists. Moreover, these smart sanctions cannot be described as targeted or smart because, even though they are expected to be directed against specific individuals and firms which may have some association with the ruling elite of the country where a terrorist organisation is based, they have been mainly used against vague entities such as the Al Qaeda network and its associates (Bures, 2010, p. 427).

Blacklisting mechanism

In addition to the criticism and shortcomings of the so-called smart sanctions regime, the effectiveness of the blacklisting mechanism as part of the sanctions regime has also been disputed. There is no clear and/or substantial evidence to show that the blacklisting mechanism has had a significant effect on CTF (House of Lords Select Committee on Economic Affairs, 2007), and the existing CTF blacklists are both under and over inclusive (Bures, 2010, p. 428). Subsequently, this regime causes difficulties in terms of determining the targets of the sanctions. Another problem related to the current blacklisting approach is that it has not proven to be smart or targeted as was expected. On the one hand these measures can be implemented against targeted individuals and entities yet experience shows that sanctions have unwittingly or incidentally had implications for individuals who may have unknown and/or unintentional relationships with terrorists and terrorist groups (Bures, 2010, pp. 428–429). For example, a seemingly legitimate business which the public may not suspect may be a disguised platform for terrorist funding. Thus, following an investigation, anyone affiliated with that business may become a suspect. As Passas (2006b, p. 283) notes, the designation lists formed by the UN, the EU and states such as the US were so long, included so many common and similar names which provide limited assistance and caused due process and enforceability problems.

Asset freezing mechanism

According to a UN report in 2004, even though $112 million was frozen in the first three months after the 9/11 attacks, this amount significantly decreased over the next two years, until only $24 million of assets were frozen (United Nations, 2004, p. 49). One reason for this drop might be the officials' illegal freezing and seizure decisions, which have been overturned by the courts. It is also rightly criticised that even though there is an already established international monitoring system, which has been led by FATF and other organisations since the 9/11 attacks, it seems impossible to reach the exact amount of the money frozen or released and the number of the cases which ended with convictions and sanctions. It is claimed that without acquiring the accurate financial figures, it will not be possible to measure the impact of any CTF policy. Additionally, it can be argued that if the existing law enforcement measures cannot destroy terrorist organisations but only disrupt their activities or provide an opportunity for the other organisations to take their place, then these measures should be examined for the possibility of being used to change the way the terrorist organisations are structured (Tupman, 2009, p. 203).

Gurule (2009) noted that despite the initial effectiveness of counter-terrorism efforts by the UN, this strategy, emboldened by the ICSFT (1999) and the FATF Special Recommendations, does not seem to be working as well against terrorist financing. The first reason is the progressive decrease in the number of names added to the sanctions list by the member states.[41] Secondly, the reluctance of member states to implement a sanction regime is another important reason for

41 For example, after the 9/11 attacks, the number of designated persons and entities was 278, whereas in 2007 only 8 names were added to this list. These improvements were introduced to ameliorate the existing problems regarding the designation and listing processes such as

the failure. Normally when an individual or organisation is placed on the designation list, member states are required to freeze the assets of those listed quickly. If they do not take urgent action, there is a real risk that terrorists may avoid these sanctions by transferring or hiding their assets.

Furthermore, the legal challenges threaten the application of the current sanctions regime, which is based on designations and asset freezing. The lack of administrative capacity, the lack of identification information of listed names or human rights and privacy concerns might have some merit for states' unwillingness to adhere to the sanctions regime. The UN Sanctions Committee is also sensitive about such issues because the quality of evidence and reasons for entities' designation can differ from country to country, and in numerous countries due process and the rule of law may not operate to the level required by international legal instruments. While the decline of the states' will and the lack of motivation for implementation of sanctions are evident, it should also be noted that states find these measures ineffective and costly on operational levels. Given the uncertainty of the success and the effectiveness of listing and asset freezing, it can be claimed that the present CTF practices may be deemed dubious by some enforcement agencies. On the other hand, it does not mean that these measures are totally ineffective for countering terrorist financing: even if CTF sanction may not bear an immediate result, they do put pressure on terrorist organisations, which may force them to make mistakes.

Gurule (2009) argues that the failure of the sanctions regime is caused by the decrease in the number of listed names and the lack of states' implementations. However, it can be claimed that it is not possible to say with certainty that the numbers of listed names and related government implementation are clear indications of the success of the sanctions regime. Therefore, it is important to understand why listed names and states' willingness are decreasing. Correspondingly, it is also important to examine whether applying these measures to the letter would provide the ultimate success for winning the struggle against terrorists and their financial activities. This is one of the aims of this monograph in the context of Turkey's CTF measures.

According to Bell (2003, p. 115) the freezing of terrorist asset strategy provides advantages for governments. For using sole intelligence information governments can justify inclusion of any suspected individual or organisation on the sanction lists without showing any evidence or linking terrorism and the suspected property. However, the disadvantage of this blunt approach is that the governments can only freeze property and assets which are held overtly and the authorities are able to trace, detect and link to a terrorist entity. On the one hand, it is claimed that the asset freezing strategy deters potential donors who will finance terrorists; on the other hand, since 2001 attacks, it is evident that terrorist

establishment of focal point, requirement for increasing the quality, accuracy and consistency of identification information and petitions for de-listing.

organisations such as Al Qaeda and ISIS have been acquiring and generating great amounts of assets, which has not prevented by the asset freezing measures.

Furthermore, Williams (2005) notes that the usage of freezing and seizing the assets of terrorists was deemed to be a significant strategy to disrupt and weaken terrorist networks. It has been claimed that following the money can provide far better outcomes in terms of preventing future terrorist attacks. However, just because terrorists cannot transfer or move frozen assets does not mean intelligence and law enforcement agencies automatically gain all the information they need to prevent and prosecute terrorists. Therefore, it is claimed that monitoring money transactions could provide better information for detecting prospective terrorist attacks than freezing assets. Moreover, it is still not clear whether targeting terrorist finances can produce anticipated results for preventing future terrorist attacks. It is claimed that the freezing and seizing approach not only has been a failure but also has produced adverse effects. Williams (2005) explains this situation by the terrorists' ability to adapt to the conditions and operate according to the rules. In this context, it is claimed that as a result of the freezing and seizing strategy, terrorists now are more able to and successful in hiding their money from the eyes of the officials, and therefore it is not easy to monitor them. In other words, by freezing assets, terrorists may be pushed further underground. It should also be noted that the figures related to frozen assets do not reflect the effectiveness of these measures, yet these figures are given more importance than they should be and give a false impression to the public about the real success of the CTF strategy.

Anti-money laundering approach

Another important CTF model used against terrorist financing is the AML model, which has been mainly established and supported by the FATF. There are differences and overlapping points between terrorist financing and money laundering, whereas, similar to the smart sanctions approach, the effectiveness of the AML model is not clear. This led a number of academics to question the suitability of the AML model and methods that are utilised in the CTF context (Roberge, 2007, p. 196; Unger & Van der Linde, 2015).

According to reports of some of the FATF member states, a major difficulty encountered by them is "that terrorists financing might not meet the definition of money laundering [which] meant that they were limited in the actions they could take against terrorist monies in the framework of anti-money laundering laws" (FATF, 2002, as cited in Vlcek, 2007, p. 106). Therefore, Bures (2012, p. 717) argues that the analogy between terrorist financing and organised crime may be misleading and moreover counter-productive. Correspondingly, some of the other scholars from politics, law, economics and sociology refuse to combine these two different concepts (Malkin & Elizur, 2002, p. 64; Roberge, 2007; Zagaris, 2004, p. 156). In contrast, some of the academics accept these two approaches as similar concepts, and this defines terrorist financing as a reverse version of money laundering (Roberge, 2007). Because of this resemblance most of the combating strategies against money laundering are deemed to be used against terrorist financing problems (Roberge, 2007, p. 196).

Even though there are differences between terrorist financing and money laundering, there are undeniable overlapping areas such as pre-9/11 classical terrorist cases. However, Bures (2010) points out that for dealing with the post-9/11 period terrorist cases, the standard organised crime money laundering approach is not effective because of the reversed nature of the process whereby money laundering by definition involves laundering of the proceeds of crime (dirty assets),whereas terrorist financing may derive from legitimate sources. The policies against money laundering mainly concentrate on the financial service sector professionals and oblige them to report and identify suspicious money transfers. According to Roberge, this type of strategy that targets the financial sector is less appropriate against terrorist financing.

It is undeniable that an AML regime must involve financial institutions and professionals therein as enablers, and their reports are important tools for law enforcement agencies. However, at the same time, these reports and entities have proven to be unsuccessful against financing of terrorism because, as an alternative to formal financial system, terrorists can use informal value transfer systems or cash couriers without leaving any paper trail on financial systems. In addition, it is difficult to detect low amounts of legitimate money transferred by terrorists in the formal financial system. In this situation, intelligence and law enforcement efforts become key tools for governments combating the financing of terrorism. If intelligence from the field is combined with financial data which is provided by financial sectors, then this process is likely to produce more successful results than focusing solely on suspicious activity reports.

As Eckert (2008, pp. 217–218) aptly observed, following the 9/11 terrorist attacks, the existing AML measures, in a broad form and without any alteration, have been put into practice for CTF purposes. This pragmatic and knee-jerk reaction is somehow understandable in the immediate aftermath of these events. However, given the significant time that has elapsed since 9/11 (seventeen years to be exact), a critical examination of the suitability and the effectiveness of the implementation of AML methods for CTF measures is well overdue. At this point the former Treasury Under Secretary Stuart Levey's words draw an explicit picture of the current difficulty of using AML measures for CTF purposes:

> The current financial regulatory regime was forged out of nearly twenty years of experience in detecting and preventing money laundering. Money laundering and terrorist financing, however, differ in significant ways. In the money-laundering field, investigators look through a telescope trying to detect the movement of large amounts of dirty cash. When investigating terrorist financing, investigators use a microscope in order to track the movement of relatively small amounts of often 'clean' [emphasis added] money, intended to support a nefarious purpose. Financial experts in the private sector have developed a set of typologies to detect money-laundering activity;

terrorist financing transactions, by contrast, may bear no inherent identifying trademarks whatsoever.

(Levey, 2004)

Consequently, Eckert (2008, p. 218) states that even though there are important differences between AML and CTF contextually, both regimes try to increase the traceability of money transfers and accumulate wider information about the main sources. In this context, the existence of these differences indicates that there may be a new specialised approach needed.

Private-public partnerships

As a natural result of the application of these two models, smart sanctions and AML measures, the inclusion of the private financial sector has become a necessity for implementing both the UN and FATF driven regimes. Therefore, both formal and informal 'private-public partnerships' have emerged to detect, deter, disrupt and deny terrorists.[42] The main expectation from this partnership is that the private financial institutions and other entities should become a guard and report suspicious activities to the corresponding authorities such as FIUs (Bures, 2012).

According to Eckert (2008, p. 220) establishing and keeping the coordination between private and public sectors is key to a successful CTF strategy. Similarly, Barrett (2012, p. 730) notes that the active and devoted participation of the private sector is one of the conditions for the success and the effectiveness of the CTF measures. In this type of partnership, financial organisations such as banks, insurance and investment companies and non-financial organisations such as casinos, lawyers, dealers and security companies are required to assist the CTF efforts by adopting a risk management process, which will be able to recognise, assess and develop alternative solutions to deal with and mitigate the possible effects of determined risks (Bures, 2012) and to address the potential financial crimes that might be perpetrated by businesses and customers. These financial institutions are expected to share suspicious activity information with government officials. On the other hand, governments must inform the private sector about risks and be willing to exchange sensitive information with them so that they can redesign their risk models and adapt more accurately. In addition, governments must provide protection for the confidential financial data and ensure the privacy of their citizens because banks know who and where their customers are and

42 Formal partnerships refer to those established by law which require particular professionals or regulated entities to report suspicious activities to law enforcement agencies and financial intelligence units. Informal partnerships on the other hand are voluntary and involve platforms for intelligence and information sharing between authorities and various enablers in the financial sector in particular. Such partnerships have been established in several common-law jurisdictions including the US, the UK, Canada, Australia, Hong Kong and Singapore. See Maxwell and Artingstall (2017).

their spending profiles, income sources, business connections and more (Barrett, 2012). The application of know your customer (KYC), customer due diligence (CDD), SARs, suspicious transaction reports (STRs) and trainings of the staff are the main elements of this risk management process. In practical terms, when implementing these measures, financial and non-financial organisations are expected to detect suspicious customers and transactions in terms of terrorist financing and report them to the FIUs. Then the FIUs examine these reports and collate information from other sources such as law enforcement, administrative or public registers and private companies, where they seek any positive links with terrorist financing. The examining processes may alter from state to state whereas the main implementation processes are similar. Even though theoretically this process may seem to be clear and simple to undertake, it is far more difficult to achieve the proper utilisation of these CTF measures in practice owing to the fact that there are many SARs to examine, information within SARs may be inconclusive and FIUs often have small teams of experts. In addition, the information exchange between the private and the public sectors is not easy because of the confidentiality of the data. Improving the relationship between these two parties is very important in order to have a better genuine risk assessment and to increase the effectiveness of the counter measures (Barrett, 2012, pp. 729–730). Furthermore, according to Levi (2010, p. 662), this situation arises from the fact that most of the CTF related data are classified and not accessible for any examination: partly counter-intelligence concerns about the analysis of technics which may reveal detection and suspicion methods and partly lack of official desire to share information with the public about the outcomes. Although publicly available details of terrorist attacks can be used in order to analyse the terrorist incidents, reaching the relevant data in terms of operational costs, the methods and sources used for financing of these attacks might not always be accessible for researchers and officials. This situation causes inevitable problems for the private financial sector and the state security and intelligence agencies.

In order to forge informal public-private partnerships that are effective, Maxwell and Artingstall (2017) have put forward key principles that must exist:

- **Leadership and trust:** Both at the public authority and private company there needs to be commitment at senior leadership levels so that trust and confidence can be built with shared objectives and risk ownership.
- **Legislative clarity:** Legal instruments and provisions therein needs to be clear with a view toward enabling and facilitating information sharing to achieve the agreed objectives.
- **Governance:** Partnership must be conducted with robust governance principles and accountability arrangements.
- **Technology and analytical capability:** Partnership needs to invest in technology and analytical capability for information flows, analysis and turning information into intelligence and evidence that is admissible.
- **Adaptability and evolution:** Partnership needs to be able to respond to ever changing threats and adopt accordingly.

Risk assessment or risk-based approach

A risk-based approach requires countries, authorities and relevant designated sectors and entities to identify, assess and understand the money laundering and terrorist financing risk to which they are exposed, and take the appropriate mitigation measures in accordance with the level of risk (FATF, 2014d).

A risk-based approach has certain difficulties in terms of the implementation of a CTF policy. Firstly, although there is data for risk assessment models for determining many types of business risks, there is no clear data to determine the CTF risks due to the fact that it is not possible to measure how much money is laundered or used for terrorist financing. Besides the difficulties of determining the burden of CTF risk, private institutions do not have any clear benchmark, which would give clues to assess the money laundering and terrorist financing risk (Bures, 2012). Levi (2010, p. 656) asserts that counter-intelligence and security concerns are the reasons why private financial partners are not provided with any clear guidance about terrorists' financial activities *modi operandi*. As a result, most of the financial institutions decide to report a large number of financial activities as suspicious without elaborate examination which creates information pollution for law enforcement agencies.

Secondly, even though there are several guidelines, which were published by international, national and private bodies, for detecting suspicious transactions, it is still not clear how and/or how easy it is to successfully identify the CTF risk as terrorist finance does not always emanate from illegal sources and activities. The financial sector is keen to help states to combat terrorism, yet they are not provided with enough direction, training and feedback (Barrett, 2012, p. 730). Therefore, financial institutions have to individually evaluate their customers and their money transfers on a discretionary basis, and they are also expected to make an assessment about their customers and the possibility of their present or future involvement with any kind of terrorist activity. Therefore, the effectiveness of a CTF reporting system often depends on the competence of the decision maker and the data available to them (Bures, 2012, p. 719).

Thirdly, even though a number of large banks have state of the art monitoring and analytical software as well as elaborate CTF/AML training programs for their staff, because of the vast number of money transfers, there is still the possibility that these institutions will have inevitable leakages (Bures, 2012).

As a result of these difficulties, financial institutions find themselves in a situation where they encounter the profit versus security dilemma. In this case, the trade-off for the profit oriented financial institutions is: by reporting less they can save money, whereas they may face the possibility of being sanctioned. On the other hand, to decrease the possibility of being sanctioned financial institutions may increase the number of their reports, but then the costs for the institution also are increased. In the current regime of regulations and penalties it can be claimed that most of the financial institutions choose to act in accordance with the latter option given the possibility of facing the heavy fines and serious consequences for non-compliance. In other words, the reputational and economic effects, which are built-in CTF measures, drive institutions to act in accordance with the CTF provisions. However, this does not mean that these reports based on individual assessments and vague concepts will contain high value intelligence and admissible evidence for the law enforcement agencies and the judiciary. Furthermore, financial institutions can only become responsible for false negatives for which they did not report illegal financial activities, which are prosecuted later on for terrorist financing or money laundering. On the contrary for false positive reports, totally legal transactions, there is no coercive action against financial institutions (Bures, 2012). This trend has led to reflex action – the 'when in doubt, file syndrome' – whereby many financial institutions from smaller to larger ones choose to file suspicious reports rather than to face criticism or criminal consequences.

In this context, the effectiveness of the highly efficient report mechanism becomes important. At this point, Eckert (2008, p. 219) asks whether the existing reporting mechanisms such as SARs, STRs and CTRs are effective tools to achieve quality information and evidence. The thresholds and benchmarks for suspicious reporting may alter from country to country, country; however, by dividing a large transfer to smaller fractions or pre-transfers from high risk countries to safe jurisdictions by informal remittance and transfers methods, these CTF measures can be evaded easily.

Efficiency of the institutions complying with the requirements of the CTF measures is high by filing many reports. However, the number of these SARs cannot be interpreted as effective implementation of the CTF measures. Similarly, the increased amount of data which is sent by private institutions raises the question of whether governments' capacity will be enough to examine and use this data properly (Eckert, 2008). Moreover, the high number of reports become a significant burden for national FIUs, which are tasked with examining a large amount of suspicious data. Also, the increasing number of reports can hide the very limited number of actual SARs, which may contain significant operative intelligence about terrorist financing (Bures, 2012). Takáts' research about money laundering illustrates that financial institutions use a self-protective approach with the "Crying Wolf" analogy: "In the tale, the boy cried wolf so often, that his cries became meaningless. Similarly, excessive reporting, which will be referred to as 'crying wolf', fails to identify what is truly relevant" (Takáts, 2007, p. 4). Furthermore, Bures (2012) finds that according to the available data, financial institutions' high efficiency of reporting neither causes deprivation of terrorists from more funding nor puts them in jail in larger numbers. In terms of the former, the fact that higher numbers of SARs have not resulted in higher amounts of frozen terrorist assets is confirmed by the available data. Furthermore, the conviction rates related to violations of CTF laws are so minimal, and numerous prosecutions are quashed by the courts owing to inadequate and/or inadmissible evidence. These facts lead us to a conclusion that the current CTF strategies have not delivered the desired results yet.

According to Passas (2006b), although some government agencies have announced numerous success stories, the CTF initiatives on the international level have had limited effect. As we mentioned before, even if the FATF recommendations had been in practice before the 9/11 attacks, the hijackers would not have been arrested owing to their small number of money transactions which would be very insignificant compared to daily transfers of the trillions of US dollars around the globe. Consequently, if these measures or reporting systems do not intercept and prevent terrorists, then it is important to ask what the purpose of the special recommendations is (Passas, 2006a). On the other hand, Barrett (2012, p. 721) feels that if an investigator had had any suspicion about one of the terrorists, then the 9/11 attacks could have been prevented and the overseas supporters unquestionably unveiled.

Due to the fact that the perpetrators of the 9/11 attacks did their financial activity inside the legal limits, they could not be detected by the security agencies. So the real failure was not about investigating Al Qaeda's financial records but was about connecting the dots before the attacks. Additionally, even though there had been a situation which comprised increased awareness and alertness against terrorism in the wake of the attacks, it is claimed that these kinds of normal and legal financial activities would not have been detected either.

Barrett (2012, as cited in 2012, pp. 721–722; Gordon, 2012) mentions a study undertaken by Eckert et al., which examines the potential terrorist financing indicators. According to this study, even though there is a small portion of overlapping similarity between money laundering and certain terrorist financing activities, it is not possible to find any reliable indicator for detecting terrorist financing. From this perspective, Passas's approach looks more proper and clearer with the examples of unfortunate terrorist attacks such as the London and Madrid bombings. When these attacks happened, the CTF measures were already in force; however, they did not detect and prevent these attacks.

In contrast to the previous claims, Acharya (2009, p. 295) argues that the measures and countering efforts implemented against terrorist financing have deterred potential sympathisers and supporters from providing money to terrorists.[43] Because of the successful implementation of CTF measures, terrorist financing has become more risky, costly and time consuming for terrorists. Therefore, the operational ability and the capability in terms of planning and undertaking spectacular attacks have been challenged and restricted.

It can be claimed that the argument of Acharya (2009) emerges from the main assumption, generally accepted by many experts and scholars, that if the money can be cut, the terrorists' activities can be prevented or decreased. In addition, this claim is supported with the examples of allegedly failed terrorists' attempts or attacks. The first example used by Acharya (2009, p. 293) is the 1993 World Trade Center terrorist attack which was partly successful: because

43 Consequently, not only has the amount of the available money for terrorists been decreased, but also the costs of raising and transferring this money have been increased for terrorists. Local cells and operatives have started to raise funds themselves rather than using financial systems (Acharya, 2009).

of lack of money the terrorists could not build a strong bomb, and they initiated the attack earlier than planned. The second one is the Strasbourg Market attack attempt, which was disclosed before it was committed due to a careless phone call by one of the perpetrators to demand extra funds for the attack. Even though these two cases seem to support the idea that decreased amounts of money result in less terrorist capabilities and sophistication, it may be argued that these two examples are not enough to demonstrate explicitly the link between the amount of money and number of terrorist attacks. The other problems, which may occur because of wrong planning, corruption and other human related deficits, might affect the development of these partial terrorist attacks. Additionally, the main terrorist actor in both of the examples is Al Qaeda; thus, it is important to answer whether it would be the same outcome if attacks were committed by other terrorist organisations. There is not an easy to answer this question with the existing data provided by Acharya. However, this does not mean that we should deny the possibility that Acharya's understanding of the mechanism might have some validity. In addition, this approach is one of the common assumptions accepted by most of the experts and scholars: the increase of the money in terrorist coffers can provide broad opportunities for terrorists and their organisations.

In the EU context, the current CTF measures which are implemented in light of the FATF Recommendations and follow a risk based approach may not be effective because they are not suitable for and specific to the EU member states' terrorist financing threat requirements.[44] Similarly, Vlcek (2007, p. 110) argues that the 'one-size-fits-all' approach does not work for the EU. According to Wesseling's (2014) analysis of the EU's main CTF tools there is a need for publicly available evidence which illustrates the effectiveness of current CTF strategy. Because of methodological and confidentiality problems it is hard to collect evidence for assessment of CTF measures. However, Wesseling draws attention to the fact that according to the qualitative analysis, the implementation of the risk based analysis of the Third Anti-Money Laundering Directive and TFTP has a number of significant problems, even though there is limited evidence (both quantitative and qualitative) on the effectiveness of existing CTF practices.[45]

3.4.2 *Measuring the effectiveness of CTF*

It is important to inquire as to how one can measure the effectiveness of a CTF strategy or whether it can be measured at all. Bures (2010) notes that measuring the effectiveness of CTF by using dubious methods and a lack of publicly

44 Bures (2010, p. 430) notes that the EU currently uses the existing US AML approach because the EU does not have its own strategic terrorism threat analysis and suggests that the EU needs to reform its CTF policy by analysing its threat assessment in order to address the real and relevant threats of terrorism and terrorist financing across the European Union.

45 Note that the Third Anti-Money Laundering Directive was repealed by the Fourth Anti-Money Laundering Directive in 2015, which was subsequently repealed recently by the Fifth Anti-Money Laundering Directive in 2018 (EUR-Lex, 2018).

available official data (e.g. the amount of frozen terrorist assets) is not desirable nor accurate. Moreover, according to Brzoska (2011, pp. 10–11) owing to the difficulty of establishing a causal relationship between output, outcome and their actual impacts, determining the effectiveness benchmarks for CTF efforts is still academic.

Correspondingly, Eckert (2008, pp. 215–216) notes that measuring the success level of the sanctions approach, which is a list based strategy, focuses on the terrorists and their support systems, whereas considering the amount of frozen or blocked money as an indicator for success is wrong and could be regarded as a misleading effort. The volume of the money confiscated and/or frozen is not an accurate measure for demonstrating the success and the effectiveness of a CTF regime. The main aim of this approach is initially based on identifying terrorist financiers publicly and then isolating terrorist supporters and deterring others from financing terrorists.

According to Donohue (2006, p. 307) the parameters for measuring the efficacy, effectiveness and success fail to determine suitable goals for CTF. That is why the focus or the benchmark ought to be on the number of terrorist convictions, the significance of individuals arrested, the percentage of overall confiscated properties and disrupted operations and their level rather than measuring success by the number of entities blocked and the value of the frozen assets. On the other hand, Sproat (2010, p. 321) does not agree with Donohue and asserts that these two criteria are too difficult to measure and find admissible evidence. Regarding the level of disrupted operations, it is claimed that acquiring such a figure is impossible because it is hard to know terrorists' plans and intentions and to find out the number of deliberately and accidentally prevented attacks. Probably, Sproat's criticisms of Donohue's idea are a result of Donohue's lack of clear explanation of how the term 'level' should be interpreted. However, it may be also claimed that this does not mean the officials who will assess the success cannot classify disrupted terrorist attacks or plots according to their levels. It may be suggested here that the level of terrorist operations can be categorised to: pre-attack or preparation level, implementation level and post-attack level, and for each category indicators might be found to identify these categories. This does not seem to be impossible as Sproat argues. Regarding the importance of the arrested terrorists, without providing any broad explanation, Sproat claims that it is also impossible and too difficult to reach the information about the level of importance of the terrorists arrested. Whereas it may be claimed that a clear answer for detecting the importance level of a terrorist can be drawn from the various sources, which can be reached by the government officials responsible for assessment of CTF policies, such as the terrorist's rank and positions in the organisation, information related to communication, location and tasks implemented and background information such as family, education, profession and intelligence.

Clunan (2006, p. 578) supports Eckert's (2008) idea, which finds the evaluation of CTF inaccurate according to the amount of frozen assets. Furthermore, it seems that there was a remarkable international reaction in which more than

100 countries adopted legislations in response to the UNSC Resolutions regarding counter terrorist financing and money laundering in the wake of the 9/11 attacks; this was commonly accepted as a successful reaction. Correspondingly, for evaluating their CTF success, the US officials have been using the same criteria such as the amount of nationally and internationally frozen assets, creation of national FIUS, signed conventions or treaties and passed legislations, technical assistance programs implemented and the IMF and WB compliance assessments. Accordingly, Clunan (2006, p. 596) suggests a comprehensive standard or model for assessing the international CTF regime by indicating how the CTF regime should be. We suggest that a successful international regime should have the ability to change the operative dynamics for terrorists by coercing them to move towards a criminal environment where it is easier to detect, arrest and prosecute them rather than struggling with pseudo-legal financial activities. For creating a successful international CTF regime on the national level, states should accept and be aware of the fact that terrorist financing is their own problem, not someone else's. Nevertheless, Levi (2010, p. 659) highlights the point that the threats in and terrorist groups of the US and Western Europe may be different from the terrorism threats in other parts of the world. The effects of these threats may be more significant for the West, whereas the same threats may produce only limited economical or business related problems for these states.

Croissant and Barlow (2007, p. 139) claim that countries with effective CTF legislation utilise financial records which are incorporated in their AML system to monitor and trace terrorist networks. Therefore, terrorists who would have not been detected normally due to their indirect position in the attacks would possibly be detected by using paper trails. Moreover, they claim that forfeiting terrorist funding decreases terrorists' capability to recruit, sustain their camps and establish safe havens. In this framework, Croissant and Barlow have conducted a comparative study of ten Southeast Asian countries, which have been analysed according to their CTF compliances and implementation levels of international standards.[46] By using public source documents it has been found that the CTF and AML approaches vary in Southeast Asia. One of the interesting outcomes is that although most of the countries are found to be in compliance with international standards on paper, late or inadequate practices of these measures and their ineffectiveness are the main problem for these countries from the CTF perspective. It seems that most of these governments[47] in Southeast Asia, which mainly depend on foreign economic assistance, may adopt international regulations

46 For this purpose, they have applied an analytical model developed by the "Targeting Terrorist Finances Project" (as cited in Croissant & Barlow, 2007, p. 139), and they conducted their analysis on four categories: (1) the legal frameworks; (2) sophistication level of administrative infrastructure; (3) diversity of the regulative measures in order to provide formal banking compliance and regulation of IVTSs and charities and (4) evidence regarding level of enforcement.

47 These countries are; Brunei, Burma, Cambodia, Indonesia, Laos, Malaysia, Philippines, Singapore, Thailand and Vietnam (Croissant & Barlow, 2007).

established by Western states and amend their legal system accordingly because compliance and re-writing legal books is less costly than non-compliance.

Additionally, there has been evidence that the development levels of the formal financial sector and the speed of the government reaction to prevent money laundering and terrorist financing have an impact on CTF success.[48] Furthermore, it has been shown that if the countries' economies depend on foreign money remittances or IVTSs, then it is more likely that these states may abstain from interfering with these kinds of money flows due to their economic concerns. Accordingly, what transpires is that the 'misfit' between national context and the international obligations can determine the factors for inadequate compliance and implementation as well as the success of CTF regimes (Clunan, 2006; Croissant & Barlow, 2007; and Bures, 2010). It can be asserted that the domestic factors may be more significant for explaining the differences in terms of compliance, enforcement and effectiveness than the coercion ability of the international actors and the legal status of the CTF provisions.

Levi (2010, pp. 663–664) argues that the lack of open source data related to financial intelligence and investigations hinders the production of evidence to assess whether CTF measures are effective or not. In addition, in order to evaluate the impact and success of CTF, law enforcement data alone is not an adequate measure. In this context, there are numerous issues to be raised. For example, it is important to know if data are based on background intelligence, which is independent of any legal prosecution mechanism, and if and how one can disprove or confirm the claim that the money has links with terrorism. Another practical problem is how one assesses the evidence; if the evidence obtained is not admissible in court, can it still be utilised as intelligence for further investigation and monitoring of suspicion activity?

Findings by Tupman (2009, pp. 195–196) confirms the above statements that the available data regarding terrorist financing are not adequate for researchers to understand the real nature of the issue. Sources related to terrorist financing are problematic at some times because CTF practitioners provide information to researchers in different times and in contrasting environments.[49] In this case it is important for researchers to confirm and to check whether this information is reliable; if not, then they should be aware of the possibility that they are being

48 Countries with underdeveloped formal financial sectors are reluctant and slow to amend their legislations to prevent terrorist financing, and it can be claimed that even if they adopted these regulations swiftly their implementation would not be effective due to the inadequacy of their financial system (Croissant & Barlow, 2007).

49 Another source is newspapers, but the problem with newspapers is that the sources or references given can be dubious, and the same event can be expressed very differently in different newspapers. In addition, newspapers have commercial interests, which may cause them to exaggerate stories in order get the attention of more readers to increase their profits. Intelligence services may provide highly exaggerated information in order to acquire more sources and more freedom of movement against this threat. From a political perspective, both trivialising and increasing the importance of the threat may produce some interests for the governments. (Tupman, 2009).

used as a propaganda or political tool. Therefore, confirmation of the information should always be a priority for the researchers if they are to make reliable and valuable research about terrorist financing.

Bell (2003, pp. 120–121) is one of the few scholars who asks how the success and the progress for denying terrorists money can be measured. Firstly, the number of confiscation and the forfeiture orders might imply a degree of CTF success. The value and types of assets taken from terrorist organisations are suggested as the second measure. Thirdly, a rather challenging aspect is establishing whether and how the disrupted amount of money and assets would have been used by terrorists. Lastly, the degree of international cooperation beyond ratifying international legal instruments may be utilised to measure success. For example, the willingness of countries to obtain and implement court orders and provide assistance to investigations and the number of orders issued may be used for the assessment of the international cooperation.

Contributing to the debate, Freeman (2012, p. 241) accepts the current challenges for measuring effectiveness and asks what determines success or failure. He states that there are so many outcomes which may be assessed as success, such as disruptions which could delay a terrorist attack or decrease the impact of the attack, efforts which could force terrorists to focus on more illegitimate kind of financing activities or efforts which then make terrorists use more internal resources for raising money or the defeat of the terrorist organisation. However, it is claimed that even if one or another of these definitions of success is valid, there is still a gap in measuring success. According to current practices, 'success' is perceived through the amount of the frozen or seized assets and the number of prosecuted non-profit organisations or confiscated drugs. Even though all these kinds of actions can be useful, Freeman (2012, p. 241) emphasises that it is important to differentiate between "operational outcomes and successful strategies". Moreover, if a strategy is successful, then it must have an explicit effect on the targeted entities. Although security forces might have seized drugs coming to a country, that does not necessarily show that these efforts were successful in addressing the illegal drug usage in that country. Therefore, it is important to distinguish operational achievements and strategies for endgame.

It is argued by de Goede (2012) that the 'new' security environment has emerged in the wake of the 9/11 terrorist attacks related to counter-terrorist financing practices and their outcomes. Consequently, CTF has created a 'new' security environment, called 'the finance-security assemblage', which has established a new security intervention domain against uncertain futures and worst-case scenarios. Beside the arguments above, de Goede (2012, pp. 197–200) aptly states that the current CTF regime has not been evaluated by the traditional policy success and cost-effectiveness measures for two reasons. Firstly, it is claimed that if the main goal of this assemblage is an expansion of the application of security in time and space in order to enable pre-emptive disruption, then the assessment of the efficiency according to the number of successful prosecutions and amount of money forfeited would be no longer in use. And according to this rationale, any act of disruption, if it has even the slightest possibility of harming a future terrorist plot, would be justified even though there would be no prosecution or confiscation at the end. Secondly, avoiding the possibility of encountering the worst-case scenario makes everything legitimate. Even if there is a 1 percent possibility for a potential disaster, then according to this understanding all the resources should be used to prevent this disaster. "This logic exceeds calculation, meaning that the financial, political, and human costs involved in the apparent prevention of terrorism financing can never measure up to the disaster purportedly prevented" (de Goede, 2012, p. 199). The present lack of comprehensive assessment of the current CTF regime appears to support these claims.

Eckert (2008, p. 227) agrees that it is very difficult to measure how effective the CTF efforts are. As terrorist groups' tactics and strategies are continuously transforming, CTF policies need to be re-evaluated incessantly. Accordingly, within this organic context, it is difficult to establish a comprehensive and systematic assessment and impact analysis of CTF. In short, it is pointed out that gauging the costs and benefits of CTF measures and modifying and tailoring them when needed are a great and a collective challenge.

On the whole, it is widely accepted that there is not a comprehensive methodology to evaluate the effectiveness and the impact of the CTF framework implemented at both the international and domestic levels. In addition, some of the tools and standards used to measure the success of the current regime such as the amount of money seized and the number of people and organisations listed are not enough to provide researchers and policy makers a clear view about the success of current CTF practices. Furthermore, the lack of publicly available data and/or obstructions to reaching such information (which is essential to making an insightful and objective assessment), dent the quality of the critical assessments of CTF regimes.

In light of the above analysis, it can be argued that before measuring the effectiveness of CTF policies or framework, two main questions have to be answered. The first question is: What are the indicators of success or effectiveness of CTF? Answering this question would help to define success and failure. The second question is whether the method or the technique used for gauging the effectiveness of CTF strategy is reliable for this purpose. After properly defining success and failure and if the answer to the second question is positive, then the second part of the process, which is implementation of the measurement, can be started. At this stage, two main components of assessment become significant on the international and national level. Firstly, it should be determined what the competent and current existing legal, administrative and executive CTF systems are. In this context, relevant institutions, staff, trainings, technological tools and degree of awareness of the CTF should be analysed. In other words, the focus should be on whether there is enough capacity for CTF. If it is found that capacity is enough for practising CTF operations, then it should be examined whether law enforcement, intelligence officials, prosecutors or judges and private sector undertake the implementation and practices in a timely and effective manner. This element of the assessment of the effectiveness of the CTF regime concentrates on implementation by practitioners. For example, even though there is enough capacity in terms of legal, administrative and executive means, if the responsible agencies and institutions do not share information and keep this to themselves, this situation can have implications for the effectiveness of that CTF regime. Consequently, if the answers to these two questions are positive, then as the third component of the assessment process, it should be analysed whether these effective CTF measures have expected outcomes and minimised terrorist threats. Additionally, and importantly, any adverse impact of these CTF practices on the society (e.g. fundamental freedoms and human rights of people) should be examined. Generally, this assessment model can be formulated as follows: definition of the success and failure, determining the measuring tool, capacity analysis implementation analysis and impact assessment. The important part of running this evaluative model is that the feedback mechanism should be active continuously at every step and all along the assessment process with a periodic review mechanism built in.

As Sproat (2010) rightly noted, utilisation of both qualitative and quantitative sources for evaluating the success of CTF measures is important. Yet even though

Figure 3.1 Assessment Model for Measuring Effectiveness in CTF

in his study, it is claimed that the UK's CTF is effective and successful, this can be contested if one was to measure the UK's CTF measure against the decline of the terror threat level (which is currently at 'severe' and likely to remain so in the feasible future) (MI5, 2018), the number of deaths by terrorist attacks,[50] or the level of the UK's public worry about terrorism[51] as a benchmark.

Importantly, it may be asserted that in contrast to 'one-size-fits-all' CTF strategy, there should be a tailored assessment model and analysis based on the jurisdiction concerned which takes into account the specific conditions of the targeted environment *inter alia*, social, cultural and economic factors. In other words, for each state, region or any specific threat or terrorist organisation, a new assessment model should be designed.

3.4.3 Financial intelligence and investigation

Another important component of the current CTF practices is the usage of financial intelligence and investigation methods. As Parker and Taylor (2010, p. 949) noted, the increasing emphasis on the importance of using financial intelligence on operational and strategic levels has caused revision of the existing CTF strategy. The evolution of US CTF (Clunan, 2006; Roth et al., 2004) along with virtually all of European countries' CTF strategies can be given as examples of this trend.

It is generally agreed that by using financial investigation valuable information might be gained regarding terror attacks and crimes by looking into the timeline of and preparation for them. In this context, combining the pieces of the terrorist attack or criminal financial investigation provides discoveries from the crime scene, which can be followed by law enforcement agencies. By doing so, previous stages of a terrorist attack or crime can be examined (HM Treasury, 2007, s. 1.19, p. 10).[52] In addition, the financial investigation allows officials to 'look sideways' in order to identify, detect and perceive the terrorist networks and their links with the plots. Another function supported by financial investigation is 'looking forward' which can warn the officials about possible future terrorist attacks (HM Treasury, 2007, s. 1.19, p. 10). In other words, by using financial investigation, law enforcement officials can look back at the terrorist attack, can look sideways to determine and locate the network and links between those responsible and can look forward which provides an opportunity for detecting future terrorist attacks.

Similarly, Levitt and Jacobson (2008, p. 80) argue that financial intelligence is a valuable counter-terrorism instrument with the ability to disrupt and prevent terrorist attacks. Due to the fact that law enforcement agencies have been using

50 See Bond (2017).

51 See Statista (2018).

52 It is also claimed by the UK government that the enquiries of the 7 July London bombings and the 21 July terrorist attempts exposed the importance of the financial investigation for the advancement of the investigations and for providing a bigger intelligence picture (HM Government, 2006, s. 20, p. 78).

financial means in order to solve crimes and establish prosecutions successfully for a long time, intelligence agencies have increased their capacity and efforts to use financial intelligence effectively in order to act pre-emptively. In addition, it is claimed that the post-attack period utility of the financial tools was confirmed with concrete results recently. It is noted that by using financial data, the investigators reached significant and immediate results regarding the post terrorist attack investigations of the 9/11 attacks and the bombings in Madrid and London along with other terrorist attacks. Moreover, under the preventive intelligence title, it is claimed that a financial transaction is a clear fact compared to the intelligence collected from humans or satellites, which needs a serious and lengthy confirmation period. It is also claimed that raising, moving, hiding and keeping money and other financial assets leaves a trail which can be followed by the investigators. They can then connect people with account numbers or determine cash couriers. Such methods can be powerful pre-emptive tools which may direct law enforcement agencies towards money movements between terrorist organisations and terrorist cells (Levitt & Jacobson, 2008, p. 81). For instance, under the TFTP program, the transferred financial data are examined with link analysis or social network analysis which allow analysts to identify terrorist groups and individuals who have links with terrorist organisations, after which this information is converted to a network map and analysed by experts to find out the characteristics and trends of the terrorists' activity (Wesseling, de Goede, & Amoore, 2012).[53]

Utilisation of financial intelligence in this way may have certain advantages, yet the comparison between the financial transaction and the other types of intelligence and evidence needs extra work for confirmation which does not seem to be correctly formulated. Like other types of intelligence gathered for criminal investigation and prosecution, the evaluation and validation of the financial transactions require human involvement for validation and analysis. In other words, the intelligence analysts give meaning to numbers, dates, transactions, the linked accounts and people and their other connections. Consequently, their interpretation of the data can change according to their background, competency and mental capability. Therefore, it may be claimed that assumption of the usage of financial transactions is better than other types of intelligence (owing to their alleged certainty) may be false and that Levitt and Jacobson do not provide clear evidence to support their claim. Correspondingly, in the context of the TFPT programme, Wesseling et al. (2012, p. 54) argue that "[. . .] how financial data are redeployed and re-inscribed with new meanings and the riskiness of such

53 The main purpose of the link analysis is not to trace terrorists; instead it is used for visualising terrorist networks and identifying the unknown ones. Moreover, link analysis has become a key tool to deal with the dispersed, global, mobile and networked terrorists since the numbers of suspects and scope of the investigations was broadened. Discovering network organisations with link analysis system also provides possible connections and signs in regards to terrorists' future intentions or plans (Wesseling, de Goede, & Amoore, 2012).

interpretative force, that is wholly masked by the injunction that 'money trails don't lie".

Parker and Taylor (2010) note that collecting financial intelligence by using different types of surveillance techniques has become an essential feature of current CTF practice.[54] Even though asset freezing and sanctions are mainly used as favourable measures against terrorist financing by states, the latest shift has been towards micro-financing activities such as low-level criminal and autonomous cell activities. In this context, it can be argued that there is still a need for more research on the real value and importance of the utilisation of financial information and financial surveillance as an intelligence tool for CTF purposes. Nevertheless, the investigators use financial data to perceive serious crimes and terrorist attacks and to map them by their phases. As a result of this trend, it is argued that a new security paradigm has emerged along with the on-going emphasis on the usage of financial information. De Goede (2008, p. 100, 2012) calls this new paradigm "complex assemblage or finance-security assemblage" where the private financial institutions have authority and discretion to make decisions regarding security. Therefore, Parker and Taylor (2010) conclude that data harvesting and financial intelligence gathering are essential elements for public security and law enforcement activities. Having said that, it is important to found a system in which intelligence and investigations will contribute to operational activities and still will be able to conceive existing difficulties to unify security and liberty.

Levi (2010, p. 667) argues that the role of financial intelligence and investigation moves beyond harvesting more SARs, freezing assets and prosecuting people for terrorist financing activities. It is formulated that how far this role should be broadened depends on the choice of how to solve this problem.[55] The first solution is a tactical approach which would make acquiring the sources and materiel harder for would-be terrorists, and the second solution is a strategic/geopolitical approach which would focus on eliminating conditions causing violent extremism (Levi, 2010, p. 666).

Roberge (2007, pp. 200–201) points out the importance of conventional intelligence for countering terrorist financing. He argues that analysing a vast amount of transaction data for detecting some illicit financial activities looks like finding a needle in a haystack. In this case the data can only be useful if the analysts have the accurate criteria, such as the names of the suspects and their movements. It is argued that even if terrorists do not use formal financial systems, the only way

54 From the law enforcement and intelligence agencies' perspectives, the financial information is very useful at the initial stages of the investigations to determine information regarding the identity and lifestyle of suspects, which can be also used for establishing further risk definition and categorisation (Parker & Taylor, 2010).

55 Levi (2010) believes that the best results can be achieved by following the money technics which may provide arresting and the broader network map of terrorists, allow physical observations, prevent terrorists from raising money for sophisticated attacks and increase the risks for their financing activities.

for collecting terrorists' financial transactions and other activities will be sound investigative intelligence.[56]

As Roberge (2007, p. 201) rightly states the importance of the intelligence collected from the ground should not be underestimated. Financial intelligence, which is acquired mainly from financial records and reports, is also important, whereas the integration of both types of intelligence is believed to produce more positive outcomes in terms of CTF. In this context, it is asserted that financial intelligence and investigations are important tools against terrorist financing; however, other types of intelligence, especially human intelligence, should be taken into account for CTF efforts due to their ability to reach information that financial intelligence cannot. Additionally, as Vlcek (2007, pp. 110–111) points out, even though terrorists can circumvent risk analysis methods, human intelligence can be used as a useful tool addressing terrorist organisations rather than recording and analysing vast amount of data of financial transactions.

3.5 Conclusion

In this chapter the CTF efforts were examined. First of all, the US CTF system and its applications were analysed. Especially in the US case, the transformation of terrorist financing perception was highlighted. In this part, how terrorist financing became an urgent security threat for the US and its implications were also discussed.

Next, the multilateral efforts were deliberated from the perspectives of international bodies. The UN and its efforts for establishing a global CTF regime were examined through its conventions and resolutions. Furthermore, the FATF as a global standard setting organisation with its soft power was explained. Interestingly, it emerges that the US has a significant leading role and force on determining the agendas of these two organisations. In this context, it may be claimed that the US also has successfully exported its own threat perception and countering strategies by utilising these organisations in order to make its own security threat a global threat. Consequently, the AML measures which target offshore banking, IVTSs, wired bank transfers and charities have become global CTF methods. Moreover, the SWIFT affair and the US-EU TFTP agreement were chosen to illustrate some of the contentious issues and challenges in creating a cooperative and global CTF policy and practice.

The effectiveness of current strategies was discussed from the AML and smart sanctions models and private-public partnership perspectives. Even though there are conflicting views and a lack of data about the success level and effectiveness of these CTF strategies, it seems that the current methods used may not be as effective and successful as they are purported. It may be claimed that adoption of one

56 For example, one of the successful operations against terrorist financing was a Dubai based, CIA owned and operated hawala business, which provided valuable intelligence to the US (Suskind, 2006, p. 161).

size for all CTF strategy which does not take into account social, economic and political differences, may be a key reason for this shortcoming.

The assumptions regarding terrorists' financing help officials and policy makers to form global and national CTF strategies. However, some of these assumptions do not reflect reality as they are supposed to. The generally accepted idea that cutting off the terrorists' money can destroy terrorist organisations and disrupt and decrease the impact of terrorist attacks seems not to be supported with strong evidence, and in light of the on-going terrorist attacks. Both the destruction of terrorist organisations and more marginalised terrorist attacks can be possible outcomes of decreasing terrorists' money; the outcome depends on the various conditions. In addition, as Wittig (2011) perceptively argues, another accepted assumption is that the money is the main target of the current CTF strategies, and money is accepted as the only exchange value form. That is why Wittig (2011) claims that the CTF framework, which is formed to pursue money, cannot be successful. As Wittig correctly posits, terrorist finance is not only about money interactions; rather it is about the exchange of any form of value, and that value can be in many forms: material ones "[. . .] cash, non-cash monetary instruments, value added commodities and raw materials or non-material values such as services, profit-or route sharing agreements and simply feelings of contributing to a cause [. . .]" (Wittig, 2011, p. 47). It is worth noting that money has a secondary or sometimes even no role in the economic relations of terrorists. In non-Western regions, different value change models are used rather than the Western formal financial systems. Therefore, adopting a Western style monitoring system in non-Western regions does not seem to be a successful approach in the context of CTF. Thus, putting value exchange into the centre of the issue and rebuilding the CTF strategy from this outlook seems logical and acceptable.

It should be noted that every state has different security dynamics and terrorist threats. Therefore, countering all of these different terrorist organisations and their financial activities using a globally determined single CTF model, which was created by the UN's convention and resolutions and FATF recommendations, may not be enough to deal with terrorist threats effectively. At this point it can be claimed that there is a need for CTF **strategies**, which would be designed for individual states taking into account the unique security environments and dynamics in which they operate. While international cooperation is essential, states should design their own CTF frameworks, combining existing measures and methods to fit particular terrorist trends and threats in their respective jurisdictions. Importantly, the CTF policies should be evaluated according to their effectiveness and impact on terrorist financing and the rights and interests of their citizens. Decreasing the adverse effects of determined measures should be a main concern to prevent and mitigate these adverse effects on their society.

Furthermore, the position of the CTF efforts in the overall counter-terrorism law and practice is another issue to be analysed carefully. Over emphasis on the role of CTF should be avoided. From this perspective, CTF should take its place as an auxiliary and complementary tool in the main counter-terrorism strategy, with the role of providing assistance for on-going counter-terrorism efforts.

Notably, it may be claimed that CTF measures and applications can provide very valuable intelligence; thus, using and improving CTF mechanisms for intelligence and admissible evidence may be more useful than freezing or forfeiting the assets of terrorists. In addition, CTF practices that may push terrorists out of formal financial systems should be avoided.

As this chapter demonstrated, there are certain gaps in the literature regarding the success and the effectiveness of the CTF strategies and practices, on both the international and domestic levels. On the one hand, some of the states have exerted huge effort to raise awareness about international terrorism and to create a global CTF regime and to ensure compliance with these international CTF provisions. On the other hand, some states do not share this motivation and have not shown the same degree of commitment albeit, at least on paper, they comply with the minimum CTF standards. This leads to the question of whether being fully compliant with international CTF framework means that these states are effective in their struggle against terrorist financing. It seems that as key actors, states are affected from their own internal dynamics and international dynamics as well. Thus, this situation brings about two further questions:

Firstly, whether states have successful CTF implementation against their self-determined terrorist financing problem; and

Secondly, whether the international milieu assesses individual states' efforts in CTF as successful and effective.

These two considerations lead to an important conclusion that the suitability and effectiveness of CTF systems should be studied from social, political, economic and international perspectives, which may provide a more comprehensive understanding of terrorist financing. Accordingly, in the following chapters, we look at the case of Turkey and analyse its CTF regime with these considerations in mind.

4 The background of the Turkish case

4.1 Introduction

In this chapter, Turkey's terrorism problem and relevant terrorist organisations therein and Turkey's CTF regime will be described from a historical perspective before analysing its CTF system and approach in detail, as a case study. Turkey has been targeted by different types of terrorist organisations and suffered innumerable terrorist attacks for decades. Inevitably, this unfortunate experience has created its own lessons for Turkey, leading to its current counter-terrorism and CTF strategy. Before delving into a detailed analysis of Turkey's CTF law and practice, examining these threats and Turkey's position are important. Therefore, in this chapter Turkey's response to terrorist threats and its counter-terrorism structure and the main CTF basis in terms of existing legal procedures and regulations are explained. By doing so, it is hoped that understanding the basic foundations of the Turkish counter-terrorism system and its current threats (which are complex to say the least) will be easier for the readers.

4.2 Terrorism threat in Turkey

Terrorism and terrorist organisations are not new phenomena for Turkey due to the fact that it has been targeted by many terrorism waves.[1] During the first years of the new republic in the 1920s, numerous rebellion and uprising attempts against the new state took place. However, it can be claimed that Turkey's terrorism problem started to increase significantly in the 1960s and 1970s (Rodoplu, Arnold, & Ersoy, 2003, p. 155). In order to understand Turkey's terrorism problem, it is worth considering these periods briefly. According to Rodoplu et al.

1 For example, on 26 August 1896 the nationalist Armenians, who were members of Dashnaktsutiun, conducted a terrorist attack with bombs and arms against the Ottoman Bank in Istanbul and as a result two bank porters were killed and two wounded (Sonyel, 1987, pp. 210–214). Similarly, on 21 July 1905, Armenian terrorists had attempted to assassinate the Ottoman Sultan Abdulhamit II by using 80 kilos of explosive at the Selamlik of Hamidiye Mosque in Istanbul. While they failed to kill him, because of the explosion, 26 people were killed and 58 people were seriously wounded (Sonyel, 1987, pp. 261–263).

(2003, p. 155) increasing urbanisation and migration from rural areas, economic difficulties, a high unemployment rate, growing disturbance in some parts of the country and religious and leftist student movements were the main causes for the social disorder. They also claim that the 1961 Constitution, which had provided a comprehensive political protest right to Turkish citizens, functioned as a catalyst.

Due to Turkey's political transformation towards a multiparty system and emerging problems relating to this process, until the late 1960s terrorism did not seem to cause significant consequences for Turkey. In the beginning of the late 1960s and early 1970s as a Western-inspired student movement and violence started to take place on Turkish soil (Mango, 2005, p. 10). By the end of the 1970s, many right- and left-wing terrorist organisations emerged, and as a result, bombings, armed attacks and threats became common in the country, and this situation could not be prevented by the governments and agencies of the day until the military *coup d'état* on 12 September 1980 declared martial law in the country (Rodoplu et al., 2003).[2]

At the same time, besides this domestic radical left- and right-wing violence, Turkey became the target of an Armenian terrorism campaign between 1975 and 1985. During this period mainly Turkish diplomats, military personnel, their family members and some other soft targets were killed and attacked by several terrorist groups such as the Armenian Secret Army for the Liberation of Armenia (ASALA) and Justice Commandos of the Armenian Genocide (JCAG), Armenian Revolutionary Army (ARA) and their main supporter Armenian Revolutionary Federation (ARF).[3] The Armenian terrorists' justification for these attacks was to attract other countries attention to the events in 1915 (Mango, 2005, p. 11). From the beginning, these movements were supported by other terrorist organisations[4] and ignored by some states.[5] Furthermore, in a press conference in South Lebanon in 1980, ASALA also announced that it would

2 According to the Turkish Ministry of Foreign Affairs, the National Security Council recorded 43,000 terrorist attacks between 1978 and 1982 in which approximately 28 victims were killed per day (2003, as cited in Rodoplu et al., 2003, p. 155).

3 Additionally, between 1973 and 1986 approximately 200 terrorist attacks were conducted by these organisations, and as a result 58 Turkish nationals, of whom 34 were Turkish diplomats, and 16 non-Turkish people were killed and hundreds of innocent people wounded. Interestingly, besides Turkish citizens, Armenians who denied providing financial support also were targeted by these Armenian terrorist organisations (Center for Strategic Research, 2007, p. 49).

4 For instance, according to Mango (2005, p. 11) the Palestinian Liberation Organisation (PLO) and especially its more violent faction the Popular Front for the Liberation of Palestine (PFLP) provided significant support for the ASALA and its attacks.

5 As French terrorism expert Moniquet (2002, as cited in Mango, 2005, p. 7) notes, French officials and ASALA reached "a sadly classic agreement" about turning a blind eye on terrorists' activities as long as ASALA did not conduct attacks in France. However, as Moniquet puts it, "[t]he blindness of the [French] government was to be fully rewarded by the attack at Orly [airport] in July [1983, which killed 8 and injured 52], proving that it is not only immoral, but also totally vain to negotiate with a terrorist group" (2002, as cited in Mango, 2005, p. 7).

cooperate with the separatist terrorist organisation Kurdistan Workers' Party (also known as the PKK – *Partiya Karkeran Kurdistan*). According to a report released on 30 April 2013 by the CIA, it is claimed by ASALA that as a result of this cooperation, a joint attack was conducted with PKK against the Turkish Consulate in Strasbourg, France, in November 1980 (Terrorism Analysis Branch, 1984, p. 4).

As already mentioned, domestic terrorism in Turkey was halted for a short period of time after the military coup in 1980; however, the Armenian international terrorism against Turkey only ended around 1986. After the military coup, a new constitution was created, the civil order was reinstated and the government started to run the country in 1983. Although initial positive economic and democratic developments and changes in the country occurred, Turkey became the target of terrorist organisations once again in the late 1980s (Rodoplu et al., 2003, p. 155). While the military coup had cracked down many left- and right-wing extremist groups and terrorist organisations, a new terrorism movement has emerged not only by following the footsteps of the old terrorist organisations but also by the creation of new ones, which caused many losses of Turkish citizens' lives since the mid-1980s (Mango, 2005, p. 21).

Even though there are different classifications and names in the literature regarding the types of terrorism trends and terrorist organisations in Turkey since the end of 1983, these can be stratified under three main titles:

- left-wing;
- ethno-nationalist and separatist; and
- religiously inspired terrorism.[6]

These are explained below.

4.2.1 Left-wing terrorism

Firstly, left-wing terrorism and its roots go back to the 1970s student movements. Their main objective has been to change the current political regime of Turkey to a communist state system where the distribution of the wealth would be regulated according to Marxist-Leninist ideology (Özeren, Sever, & Başıbüyük, 2011, p. 151; Sözen, 2006, p. 138). While the military rule between 1980 and 1983 seemed to have diminished these organisations to great degree, those members who managed to escape to safe haven countries such as Syria, Germany, Iran, Iraq and Greece survived and continued their terrorist activities after 1984 (Göktepe & Erçıktı, 2007, p. 385). In this context, the main left-wing terrorist organisations operating against Turkey from inside and outside of the country currently are the Revolutionary People's Liberation Party/Front (DHKP/C),

6 The terms used here are taken from the European Union Terrorism Situation and Trend Report (TE-SAT) 2014's classification (Europol, 2014).

Marxist Leninist Communist Party (MLKP), and the Turkish Communist Party/Marxist-Leninist (TKP/ML) (Çağlar, 2008, p. 100).

The Revolutionary People's Liberation Party/Front (DHKP/C)

DHKP/C is a prominent terrorist organisation. DHKP/C has a similar ideology to those of the other left-wing terrorist organisations which aim to change Turkey's political system. Even though it initially had two bases inside and outside the country, because of successful operations by the Turkish security forces, they moved their command centre to Europe and established units in several countries including Germany, Belgium, the Netherlands and Greece, where large Turkish populations live. This organisation mainly uses armed attacks, suicide bombing, bomb traps and assassination tactics (Özeren et al., 2011, p. 152). Their targets are mainly Turkish security forces, ex-military, government and politicians, as well as strategic state institutions. Moreover, because they perceive the US as a leading imperialist and capitalist actor that is responsible for problems in Turkey and beyond, any NATO or US related person or institution such as the Turkish-American Friendship Association and General Motors' buildings have been among their targets (Çağlar, 2008, p. 101).[7]

Although, DHKP/C is recognised and designated as a terrorist organisation by the US and the European Union, European countries continue to be important places for them to conduct their activities such as propaganda, financing and recruitment (Europol, 2014, p. 9).[8] For these purposes, they often use associations, cultural centres and media organisations (Özeren et al., 2011, p. 153). According to the latest investigations, DHKP/C has a number of illegal structures in some of the EU member states to provide its logistical and financial requirements. However, it is important to indicate that these structures are supported by organisations which are legal and legitimate. An example of this kind

7 Some of the striking terrorist attacks of this group: During the Gulf War, two US military contractors were assassinated, one US airman wounded and more than 20 US and NATO facilities were attacked by this group (Özeren, 2008, p. 156). DHKP/C terrorists assassinated the former Minister of Justice, Osman Topac, on 29 September 1994. Ozdemir Sabanci, who was a prominent businessman and a board member of one of the leading holding companies in Turkey, was murdered with his secretary in his office in Istanbul on 9 January 1996 by three DHKP/C terrorists (Özeren et al., 2011, p. 153). It is observed that suicide bombing attacks started to be used by DHKP/C in 2001 (Özeren, 2008). On 29 April 2009, for instance, two DHKP/C suicide bombers attempted to assassinate former Minister of Justice Professor Dr. Hikmet Sami Turk, with eight kilos of explosives (Özeren et al., 2011). The last example was on 26 January 2013, when a DHKP/C suicide bomber exploded himself in the entrance of the US Embassy in Ankara as retaliation against US activities in Iraq, Syria, Egypt and Libya, killing one guard and wounding three others (National Consortium for the Study of Terrorism and Responses to Terrorism, 2013).

8 Sixteen members of DHKP/C were arrested in 2013 in Austria, Germany, Greece, Italy and Spain (Europol, 2014, p. 36).

of organisation is the 'Solidarity Committee for Political Detainees in Turkey and Kurdistan' which is stationed in Greece (Europol, 2014, p. 36).

In regard to its finances, this organisation acquires its funds from different sources. DHKP/C collects racketeering and extortion money from Turkish citizens who mainly live abroad, especially in Europe. Another financial source is money obtained from members and sympathisers in Turkey. DHKP/C generates income by selling publications such as magazines and newspapers and organising social activities such as concerts, picnics and other social events. Beside donations both from Turkey and abroad, criminal activities are important means for raising money for the organisation. These range from petty crimes to more serious and organised crime activities such as drug trafficking, burglary, robbery, extortion and smuggling (Özeren, 2008, p. 157; Özeren et al., 2011, p. 153). Moreover, according to the EU Terrorism Situation and Trend Report ((Europol, 2014, pp. 12–13), DHKP/C misuses some charities for supporting its activities. In the light of this background information, it can be clearly claimed that DHKP/C and other left-wing terrorist organisations are actively engaged in financing activities and are at large continuing to be a terrorist threat for Turkey.

4.2.2 Ethno-nationalist and separatist terrorism

According to Gürses (2008, p. 75), the end of the Cold War period gave rise to a new world order which stimulated many ethnic groups to move towards finding an autonomous place in this renewed international system. Some of these groups have chosen to use guerrilla tactics and/or violent methods to pursue their aims. Even though this type of terrorism has similar orientations such as compelling their rival groups and governments towards their objectives, unlike other types of terrorist organisations (e.g. religiously inspired terrorist groups and radical left/right-wing terrorist organisations), they concentrate on creating a separate ethnic identity and mobilisation of their constituencies (Byman, 1998, p. 150).[9]

In this context, ethno-nationalist and separatist terrorism has been another significant security concern for Turkey since the early 1980s. The Kurdistan Worker's Party (PKK), as one of main terrorist threats in Turkey, fits into this category of ethno-nationalist and separatist terrorism. The PKK has been responsible for high number of deaths since 1984. The PKK was formed in Diyarbakir (a city in the southwest of Turkey) on 27 November 1978 by a group of Marxist and Leninists terrorists who were led by Abdullah Öcalan (Ruehsen, 2012). Even though the above-mentioned date is the official one, the first elements of this movement can be found in the early 1970s when right/left wing terrorism densely occupied the daily life in Turkey (Gergin, Balcı, & Eldivan, 2009, p. 269). According to its

9 The Liberation Tigers of Tamil Eelam (LTTE) in Sri Lanka, the Irgun in Palestine, Provisional Irish Republican Army (PIRA) in Northern Ireland and Basque separatist organisation Euskadi Ta Askatasuna (ETA) in Spain can be given as examples in this category (Byman, 1998, p. 149).

'Foundation Manifesto' (PKK Merkez Komitesi [PKK Central Committee], 1978) the PKK terrorist organisation's main aim is to establish an independent unified Kurdistan, which covers territories of four different countries, namely Iran, Iraq, Syria and Turkey. Even though the PKK informed its vision with Marxist/Leninist ideology in the initial foundation phase, after the collapse of the Berlin Wall and the subsequent dismantling of the Soviet Union, the PKK has transformed its ideology and started to use religious elements especially for recruitment and propaganda purposes in countries where the majority of the populace are Muslims. It can be claimed that presently, the PKK has a pragmatic approach and uses both religious and leftist ideology for its separatist aims (Özeren et al., 2011).

Interestingly, shortly before the military coup in 1980 took place; the PKK and its senior leadership left Turkey and went to Syrian controlled Beqaa Valley in Lebanon. It is not clear whether they took this decision deliberately by foreseeing the oncoming military intervention or whether they were looking for a safe haven at that period. However, ultimately, they saved themselves from the fate of the other terrorist organisations in the aftermath of the military coup and found a safe haven where they could enhance their capabilities and develop their training (Criss, 1995, p. 19).[10] Subsequently, the PKK commenced its first full-scale campaign on 15 August 1984 by attacking two districts, Eruh and Şemdinli, of Turkey (Bacık & Coşkun, 2011, p. 249).[11] From this date onward, the PKK increased its armed attacks on villages and killed many people including women and children. The clear message behind these terrorist attacks was that whoever supports the Turkish state will be harmed and destroyed by the PKK (Durna & Hançerli, 2007, p. 328).

With the escalation of armed attacks, PKK terrorism has become a very serious problem for Turkey's security and safety. Beside Turkish and Kurdish origin citizens and security forces, different professionals such as city mayors, religious scholars, teachers, journalists, doctors, nurses, public servants and foreign tourists have become victims of PKK terrorism. In addition, PKK has attacked important public and commercial infrastructures such as bridges, hospitals, schools, electricity plants, oil refineries and pipelines in order to deter and destroy investment in the southeast part of the country (Rodoplu et al., 2003, p. 157; Türkiye Büyük Millet Meclisi İnsan Haklarını İnceleme Komisyonu, 2013).[12] According to a

10 In Beqaa Valley, the PKK got a significant amount of training and support from the Palestinian Liberation Organisation (PLO) until Israel's invasion of Lebanon in 1982. However, the PLO was compelled to move to Tunisia. The PKK stayed there with other Marxist Palestinian and Hezbollah militia groups in the Syrian controlled part of the valley and continued its preparations for terrorist campaign (Mango, 2005, p. 36).

11 Eight months after its founding, the PKK first appeared on the public scene with an attack on a parliament member, Mehmet Celal Bucak. This was the PKK's initial attempt to gain support and attract the attention of the Kurdish population (Gergin, Duru, & Çetin, 2014).

12 For more information, see the Global Terrorism Database, which provides a clear line chart about PKK targets (National Consortium for the Study of Terrorism and Responses to Terrorism, 2018).

report by the Turkish Grand National Assembly's Sub-Committee on Human Rights, 35,576 people lost their lives because of the PKK terrorism between 1984 and 2012 (Türkiye Büyük Millet Meclisi İnsan Haklarını İnceleme Komisyonu, 2013, p. 78). Furthermore, according to the recent Global Terrorism Index report, the PKK was responsible for 29 percent of all terrorism-related deaths in the OECD countries between 2009 and 2014 (IEP, 2014, p. 36).[13] These striking figures and reports are enough to explain the seriousness of the danger and the threat of PKK terrorism for Turkey.

Since its inception, in order to establish a separate Kurdish state, the PKK[14] has envisioned that defeating the Turkish Army in the southeastern part of Turkey is necessary (Ozcan, 2009, p. 9).[15] Accordingly, the PKK have been using many tactics and methods including ambush, sabotage, use of Improvised Explosive Devices (IEDs), bomb attacks, mines, kidnapping, assassination of public figures or officials, suicide bombings and riots and protests (Durna & Hançerli, 2007, p. 330). Additionally, various media tools such as satellite TV channels and websites are used by the PKK leadership as effective propaganda tools to convey their orders and messages to the PKK terrorists on the ground and their sympathisers further afield (Özeren et al., 2011, p. 156).

Even though Turkish security forces incarcerated the leader of the PKK in 1999 and defeated the PKK terrorists, who mainly adopt guerrilla tactics especially in southeastern and eastern parts of the country since 1984, the terrorist organisation has managed to find a way to revive its violent struggle. Different reasons might be listed for this resurrection *inter alia*, problems related to capacity and capability of security and intelligence services of Turkey as well as administrative failures and the historical background of the issue, whereby factions of the society at a local level have continued to support PKK. However, the external dimensions of the issue including the role of the PKK's organisational and financial structures outside Turkey, facilitation of these by foreign governments, and providing safe haven to PKK terrorists since its inception by numerous countries within the

13 This total number is the sum of the numbers of losses of security forces (7,918), civilians (5,557) and PKK terrorists (22,101).

14 From a structural perspective, the PKK is a hierarchical organisation, which starts from the top with the leader of the organisation, Abdullah Öcalan; under this position there are in order a chairmanship council, a central committee and a central disciplinary board (Roth & Sever, 2007, p. 905).

15 To reach this goal the PKK has adopted a Maoist Protracted People's War Strategy, which consists of three would be phases: strategic defence, strategic balance and strategic attack. Even though the PKK implemented various hybrid tactics to fulfil the first phase, they could not pass to the second phase, strategic balance, due to military losses against the Turkish army and Turkey's counter-terrorism strategy. As a result, the PKK left Maoist strategy and decided to follow a strategy which focuses merely on creation of an ethnic identity of Kurds in its 5th Congress in 1995 (Özcan, 2009, pp. 9–11; Özeren, *et al.*, 2011, p. 156). Thus, this strategy alteration increased the organisation's recruitment ability of the youngsters from rural areas and widened the support network in a way which included Iraqi and Syrian Kurdish population (Eccarius-Kelly, 2012).

region and in Europe, should be pointed out as key factors which have enabled the longevity of PKK terrorism. These safe environments have allowed PKK to sustain its recruitment, propaganda, logistical, financial and political activities.[16]

Since the key focus of this monograph is CTF, the key features of the financing activities of PKK ought to be mentioned. It can be claimed that the wide spectrum and variety of financial sources, sophisticated and well running organised crime networks (armed robbery, heroin production, drug trafficking, money laundering, people smuggling and extortion, to name a few) (Criss, 1995, pp. 18–19), and the financial activities therein have been significant factors behind PKK's survival. Even though there is no clear data regarding the amount of PKK's annual income, there are varying estimations. Some predict that PKK's annual income is around $100 million (Eccarius-Kelly, 2012, p. 241). Zehorai (2018) indicates that PKK generates around $180 million per annum. According to the Anti-Terrorism Briefing of the Turkish Ministry of Interior, June 2007, PKK's income is estimated at approximately 400–500 million euros annually (as cited in Saygun, 2008, p. 229).[17] In addition, the NATO Terrorist Threat Intelligence Unit 2007 report predicts a more modest amount around $50–100 million in income per year. The United Nations Office on Drugs and Crime (UNODC) and NATO intelligence analysts estimated that PKK makes between $50 to $100 million annually from heroin alone (UNODC, 2010). Tupman (2014, p. 6) notes that the differences between amounts are caused by different understandings and calculations of the drug trafficking business, whereby the higher predictions are calculated under the assumption that all profits go to PKK's coffers and conversely lower amounts are the result of calculations in which PKK is accepted as only getting a share of the profits. Nevertheless, Tupman puts PKK on his list of the top five terrorist organisations in the world from a financial success perspective (Tupman, 2014, p. 6).[18] Besides its ability to finance its activities effectively, PKK has managed to be a well-established formidable force with international links and networks, thanks to financial and logistical support from foreign governments. Tupman (2014, p. 6) highlights the fact that after declining state sponsorship in the post–Cold War era, the PKK concentrated its efforts on raising funds

16 As Mango (2005, p. 35) notes, during the Cold War period, Russia used three proxies, namely Bulgaria, Syria and Palestine, for supporting the PKK. During this period Syria and Iran provided support for the PKK via Masud Barzani and Jalal Talabani. In addition, Greek Cyprus and Greece intelligence took part in supporting the PKK terrorism due to their national disputes with Turkey (Mango, 2005, p. 35). Moreover, Mango (2005) claims that Western Europe became a safe haven, which provided a base for training, financial sources and propaganda opportunities against Turkey to acquire the support and the sympathy of the Europeans for the PKK terrorists.

17 "It is estimated that [. . .] 200–250 million euros are provided through drug smuggling and 100–150 million euros are provided through smuggling (fuel oil, tobacco and human trafficking), while 15–20 million are procured from donations and 20–25 million from other activities" (Turkish Ministry of Interior, 2007, as cited in Saygun, 2008, p. 229).

18 Tupman's top five terrorist organisations list consists of: "1. The Taliban 2. The Al Qaeda Brands 3. Syrian Jihadists 4. Hezbollah 5. The PKK" (Tupman, 2014, p. 6)

from the Kurdish diaspora, mainly populated in Europe, and other self-funding methods.

Marcus's (2007, pp. 181–184) interviews with the PKK terrorists indicate that PKK terrorists in urban cities might have salaries to support their basic needs and activities; however, other terrorists who are in the rural areas depend on money and goods donated by and/or collected from individuals and businesses as tax or protection money. According to these interviews, especially wealthy people, private companies, contractors, smugglers and drug traffickers have to pay so-called revolutionary taxes to the PKK (Marcus, 2007, pp. 182–184). Moreover, as Roth and Sever (2007, p. 906) point out, the PKK has been compelled to raise majority of its funding from different sources (including legal and illegal proceeds) which has steered the PKK towards transnational organised crime, notably after the collapse of the Soviet Union. In this context, it has been observed that the PKK undertakes various transnational criminal activities such as drug trafficking, trafficking; smuggling of arms, humans or other kinds of commodities (oil, cigarettes, sugar etc.); robbery; extortion and money laundering (Roth & Sever, 2007, p. 906 and Europol, 2010, p. 31, 2011, pp. 12, 22, 2012, p. 24, 2013, p. 11). Roth and Sever (2007) and Eccarius-Kelly's (2012, p. 246) emphasise the importance of the geographic and logistical features of the PKK's financial activities. Having borders with eight different countries and a 5,000 milelong coastline, Turkey's location provides a significant geographical advantage for transferring drugs, humans and other illegal commodities from South Asia and the Middle East towards Europe (Eccarius-Kelly, 2012, p. 246).[19] In addition, according to the Turkish Ministry of Foreign Affairs (2014) website, the PKK has been generating revenues from its media outlets such as dailies, periodicals, TV and radio channels and its various propaganda activities in different parts of the world.

Moreover, MFA (2014) indicates that Europe is a significant place for the PKK because it is not only a lucrative market for its illegal drugs trade but also hosts most of its supporters and affiliated organisations. While the PKK has been designated as a terrorist organisation by the EU since 2002, the EU TE-SAT report accepts the fact that the European countries are still used and exploited by the PKK, for its financial, logistical and other vital requirements (Europol, 2014, pp. 9, 12, 29). It is indicated that the Kurdish communities in Western Europe in particular have been raising substantial amounts of money for the organisation, via membership fees, sales of publications and special events (Europol, 2014, p. 12). For transferring the money collected under the name of so-called donations, mainly PKK affiliated charities and NGOs are used (Ruehsen, 2012, p. 69).[20] Notably, even though the EU countries try to hamper the activities of

19 Turkey is positioned at the transection of Asia, the Middle East and Europe as a bridge, which connects all of them. The neighbouring countries are Georgia, Armenia, Azerbaijan, Iran, Iraq, Syria, Greece and Bulgaria.

20 It is reportedly claimed that some of these organisations, such as European Kurdish Democratic Society Coordination (CDK), European Kurdish Associations Confederation (KON-KURD), International Kurdish Businessmen Union (KARSAZ) and Kurdish Red Crescent

the PKK, its network is still able to raise and transfer the money, gathered in different legal and illegal ways, all around the EU.

Overall, it can be argued that PKK's diversified and professionalised financial activities are important factors for empowering PKK's organisational capabilities and prolonging its lifetime.

4.2.3 *Religiously inspired terrorism*

Religiously inspired international terrorism is recognised as the most recent wave of terrorism by Rapoport (2004) who presents four different waves of modern terrorism, namely: 1. Anarchist Wave 2. Anti-Colonial Wave 3. New Left Wave and 4. Religious Wave. This latter trend of violence has been another problem for Turkey's security and its security and law enforcement agencies.[21] Karmon (1998, p. 102) notes that religiously motivated terrorist organisations with implications for Turkey emerged in the 1960s. The incarceration of the Hizb-ut Tahrir (Islamic Liberation Party) leaders for attempting to change the state system to a religious one (namely Sharia governance) as early as 1967 and 1973 can be given as examples. After the Iranian Islamic Revolution, many of the religiously inspired terrorist groups started to appear in Turkey in line with Rapoport's (2004) fourth wave theory (Çağlar, 2006).[22]

The main purpose of these kinds of terrorist organisations targeting Turkey is to destroy the current secular and republican constitution of the Turkish state and replace it with a theocratic state which governs according to a certain interpretation of the religious rules (Özeren et al., 2011, p. 151; Rodoplu et al., 2003, p. 156). According to the ideology and aims of these groups, everything which constitutes modern Turkey would be destroyed and a new state system would be reconfigured according to Sharia law. Some of these groups also operate outside Turkey and use Turkey as a platform to recruit new members and reach further targets in Europe. Karmon (1998, p. 103) notes that the religious movements

(Heyva Sor A Kurdistan-Heyva Sor), Scandinavian Kurdish Peace Council, Council of Solidarity with the Kurdish People in France, London Kurdish Relationship Group, Kurdistan Human Rights Project, Council of Say No to the War Against Kurdish People, A Kurdish Information Network (AKIN), Kurdish Foundation Trust, are used for depositing so-called donations and moving this money through them ("Intelligence Report on PKK Alarms Turkey," 2014; Özeren, *et al.*, 2011, pp. 158,159; Kochan, 2005,p. 93; Ruehsen, 2012, p. 69).

21 As Mango (2005, p. 58) points out, Turkey has a long fight against exploitation of Islam for political interests. Due to this fact, Turkey is aware of the danger of the religious fanatics who try to prevent the development of the society. Even in the Ottoman period these religious fanatics such as the Wahhabis in Saudi Arabia and the Zeydis in Yemen, tried to be put under control. While there are no available statistics in Turkey, in 2017, 62 people were killed in 33 religiously inspired terrorist attacks in the EU, compared to 135 deaths in 13 attacks in 2016, according to Europol figures (Europol, 2018).

22 According to Rapoport (2004) the four waves of modern terrorism are: 1. Anarchist Wave 2. Anti-Colonial Wave 3. New Left Wave and 4. Religious Wave.

similar to other left- and right-wing movements were initially affected seriously by the military coup in 1980; yet they resurfaced shortly after.

Hizbullah, the Great Eastern Islamic Raiders' Front (IBDA-C) and Al Qaeda are the most prominent international and religiously inspired terrorist organisations, which Turkey has to deal with. Hizbullah emerged in 1984 as one of the major terrorist organisations (Karmon, 1998, p. 103). Even though the name they are using is identical to Hizbullah in Lebanon, the one in Turkey has no organisational connection to Hizbullah in Lebanon (Cline, 2004, p. 323).[23] Similar to other religiously inspired terrorist organisations, Hizbullah's aim is to replace the secular regime with a religious one (Başıbüyük, Karakuş, & Akdoğan, 2007). Hizbullah mainly operates in southeast Turkey, especially in the cities and towns of Diyarbakır, Silvan, Cizre, Kızıltepe, Van, Batman and Mardin, where the majority of the population are young and unemployed (Karmon, 1998, p. 104; Özeren, 2008, p. 159). Hizbullah has a hierarchical style of organisation similar to the PKK. This structure consists of three main parts: the leadership, the top council or '*şura*', and the lower-level councils (Özeren & Van De Voorde, 2006, pp. 82–84).[24]

Between 1980 and 1991 Hizbullah prioritised strengthening its leadership base and recruiting new members for the organisation and thus did not conduct any attacks or engaged in violence (Sözer & Sever, 2011, p. 23). Additionally, Hizbullah attempted to expand its operative area towards the western regions and commercial centres of Turkey, such as Istanbul, in the late 1990s (Özeren & Van De Voorde, 2006). In 1991, it was observed that two terrorist organisations, Hizbullah and the PKK, which operate in the same region with different ideologies, started to see themselves as competitors and attacked each other (Sözer & Sever, 2011, p. 23). It can be claimed that the majority of Hizbullah's attacks were aimed at the PKK until the signing of the 'cooperation protocol' between the two organisations in March 1993 (Cline, 2004, p. 324). This is a small but important detail which CTF and terrorism studies have given scant attention. While terrorist organisations often target governments, state institutions and citizens to pursue their agendas, they also compete for power, control and financial resources, which can culminate in armed conflict between terrorist organisations. In contrast, if and when agendas and aims converge, terrorist organisations may merge and join forces in order sustain their operations. Karmon (1998, p. 108) notes that after the conflict between Hizbullah and the PKK, Hizbullah's main aim was to end the conflict with the PKK and to conduct a joint struggle against the Turkish state, because Hizbullah reckoned that this conflict only served the interests of 'colonialists' and was harmful for their Islamic cause. Therefore, in

23 Moreover, there is a difference between the religious approaches of these two parties. While the Lebanese follow Shia based Islam and consist of Shia Muslims, Hizbullah in Turkey embraces the Sunni type of Islam.

24 Detailed information and a complete organisational structure diagram of Hizbullah can be found in Özeren and Van De Voorde (2006, p. 83).

accordance with this development, Hizbullah started to murder mainly secularist, moderate Muslims, representatives of Kurdish religious charities and clerics from other religious beliefs (Özeren & Van De Voorde, 2006, p. 84).

The main tactics of Hizbullah are contracted armed attacks, shootings, assassination, arsons, kidnappings and torture. Until 2003, 696 people were killed and 434 people were wounded as a result of Hizbullah terrorist attacks (Özeren et al., 2011). While Hizbullah was engaged in these terrorist attacks, in 1998 the Turkish government started a concerted operation against Hizbullah (Cline, 2004, p. 324). Because of these operations between 1999 and 2003, so many terrorists[25] were arrested and security forces acquired granular intelligence which resulted in Hizbullah operations and attacks virtually coming to an end. Some of their high-ranked leaders managed to escape to Europe and since 2003, they have changed their tactics by avoiding direct armed conflict with the state and other terrorist organisations (Sözer & Sever, 2011, p. 24).

Even though Iran has strongly denied it, Mango (2005), Cline (2004) and Karmon (1998) claim that Iran has provided financial/logistical and material support for Hizbullah to act against Turkey. Moreover, Hizbullah has received money from different illegal sources and activities including extortion, taxing, donations collected from sympathisers, selling of publications and CDs. Moreover, kidnapping businessmen and smuggling goods are identified as other types of financial revenues for the organisation in recent years (Mango, 2005, p. 66; Özeren et al., 2011, p. 160).

Besides Hizbullah, another significant religiously inspired terrorist organisation is the Great Eastern Islamic Raiders' Front (IBDA-C) which operates in Turkey (Cline, 2004, p. 324). As a Sunni religious movement, IBDA-C was created in 1984 (Orhan, 2010, p. 153). Although IBDA-C has been an active since the 1970s, it can be observed that only since the early 1990s has it been engaged in violent and extremist activities. Even though they have been following a similar cause to that of Hizbullah (i.e. abolishing the democratic, secular and republican governance in Turkey and establishing a Turkish caliphate and an Islamic state instead), interestingly, different than other Islamic terrorist organisation, it has been using leftist slogans in its publications and let ex-Marxists to join its cadre (Karmon, 1998, pp. 105–106). While IBDA-C has rejected ideologies of other Islamic terror groups, this rather unusual opposition has not prevented it from cooperating with other terrorist organisations which aim to destabilise Turkey. For example, KADEK, the Kurdistan Labour Party, is known to have collaborated with IBDA-C (Fighel, 2003).

Similar to Hizbullah, IBDA-C has attacked Alevite, Jewish, Christians and public secular figures such as the assassination of Ahmet Taner Kışlalı, a prominent figure who was a newspaper columnist, academic, former minister and Member of Parliament, on 21 October 1999. Besides that, churches, publishing houses,

25 Reportedly, 1,366 suspected of being Hizbullah members and supporters were arrested by security forces in the first month of the operation (Cline, 2004, p. 324).

foreign consulates, state sponsored mosques, secular TV transmitters, secular newspapers, Ataturk statues, bars, brothels and businessmen have been other targets for IBDA-C (Cline, 2004, p. 325). It should be noted that unlike other terrorist organisations, such as Hizbullah and the PKK, IBDA-C does not have a hierarchical organisational structure. Rather IBDA-C uses a cell type structure where individuals have a high level of autonomy and independence which makes it difficult for security forces to infiltrate (Cline, 2004). While there is no clear data regarding the real strength of the organisation, Cline (2004, p. 325) argues that IBDA-C may have not more than a few hundred members and sympathisers.

In addition to the terrorist organisations exploiting religious beliefs, there has been another grave threat to Turkey's security: the Fetullahist Terrorist Organisation and the Parallel State Structure (FETO/PSS). This terrorist organisation has attempted to topple the legitimate government of Turkey by killing 250 innocent Turkish citizens and injuring 2,193 of them. These victims were murdered and maimed by the Turkish State's own aircrafts, helicopters and tanks[26] which were operated by FETO/PSS's uniformed terrorists who had been infiltrated into the Turkish State system systematically over nearly forty years (General Prosecution Office of the Supreme Court of Appeal, 2018, p. 1). It might be also claimed that in terms of its capabilities, *modus operandi* and devastation, this terrorist organisation has posed a unique and significant security threat to Turkey. The impact of this terror group has encompassed socio-economic, socio-political and socio-psychological aspects unlike any other terrorist organisations which Turkey has encountered (Turkish National Police Academy, 2017, p. 5).

FETO/PSS was established by a preacher named Fetullah Gülen in 1966 (General Prosecution Office of the Supreme Court of Appeal, 2018, p. 6; High Council of Judges and Prosecutors, 2016, p. 6). According to the General Prosecution Office of the Supreme Court of Appeal (2018, p. 7) the main aim of this terrorist organisation is "[. . .] to establish a totalitarian state order based on the oligarchy of the congregation and to become a political and economic power effective at the international level". In this framework, it can be noted that since its creation the FETO/PSS gained its legitimacy and power through systematic exploitation of the religious allegiances of Muslim communities. In addition, it established an international network of educational institutions and opportunities for youngsters from particularly poor families. These students were educated according to the aims and principles of the FETO/PSS and recruited into the ranks of the organisation (High Council of Judges and Prosecutors, 2016, p. 7).

26 In addition to the civilian casualties and serious injuries people had, the Grand National Assembly of Turkey (TBMM), Presidential Complex, National Intelligence Organization (MİT), Ankara Security Directorate, Special Operations Department of the Security Directorate and other strategic public buildings and Istanbul's Bosphorus Bridge were targeted and attacked with more than 8,000 military personnel, 35 fighter jets, 37 helicopters, 74 tanks, 246 armoured vehicles and almost 4,000 weapons during this heinous terrorist attack (coup attempt) (General Prosecution Office of the Supreme Court of Appeal, 2018, p. 1).

In the beginning the main focus of the organisation was attracting school-age children and youngsters to become full-fledged members with operational duties. Later on, Fetullah Gülen also succeeded in gaining support from the public via sermons, books, speeches and secret meetings. (General Prosecution Office of the Supreme Court of Appeal, 2018, p. 6). In the early 1990s it can be seen that the reach of FETO/PSS abroad was expanded and subsequently, in a very short period of time, it managed to operate in nearly 160 states (General Prosecution Office of the Supreme Court of Appeal, 2018, p. 7).

Although the hierarchically organised structure of FETO/PSS is stricter than those of other international terrorist organisations (General Prosecution Office of the Supreme Court of Appeal, 2018, p. 7), it comprises two separate autonomous spheres of operation in two distinct structures, namely in public and private institutions. The sub-units of the organisation covertly continue their operations in autonomous cells which are agile and resilient against traditional counter-terrorism measures. Therefore, in case of any disclosure of a unit or number of units, the organisation can continue its operation with ease (Ankara Chief Public Prosecutor's Office, 2017, p. 255).

The FETO/PSS, similar to other terrorist organisations, undertakes its activities in a secret and hierarchical structure, and these are directed through organisational tactics such as communication through onionskin papers, crypto communication programs and using code names (High Council of Judges and Prosecutors, 2016, p. 9). However, unlike other terrorist organisations, FETO/PSS has managed to infiltrate key state institutions whereby most of its activities have been conducted through the state organs as an alternative state or a parallel state model.[27] In addition, it is a well-known fact that members of FETO/PSS practice *taqiyya*[28] in order not to be exposed by police and security forces (Yavuz & Koc, 2016, p. 137). In this framework, FETO/PSS has mainly based its activities on religious principles and references which it interpreted in accordance with its aims and objectives. To this end, being part of the secular and democratic state system was necessary, albeit the main aim was to abolish it. In

27 The instructions by Fethullah Gülen include: "Be flexible, move around the vital parts without coming into prominence!; Move forward to the essential parts of the [state] system without being noticed until all power centers are reached! Until you have all power and authority in Turkey by your side, each step is deemed to be early.

> Each step is deemed to be early until we have the power and competence in all constitutional institutions by our side relative to the state structure criterion in Turkey. (. . .) in such a crowd, I told you this world and my thought in so-called privacy. (. . .) Your secret is your secret. If you reveal it, you become bond slave.
>
> The existence of our fellows in judiciary, civil service or other vital institution should not be considered as individual existences. So these are our guaranties in those units for the future. At some point, they are the guaranty of our existence" (High Council of Judges and Prosecutors, 2016, p. 1).

28 In short, '*taqiyya*' can be defined as "concealing one's intentions and goals in order to control key power positions" (Yavuz & Koc, 2016, p. 137).

addition to being managed from abroad,[29] their targets are put under pressure by blackmailing and various illegal activities (General Prosecution Office of the Supreme Court of Appeal, 2018, p. 13).

In terms of its financial sources, FETO/PSS has many different channels for undertaking and sustaining its activities. FETO/PSS has more than 9,000 companies established in many different sectors across the world such as banking, financial institutions, energy, infrastructure, transportation, logistics, construction, healthcare, food, tourism, textile, media and private education. In addition, donations, in the name of 'benevolence, alms and scholarship money' are collected from wealthy businessmen, their members and sympathisers. Moreover, it is known that FETO/PSS raises funds through their NGOs, associations, and foundations (General Prosecution Office of the Supreme Court of Appeal, 2018, p. 12).

In terms of its *modus operandi*, this organisation can be called a *sui generis* criminal/terrorist organisation. Moreover, FETO/PSS is a unique terrorist organisation because of its ability to use legal means to cover its illegitimate objectives. Unlike any common terrorist organisations, FETO/PSS does not need to acquire weapons, power and intelligence to achieve its objectives because the FETO/PSS terrorist organisation already has loyal members working as civil servants, military and police officers who have direct access to these means (Mert, 2016, p. 5).

FETO/PSS has been using its official and civilian structures and members such as judges, prosecutors, police officers, military and media very effectively to achieve its aims. For instance, it can be noted that the Turkish Army and its command chains and influence were crucially deteriorated by fabricated court cases comprised of fake and fictitious evidence. Cases such as 'Sledge Hammer', 'Ergenekon' and 'Izmir Espionage Affair' are some of the well-known cases in which high-ranking military personnel were convicted for espionage and plotting a coup against the Turkish state (Yavuz & Koc, 2016, p. 136). Following these convictions, members of the FETO/PSS were appointed to strategic positions in the army. In order to achieve this, experienced and competent generals and officers who were due promotion (but were not sympathisers of FETO) were either forced to retire or incarcerated in fabricated cases. Moreover, it became obvious that most of these FETO/PSS generals and officers who were appointed at the time were also the main perpetrators behind the attempted coup on 15 July 2016 (Uzun, Akgün, & Yücel, 2017, pp. 27–28).

While the majority of the operations against this terrorist organisation took place following the attempted coup plot in 2016, the Turkish State was undertaking counterterrorism operations against FETO as early as December 2013 in order to crack down on its financial, media and parallel state structures in Turkey and beyond.

29 Fetullah Gülen continues to instruct its members from his residence in Pennsylvania, US, despite the fact that Turkey has demanded his extradition.

In addition to these local-national terrorist organisations, Turkey has become a target of religiously inspired international terrorism: namely Al Qaeda, and ISIS (Çağlar, 2006). It is claimed that Turkish security forces have been taking the Al Qaeda threat seriously and focusing their efforts on preventing their infiltration to Turkey since 1999 (Cline, 2004, p. 322). However, Al Qaeda managed to hit Turkey using its clandestine members in two separate suicide attacks with trucks loaded explosives on 15 and 20 November 2003 (Mango, 2005).[30] Following the police investigation, the perpetrators were identified in a very short time, and it emerged that these attacks had been elaborately planned and executed. Even though in the aftermath of the attacks, Hizbullah (Turkey), IBDA-C and another less known foreign terrorist organisation, Abu Hafs al Masri Brigades, announced that they were responsible for these attacks (Cline, 2004, p. 322), investigations showed that the perpetrators of these attacks had established an organisation which had direct links with the Al Qaeda network (Özeren, 2008, p. 160). Moreover, investigations revealed that these terrorists had gone to Al Qaeda camps for training in Afghanistan and Pakistan (Mango, 2005). It is also claimed that in order to finance these attacks, Al Qaeda paid a total of $150,000 (Güven, 2004).

Terrorists who are based in Turkey who join to the ranks of ISIS to fight the Syrian and Iraqi governments from Turkey may emerge as a significant threat for the future. In 2014, the Turkish Ministry of Foreign Affairs reported that 600 Turkish citizens had joined ISIS and more than 100 of them have already been killed (*Hurriyet Daily News*, 2014b). These details indicate that even though the numbers are small, the possibility of Turkish citizens joining and supporting ISIS is real, and recruitment, radicalisation and exploitation through religion do work, which poses a serious security threat for Turkey.

In this section, terrorist organisations that operate in Turkey and their activities and the spectrum of their threats were examined. In this context three main types of terrorism – left-wing, ethnic nationalist and separatist, and religiously inspired models – were identified. While all of these forms of terrorism are serious threats for Turkey, it might be asserted that the ethnic separatist terrorism takes the first place given its financial and organisational sophistication compared to other types of terrorist organisations.

4.3 Counter-terrorist financing structure of Turkey

Examination of the types of terrorist organisations in Turkey as well as their specific aims and targets illustrates clearly that both national and international

30 On 15 November 2003, terrorists targeted two Jewish synagogues, Istanbul Şişli Beth Israel Synagogue and Istanbul Beyoğlu Neve Shalom. On 20 November 2003, they attacked the British Consulate in Istanbul and HSBC Bank Beşiktaş Branch in Istanbul (Özeren, 2008, p. 160). Because of these terrorist attacks, 65 people (including the British Consul General, Roger Short) were killed, and more than 650 people were injured (Cline, 2004, p. 322; Mango, 2005, p. 68).

terrorism have been a significant threat for Turkey. Consequently, Turkey has been trying to counter these threats since the 1970s with mainly military based tactics and measures which have to certain degree altered over time, in line with specific and changing threats faced by the country. In this context, among other terrorist organisations, the PKK threat has been perceived as the most serious threat by the Turkish state because of PKK's protracted existence, strong foothold and financial and armed power on Turkish soil and abroad. In addition, PKK's ultimate aim of establishing an independent state by partitioning Turkish territory in the southwest of the country is undoubtedly seen as a serious threat to Turkey's territorial integrity and political unity. When these factors are coupled with the huge death toll and thousands of victims of PKK terrorism, it is understandable why Turkey views PKK as the greatest threat to its national security and the well-being of its citizens and why it has adopted coercive methods to counter this threat.

Crelinsten (2009, p. 48) classifies coercive counter-terrorism strategies under two categories:

1 the criminal justice model where terrorism is treated as a crime; and
2 the war (large scale armed conflict) model whereby the military has the main responsibility.

In the former model the law enforcement agencies have the main responsibility and entities of the criminal justice system such as prosecutors, courts and prisons are the key actors of this system. In the latter model, the main responsibility belongs to the military, and the rules of war embodied in international human rights and humanitarian laws are implemented (e.g. the provisions of Geneva Conventions) (Crelinsten, 2009, pp. 48–49). In this context, it can be claimed that the criminal justice model has been implemented as Turkey's counter-terrorism strategy in general. Evidence of this can be found in the criminal code of Turkey. According to Turkish criminal law, terrorism is seen and defined as a crime; thus terrorists, and those who aid them, are perceived as criminals. Moreover, according to Turkey's counter-terrorism legal regime, the task of countering terrorism is the responsibility of law enforcement agencies, which are organised under the Turkish Ministry of Interior. However, as Cerrah (2008, p. 141) points out, the Turkish Armed Forces also has been used as one of the instruments against terrorism in general and against PKK in particular, partly because of the unique operational challenges of this endeavour; PKK operates mainly in the rural and mountainous areas of Turkey, and operational capability in this environment requires military training, expertise, tools and tactics. Indeed, the utilisation and deployment of the military in counter-terrorism missions are stipulated by the Provincial Administration Law (*İl İdaresi Kanunu*, 1949) which confers the power and responsibility to the city governors to determine the size of the military force and the time limits and frames for deployment in the event that regular law enforcement agencies would not be adequate to deal with terrorist threats.

While the Turkish counter-terrorism strategy and policy have been designed as a criminal justice model, dense and frequent usage of military units along with law enforcement agencies, especially in the context of tackling PKK terrorism, has created a conflation between these counter-terrorism models. It can also be asserted that the hybrid nature of this counter-terrorism model which involves two different institutions (i.e. police gendarmerie and military) has at times led to operational difficulties for personnel involved. This does not mean that Turkey's law enforcement and military forces are the only counter-terrorism instruments used. Beside these actors, other substantial dimensions of counter-terrorism have emerged ranging from political, social, and economic development initiatives and the usage of intelligence, diplomacy and financial agencies to terminate or at least to limit the terrorist threat in Turkey.

Turkey's legal framework on CTF

Before starting to examine the CTF related legislation, it would be useful to examine how the Turkish legal system interprets 'terrorism' and defines this term. The Turkish Criminal Code (TCC) (2004) and Anti-Terrorism Law (1991) (which has been amended several times) defines terrorism as follows:

> Terrorism is any kind of act done by one or more persons belonging to an organization with the aim of changing the characteristics of the Republic as specified in the Constitution, its political, legal, social, secular and economic system, damaging the indivisible unity of the State with its territory and nation, endangering the existence of the Turkish State and Republic, weakening or destroying or seizing the authority of the State, eliminating fundamental rights and freedoms, or damaging the internal and external security of the State, public order or general health by means of pressure, force and violence, terror, intimidation, oppression or threat.
>
> (Translated from Turkish by MASAK, 2014)

According to this definition, while the Republic of Turkey is protected against acts of terrorism, any other international organisations or foreign states are not included in the sphere of this protection. Thus, it may be claimed that the acts of terrorism against other states and international bodies are excluded from this definition. And this feature of the act has been criticised on domestic and international platforms (Akın, 2009, p. 370; Yıldırım, 2012, p. 258).

Moreover, Article 7 of the Anti-Terrorism Law (1991) mentions terrorist organisations and stipulates that establishing a terrorist organisation, managing and being a member of this organisation are terrorist crimes. Any related act will be punished according to Article 314 of the TCC (2004), which regulates 'Armed Organisations'. This regulation under Article 314 of TCC (2004), makes reference to Article 220 of the same statute which provides that organised groups formed with the intention of committing crime are armed organisations.

According to Article 220 of TCC (2004) beside terrorist leaders, members of a terrorist organisation, and the ones committing crime on behalf of a terrorist organisation, any person who knowingly and willingly helps an organised criminal group, even though it doesn't take place within the hierarchic structure of the group, is to be punished as if he/she is a member of the organised group.

Under the Anti-Terrorism Law (1991) and TCC (2004), terrorism, terror crime, terrorist and being a member of terrorist organisation are defined broadly. In addition to these domestic legal instruments against terrorism, Turkey has signed and ratified numerous international legal instruments including conventions, resolutions and treaties of the UN, the EU and the Council of Europe (COE, 2005).

When the Anti-Terrorism Law (1991) was amended in 2006, financing of terrorism was embodied as a specific crime, and subsequently, this criminal act has been regulated under different provisions of the criminal code. For example, the perpetrators of financing of terrorism were punished according to Article 169 titled 'Help to Armed Gangs'. According to this provision, crimes of supporting an armed gang included: offering accommodation, 'helping', or providing provisions or weapons, ammunition or clothes or doing anything else which would facilitate activities of the armed gangs. Even though the article seems to be clear and broad enough, it was not easy to determine what the term 'helping' encompassed. As a result of this, different interpretations and court judgements ensued (Yıldırım, 2012, p. 281).

The rise of terrorism in Turkey in the 1980s and the need for a more effective law addressing this phenomenon resulted in the enactment of the No: 3713 Anti-Terror Law, 1991. Correspondingly, it should be noted that this law did not contain a specific provision in terms of criminalisation of terrorist financing. However, according to this legal instrument, until its amendment in 2006, helping the members of a terrorist organisation was regulated as an independent crime under Article 7. Under this article, the acts which amount to 'help' were not clearly listed; instead a general approach was used to describe all types of support activities (Yıldırım, 2012) similar to the US approach which employs the term "providing material support".[31]

The amendment of the Anti-Terror Law in 2006 provided for the first time the offence of 'Financing of Terrorism' under Article 8:

> Whoever provides or raises funds with knowledge and intent that these will entirely or partially be used in the commission of terrorist offences shall be punished as a member of the organisation. The perpetrator shall be punished accordingly, even if the funds have not been used. The term "funds" as mentioned under paragraph 1 of this article signifies any goods, rights,

31 "Providing material support" for terrorism is a crime prohibited by the US PATRIOT Act, 2001 and codified in Title 18 of the United States Code, sections 2339A and 2339B.

claims, revenues, benefits, or benefits and values derived from the conversion of those.

(Translated from Turkish by Legislationonline, 2004)

Prohibition of terrorist financing was inserted to the general anti-terrorism law to comply and integrate the norms and obligations under the International Convention for Suppression of the Financing of Terrorism (1999), which was signed on 27 September 2001 and ratified on 1 March 2002 by Turkey, and then was transposed into the domestic judicial system (Akın, 2009, p. 370).

The punishment for financing of terrorism crime is stipulated by TCC (2004) Article 314. Article 8 of the Anti-Terrorism Law (1991) clearly emphasises the perpetrator of financing of terrorism "shall be punished as a member of the organisation", and Article 7 provides that being a member of organisation is punished according to TCC (2004) Article 314 which determines the penalty for being a member of an armed organisation. Thus, according to TCC (2004) Article 314, the members of armed organisations can be punished by a sentence of five to ten years of imprisonment. Moreover, these penalties are increased at a rate of half according to Article 5 of Anti-Terrorism Law (1991).[32] Article 5 provides that:

> Penalties of imprisonment and judicial fines to be imposed on perpetrators of offences specified under articles 3 and 4 shall be aggravated by one half. Penalties to be determined accordingly may thereby exceed the regular upper limit of the penalty prescribed for that offence for any type of punishment. However, in case of life imprisonment, the sentence shall be transformed to aggravated life imprisonment.
>
> If the article defining the offence prescribes that the sentence shall be aggravated when the offence is committed within the framework of activities of a criminal organisation, the sentence will solely be aggravated according to that article. However, the aggravation may not amount to less than two thirds of the penalty.
>
> The provisions of this article are not applicable to children.

Until the enactment of Law No. 6415 on Prevention of the Financing of Terrorism Law (2013) in 2013, the offence of financing terrorism regulation in the Anti-Terrorism Law (1991) was used in accordance with other related statutes

32 In different jurisdictions, the punishments can vary. For instance, according to the UK Terrorism Act (2000, p. 11), the maximum sentence for financing terrorism is 14 years of imprisonment; in the US, the penalty for terrorist financing can be up to 20 years of imprisonment (FATF, 2016b, p. 187); according to the Australian Criminal Code Act (1995), a terrorist financier can face between 15 and 25 years of imprisonment; in Canada, the Criminal Code (2017, p. 80) imposes a prison sentence no more than 10 year for the offence for terrorist financing.

such as TCC (2004), the Prevention of Laundering Proceeds of Crime (2006) and Turkish Criminal Procedure Code (2004). Although Article 8 of the Anti-Terrorism Law (1991) has been repealed, other related laws have continued to be used in conjunction with the Prevention of the Financing of Terrorism Law (2013).

Article 8 of Anti-Terror Law was criticised because of the limited scope of 'terrorist crimes' which viewed terrorism only from Turkish and local perspectives (Özgenç, 2013, p. 176) thus omitted the spirit of Article 2 of the International Convention for Suppression of the Financing of Terrorism (1999), which is designed to address the acts of terror. In order to address this shortcoming, Turkey has adopted its terrorist financing law relatively recently, on 16 February 2013.[33] Accordingly, Article 1 of Law No. 6415, Prevention of the Financing of Terrorism (2013), under the title "Purpose and Scope", the effective prevention of terrorist financing and freezing of assets are emphasised in the context of the UN's International Convention for Suppressing Financing of Terrorism (1999) and the relevant United Nations Security Council Resolutions.

Under Article 2, definitions of the terms used in this act are explained[34] and Article 3 provides a list of prohibited acts of providing funds or supporting terrorist organisations. According to this article "[a]cts intended to cause death or serious bodily injury for the purpose of intimidating or suppressing a population or compelling a government or an international organisation to do or to abstain from doing any act"; acts which are accepted as terrorist offences according to the Anti-Terrorism Law (1991); and the acts which are accepted as forbidden and unlawful in the nine UN Conventions[35] to which Turkey is a signatory are

33 Firstly, this new law has been adopted with the aims of synchronising the Turkish legal system with the requirements of the UN's International Convention for Suppressing Financing of Terrorism (1999). Secondly, this legal instrument, by transposing UN law into the domestic judicial system, regulates the implementations of decisions and demands, which have been taken by the UN Security Council Sanctions Committee regarding freezing the assets of Al Qaeda, and Taliban related individuals and organisations and other terrorist organisations. Thirdly, the process regarding the asset freezing demands of foreign states and foreign organisations in terms of terrorist financing is put into order. Lastly, how Turkey's own asset freezing demands from other states and organisations will be implemented is organised.

34 'Fund' is defined as "[the] means money or property, right, claims of every kind whether movable or immovable, tangible or intangible which could be represented by money and all kinds of documents representing them" and 'asset' is defined as "[the] fund, proceeds, benefit and value derived from inter-conversion of them, owned or possessed or directly or indirectly controlled by a natural or legal person." Moreover, freezing of assets is described as "[the] removal or restriction of the power of disposition over the asset for the purpose of preventing obliteration, consumption, conversion, transfer, assignation, conveyance and other dispositional actions of the asset" ("Law on the Prevention of Financing of Terrorism", 2013).

35 These UN Conventions are: Convention for the Suppression of Unlawful Seizure of Aircraft (1970), Convention for the Suppression of Unlawful Acts against the Safety of Civil Aviation (1971), Convention on the Prevention and Punishment of Crimes against Internationally

accepted as the terrorist offences. With the introduction of these provisions, it can be asserted that the limited and criticised scope of the definition of terrorism under the Anti-Terror Law 1991 was broadened, and international norms have been transposed into national laws. Notably, the first part of Article 3 has a degree of resemblance to Article 2/1/b of the International Convention for Suppressing Financing of Terrorism (1999).[36]

Article 4 stipulates the conditions of the financing of terrorism offence. According to paragraph 1 of Article 4, 'financing of terrorism offence' occurs when "[a]ny person who provides or collects funds for a terrorist or terrorist organisations with the intention that they are used or knowing and willing that they are to be used, even without being linked to a specific act, in full or in part, in perpetration of the acts that are set forth as crime within the scope of Article 3 [. . .]". The legislation clearly states that providing or collecting funds for any terrorist offence is not enough to form the financing of terrorism crime. In order to establish culpability and guilt for crime, the perpetrators must have knowledge and intent as necessary conditions. In the continuation of the paragraph, the punishment for this crime is clarified. If the crime is committed, then it will "[. . .] be punished by imprisonment for a term of five to ten years, provided that his/her act does not constitute another offence requiring a heavier punishment".

Moreover, according to paragraph 2 of Article 3, it is not necessary for the funds to be used for a terrorist crime for the court to impose a sentence outlined in paragraph 1 (Law on the Prevention of Financing of Terrorism, 2013).

Another important change regarding this legal instrument is the introduction of an administrative asset freezing provision, which the Turkish counter-terrorism regime did not have before. In this context, Articles 5, 6 and 7 stipulate asset freezing applications in three different situations.

Article 5 outlines the implementation of the UNSC's asset freezing decisions, which originally emanated from Resolutions 1267 (1999), 1988 (2011) and 1989 (2011). According to this article, the UNSC's asset freezing decisions will be executed immediately through the decisions given by the Council of Ministers and published in the Official Gazette. MFA is responsible for notifying the

---

Protected Persons (1973), including Diplomatic Agents, International Convention against the Taking of Hostages (1979), Convention on the Physical Protection of Nuclear Material (1980), Protocol for the Suppression of Unlawful Acts of Violence at Airports Serving International Civil Aviation (1988), Supplementary to the Convention for the Suppression of Unlawful Acts against the Safety of Civil Aviation (1988), Convention for the Suppression of Unlawful Acts against the Safety of Maritime Navigation (1988), Protocol for the Suppression of Unlawful Acts against the Safety of Fixed Platforms Located on the Continental Shelf (1988), International Convention for the Suppression of Terrorist Bombings (1997).

36 Article 2/1/b: "Any other act intended to cause death or serious bodily injury to a civilian, or to any other person not taking an active part in the hostilities in a situation of armed conflict, when the purpose of such act, by its nature or context, is to intimidate a population, or to compel a government or an international organization to do or to abstain from doing any act".

UNSC of implemented resolutions. The Financial Crimes Investigation Board (MASAK – the FIU of Turkey which operates under the auspices of the Ministry of Finance)[37] applies the resolutions against relevant entities.

Article 6 deals with asset freezing requests by foreign countries. When such a request is made, the Assessment Commission, which was established by the Law on the Prevention of Financing of Terrorism, 2013, evaluates the request. If it deems the request to be warranted, then the formal decision regarding the request is made by the Council of Ministers. Article 6 emphasises that in reaching such decisions, the reciprocity principle will be taken in consideration. To be able to make a decision the justifications regarding the request have to be delivered by a competent authority of the foreign state to Turkey. If the foreign state does not initiate an investigation one year after the asset freezing decision has been given and published in the Official Gazette, the application of the freezing decision may be revoked.

Article 7 determines the process of Turkey's asset freezing requests from other states and the procedure for the asset freezing in Turkey. Article 7 thus provides that assets belonging to persons and organisations believed, based on reasonable grounds, to have committed offences listed in the third and fourth articles, may be frozen by the Council of Ministers following a proposal from the Assessment Commission. Additionally, those linked with the assets in Turkey may be investigated pursuant to the Turkish Criminal Procedure Code (2004). The Ministry of Foreign Affairs is responsible for notifying foreign states about asset freezing requests by the Turkish Council of Ministers.

Under these three provisions, the administrative processes of the asset freezing mechanism are addressed. It is clear that the UNSC Resolutions shall be implemented, and in accordance with Turkey's obligations under international law, requests from foreign states would be considered by competent authorities. However, in the case of terrorist and suspect assets in Turkey, the Turkish Criminal Procedure provisions is used for seizure and confiscation of such assets. In other words, in the first two situations, the UNSC decisions and foreign requests, administrative asset freezing procedures, without the involvement of the judiciary, are employed. If the financing of terrorism offence is suspected and/or committed in Turkey, then the Turkish judicial officials are involved.

The law on the Prevention of Financing of Terrorism, 2013 recognises wider forms and implications of the financing of terrorism offence within and beyond Turkey and encompasses offences by all designated terrorist organisations and terrorist activities recognised by the international community. This is a welcome change and progress when compared to the older regime under the Anti-Terror Law 1991 which had a narrower interpretation of terrorist offences and omitted

37 On 10 July 2018, the Presidential Decree No: 1 (2018) the Ministry of Finance and Ministry of Treasury have been merged and become the Ministry of Treasury and Finance. MASAK's responsibilities, tasks and bureaucratic position have not been changed under this new structure.

financing of terrorism and international cooperation altogether. In addition to the existing asset seizure and confiscation applications by the judiciary, asset freezing has been introduced as an administrative measure where there is no need for judicial oversight. While this administrative mechanism may speed up investigation and enforcement measures in countering international terrorism, it relies on information produced by external bodies and assumes that requests from foreign jurisdictions are a product of the rule of law and due process whereby the rights of organisations and persons have been protected. Given the fact that there are countries around the world which use their counter-terrorism measures to punish and silence legitimate opposition and/or extract evidence against people by illegal methods, there is a risk that the asset freezing mechanism in Turkey may inadvertently contribute towards such practices. Thus, the Turkish CTF legislation needs to include the necessary safeguards when dealing with asset freezing requests from authorities beyond its control.

Article 8 of the Law on the Prevention of Financing of Terrorism, 2013, designates MASAK, the Turkish FIU, as the responsible institution for analysing suspicious activity reports, investigating financial crimes and executing asset freezing decisions. When information is requested by MASAK from public institutions and natural and legal persons, such information must be provided immediately. Justice, Interior and Foreign Affairs Ministries, the National Intelligence Agency and other related institutions and agencies have to provide their assessments, findings and any related information and documents for the asset freezing requests and decisions mentioned in Articles 6 and 7. The results of the such investigations and analyses are presented to the Assessment Commission by MASAK. According to Article 12, once published in the Official Gazette, the asset freezing orders become legally binding and in effect.[38]

Another important legislation which precedes the Law on the Prevention of Financing of Terrorism, 2013, is Law No. 5549 on the Prevention of Laundering of Proceeds of Crime (2006) which encompasses CTF measures.[39] Law No. 5549 outlines the responsibilities and duties of MASAK whereby MASAK also has the task of countering financing of terrorism (beside AML activities) by data collection, analysis and evaluation of SARs.

38 "The Assessment Commission is composed of General Director of Security Affairs in Prime Ministry, Deputy Undersecretary of National Intelligence Organisation, Deputy Undersecretary of the Ministry of Interior, General Director of Criminal Affairs in the Ministry of Justice, General Director of Research and Security Affairs in the Ministry of Foreign Affairs and General Director of Financial Sector Relations and Exchange in the Under Secretariat of Treasury under the chairmanship of the President of MASAK" ("Law on the Prevention of Financing of Terrorism", 2013).

39 After becoming a member of the FATF in 1991, Turkey enacted its first anti-money laundering (AML) legislation, Law No. 4208 on Prevention of Money Laundering, in 1996. Depending on the developments in terms of money laundering techniques and increasing financial and economic relations forced Turkey to address these changes. Therefore, the current legislation, Prevention of Laundering Proceeds of Crime, was enacted in 2006 (Aykın & Sözmen, 2009, p. 149).

The main purpose of Law No. 5549 is to determine the procedures and principles for preventing money laundering and terrorist finance, and it provides the list of parties obliged with reporting and monitoring duties for AML and CTF.[40] In line with FATF Recommendations, this legal instrument outlines the 'Customer Identification' and KYC procedures as a legal requirement. According to Article 3, obliged parties must identify the person/s who make money transaction and the persons on behalf of or for the benefit of whom the transfer will take place before the transfer is conducted. Article 4 provides the 'Suspicious Transactions Reporting' (STR) procedures.[41]

Article 17 deals with 'Seizure' of assets. According to Article 17, paragraph 1: "[i]n cases where there is strong suspicion that the offences of money laundering and financing of terrorism are committed, the asset values may be seized in accordance with the procedure in Article 128 of Criminal Procedure Law No. 5271". Under Articles 19 and 20, the duties and powers of MASAK and the Coordination Board for Combating Financial Crimes are stipulated.

Another relevant legal instrument which needs to identified in the context of CTF is Law No. 5271 – Turkish Criminal Procedure Code (2004). Article 128 of Law No. 5271 regulates the seizure of criminal assets[42] and complements Law No. 5549 on Prevention of Laundering Proceeds of Crime (2006).[43]

40 According to Article 2 of this legislation, the obliged parties are listed as those which operate in the "[. . .] banking, insurance, individual pension, capital markets, money lending and other financial services, and postal service and transportation, lotteries and bets; those who deal with exchange, real estate, precious stones and metals, jewellery [*sic*], all kinds of transportation vehicles, construction machines, historical artefacts [*sic*], art works, antiques or intermediaries in these operations; notaries, sports clubs and those operating in other fields determined by the Council of Ministers" ("Law on Prevention of Laundering Proceeds of Crime", 2006).

41 Obliged parties are required to report to MASAK any transaction which "there is any information, suspicion or reasonable grounds to suspect that the asset, which is subject to the transactions carried out or attempted to be carried out within or through the obliged parties, is acquired through illegal ways or used for illegal purposes". It is forbidden for the obliged parties to share the information of their Suspicious Transaction Report with MASAK, other than supervisors who are tasked with checking obligations and courts. It is stated that the principles, procedures of reporting and parties required to implement this obligation are clarified in the regulation.

42 According to this Article, the assets of the suspects or accused ones may be seized if there is strong evidence which demonstrates that the crime investigated or prosecuted has been committed and these properties have been acquired from this crime. It should be noted that "[e]ven in cases where these immovable assets, rights, credits and other values of belongings are in possession of individuals other than the suspect or the accused, the seizure is also permitted".

43 Types of properties are listed in the Article 128(1): a) Immovable goods, b) Transport vehicles of land, sea or air, c) All kinds of accounts in banks or other financial institutions, d) All kinds of rights and credits by real or juridical persons, e) Valuable documents, f) Shares at the firm where he is a shareholder, g) Contents of the rented safe, h) Other assets belonging to him (Turkish Criminal Procedure Code, 2004).

Articles 54[44] and 55[45] provide the mechanism for confiscation orders which can be imposed on properties and income.

4.4 Conclusion

This chapter provides an introduction to Turkey's CTF regime. Firstly, the terrorist threat to Turkey is explained. Following this, the legal system and relevant provisions are identified. The purpose of this chapter is to give an idea of and information about Turkey's developing counter-terrorism efforts and terrorist financing structure in the face of the terrorism threat Turkey faces at present. After outlining the legal base for CTF measures at the domestic and international levels, in the next chapter, the effectiveness and efficacy of the CTF system are going to be evaluated. In this context, Turkey's national and international efforts will be analysed from legal, administrative and international dimensions. Ultimately, the effectiveness and success of on-going practices of CTF structure in Turkey will be assessed.

44 In Article 54, the provisions for confiscation of property are provided. Accordingly, it is stated that for the court to decide to confiscate the property and tools, they must be used in or reserved for the perpetration of a crime. Moreover, this property should not belong to third parties who have good faith. Furthermore, if it is decided that the property and tools arranged for committing a crime are hazardous to public safety, health or morality, then these can be confiscated also. In case of concealment, disposal, consumption of the property defined in the first subsection, or avoidance of seizure in any other manner, the court may adjudicate confiscation of a sum corresponding to the value of this property (TCC, 2004).

45 Correspondingly, pursuant to Article 55, confiscation of income may be ordered. The court may decide confiscation of economic benefits acquired through committing the offence, or forming the subject of the crime, or provided for perpetration of crime, as well as the economic gains recorded as a result of usage or transformation of these benefits. Confiscation decision could only be given where it is not possible to return the economic gains to the victim of the offence. In addition, if the seizure of the property or economic benefits subject to confiscation is not likely, or not possible to convey the same to the related authorities, the court may decide confiscation of the values considered as the equivalency of this property (TCC, 2004).

5 Critical analysis of CTF system of Turkey

5.1 Introduction

In Chapter 4, institutional arrangements and domestic and international legal provisions of the CTF regime in Turkey were explained. For a comprehensive analysis of the CTF regime in Turkey, there is a need for further elaboration of how well this system functions and how it affects the daily life of ordinary citizens. In order to achieve this task, this study has gone beyond the examination of 'law in books' and conducted 35 semi-structured interviews with 37 CTF experts and practitioners, coming from law enforcement, financial intelligence, judicial, customs and border control, financial sector and academic backgrounds. Most of the interviewees agreed to be interviewed on the conditions of confidentiality and anonymity in regard to their identities because of the sensitive nature of the subject matter. These interviews provide good empirical data responding to the question of to what extent the current CTF regime in Turkey is effective. Firstly, the TF and CTF perceptions are analysed so as to find out how these experts conceive and interpret these terms; what importance they give to these terms; and what elements should be present in a well working and successful CTF regime. Secondly, this chapter reveals the key areas in which CTF practice is concentrated in Turkey's long struggle with terrorism. After examining the perceptions and the place of CTF in the overall counter-terrorism practices in Turkey in the last to three decades, the level of administrative and legal structures addressing terrorist financing and their effectiveness are examined in order to have a clearer picture of the adequacy of the current administrative structure and legal basis for conducting CTF efforts. Following this, the current implementation of counter terrorist financing is analysed critically by looking into whether the current practices are feasible, manageable and delivering the anticipated outcomes. In addition, the degree of applicability of the current laws and regulations, capacity, education, technology, cooperation and coordination between related institutions and elements are examined in detail. Furthermore, the impact of the CTF practices on terrorist organisations operating in Turkey is examined so as to find whether it is possible to speak of tangible successes.

5.2 Historical background of CTF in Turkey

Turkey has been fighting different types of terrorism since the 1970s; thus, it is important to establish if and how new the current Turkish CTF efforts are. In other words, what has been the place of CTF efforts within Turkey's counter-terrorism strategy for nearly 50 years? The main aim of answering this question is to explore the past efforts and initiatives of the Turkish state and governments and tease out if any of them have been successful. In answering this question, two main responses emerge.

Firstly, it is claimed that financial activities of terrorist organisations were neglected and were not a part of Turkey's main counter-terrorism strategy.[1] Another scholar supports this claim by giving an example from the Anti-Terrorism Law of Turkey enacted in 1991 following the escalation of terrorist attacks by PKK. The sudden wave of PKK terrorism in 1984 meant that Turkey could not have conceived the real nature of this terrorist threat initially. Consequently, as the first reaction, Turkey had used security forces such as the army and police forces similar to Spain and the UK during the 1970s and 1980s. When enacted, the Anti-Terrorism Law (1991), which is the main legislation against terrorism in Turkey, did not contain provisions which specifically target the financial aspect of terrorist organisations. It is claimed that Turkey has become aware of the financial dimensions of terrorism due to the external factors.[2] As mentioned in the previous section, 'Financing of Terrorism' provisions were incorporated into Anti-Terror Law only in 2006 when it was amended in order to fill this gap. Consequently, it can be claimed that the financial dimension of terrorism was neglected to a certain degree, and the counter-terrorism efforts were mainly concentrated on military and/or law enforcement agencies' engagement in the hot pursuit of terrorists, which often was operationally difficult.

The observation above is supported by a senior level judge who indicated that the novelty of the legislation on Prevention of Financing of Terrorism (2013) illustrates that Turkey did not have any specially designed law for the prevention of financial sources of terrorism until then. He adds that while different types of terrorist groups, such as PKK, DHKP/C and Hizbullah, were financing themselves using various methods such as taxation for revolution, bank robbery and stealing under the name of expropriation, these efforts were not providing them adequate income for their needs.[3] It is also mentioned that Turkish courts were trying to punish these kinds of activities heavily by using provisions in the existing Turkish Criminal Law (1926), such as Article 169, which prohibits providing

1 Interview with a Scholar who is an Expert on International Relations, Security Studies and Terrorism – Professor at a University No: AC3.

2 Interview with a Scholar who is an Expert on Security Studies – Professor at a University No: AC4.

3 Interview with a Senior Level Judge from the Department of Justice No: JD2.

help to armed gangs.[4] However, in general, Turkey did not perceived CTF as an important issue and no large- or small-scale economic and financial operations towards terrorist groups were conducted. These findings indicate that Turkey had a rather passive approach to CTF and did not take prevention of financial capabilities of terrorist organisations as a priority partly because of the trivial or inadequate amount of income terrorist organisations had in that period. Furthermore, in the PKK example, it is claimed by a scholar that Turkey could not prevent PKK's financial activities effectively, and consequently, PKK managed to raise funds from both internal and external sources such as smuggling and collecting donations.[5]

At this point, a senior level CTF expert's words are important in terms of reflecting Turkey's position against financing of terrorism:

> In this context, as you have rightly mentioned, Turkey has been struggling [with terrorism] since 1970s, however, I become sad when I start to think about the confiscation figures and I think that these figures should be taken into account more seriously, because, as far as I know, we were trying to collect data and statistics from different institutions in order to show our successes during the [international] negotiations. [. . .] [W]hen we looked at these figures there were some success stories but in comparison to the total number of cases, the number of these stories are so limited. My personal opinion, which can be seen so pretentious to you, is that during this period, we failed in this business. [. . .] For example, in the case of PKK terrorist organisation, even though we have so many success stories in terms of military responses and operations on the ground, presented with honour, we do not have the same success stories when it comes to the court processes, sentencing these people and confiscation of funds used for terrorism. Therefore, there is a situation that whether we do not know how to deal with financing of terrorism or we are simply not good at this.[6]

In addition, it is claimed by the same expert that the lack of significant amounts of confiscated assets or funds used for terrorism or terrorist organisations is one of the indicators which demonstrates that in historical perspective CTF was neglected in Turkey.[7]

The second main approach is that Turkey was aware of the importance of finance for terrorists and their survival; however, they could not have conducted a systematic CTF strategy in practice. According to a senior level director at the

4 The article of 'Help to Armed Gang' which criminalises the actions of supporting and helping an armed gang by showing a place for accommodation, providing weapon, ammunition, dress or any other kind of assistance which would facilitate the acts of armed gangs in annulled Turkish Criminal (1926) Law No: 765.

5 Interview with a Terrorism/Counterterrorism Scholar from a University No: AC2.

6 Interview with a Senior Level CTF Expert from the Turkish FIU – MASAK No: FIU1.

7 *Ibid.*

MFA, there were efforts to fight financing of terrorism in Turkey in the past; however, this struggle could not be undertaken in a systematic way. In addition, it is claimed that Turkey was aware of CTF and knew the importance of the financial sources for terrorists.[8] Similarly, as the CTF experts express above, Turkey's CTF efforts against financial sources of terrorism were not systematically designed and conducted in this sense effectively.[9]

Regarding Turkey's awareness of the importance of CTF, Turkey's proposal presented at the deliberations in order to form the United Nations Convention against Transnational Organized Crime, Resolution 55/25 which was adopted by the General Assembly on 15 November 2000, also known as the Palermo Convention, can be given as an example. In its proposal Turkey demanded that terrorists' financial activities be incorporated into the main body of the convention explicitly in order to prevent terrorist financing and their sponsors. However, other countries did not accept this proposal (United Nations General Assembly, 1998, p. 14, 1999, p. 5, 2000a, pp. 4, 5, 2000b, pp. 8, 9).[10] This example clearly shows that Turkey was aware of the role of financing of terrorism and the importance of preventing it and indeed, tried to address the issue at an international platform.

In the earlier period, regarding the financing of terrorism, the National Police reports on illicit drug trafficking pointed out the link between terrorist organisations, especially PKK, and illicit drug trafficking (Narcotic Division, 1994, pp. 111–112). It was noted in these reports that terrorists were financing themselves by conducting drug trafficking (Narcotic Division, 1994, pp. 130–132). While these reports show that Turkey was aware of the financing of terrorism and their financial activities domestically and internationally, it is not so clear how Turkey was trying to counter these.

Both perspectives on Turkey's past CTF efforts have some validity. It seems that even though Turkey was aware of the importance of financial activities for terrorist organisations and was trying to create awareness even on the international arena, it could/did not conduct a systematic CTF strategy to curb the money flows into the terrorist organisations' coffers. It is important to ask here therefore why CTF was not part of Turkey's overall counter-terrorism strategy.

5.2.1 Prominence of armed type counter-terrorism struggle

One of the frequently emerging opinions during the interviews was that the Turkish national security approach focused primarily on the use of military means

8 Interview with a Senior Level Director from the Ministry of Foreign Affairs No: MFA1.

9 Interview with a Senior Level CTF expert from the Turkish FIU – MASAK No: FIU1.

10 According to a senior director from MFA, Turkey was aware of the danger posed by terrorist organisations' financial activities and their links with criminal world. Even though Turkey insisted on putting terrorist financing into that convention, most of the Western countries, most of which seem strictly against terrorist financing these days, rejected and declined Turkey's demand. This interviewee believes that Turkey's sincere efforts against terrorism were not supported, and Turkey was left alone in its fight that time.

as the main counter-terrorism instrument. Thus, addressing the financing of terrorism took a back seat in Turkey's counter-terrorism strategy.

As one of the academics noted, the main coordination responsibility and conducting the fight against PKK and its terrorism were put on the shoulders of soldiers for many years. It was also noted that, even though soldiers might have been aware of other types of non-military methods such as preventing financing of terrorism, they could not do anything other than asking the civilians about this dimension of the issue in the regular senior level security meetings such as the Turkish National Security Council (NSC) meetings. Furthermore, it was noted that normally, military personnel were not trained for or did not have any capacity to conduct operations on the financial aspects of terrorism either. In tandem, the civilian authority did not take proper CTF action, probably because they did not know much about how to carry out a CTF campaign.[11] Prominent Turkish journalist Bila's (2007, pp. 42, 43, 73,74) interview with former Turkish Chief General Staff Retired General Güreş supports the claims that politicians left the responsibility to the soldiers in the early 1990s without giving them the official authority to so. He expressed that even though he was not given official authority to conduct the counter-terrorism efforts, the Prime Minister and governors were not disturbed that he was undertaking this responsibility, and they had no reservations about this situation. He describes the situation and his discomfort as follows: "[w]hen I went to the NSC meetings, I observed that everyone was so content. [However] Mother of the martyr at the funeral was looking at me [and waiting for an answer for her loss]. In the NSC meetings, I was asking [directly] to the President and Prime Minister how they could be all content!" (Bila, 2007, p. 73).

Similarly, it was noted by one of the law enforcement professionals who was interviewed that "[n]early since its foundation in the 1920s, Turkey has been fighting terrorism, yet we could not perceive the concept of counter-terrorism properly. The idea that counter-terrorism is equal to the countering financing of terrorism could not be understood, instead an armed style struggle came to the fore for a while".[12] In addition, another law enforcement official points out that the financial aspect of counter-terrorism was not the key focus, and it was not seen as an important issue; on the contrary mainly the military and law enforcement forces were used to conduct the armed struggle against terrorists. Even though there were some limited efforts regarding curbing financial sources, the usage of military means was much more important for the security forces. He indicated the main mentality of that era by noting that "[w]e as being soldiers and police were trying to deal with mosquitos rather than the bog".[13]

11 Interview with a Scholar who is an Expert on international relations, security studies and terrorism Professor at a University No: AC3.

12 Interview with a Middle Level CTF Practitioner from a Law Enforcement Agency No: LE11.

13 Interview with a Senior Level CTF Practitioner from a Law Enforcement Agency No: LE3.

According to one interviewee, before the Turkish Republic was founded in 1923 there had been already separatist movements within the Ottoman Empire. Such separatist and terrorist movements continued after the establishment of the republic. In this context, it is noted that Turkey's efforts against terrorism were mainly formed by focusing on solutions regarding using armed security forces and criminal prosecutions, whereas Turkish officials and political elites ignored the root causes of terrorism. Arresting, punishing and eliminating terrorists were the main goals of this security oriented counter-terrorism approach. However, eliminating or prosecuting terrorists by the army and law enforcement units did not counter terrorism, because the main causes of this phenomenon emanate from *inter alia* economic, political and cultural factors as well. It is claimed that this was the mistake of the Turkish executive during that period.[14] Another scholar noted that terrorism had been understood as a mere security problem where its financial part was ignored. Terrorism was seen as a direct military threat, and thus solutions to eliminate it came primarily from military and law enforcement perspectives excluding its social, economic and financial dimensions. Because of experiences gained from the on-going struggle across several decades, these shortcomings were noticed by the state mechanism.[15] As one of the interviewees noted, Turkey focused on finishing terrorism rather than addressing the main causes which produce this violence, and counter-terrorism strategy has been formed by the process of 'trial and error' in Turkey until now.[16]

A senior level judge explains that Turkey did not apply CTF tactics in the past and rather implemented a military based approach by saying, "[h]owever, in that period an intensified armed struggle had been adopted as the main combating [terrorism] strategy".[17] Similarly, it is stated by another senior level judge that armed struggle which was conducted by military and law enforcement forces was the main approach of Turkey's fight against terrorism, and the main aim of this was only to capture and punish terrorists. It is also noted that there was no judicial action or court case in terms of investigating internal and external financial sources of terrorism until the 2000s.[18]

In addition, a retired law enforcement director stated that even though the security dimension only constitutes 10 percent of the whole counter-terrorism efforts, the other 90 percent comprise the other important dimensions such as social, cultural, political and economic efforts. However, it was argued that Turkey only concentrated its efforts and sources to cover 10 percent of the security dimension, rather than 90 percent of other kinds of efforts.[19]

14 Interview with a Scholar who is an Expert on International Law – Professor at a University No: AC7.

15 Interview with a Scholar who is an Expert on Security Studies – Professor at a University No: AC4.

16 Interview with a Senior Level CTF Practitioner from a Law Enforcement Agency No: LE3.

17 Interview with a Senior Level Judge from the Department of Justice No: JD2.

18 Interview with a Senior Level Judge from the Department of Justice No: JD1.

19 Interview with a Senior Level (retired) Director from a Law Enforcement Agency No: LE5.

According to one academic who also has a law enforcement background, Turkey's main counter-terrorism efforts and strategy were based on eliminating terrorists shaped by a security-based framework. Consequently, he claimed that as it was a technical issue, countering terrorist financing was not taken into account at the operational level. On the macro level, the issues in terms of preventing terrorists' weapon and ammunition procurement and international supports of sponsor states were deliberated in the State National Security Council meetings. In addition, even though the roles of European based drug trafficking and human smuggling networks which funded terrorist organisations were well-known, tackling these issues did not form a significant part of the main counter-terrorism strategy. Additionally, it is claimed that this situation was related to the mind-set of Turkey's counter terrorism struggle. In this type of struggle, it was envisaged that targeting and eliminating the violence caused by terrorists by either killing or arresting them would finish terrorism.

Correspondingly, another senior level law enforcement official pointed out that especially in 1990s a result-based approach to countering terrorism, which was aimed at solving the problem in a short period of time, was endorsed by the Turkish bureaucracy. This approach was in contrast with a process oriented approach, in which the state can sustain the counter-action consistently such as protracted war types of armed conflicts. In this context, it is claimed that both governments and the security bureaucracy deemed that increasing the powers of security institutions would be enough to solve terrorism problem in a short timeframe. However, as the case of PKK terrorism demonstrates, this struggle can continue over many decades. According to the same interviewee, the Turkish security bureaucracy did not perceive this fact until the 2000s. One of the main reasons for opting for this short-term approach was the success that had been experienced against leftist terrorism since the 1970s whereby the goal-oriented approach of 'sweep and destroy' was successful in dismantling small units of these terrorist organisations. Thus, with the confidence of this success, Turkey deployed the same strategy against PKK terrorism. However, PKK terrorism required a different approach, a process oriented approach, which sets its strategy for a long-term period. After the 2000s, Turkish bureaucracy eventually understood that they had been fighting against terrorists on the individual level but not terrorism with a holistic strategy. In this context, it is claimed that the Turkish bureaucracy could not understand that the dynamics of the Cold War era and failed to adapt to the requirements of the new post–Cold War environment.[20]

The claims and statements mentioned above emphasise the role of a security-based approach and using military means as the main instrument against terrorism. It seems that political elites had left the responsibility of addressing terrorism to the military and security forces; thus, it may be claimed that these institutions tried to fulfil this responsibility in the scope of their key capacities and capabilities and organisational experiences. However, these organisations did

20 Interview with a Senior Level CTF Practitioner from a Law Enforcement Agency No: LE9.

not have the ability and knowledge to conduct a financial operation against the financial resources of terrorists. Moreover, the mentality based on destroying terrorist organisations by military means (i.e. lethal force) could be another possible reason not to have a CTF strategy. In addition, the concept of terrorism was conceived from only a military perspective owing to the nature of PKK terrorism which has been conducted as a protracted armed conflict; however, other root causes of this violence had been neglected during that time.

In accordance with these arguments, Aktan and Köknar (2002, pp. 272–280) describe Turkish counter-terrorism efforts used against PKK terrorism as being mainly based on coercive usage of military and its technological improvements and intelligence collection to support these efforts. There were, however, other efforts to improve the international cooperation and legal provisions in order to control the terrorism threat in Turkey. Regarding the activities undertaken in order to prevent financing of terrorism, Aktan and Köknar (2002, p. 77) identify that in the 1990s, Turkish security forces evacuated residents from their remote villages and hamlets in the conflict areas to safer zones which resulted in curbing the logistical, propaganda and recruitment capacity of the PKK terrorist organisation in these areas significantly. However, even though the purpose of this strategy claimed to be protecting the people against PKK terrorism, the Turkish state was criticised by Western countries for imposing forced migration and violation of human rights (EU Commission, 1998, pp. 19–20).

Aktan and Köknar (2002) also mention that Turkey failed to address money laundering, organised crime, and related corruption, which facilitate the activities of terrorist organisations. Furthermore, they explain that there was not a systematic financial approach against terrorist organisations other than using diplomatic means for gaining support and cutting sponsor states activities. Similarly, Kundakçı (2005), who is a retired Lieutenant General, explains the importance of money and PKK's financial activities and sources in a very detailed way in his book. However, there is no relevant information regarding how these financial activities had been encountered by the Turkish state during that period. It is only briefly mentioned that Turkey had warned countries diplomatically in order to prevent support for PKK. Kundakçı (2005) also provided the account of the military condensed response, and the adaptation of the Turkish army against PKK is provided in a very detailed way. These examples indicate that due to militaristic interpretation of the counter-terrorism efforts, the option of addressing financing of terrorism had not been an important part of these activities in the past.

5.2.2 Turkish state perception and state sponsorship

In addition to the military based approach which has been adopted as the main method against terrorism, another factor which underpins the Turkish counter-terrorism regime is the interpretation of counter-terrorism and CTF. From a legislative perspective, financial activities of terrorists were not specifically classified under the financing of terrorism offence. There was no specific definition for this kind of activity, yet not only the financial assistance but also all kinds of material and intangible types of support provided to terrorists and their supporters had been interpreted in the context of aiding and abetting offences by the courts. As one of the interviewees noted, in the initial phase of the counter-terrorism campaign of Turkey, the issue of terrorist financing was assessed as an act of providing any kind of support and assistance to terrorist organisations in general. There was no systematic examination of these activities from a separate financial perspective. It is believed that developing and changing economic conditions such as the introduction of advanced wired money transfer technologies and other financial activities have effects on the increasing awareness of Turkey in terms of addressing terrorist financing.[21]

Coupled with this broad understanding of financing of terrorism, the Turkish state mechanism approached the issue from the international state sponsorship perspective. In other words, it disregarded other ways and methods of financing, whereby it was believed that terrorist organisations operating in Turkey were mainly supported by foreign states for acquiring weapons, logistics and their financial needs. As one scholar pointed out, at the beginning, PKK had been evaluated by Turkey as a state sponsored terrorist organisation. It was noted that because of this perception, Turkey prioritised external dynamics of PKK terrorism and its financial capacity supported by foreign countries. Thus, Turkey could not understand the significance and the role of internal dynamics for the financial activities and sources of terrorism. After being aware of the internal dynamics of the issue, Turkey has started to perceive the importance of the financial capacity and activities of PKK.[22] In the case of PKK, it is noted that while villagers who were living in terrorism affected areas did not have enough money to give to terrorists voluntarily, terrorists collected money and other needs from them forcefully. The main armaments of terrorists such as weapons and ammunition were already provided from abroad. However, it is claimed that Turkey could not act decisively against this support either.[23]

One of the scholars emphasised the negative influence of other countries on Turkey's counterterrorism efforts by stating that especially after the first Iraq War, some of the countries operating in Northern Iraq in order to provide safety to the people living there in the context of 'Operation Provide Comfort', supported PKK terrorists by providing food, and weapons and warned them against Turkish military operations.[24] The former Chief of General Staff Retired General Güreş asserted that during an operation in Northern Iraq in 1992, they detected that a US helicopter was airdropping supplies to the terrorists in the night, and later these assertions were confirmed by the statements collected during

21 Interview with a Senior Level Director from the Ministry of Foreign Affairs No: MFA1.
22 Interview with a Scholar who is an Expert on Security Studies – Professor at a University No: AC4.
23 Interview with a Senior Level CTF Practitioner from a Law Enforcement Agency No: LE7.
24 Interview with Scholar who is an Expert on Security and Intelligence – Professor in a University No: AC8.

interrogations of PKK terrorists (Bila, 2007). In terms of states' supporting activities of terrorist organisations active in Turkey, the same scholar claimed that:

> These terrorist organisations [in Turkey] were also supported by states. Especially in the context of PKK, the US, Germany, the Netherlands and Sweden were the main countries supporting the PKK during that period. These countries provided the PKK with financial, recruitment, arms supply and logistical support. Especially in terms of left wing terrorist organisations, Dev-Sol and DHKP/C were supported by Belgium. Armenian terrorist organisation, ASALA, still exists and it has been supporting the PKK and other left wing organisations. Moreover, Bulgaria supported left wing organisations and the PKK; the arms and ammunition dimension of this support is especially important. Between 1990 and 2000, Syria had been providing a significant support to the PKK until the head of Turkish Armed Forces threatened them on the Syrian border.[25]

Aktan and Köknar (2002, pp. 268–270) list the support activities of foreign states for terrorist organisations, especially PKK, operating in Turkey under four main categories: namely, moral, political, resource and sanctuary support. It is claimed that in addition to the moral support provided by Greece and Greek Cypriot to PKK, these provided training and military supplies to PKK and other leftist terrorist organisations in Lebanon's Bekaa Valley (Aktan & Köknar, 2002, pp. 268–269). Even though the Greek government rejected the claims of supporting terrorism, the confessions of the incarcerated leader of the PKK terrorist organisation, Abdullah Öcalan, evidenced the Greek support regarding training facilities and camps (Wood, 1999) and revealed the funding activities provided by the Greek churches to PKK (BBC NEWS, 1999). Politically it is also claimed that the members of parliament and diplomats of countries such as Greece, the United Kingdom, the United States, France, Germany, Italy, Russia, Netherlands, Norway and South Africa, provided indirect or direct assistance to Turkish terrorists for spreading their messages internationally (Aktan & Köknar, 2002, p. 269). Aktan and Köknar indicate Iran, Syria and Greece as the countries providing support to religiously motivated, leftist and separatist terrorist organisations in Turkey. Finally, Aktan and Köknar (2002, pp. 269–270) note that Syria, Iran and Armenia have provided safe havens to PKK terrorists. As argued in the previous sections, terrorist organisations operating in Turkey managed to find a significant amount of support from abroad. These examples, to a certain degree, explain why Turkey interpreted financial and other types of support as a mere state sponsored activity.

In relation to Turkey's inclination towards treating terrorist finance through the lens of a foreign state sponsorship framework, another scholar held the view that, one of the significant mistakes regarding main counter-terrorism efforts by

25 *Ibid.*

Turkish political and security elite was that the terrorism issue was not analysed comprehensively and systematically. According to him, terrorism in Turkey is not only political but also has a mechanical dimension. Consequently, the terrorism problem was perceived as a political project of terrorists, the main objective of which was forging a separation state in Turkish territory. Therefore, the mechanical dimension of the financing of such activities was not considered along with the political agenda. Focusing merely on the prevention of political objectives of terrorist organisations resulted in the implementation of military based counter-terrorism strategy whose ultimate aim was to suppress this terrorism wave in order to maintain territorial integrity of the state, rather than dealing with its financial sources and the root causes of this violence.[26]

As being another possible reason, an interviewee reflected on whether addressing financing of terrorism was a priority for Turkey in the past and asserted that financial capabilities and capacities of terrorist organisations operating in Turkey were not perceived as a problem because the amount of these financial activities was never at a level which could create disturbance and force Turkey into an imminent counter-action. In other words, the amount of the financial activities of terrorists was not perceived as a significant threat; thus, Turkey focused on addressing terrorist organisations' comparative advantages.[27]

At the same time, these accounts have eventually led to high expectations for countering terrorist financing which was seen as a panacea for addressing terrorism for many of the practitioners and scholars due to uncritical, superficial acceptance of these concepts. However, CTF is only a part of the on-going counter-terrorism efforts rather than being the main instrument of the overall counter-terrorism struggle. CTF is about prevention of terrorism by targeting the terrorist organisation in contrast to the broader approach which ought to tackle the root causes of terrorism, therefore lessening the appeal for radicalisation, terrorism and violence. As one scholar interviewed pointed out, believing that the prevention of financing of terrorism can destroy [terrorist organisations] and solve all related [terrorism] problems is misleading,[28] such as expecting the same outcome from a military based approach alone.

In contrast to the views that accept CTF as the main instrument of the overall counter-terrorism strategy, some of the interviewees expressed that CTF efforts should be positioned under the main counter-terrorism strategy as a component of it.[29] In addition, it is noted that being a multidimensional problem, countering terrorism needs an elaborately planned holistic approach, which includes every

26 Interview with a Scholar who is an Expert on International Relations, Security Studies and Terrorism – Professor at a University No: AC3.

27 Interview with an Expert on EU-Turkey Relations and Terrorism, No: EU1.

28 Interview with a Scholar who is an Expert on International Relations, Security Studies and Terrorism – Professor at a University No: AC3.

29 Interviews with a Middle Level CTF Practitioner from a Law Enforcement Agency No: LE8 and (former) Senior Level Director from MASAK No: FIU2.

detail from the root causes of terrorism to its results.[30] The main argument here is that it is not possible to finish terrorism by only preventing financial activities of terrorism, especially in situations where a terrorist organisation reached a significant level of autonomy and financial independence, such as PKK. It is believed that by applying CTF measures, the capabilities of terrorist organisations may be limited, and financial intelligence can be utilised in order to disclose and disrupt their activities, support systems and contacts and their links.[31] As mentioned above, without denying the importance or the benefits of the application of CTF against terrorist financing, the prevention of terrorist financing can harm terrorists as a sub-element of the main counter-terrorism strategy rather than destroying them. Passas (2006b, p. 282) rightly points out:

> [I]f the root causes of terrorism are ignored, the problems the international community faces will remain in place despite apparent successes [against Islamist terrorism], [. . .] other groups or secular radicalism may follow. [. . .] An over-emphasis on the supply-side led to a comparative neglect of demand side approaches (e.g. what fuels militancy and the willingness of so many individuals to engage in extreme acts or suicide in the name of a given cause). Short-term, military and law enforcement approaches were not sufficiently supplemented by long-term socio-economic and political strategies and tactics.

In this context, rather than applying a broader holistic approach, the terrorism problem was seen by Turkey as a diplomatic issue which could be solved by using soft and hard power applications on sponsor states rather than dealing with the mechanics of financing of terrorism. In addition, the narrow scope of Turkish anti-terrorism legislation which omitted various types of support activities for terrorism (such as assisting and abetting a terrorist organisation) hindered the success of CTF measures in Turkey.

5.2.3 *The inadequacy of the legal and institutional structures in Turkey*

The adequacy of the legal and administrative structures in Turkey is identified as one of the significant factors as to why Turkey could not conduct an effective CTF against terrorism in the past. In terms of the legislative system, the interviews revealed two different schools of thought: while some of the interviewees supported the idea that in the past Turkey's legislative system had some deficiencies for addressing financial activities of terrorist organisations and was not designed for tackling this problem, others contended that the existing legal system was sufficient for addressing funding activities of terrorists in Turkey.

30 *Ibid.*
31 Interview with a Middle Level CTF Practitioner from a Law Enforcement Agency No: LE8.

According to a judge, the legislation was not adequate for carrying out a CTF campaign. Moreover, he stated that there had been no infrastructure to support an effective CTF regime, and the limited understanding of the mechanisms of terrorist financing resulted in very limited, if any, CTF operations in the past.[32] In accordance with this assertion, a law enforcement officer pointed out that Turkey as a victim of terrorism for years could not address the financial sources of terrorists because of the lack of adequate legislation for dealing with terrorist financing. He claimed that the enactment of the Law of Criminal Procedure in 2005 was a milestone for implementing and enacting other provisions, including terrorist financing.[33] Similarly, another law enforcement member supported this statement by saying that before the Law of Criminal Procedure, 2005, it was not possible to seize any money acquired from crime even if it was found in the house of criminals.[34]

However, other interviewees opined that the overall legal system and relevant provisions were sufficient for curbing funds of terrorist organisations in Turkey. According to this view, another judge noted that countering financing of terrorism is an important issue; however, this is not a completely new phenomenon for Turkey. According to him, Turkey has had the legal base for a long time in order to prevent aiding and abetting terrorists and terrorist organisations.[35] Similarly Yenidünya and Değirmenci (2008, p. 1275) and Özgenç (2013, pp. 174–175) note that there was no need to enact a new special legislation for penalising terrorist financing because this offence could be punished by the existing provisions of the Turkish Penal Code and Anti-Terror Law. In addition, it was claimed by a scholar that Turkey could have done many things to prevent terrorist financing without enacting new laws. Moreover, he claimed that if the existing legislation had been applied properly by the law enforcement agencies, there might have been an effective CTF as the existing legal base allowed the confiscation of the proceeds of crime in Turkey. It was thus argued that the main problem was not the legal system; rather it was the inadequate implementation of the existing legislations and the capacity of the practitioners.[36]

It can be claimed that both approaches have a certain validity. It is true that in the past Turkey had adequate legislation and measures in order to investigate and punish most offences regarding terrorism and terrorists. As mentioned above, these legal instruments also had provisions for addressing all types of support activities for terrorist organisations, which also contained financing of terrorism. However, it is also true that there was not any specific legislation in order to carry out coordinated and complex operations against terrorist financing. In addition, it is true that the level of capacity and the enforcement of these laws were

32 Interview with a Senior Level Judge from the Department of Justice No: JD1.

33 Interview with a Senior Level CTF practitioner from a Law Enforcement Agency No: LE2.

34 Interview with a Senior Level CTF practitioner from a Law Enforcement Agency No: LE1.

35 Interview with a Senior Level Judge from the Department of Justice No: JD2.

36 Interview with a Scholar who is an Expert on International Law – Assistant Professor at a University No: AC1.

problematic. Therefore, legal deficiencies might be stated as a probable reason for why Turkey could not conduct an effective CTF in the past. However, it should be noted that the multitude of terrorist organisations which are active in Turkey and supported and financed by states did also dent the effectiveness of Turkey's anti-terrorism campaigns.

Beside dealing with terrorism by using a security oriented approach and military strategy and wrongly thinking that the roots of terrorism finance were only harboured outside of Turkey, Turkey did not deem it necessary to enact a special legislation for CTF at all and continued to enforce existing legal provisions. As one senior level law enforcement officer noted, the offence of terrorist financing was not classified as a special crime in Turkish criminal law.[37] According to him even though Turkey has been dealing with terrorism since the 1970s, the Turkish bureaucratic system did not assess the financing of terrorism as a different and serious crime. It was thought that arresting criminals and jailing them would suffice to deter and prevent future attacks. However, when PKK reached a level of robust bureaucratic structure and financial capacity, it was only then the Turkish state realised the seriousness of the issue and the failure of its counter-terrorism approach. It is stated that only after the 2000s, has Turkey developed a more technocratic approach which focuses on the establishment of specialised institutions (e.g. the Turkish FIU, MASAK) and training of financial experts.[38]

Novelty of the CTF applications, knowledge, awareness and expertise

Since its foundation, the Turkish FIU, MASAK, has been fighting money laundering and other types of financial crimes. However, financing of terrorism was not one of these tasks until the enactment of the Law on Prevention of Laundering Proceeds of Crime, 2006.[39] Regarding this additional CTF mandate, an FIU practitioner pointed out that, when Turkish FIU was tasked with CTF, beside AML duties, it started to forge and establish avenues for communicating and cooperating with other domestic and foreign CTF institutions in order to learn and improve its capacity for dealing with terrorist financing. However, it was claimed that before the 2000s, the CTF measures and operations were not known or implemented in Turkey. It is clear that there was a degree of uncertainty regarding how to fight against financial sources of terrorists at that time.[40] Additionally, a judge highlighted the lack of information at that period by noting that Turkey did not know the details and the information regarding terrorist

37 Interview with a Senior Level CTF Practitioner from a Law Enforcement Agency No: LE9.

38 *Ibid.*

39 Before the enactment of the Law on Prevention of Laundering Proceeds of Crime (2006) the main legal base for MASAK was the Law on Prevention of Money Laundering, which had been in force since 1996. While the latter legislation was being used as the main base for the anti-money laundering campaign, there was no article or regulation dealing with financing of terrorism in the main content and the spirit of this legislation.

40 Interview with a Senior Level CTF Expert from the Turkish FIU – MASAK No: FIU1.

organisations, their resources, how to cut them and how to organise a counter-plan, which would include domestic and international dimensions, which made Turkey weak on the CTF front. In other words, Turkey did not know much about the terrorist organisations' financial activities and how to intercept and prevent them.[41] Rather, Turkey only approached the terrorism problem from a military perspective by military means which are more suited for a battlefield.

Coupled with the lack of awareness and understanding (by the Turkish security bureaucracy and the political elite) of the significance of financing of terrorism and terrorists' funds, the past CTF regime was doomed to fail. This was reaffirmed by a senior law enforcement officer, who stated that in the beginning of Turkey's fight against terrorism, Turkish officials could not perceive the role and importance of smuggling and other criminal activities that feed terrorist organisations, because terrorists have been raising the majority of their financial income from these activities.[42]

5.2.4 CTF – a new subject for everyone

It would not be a far-fetched idea to suggest that countering financing of terrorism was a new phenomenon for the entire world during the 1970s, 1980s and most parts of the 1990s. Even though there were many conventions and resolutions regarding terrorism, the first time a convention regarding countering financing of terrorism was put on the table in the international arena was 1999.[43] Therefore, it can be noted that, as already mentioned in the previous chapters, financing of terrorism and countering this dimension of terrorism was relatively new for many countries, including Turkey, despite its first-hand experience with terrorism for many decades.

Conducting a CTF campaign requires particular bureaucracy and technical expertise. In this context, it is noted that the expertise learned from the use of economic sanctions and financial measures firstly on Sudan and Cuba, later on Iran and ultimately on Russia, resulted in the development of the financial expertise and bureaucracy for AML and CTF in the world.[44] These implementations and applications of economic and financial sanctions have created advanced specialisation and expertise and, especially, OFAC was one of the institutions in the US where this experience has been accumulated. However, Turkey did not manage to develop such an expertise and put in place the bureaucracy and cooperation needed, and thus failed to conduct a systematic CTF campaign in the past.[45]

41 Interview with a Senior Level Judge from the Department of Justice No: JD1.

42 Interview with a Senior Level (retired) Director from a Law Enforcement Agency No: LE5.

43 The International Convention for the Suppression of the Financing of Terrorism was adopted by the UN General Assembly in Resolution 54/109 of 9 December, 1999.

44 Interview with a Scholar who is an Expert on International Law – Assistant Professor at a University No: AC1.

45 *Ibid.*

5.2.5 The role of international developments

As one senior level CTF expert indicated, "the September 11 terrorist attacks has become a milestone both for the globe and Turkey for tackling financing of terrorism".[46] This opinion might be true, because despite the fact that the UN opened the ICSFT (1999) for signature on 10 January 2000, only four states signed this convention before the 9/11 attacks, and Turkey was not one of these four countries.[47] Rather, Turkey signed this convention on 27 September 2001 after 9/11 and then ratified it on 28 June 2002 (United Nations, 2016a). In addition, it was asserted by a senior FIU director that the term 'financing of terrorism' is a new concept developed within the Western countries, most of which are members of FATF.[48] This shows that financing of terrorism and prevention of the financial activities of terrorists were a new notion and consideration for Turkey only after 9/11.

Furthermore, it was claimed that CTF has emerged as an issue in Turkey because of the pressure created by international organisations and international agreements and legal instruments. In particular, the UN Security Council and the FATF have been instrumental in this process. As one senior level bank director stated, "CTF is an issue which has not been practiced for a long time in Turkey. Actually, the application of CTF has started because of the FATF and UN and their decisions. [. . .] [I]n this sense it cannot be said that CTF has been conducted in Turkey for a long time. Rather, it can be said that CTF has become an issue in Turkey recently by the inducement of international organisations and their instruments".[49] A law enforcement practitioner supported this by saying:

> Due to the fact that as a member of international institutions, organisations and other kinds of structures established by foreign states, it has been expected from Turkey to respond to their demands by providing information regarding what we have been doing on this issue. Hence, this might have had a coercive force for CTF to become a prominent issue in Turkey. As a result, Turkey is forced to fulfil the requirements emanating from these structures and measures.[50]

In addition to the general international CTF standards, it was also pointed out that the application of CTF methods in specific context has become an important issue as a result of external demands made by Western countries: for example, the freezing assets of Al Qaeda and affiliated organisations was initiated by the US but required concerted effort by several countries. Especially after the 9/11

46 Interview with a Senior Level CTF Expert from Turkish FIU – MASAK No: FIU4.
47 According to the UN records Botswana, Sri Lanka, the UK and Uzbekistan were the countries which ratified the Convention before 11 September 2001 (United Nations, 2016a).
48 Interview with a (former) Senior Level Director from MASAK No: FIU2.
49 Interview with a Senior Level Manager of a Bank Branch No: BS1.
50 Interview with a Senior Level CTF Practitioner from a Law Enforcement Agency No: LE3.

terrorist attacks, the demands from the US government and international organisations such as the UN and the FATF, asset freezing orders and blacklisting of terrorists and their financial supporters could not be ignored by Turkey. Thus, Turkey started to work on the issue to find out what kind of legal instruments it could use to respond to these demands and adhere to its international responsibility and obligations.[51]

One of the interesting and important issues that emerged during the interviews is the difference between Turkish and Western understandings and perceptions of financing of terrorism. In this context, it is noted that in the West, the term CTF is used and understood as the efforts for preventing religiously motivated terrorism and its financial sources. However, in Turkey this term is perceived as cutting off the funding of terrorist organisations, which have been imminent national threats for Turkey such as PKK and DHKP/C. Therefore, the expectations and perceptions between Turkey and the US dominated FATF are different and sometimes contradictory. Consequently, priorities end up being different, and it is believed that this contextual difference is the main cause for the problems experienced. Furthermore, these different approaches inevitably affect the efficacy of the international CTF measures and the expectations therein. Regarding this aspect of the CTF, an EU expert expressed the following:

> However, Turkey's interpretation of classical terrorist financing is different than the one that is formed and governed by FATF as a West referenced interpretation. Well, what we understood merely from this issue in the past, in accordance with our classic threat perception, was that it was related with terrorist organisations such as PKK and DHKP/C and their financial activities and money flows between their diaspora communities and Turkey. Nevertheless, now the new legislation proposed by the US and the UK shows that their real concern and the significant point is, although it is not written in the proposal explicitly, the relation between globally Islamic referenced jihadists and home-grown terrorists in Turkey and their financial activities. Our country [Turkey] and West understand the subject differently and we have a problem here.[52]

Another critical issue is that the application of the CTF regime has been mainly concentrated on the international level and/or based on perceived threats and priorities of mainly Western countries. It is understood that Turkey's CTF is not successful in addressing its domestic terrorist threats, especially PKK terrorism. However, the compliance of Turkey with the international standards and the more recent efforts against international terrorist organisations, such as Al Qaeda and ISIS, have been developed, mostly as a result of the pressure from

51 Interview with a Scholar who is an Expert on security studies – Professor at a University No: AC4.

52 Interview with an Expert on EU-Turkey Relations and Terrorism, No: EU1.

the Western countries. One CTF practitioner made the following point in this context:

> To be honest, I have a sense that Turkey could not combat financing of terrorism adequately. Our struggle for cutting off terrorist organisations' funds, which are more dangerous threat for our country, is inadequate and ineffective. Moreover, due to the increasing pressure and coercion of great powers such as the US and the UK on Turkey for prevention of the financial activities of [terrorist] organisations such as Al Qaeda and ISIS has paved the way for Turkey to concentrate its efforts on this issue in the last five or six years, and I think Turkey has made a significant progress since then.[53]

Therefore, it can be said that CTF is a relatively new concept and measure for Turkey. This assertion is accepted by a judge who opined that:

> Well, if I have to say the truth, this term [CTF] has been discovered very lately in Turkey. We have legislation addressing proceeds of crime, then with the Article 8 it had been incorporated into Anti-Terrorism law. Later it was removed from there and a new special legislation was enacted, you know all of these. Well, in terms of financing of terrorism essentially, it might be said that Turkey is a country, which was late for this [CTF].[54]

On the other hand, while it is accepted that CTF is a new counter-terrorism concept for Turkey, it was claimed by a law enforcement officer that the awareness regarding CTF has been increasing gradually whereby CTF practitioners have started to include the financing and financial activity elements of terrorism into their investigations. It was also asserted that Turkey is just in the beginning stage of conducting this kind of struggle.[55] On this point, a senior level FIU expert agreed and pointed out that "[e]ven though the term of combating terrorism has been a very old struggle in Turkey, on the contrary, financing of terrorism is a brand-new term. As I mentioned before, there is lack of awareness; this is so obvious".[56]

Turkey has started to apply CTF as part of its counterterrorism strategy. One scholar noted that, although Turkey was late including CTF into its counterterrorism agenda, it has recently understood the importance of dealing with the financial activities of terrorists such as PKK and other religiously motivated terrorist organisations or the ones which are supported from abroad. While this concept is quite new, Turkey has put significant effort in terms of curbing terrorist

53 Interview with a Middle Level CTF Practitioner from a Law Enforcement Agency No: LE4.
54 Interview with a Senior Level Judge from the Department of Justice No: JD1.
55 Interview with a Middle Level CTF Practitioner from a Law Enforcement Agency: LE6.
56 Interview with a Senior Level CTF Expert from the Turkish FIU – MASAK No: FIU4.

funding.[57] Similarly an FIU practitioner noted that, "[f]inancing of terrorism is a very important subject. It can be said that in terms of combating financing of terrorism there have been some efforts in Turkey in recent years, whereas there were not any initiatives before. [. . .] After 2007, new efforts have started to take place. In this context financing of terrorism became a crime in 2006".[58]

Therefore, it can be claimed that Turkey's modern CTF regime is just over ten years old, and there had been hardly any initiative to curb terrorist financing prior to that.

Besides Turkey's genuine endeavour to fulfil its international obligations, counter-terrorism experiences and regimes from other countries have had a degree of influence in Turkey's 'eventual' integration of CTF as a part of its counter-terrorism (CT) strategy. It was noted by a MASAK director that Turkey has started to implement CTF and related applications following other countries' counter-terrorism experiences, such as the UK, the US and Spain.[59] These experiences enlightened Turkey for using counter-terrorist financing methods. As one scholar stated, "[i]n addition, [countries] imitate counter-terrorism policies of each other. So, other countries' applications etc. are modelled and/or held up as an example. Once terrorism and terrorist organisations which are active in other countries have been examined, different counter-terrorism methods (e.g. CTF) have naturally been conceived; thus, Turkish executives have understood the significance of financing of terrorism for eliminating terrorist movements".[60]

As CTF has become a prominent subject within anti-terrorism strategies across the world, especially after the 9/11 terrorist attacks in the US, Turkey has contributed to this development, and CTF has taken its place in the agendas of the Turkish security bureaucracy. The determining factor for Turkey's case seems to be the mandate and pressure established by the international organisations such as the UN, the EU, the FATF, NATO and influential countries such as the US and the UK. As a member of these organisations (with the exception of the EU), Turkey had to respond to the expectations as a strategic partner in the Middle East and as a neighbour to the EU and fulfil its obligations.

While Turkey has focused on CTF at the international fora by targeting international terrorist organisations such as Al Qaeda and its affiliates, the financial activities of terrorist organisations operating inside Turkey such as PKK were given a scant attention. Thus, Turkey has approached the issue of CTF from an international perspective in light of its international responsibilities, yet as our interviews revealed, the level of CTF action on terrorist threats on Turkey's national security was in most part omitted and inadequate. Another issue which

57 Interview with a Scholar who is an Expert on Security Studies – Professor at a University No: AC4.

58 Interview with a (former) Senior Level Director from MASAK No: FIU3.

59 Interview with a (former) Senior Level Director from MASAK No: FIU3.

60 Interview with Scholar who is an Expert on Security Studies – Professor at a University No: AC4.

emerged from the interviews is that there are different threat perceptions and prioritisation of threats between Western countries and Turkey. These differences have a bearing on the terms of what might be a terrorist financing activity and how one should counter it. One of the major differences stems from the security environment in which the CTF must be instilled: While the CTF practice in the West has mainly focused on financing of terrorism in the context of a religiously motivated terrorism thus utilised CTF methods to prevent and counter these types of terrorist financing structures for potential attacks in the future, for Turkey, the financial activities of terrorist organisations constitute an active threat whereby these organisations are engaged in an armed conflict with Turkish security forces on a daily basis. Thus, the CTF methods must be part of immediate and on-going armed response to terrorism. This shows that the security environments in which the international CTF measures are meant to be implemented are different, and there is a divergence between Turkey and its foreign counterparts on this issue.

5.3 Legal and institutional structure

In this part, the current legal and administrative aspects of the CTF regime in Turkey are examined. By doing this, we aim to evaluate the effectiveness, efficacy and adequacy of the current legal and administrative structure for CTF. The analysis is informed by our findings from the interviews, official documents and reports. As is mentioned in Chapter 4, Turkey has a long and painful past as a victim of terrorism and experience experienced countering terrorism threats, yet the field of dealing with financing of terrorism is quite new for Turkey. The main question which was posed to the CTF experts, practitioners and academics was this:

> *What do you think about the provisions of legal, administrative and institutional structures for CTF in Turkey?*

By asking this generic and open question, we aimed to find out to what extent the legal system, recent amendments and regulations meet the demands of the practitioners for conducting an effective CTF regime. Generally, the mainstream answer for this question is that there is no major problem with the existing legal framework in general and the current CTF regime in particular in terms of meeting the needs of CTF practitioners. Nevertheless, there are some minor deficiencies in the legal framework that need to be addressed. Similarly, in terms of administrative structure, practitioners seem to be generally satisfied though there are some criticisms regarding the bureaucratic structure of the CTF system in Turkey.

Another question for the interviewees was whether and to what extent the FATF mandated CTF system and measures suit Turkey's unique security problems. In this regard, the influence of international organisations, such as FATF, on Turkey in terms of coercing Turkey to establish and comply with CTF standards, measures and especially the adequacy of the latest legislation on Prevention of Terrorist Financing are discussed. Furthermore, the influence of FATF, the UN, the EU and countries like the US on shaping the Turkish CTF regime as well as the pros and cons of the recent amendments and regulations of CTF are discussed. In order to understand the level of adequacy and the effectiveness of the legal system, the administrative structure is analysed separately.

It is concluded that, even though there are different ideas regarding the compatibility of the international CTF regime for Turkey, the adequacy and provisions of the legal and institutional CTF regime in Turkey is deemed to be satisfactory by the experts, practitioners and scholars of CTF. However, we opine that there is room for improvement in several areas of the CTF regime in Turkey.

5.3.1 Legal structure

In the previous chapter, the main legislative pillars of counter-terrorism and CTF (namely the Turkish Criminal Code, the Anti-Terrorist Law, the Prevention of Financing of Terrorism and the Law on Prevention of Laundering Proceeds of Crime and other key legal instruments) were described in detail. In this section, the level of adequacy and effectiveness of the CTF legal framework will be analysed.

Regarding the question on the adequacy and efficacy of the CTF legal framework in Turkey, most of the interviewees indicated that it is, by stating that the CTF legal provisions provide the necessary powers and procedures for carrying out effective CTF operations and that Turkey has an adequate legal basis for conducting CTF activities. One of the law enforcement practitioners said that: "I experienced in some cases that I dealt with, it [CTF legislations] is adequate".[61] Similarly, another law enforcement member said that: "[t]here is an adequate legal base and powers for fighting against financing of terrorism in Turkey".[62] Another practitioner also added that: "[i]n my opinion, I assess that it is enough; moreover I evaluate this as more than we should need when I compare it with the international community. The idea I have is that [Turkey] did more than enough on this issue".[63] A judge briefly noted that: "According to my assessment, the legal base is adequate".[64] Additionally, an EU expert on Turkey reaffirmed this line of thinking by emphasising that:

> Well, let me say like that while thinking the level of awareness that our politicians have on this subject, both existing legal and institutional bases are perfect. This is because we do not have such an issue in our agenda. Even though there are some on-going critics, we have a perfect, completely

61 Interview with a Middle Level CTF Practitioner from a Law Enforcement Agency: LE6.
62 Interview with a Senior Level CTF practitioner from a Law Enforcement Agency No: LE3.
63 Interview with a Senior Level CTF practitioner from a Law Enforcement Agency No: LE2.
64 Interview with a Senior Level Judge from the Department of Justice No: JD2.

FATF aligned thing. [Asked by us: awareness?] No, we have the legal system.[65]

It can be asserted that Turkey's CTF legislation mainly provides the standards of international agreements and resolutions. From a financial intelligence perspective, one FIU practitioner stated:

> When we put together both international conventions and our legislation [in Turkey] we can see that more or less the offence of financing terrorism created by us is nearly at the same level as international conventions. Especially with the latest legislation [Prevention of Financing of Terrorism Law], we see that the mechanism of asset freezing has been acquired.[66]

Our findings from the interviews indicate that the CTF practitioners think that the CTF regime in Turkey provides the necessary legal base and powers for authorities to conduct CTF operations, yet based on these provisions, it cannot be claimed that the CTF legislation in Turkey is completely compatible with the international standards owing to certain sensitivities in Turkey's unique political and security spheres and operational capabilities. It was acknowledged that every country has a degree of deficiency in their CTF regimes and it was noted that "it will be very ambitious to assert that [Turkey] has a 100 percent perfect legal base".[67] From a customs and border control perspective, it was asserted that "[i]t seems that legal and institutional situation is adequate. Especially in terms of cash controls and SARs regulated by MASAK [FIU] are important here. In customs, cash control reports can be monitored online. [. . .] In this sense, it can be said that our legislation is adequate".[68]

The interviews also indicate that there is a consensus on one of the key problems affecting the CTF: the implementation of legal provisions – in other words, law in action. One of the academic experts expressed that: "[f]rom the start [. . .] I have not believed that the problem is caused by the legal base. Rather the mentality, culture and the implementation of legal provisions are the key problematic parts of the issue".[69] Another scholar pointed out that despite the fact that the existing legislations for combating terrorism and terrorist financing are adequate, there is a need for competent and well-trained personnel and coordination between institutions.[70] One of the CTF practitioners noted that: "as long

65 Interview with an Expert on EU-Turkey Relations and Terrorism, No: EU1.

66 Interview with a Senior Level CTF expert from the Turkish FIU – MASAK No: FIU1.

67 *Ibid.*

68 Interview with a Senior Level Expert from the General Directorate of Customs Enforcement No: CO1.

69 Interview with a Scholar who is an Expert on International Law – Professor at a University No: AC7.

70 Interview with a Scholar working as a CTF Practitioner Expert on counter-terrorism and radicalisation No: AC6.

as you are implementing effectively, I think the existing legislations, regulations and Law no: 6415 [Law on Prevention of Financing of Terrorism] do not have deficiencies for now".[71] On this point the words of a senior level director from FIU are worth citing:

> I think that the legislation is adequate. Existing laws are adequate for combating but again as I said before it is not important to have an adequate legislation if you cannot address the difficulties in application of it. What these difficulties are, the lack of coordination and cooperation, turf wars between institutions, lack of training and timidity of responsible personnel.[72]

These narratives reveal that Turkey's legal base is assessed as adequate in order to combat against financing of terrorism. However, the main concern emerges from their implementation and application in practice.

Beyond our findings via the interviews, due consideration needs to be given to the FATF reports on Turkey. The Third FATF Mutual Evaluation Report on Turkey (which has been followed up by subsequent reports) finds similar trends in Turkey's CTF regime (FATF, 2007). In regards to the legal base for CTF, FATF's on-going review of compliance report reports assesses the situation as follows:

> Turkey has demonstrated progress in improving its AML/CFT regime; however, the FATF has determined that certain strategic AML/CFT deficiencies remain. Turkey has made a high-level political commitment to work with the FATF to address these deficiencies, including by:
>
> (1) adequately criminalising terrorist financing (Special Recommendation II); and
> (2) implementing an adequate legal framework for identifying and freezing terrorist assets (Special Recommendation III) (FATF, 2010a).

After this report in 2010, several other reports were published by the FATF. One of these identified deficiencies in relation to the legal base of CTF measures. The public statement about Turkey after the plenary meeting of the FATF on 17–19 October 2012 is worth mentioning here because it stated that "[. . .] [FATF] is deeply concerned by Turkey's continued failure to take action to fully criminalise terrorist financing and establish an adequate legal framework for identifying and freezing terrorist assets consistent with the FATF Recommendations" (FATF, 2012c). Moreover, in the same statement, Turkey is warned of being subject to suspension of its membership in case of not meeting the conditions demanded by the FATF (FATF, 2012c). This indicates that there were serious concerns

71 Interview with a Senior Level CTF Expert from the Turkish FIU – MASAK No: FIU4.
72 Interview with a (former) Senior Level Director from MASAK No: FIU3.

over the legal base and suitability of the existing CTF provisions at that time. As a consequence of such shortcomings, Turkey was put on a list of countries with CTF deficiencies.

Subsequently, Turkey enacted new CTF laws, issued regulations, repealed old laws and amended a number of CTF related statutes. Following the Fifteenth Report of Mutual Evaluation on Turkey in 2014, the FATF decided to remove Turkey from the list of "[. . .] jurisdictions which have strategic AML/CTF deficiencies [. . .]", and Turkey became a jurisdiction no longer subject to the FATF's on-going global AML/CTF compliance process (FATF, 2014c). According to this public statement issued on 24 October 2014, Turkey has been evaluated as meeting the legal and regulatory requirements and demands of the FATF. By October 2014 the FATF was satisfied with Turkey's AML/CTF legal framework.[73] Accordingly, it can be argued that Turkey's CTF related legal base was not interpreted as adequate until 2014, and the CTF regime was influenced and shaped by pressure from an international organisation. In the course of several evaluation reports between 2007 and 2014, Turkey's CTF regime has been transformed and improved by the FATF. As of today, it can be claimed that both domestic and international parties agree that Turkey has an adequate legal base for CTF. Although the legal base for CTF is accepted as satisfactory, some interviewees raised a couple of important issues and according to them, there are certain elements in the legislation that need to be fixed.

In order to conduct a more effective CTF campaign, it is claimed that there is a need for more flexibility and autonomy in terms of operational and bureaucratic capabilities. However, within the confines of the current CTF system, it is not possible to have this freedom. In terms of CTF or AML for example, while foreign counterparts are being able to conduct operations all around the world in order to arrest terrorists or money launderers by establishing fake firms or banks in different jurisdictions and locations, Turkey cannot conduct such operations due to its legal and bureaucratic constraints.[74] It is believed that if Turkey has this kind of capability and flexibility it might be able to conduct more successful CTF operations against terrorists and money launderers.[75]

73 According to this public statement: "The FATF welcomes Turkey's significant progress in improving its AML/CFT regime and notes that Turkey has established the legal and regulatory framework to meet its commitments in its action plan regarding the strategic deficiencies that the FATF had identified in February 2010. Turkey is therefore no longer subject to the FATF's monitoring process under its on-going global AML/CFT compliance process. Turkey will work with the FATF as it continues to address the full range of AML/CFT issues identified in its mutual evaluation report" (FATF, 2014c).

74 Operation Dinero can be given as a suitable example for an innovative law enforcement ML and drug trafficking operation. Setting up a fictitious bank, RHMT Trust, front companies and bank accounts in Antiquilla, this sting operation was conducted against the Cali Cartel by both DEA and IRS agents in 1993 in order to prevent their money laundering and drug trafficking activities (Chepesiuk, 2003, pp. 101–103).

75 Interview with a Senior Level CTF Expert from the Turkish FIU – MASAK No: FIU1.

The role of international pressure

International organisations play a significant role in setting the standards and guiding principles for CTF and determining which actors should be responsible for executing these measures. In this context, FATF, as we mentioned earlier, emerges as one of the important organisations shaping the global CTF framework. However, although the term 'task force' implies an informal, flexible and temporary organisation, with its bureaucratic structure and links with global counter-terrorism organisations, powerful states, non-states organisations, multinational businesses, banking and financial sectors, the FATF emerges as a robust organisation for managing global risks by setting global standards and building capacity (Heng & McDonagh, 2009, p. 13). Although FATF does not have any formal treaty for its establishment, in practice, with its 40+ Recommendations framework, mutual evaluation system and with the UNSC backing, it functions as a formal type organisation (Heng & McDonagh, 2009, p. 15) with a considerable degree of legitimacy and persuasion for compliance. Moreover, FATF manages risks globally, and as Heng and McDonagh (2009, p. 22) argue, "[i] t is often power and coercion rather than voluntary consensus on risk that bring about agreement and compliance" in this system. It can be claimed that Turkey has not been exempt from the FATF's influence.

It would not be an exaggeration to state that Turkey has gone through a rough time with the FATF regarding its compliance and implementation of the recommended CTF/AML measures. The FATF's Third Mutual Evaluation Report on Turkey in 2007 listed numerous deficiencies in the Turkish CTF system including the legal system and institutional regulations; preventive measures, financial institutions, designated non-financial businesses and professions; legal persons and non-profit organisations and national and international cooperation (FATF, 2007). According to this report, the total number of suspicious transaction reports sent to the FIU (MASAK) by the banking sector, given the size of the Turkish economy, was very limited in general, and there were no reports sent by and/or from the financial services community. In addition, it was stated that the number of convictions and discovered violations was very low, and the existing preventative measures were inadequate. These were core issues for FATF because by failing them, Turkey was exposing foreign financial institutions and investors to potential terrorist financing threats (FATF, 2007; Keatinge, 2014).

During the process of the mutual evaluations, which took place in February, June and October 2010, Turkey was depicted as a country with "certain strategic AML/CTF deficiencies". These deficiencies included the lack of provisions which criminalise terrorist financing and a legal framework for identifying and freezing terrorist assets (FATF, 2010a, 2010b, 2010c). Due to the unsatisfactory compliance, Turkey was placed into FATF's 'grey list' in 2011 among other countries such as Bolivia, Ethiopia, Kenya, Myanmar, Sri Lanka and Syria (Keatinge, 2014). In the beginning of 2011, Turkey was warned for not making sufficient progress in implementing its action plan and addressing the deficiencies identified (FATF, 2011c). Similarly, according to subsequent reports, it was stated that even though Turkey had taken some positive steps such as submitting its new CTF legislation to the parliament for approval, it had failed to address the earlier deficiencies adequately (FATF, 2011a, 2011b). In June 2012, Turkey was singled out by FATF to enact the proposed CTF legislation and take substantive steps to address its deficiencies by the next meeting in October 2012. Moreover, FATF explicitly announced that it would "call upon its members to apply countermeasures proportionate to the risks associated with Turkey" (FATF, 2012b). According to Keatinge (2014), application of counter measures against Turkey would have caused curtailment of foreign investment flows and obstructed Turkey's access to the international financial system. Consequently, in October 2012 FATF made the following strict statement:

> [. . .] Given Turkey's continued lack of progress in these two areas, as a counter-measure, the FATF has decided to suspend Turkey's membership on 22 February 2013 unless the following conditions are met before that date:
>
> 1 Turkey adopts legislation to adequately remedy deficiencies in its terrorist financing offence; and
> 2 Turkey establishes an adequate legal framework for identifying and freezing terrorist assets consistent with the FATF Recommendations.
>
> FATF calls upon countries to take additional steps as necessary proportionate to the risks arising from the deficiencies associated with Turkey.
>
> (FATF, 2012a)

After this statement, some financial regulators such as the US Treasury Department's FinCEN released advisories regarding FATF's warnings (Keatinge, 2014). Just before the FATF deadline expired, Turkey enacted its new CTF legislation in February 2013, and FATF decided not to suspend its membership. Turkey's progress was welcomed by FATF because most of the deficiencies identified by FATF were addressed, most importantly, by introducing provisions which criminalised financing of terrorism. However, there were still some concerns remaining in the context of the asset freezing regime in Turkey (FATF, 2013). Since this last statement in 2013, Turkey has addressed most of the issues and concerns, and ultimately it was taken off the list of 'Jurisdictions with Strategic AML/CTF Deficiencies' and became a member of the jurisdictions no longer subject to FATF's on-going global AML/CFT compliance process (FATF, 2014c).

Turkey's progress on FATF compliance took more than seven years and was subject to various interactions between Turkey and FATF. These events evidence that Turkey has started addressing financing of terrorism not by its own accord and internal dynamics but rather because of international pressure, especially from FATF. Regarding this topic, as one of the FIU staff noted:

> There were some problems in terms of, especially, defining financing of terrorism crime and establishing asset freezing institution for complying special

> recommendations [of FATF]. However, Law no 6415 [Law of Prevention of Financing of Terrorism] has been enacted after especially FATF pushed us forward, put us into the 'grey list', consequently we were downgraded from list to list, and also the serious financial pressure on us had a role for this. This clearly shows that actually, it seems that combating against financing of terrorism in Turkey did not originate because of its core dynamics and its own requirements rather it became a[n] area of reform because of the international pressure.[76]

Even though this new CTF system has undoubtedly provided benefits to Turkey in the international fora, these changes were not triggered by domestic necessities or initiatives. As was already discussed, Turkey did not have a functioning CTF system in the past. Thus, as one interviewee claimed, this lack of will and CTF legacy on Turkey's part prolonged the implementation of FATF recommendations for a considerable time.[77]

Notably, during this period, the enactment of a specific CTF legislation was a major issue. Turkey submitted an action plan regarding its CTF system in January 2010 and committed to submit a draft CTF bill, which would be enacted by the end of 2010. The action plan and the draft bill were submitted to the prime minister as was promised; however, due to technical problems regarding some of the articles of the bill, the legislative enactment process was prolonged. Even though the draft bill was submitted to the parliament in February 2011, it was not put forward for a parliamentary vote until April 2011 because of the adjournment that took place for the upcoming elections in June of that year (Aydınonat, 2012, pp. 6–7). After the elections, the process started again and with the pressure from FATF, the draft CTF bill was negotiated in different parliamentary commissions and eventually enacted in February 2013.

As Shields (2005), Clunan (2006) and Heng and McDonagh (2009) note, the US, as the main sponsor and promoter of FATF, has a significant role in shaping the international CTF regime in accordance with its expectations, priorities and interests. However, it is not always clear as to how feasible and suitable these are for other countries which operate in different security environments with different social, legal, political and economic characteristics. A CTF practitioner noted that especially after the 9/11 attacks, the US has been shaping the international arena according to its interests and addressing threats using both soft and hard power methods.[78] In this context, the US has affected the UN, the EU and other related organisations and states. It is also claimed that the current CTF legislation and regulations, which have been adopted by Turkey, are in line with the US interests mainly because Turkey is one of the US's allied countries (as a

76 Interview with a (former) Senior Level Director from MASAK No: FIU2.

77 Interview with a Middle Level CTF Practitioner from a Law Enforcement Agency No: LE11.

78 Interview with a Middle Level CTF Practitioner from a Law Enforcement Agency No: LE8.

member of NATO) which is positioned strategically to the potential threats from the Russian Federation and the Middle East. Therefore, it can be argued that the recent CTF instruments are formed in line with the US's interests. However, it is not clear if and to what extent these new legal instruments have improved the CTF operations by law enforcement agencies and the ultimate level of security in Turkey.

The role and influence of external factors which have shaped Turkey's Western-driven CTF regime were acknowledged during the interviews. During the evolution of the CTF regime in Turkey, it is claimed by an expert that the US Treasury has put great pressure on Turkey toward the enactment of new CTF legislation and improve improving its CTF regime. It is also claimed that the US Treasury asked private banks to put pressure on the Turkish government in order not to jeopardise their financial relationship with the US banks and strengthen their AML/CTF frameworks. In this context, the main concern of the US Treasury was believed to be the alleged financial links between Turkey and Iranian banks which were subjected to sanctions by the US.[79] Furthermore, creation and development of Turkey's CTF regime in line with FATF standards were imposed on Turkey by the EU. In Turkey's accession process to the EU, one of the closing criteria of the financial chapter of its accession negotiation was the requirement to comply with the FATF 40+ Recommendations. In 2009, the EU deemed the Turkish progress in the fight against money laundering and CTF to be uneven both in terms of its legal framework and with regard to its administrative capacity to implement and enforce properly the relevant AML/CTF legislation (EU Commission, 2009, p. 44). Overall, it is clear that Turkey has adopted its terrorist financing legal framework mainly because of the pressure from the EU and the US.[80]

Country specific needs

At this point, one of the emerging questions is:

> *How suitable is the new CTF regime imposed by external actors on Turkey in dealing with its unique security threats and concerns?*

The idea is that every country and every threat need to be addressed according to their exclusive and unique conditions through specifically designed solutions and approaches at the local level rather than applying one system to remedy all problems. It should be restated here that the terrorism problem which Turkey is experiencing is different than that of other countries. While general and minimum international CTF measures and standards can be applied to some extent by all countries, without taking into account the efficacy of these in different cultural, social, economic and country specific conditions, such measures are destined to

79 Interview with an expert on EU-Turkey Relations and Terrorism, No: EU1.
80 Interview with an expert on EU-Turkey Relations and Terrorism, No: EU1.

have limited effect. According to a CTF practitioner, the current FATF measures do not address the security needs and terrorist threats in Turkey:

> The problems of Turkey are different, because every country has its own reality. [. . .] In this context general issues can be applied for Turkey or others, however, one country's own history, social, economic differences and its own specifications require a specially designed structure. Therefore, I do not think that the things FATF brought are addressing Turkey's problems.[81]

Additionally, regarding the aptness of the FATF based CTF regime for addressing Turkey's terrorist financing issues, another CTF practitioner emphasised that " [. . .] at least they [FATF formed regulations] are at the level of meeting [CTF] needs of Turkey, and moreover they did not emerge from our [Turkey] requirements".[82] One possible implication can be claimed that these measures did not emerge because of Turkey's own domestic requirements or demands; moreover, this legislative and administrative structure has been established by the directions of the FATF. Moreover, this system may not be successful addressing Turkey's terrorist financing problems.

It is also thought that due to the FATF influence and pressure, Turkey concentrates its efforts on fulfilling CTF obligations at the international level rather than domestic applications of its CTF campaign against domestic terrorism. According to CTF practitioners, nonetheless, the outcomes of these international level CTF efforts do not have direct effect on Turkey's terrorist financing related problems. As one practitioner noted:

> As I said in the beginning of my speech, the struggle against terrorism conducted within Turkey is completely ineffective. While the FATF's international fight [against financing of terrorism] is gaining importance, its positive outcomes do not affect us [Turkey's struggle against financing of terrorism] directly. Now, let us assume that Turkey has cut the financial sources of Al Qaeda terrorist organisation; ok it can cut it, so?! In fact, Al Qaeda does not have any assets in Turkey and they are not an active organisation in Turkey.[83]

International drivers as the main focus

From a financial sector perspective, a practitioner agreed with the abovementioned conclusion by reiterating that Turkey's domestic security problems and threats of terrorism are not addressed by the FATF standards. Rather, the

81 Interview with a Senior Level Expert from the General Directorate of Customs Enforcement No: CO1.

82 Interview with a Middle Level CTF Practitioner from a Law Enforcement Agency No: LE8.

83 Interview with a Middle Level CTF Practitioner from a Law Enforcement Agency No: LE4.

international CTF system, designed by FATF and the UN, mainly focuses on the terrorist threats faced by developed countries of the West. In this framework, it is claimed that the FATF system has a top-down structure that does not take into consideration domestic and specific conditions of Turkey. According to him, similar to other accounts, Turkey's own requirements and needs did not shape its current CTF system. Rather, Turkey has adopted the FATF's typologies of financing of terrorism. At present, it was noted that Turkey is mainly focusing on its international responsibilities of regulating key financial actors and enacting legislation in line with those in the EU and further afield rather than addressing financial capabilities of its domestic threats.[84] It is especially important to emphasise that forming a CTF typology or system according to the different terrorist organisations, their financing methods, conditions of the country and domestic terrorist threats are essential for the CTF success therein. As mentioned before, Turkey's main concern seems to be appearing to be compliant with international requirements and responsibilities instead of finding ways to address financial activities of terrorist threats at the national level.

As Biersteker and Eckert (2008a) argue, different terrorist organisations undertake terrorist attacks or activities for various reasons, and similarly their financing methods, instruments and capabilities differ significantly. Therefore, it is not desirable to develop CTF strategies and policies which ignore the DNA of each terrorist organisation. As Biersteker and Eckert opined, "[o]ne size does not fit all" (2008a, p. 297). Therefore, it may be argued that the CTF system formed by external influences and priorities may only have a limited degree of impact on addressing terrorists' financial activities in local contexts. FATF's CTF regime has a tendency towards generalising all terrorist organisations and addressing countries having the same characteristics and conditions. However, as explained earlier, Turkey has unique and specific terrorism threats and security conditions.

Consequently, it is not possible to fight against these terrorist groups with one-size-fits-all solutions. Therefore, every terrorist organisation operating in Turkey should be analysed and examined individually by specifically trained personnel. Then a Turkey specific CTF campaign, which is designed for each terrorist group separately, should be carried out. Furthermore, this kind of approach should be reviewed and updated in accordance with the evolution of the security environment. A senior level CTF practitioner noted that:

> As we said in the beginning [. . .] there should be some specifically designed strategies for terrorist organisations separately, because countries have their unique and different conditions. In other words, you have to have *sui generis* differentiating prevention techniques for DHKP/C, for Al Qaeda and for PKK terrorist organisations, because let's say while one of them has rural structure, other has urban organisation and the last one has cell structure. [. . .] While one of them can explode a bomb with the money taken from

84 Interview with a Senior Level Manager of a Bank Branch No: BS1.

> the bank as credit, other can do the same thing by taking commission from the drug trafficking, therefore adopting same methods or strategies it is not possible to fight against them. Consequently, this is possible only taking into account your own [country's] dynamics, analysing the features of terrorist organisations in our country separately and if you have experts who live and breathe with these terrorist organisations in cognitive sense. Shortly it should be country specific. [. . .] [S]o, let's say the financing methods of the PKK 10 years ago can become invalid now. Today's money transfers methods and usage of existing techniques can be invalid later, so they must be updated according to the situation.[85]

This is one of the important criticisms regarding the FATF led CTF regime. Mostly, the adoption of FATF's one-for-all type of CTF measures is not compatible with the context specific cases of individual countries. In this framework it may be better to design CTF regimes according to the specifications of the country, its internal and external dynamics, type of terrorist organisations operating and their financing activities.

Law No. 6415 – Prevention of financing of terrorism – Hurdles and outcomes

Notably, for the compliance progress of Turkey with the FATF Recommendations, the enactment of the Law on Prevention of Financing of Terrorism (2013) has played an important part. Because of internal factors within the Turkish legislative procedures and politics, this legislation and other expected transformations could not be set up by Turkey on time, and consequently Turkey faced several criticisms from FATF and other actors. An FIU expert elaborated on this issue by explaining that the political elections in Turkey and the Mavi Marmara crisis had caused the delay of the enactment of the draft bill.[86] He noted that after the 9/11 attacks, for FATF to design and establish an overall international CTF regime, comprising its recommendations and standards, took more than two years. Turkey promised to enact a new CTF legislation by 2011 during its meeting with FATF in 2010. However, legislating this code, which refers to the coordination of multiple institutions and dimensions, was not an easy task for Turkey at that time. In addition, as has been the case for many decades, because of the unpredictable

85 Interview with a (former) Senior Level Director from MASAK No: FIU2.

86 The Mavi Marmara case, also known as the Gaza Flotilla Raid, on 31 May 2010 Israeli military forces conducted an operation in international waters against six civilian ships. The Gaza Freedom Flotilla started their journey in order to prevent an Israeli blockade of the Gaza strip, and as a result of that operation nine civilian activists were killed by Israeli commandos. Both the Free Gaza Movement and the Turkish Foundation for Human Rights and Freedoms and Humanitarian Relief (IHH), which had been listed as outlaw charity organisations by the Israeli government since 2008 (The Meir Amit Intelligence and Terrorism Information Centre, 2008), organised this flotilla (BBC News, 2014).

and changing nature of the political diary in Turkey, it generally takes a long time for legislation to be passed in the parliament. The legislation process for this law was delayed because of the general elections in Turkey at that time. A further delay was caused by the Mavi Marmara crisis, wherein the Humanitarian Relief Foundation's (IHH), one of the main actors behind this crisis, was put on the designated terrorist organisations list by Israel as a terrorist financing organisation. A CTF expert noted that authorities in Turkey deliberated at length as to what would be the position of Turkey in case requests were made to freeze the assets of the IHH Foundation. Consequently, Turkey needed more time for finding a possible answer and solution and planning a road map, before enacting the CTF legislation.[87] Correspondingly Omer Suha Altan, the main opposition party member from Mugla province in Turkey, made a similar claim about Turkey's dilemma in enacting this law (Turkish Parliament – *Türkiye Büyük Millet Meclisi Tutanak Dergisi*, 2013a, p. 648). According to him the main problem regarding this law lies in the differing perceptions between Turkey and the US and EU countries in the context of identifying Hamas and Muslim Brotherhood organisations as threats and terrorist organisations. For instance, while Hamas is listed as a terrorist organisation by the US, Israel and the EU, for Turkey, Hamas is legitimately elected political party. For the Western powers, Turkey is an important actor for detecting, controlling and preventing financial sources of Hamas. Thus, the expectation was that Turkey would put into place legal provisions to prevent and punish Hamas. From the Turkish point of view, if such legislation was created following the pressure from the West, it would lose its credibility and the trust of Palestinian people. On the other hand, refusing to fulfil the demands against Hamas might have caused Turkey to face very harsh economic sanctions enforced by the West (Turkish Parliament – *Türkiye Büyük Millet Meclisi Tutanak Dergisi*, 2013a, pp. 648–649). This illustrates that compliance with the international CTF regime is not just about enacting legislation and regulations and implementing them; it is also about finding answers by calculating their cost and effectiveness in various socio-legal and socio-political environments where terrorism is a contentious issue and various interests both domestically and internationally are at stake.

A CTF practitioner who participated in the parliament discussions and observed the situation there stated that:

> When this 6415 [financing of terrorism law] was brought to the parliament, it was an interesting period because for the first time as a bureaucrat, I experienced such a thing that for the same legislation, both opposition and governing parties, surprisingly opposed to passing it. Everyone had different reservations at that time.[88]

87 Interview with a Senior Level CTF Expert from Turkish FIU – MASAK No: FIU4.
88 Interview with a Senior Level CTF Expert from the Turkish FIU – MASAK No: FIU1.

Moreover, it should be noted that the issues revolving around the proposed financing of terrorism law were not confined to international politics. The far-reaching powers conferred on the law enforcement agencies by this new statute, without any judicial oversight, were also an important factor in delaying its enactment. According to Turkish Parliament minutes on 6 February 2013, a day before enactment of the terrorist financing law, opposition parties emphasised the possibility of abuse of this new law for political purposes in order to silence and terminate opposition in the country. Regarding this issue, Ali Rıza Öztürk, an MP from the city of Mersin for the Republican People's Party (CHP), stated that, "[t]he main problem lies in the definition of terrorism made in our country regarding legislative activities on terrorism. Everyone who is dissident against the government can be accused of being a terrorist. In our country, what is mainly understood from a 'terrorist act' is that 'the act of being opponent against government" (*Türkiye Büyük Millet Meclisi Tutanak Dergisi*, 2013a, p. 616). In other words, it was believed and highlighted that with the enactment of this law, the government and security forces would have direct authority to freeze the assets of opposition parties, media institutions without any criminal investigation undertaken or decision following a judicial process. Moreover, Öztürk stated that they had their concerns and reservations, which were not addressed in the sub-commission's meetings. He added that "not only opposition parties have these concerns but also the governing party has some reservations and concerns regarding this law as well" (*Türkiye Büyük Millet Meclisi Tutanak Dergisi*, 2013a, p. 620).

In addition, the pro-Kurdish opposition party, the Peace and Democracy Party (BDP), had similar concerns regarding misuse of this law against them. In this regard, BDP MP Sırrı Süreyya Önder expressed their concerns by stating that:

> In other words this will be against the universal principles of law [. . .] and it will be transformed to a weapon that every new government can use against opposition (*Türkiye Büyük Millet Meclisi Tutanak Dergisi*, 2013a, p. 622). [. . .] In summary, today it [law on Prevention of Financing of Terrorism] is used against Kurds, tomorrow Turks, other day to rightists, other day to Islamists, later it turns to Alevites, the essence of this law is about transferring and taxing of wealth.
>
> (*Türkiye Büyük Millet Meclisi Tutanak Dergisi*, 2013a, p. 623).

Similar to Öztürk, Önder pointed out the reservations of the governing party, the Justice and Development Party (AKP), by noting that:

> Please check the minutes of the deliberations in the Internal Affairs Commission. Especially, I would like to appeal to the commission and the parliament. Most of the motions of amendments [for the law] have been given by the AKP's MPs. Why, because in its core this legislation has been prepared with an Islamophobic reflex.
>
> (*Türkiye Büyük Millet Meclisi Tutanak Dergisi*, 2013a, p. 621).

On the other end of the political spectrum in Turkey, the nationalist opposition party, namely the Nationalist Movement Party (MHP), had concerns similar to those of the other opposition parties on this issue. Enver Erdem, MP of MHP noted that:

> Distinguished members of parliament, with this regulation for the first time in Turkish justice system, an injunction will be implemented without a judicial decision. With this regulation, it will not be possible to seize the PKK terrorist organisation's assets, money and sources that are abroad. There is a risk that this legislation can be used for political purposes. Today when it is thought that the government characterised the Chief of General Staff [of the Turkish Armed Forces] as being the 'leader of [terrorist] organisation', [we have] the worry that the government can abuse this legislation.
>
> (*Türkiye Büyük Millet Meclisi Tutanak Dergisi*, 2013a, p. 654)

According to these accounts, all the opposition parties, along with the ruling party, had reservations about human rights issues, economic consequences and international relations regarding the implementation of the new CTF regime. Interestingly, an EU expert stated that the EU Delegation of Turkey tried to persuade opposition parties to support the new CTF laws by stating that it did not have any domestic usage and that it was all about protecting Turkey's international reputation:[89]

> This is like a joke well, we convinced them like that; we went to both CHP and HDP opposition parties and told them not to object the enactment of this legislation because this legislation does not have any domestic usage, but there is a reputation problem regarding this. Republican People's Party (CHP), main opposition, members were afraid to be associated with leftist terrorist organisations, correspondingly People's Democracy Party (HDP) also was afraid of the PKK thing. Of course, we went to them and said that we had talks with Turkish government before as the European Delegation and guaranteed and convinced them [opposition parties] that this legislation has nothing with domestic application.[90]

Despite these reservations and opposition, due to the majority the governing party had in the parliament, this legislation passed in the first round of the voting.[91] It can be concluded therefore that the current CTF legislation has been designed in a way that only addresses international requirements and expectations

89 Interview with an Expert on EU-Turkey Relations and Terrorism, No: EU1.

90 *Ibid.*

91 The law on Prevention of Financing of Terrorism was passed with the participation of 254 out of 550 MPs, of whom 231 voted for and 22 voted against it on 7 February 2013 (*Türkiye Büyük Millet Meclisi Tutanak Dergisi*, 2013b, p. 871).

and does not systematically take into account the domestic terrorist financing problems and the legal and political implications of these measures in Turkey.

Regarding the discussions on domestic usage and potential implications of this new legislation, it was also stated that in light of its context and objectives, the prevention of terrorist financing legislation only covers the UN designated threats but not domestic terrorist financing crimes, demonstrating that this legislation is an internationally forced instrument about which the Turkish government is unenthusiastic.[92] It is true that by this CTF regime, a new administrative asset freezing mechanism has been incorporated into the Turkish legal system, particularly in response to the UN Security Council Resolutions.[93] In this framework, Turkey has to fulfil the requirements of the UNSC Sanctions Committee's lists and undertake the asset freezing requests made by foreign states or can apply to foreign states for such orders. It is important to stress here that for all these processes to be initiated, there is no need for any legal authority and/or judicial decision. All the actions under the CTF regime can be executed through an administrative board and process. Article 7 of the Law on Prevention of Financing of Terrorism, 2013, stipulates the procedure for freezing of assets (which are subject to financing of terrorism crime) in Turkey. Accordingly, it puts forward a process governed by the Criminal Procedure Code No. 5271. In other words, Turkish citizens who are living in Turkey and their assets are subjected to the normal legal seizure procedure, which is regulated in Criminal Procedure Code No. 5271. Therefore, it might be correct to say that the asset freezing mechanism as being a new method introduced by this law only covers the asset freezing listings of the UN Security Council Sanctions Committee and the demands of foreign states.

It is worth considering here that if asset freezing is deemed to be a significant and fast way of dealing with financing of terrorism which is incumbent upon the states owing to legal obligations (via conventions, resolutions, etc.), then why did Turkey not incorporate or apply this measure in its domestic CTF regime? According to Özgenç (2013, p. 206) who participated in the preparations of this legislation and advised relevant commissions (e.g. interior affairs and justice) in the parliament as an expert, this legislation was not prepared and enacted because of Turkey's own immediate security requirements and priorities in terms of its counter-terrorism efforts. Moreover, he opines that this legislation was enacted following the pressure by the US and the UK, using FATF as an intermediary (Özgenç, 2013, pp. 206, 207, 209).

Examination of the minutes of the meetings of the Turkish parliament and internal affairs and justice commissions reports reveals a number of important concerns. Firstly, the new asset freezing mechanism may be used against opposition or any other company both by the Turkish government and requests by

92 Interview with a Scholar who is an Expert on International Law – Professor at a University No: AC7.

93 For example, UN Security Council Resolutions 1390, 1456 and 1566.

foreign states without judicial oversight. Therefore, there is a risk to human rights (freedom of expression and the right to property, to name a few) which are protected by the Turkish Constitution (*Türkiye Büyük Millet Meclisi Tutanak Dergisi*, 2013a) as well as international and regional legal instruments. Özgenç (2013, pp. 207–208) points to the dangers of the implementation of the asset freezing mechanism by an administrative procedure. Although both governing party MPs and especially the Minister of Finance have expressed that this legislation does not have any domestic usage against Turkish citizens living in Turkey, according to Article 6, asset freezing requests by foreign states can be entertained, without undertaking any judicial process, against both Turkish citizens and companies in Turkey, and their assets can be frozen indefinitely merely by an administrative decision. Özgenç (2013, p. 207) calls this situation 'total confiscation' punishment which is clearly forbidden according to Article 38 of the Turkish Constitution (1982).[94] Although during the deliberations in the Turkish Grand National Assembly, the Minister of Finance Mehmet Şimşek denied these claims by arguing that decisions for the asset freezing demands would be made by the Council of Ministers according to the reciprocity principle (*Türkiye Büyük Millet Meclisi Tutanak Dergisi*, 2013a, p. 645), there is still a possibility that this law can be applied without due regard to human rights and constitutional guarantees.[95]

Secondly, the debates on the definitions of 'terrorism' in the Turkish legal system and with reference to the UN Convention appear as another significant concern (*Türkiye Büyük Millet Meclisi Tutanak Dergisi*, 2013a) in the context of CTF legislative initiatives. Turkey's own terrorism definition, specific to its own national security threats, is provided in the Anti-Terrorism Law (1991)[96] which has been incorporated into the new CTF law. This definition is rather conflated with international resolutions and conventions; thus, it is relatively less relevant and specific in terms of the types of terrorism which are rife in Turkey, yet it embraces some of the universal interpretations. However, it is claimed by some of the MPs that the part of the definition taken from the Anti-Terrorism Law (1991) can be interpreted broadly, and anyone can easily be subjected to this definition due to the fragile state of the legal system and the rule of law in Turkey.[97] Regarding this, while the BDP Party suggested using the terrorism term defined in the ICSFT (1999), others proposed changing the definition written in the convention by application to the UN, because the definition of terrorism under the UN Convention poses problems for Turkey (Özgenç, 2013, pp. 168–170). For instance, Article 1, paragraph 1/b of the ICSTF (Turkey put

94 Article 38 of the Turkish Constitution states that "[n]either death penalty nor general confiscation shall be imposed as punishment" ("Türkiye Cumhuriyeti Anayasası (Constitution of the Republic of Turkey)," 1982).

95 Özgenç (2013, p. 207) shares the same concerns regarding the possibility of human and constitutional rights violations.

96 See pages 20–21.

97 According to the latest 'rule of law' index 2017–18, Turkey is ranked 101 among 113 countries (World Justice Project, 2018).

a reservation on that part of that convention) provides that only attacks which are against civilians are counted as terrorist attacks.[98] Therefore, according to the literal interpretation of the Convention's definition, the terrorist attacks by PKK against Turkish security forces including police, gendarmerie and soldiers cannot be regarded as terrorist attacks. As Dilek Akagün Yılmaz, a CHP MP, noted, putting a reservation on this part of the convention represented Turkish interests and Turkey's reservation, and its security priorities were not significant matters for other countries which are signatory to this convention (*Türkiye Büyük Millet Meclisi Tutanak Dergisi*, 2013b, p. 828).

Another concern or pressure point for Turkey was the economic burden of implementing the new CTF regime. It seems that Turkey was caught between the East and the West on this issue. Some said enacting this legislation would decrease the foreign investment coming from mainly Gulf and Middle Eastern countries due to the risk created by the abusive and Islamophobic characteristics of the blacklisting system implemented in the world (*Terörizmin Finansmanının Önlenmesi Hakkında Kanun Tasarısı ile İçişleri Komisyonu ve Adalet Komisyonu Raporları*, 2013, p. 26; *Türkiye Büyük Millet Meclisi Tutanak Dergisi*, 2013a, p. 621; *Türkiye Büyük Millet Meclisi Tutanak Dergisi*, 2013b, p. 818). On the other hand, it was noted that failing to fulfil the responsibilities established by Western states could bring about higher economic ramifications for Turkey especially in terms of its integration with the international financial sector and investment from these countries (*Türkiye Büyük Millet Meclisi Tutanak Dergisi*, 2013a, pp. 616, 622, 629, 648; *Türkiye Büyük Millet Meclisi Tutanak Dergisi*, 2013b, p. 826).

Besides the economic ramifications of non-compliance with FATF recommendations, FATF's threat to suspend Turkish membership, thus the possibility of being placed along with North Korea and Iran on the same blacklist would not be good in terms of Turkey's reputation and country image. The records indicate that during the speeches in parliament, the new CTF legislation was argued to be necessary to serve the protection of Turkish interests and its reputation (*Türkiye Büyük Millet Meclisi Tutanak Dergisi*, 2013a, pp. 634–639).

What is also interesting to note is that in these parliamentary debates and commission reports the discussions were mostly about PKK terrorism and its financial capabilities and activities as if PKK was the only terrorist group active in Turkey. To some extent it is natural that the focal point of discussions was PKK because in comparison to other terrorist organisations, PKK is the most significant and imminent threat to Turkey's national security. However, this kind of approach might give clues how narrow the perceptions are regarding the existence of other

98 According to the Article 2 paragraph 1/b of the International Convention for Suppression of the Financing of Terrorism (1999), "[a]ny other act intended to cause death or serious bodily injury to a civilian, or to any other person not taking an active part in the hostilities in a situation of armed conflict, when the purpose of such act, by its nature or context, is to intimidate a population, or to compel a government or an international organization to do or to abstain from doing any act".

threats and transformation of terrorist organisations other than PKK. Another issue is that some experts [99]interviewed believe and state similar to the MPs, that in order to finish terrorist organisations, cutting off their financial sources would be enough. However, the validity of this presupposition is open to debate given the wide range of financing opportunities that are available to terrorist organisations.

Contrary to the claims that the FATF's CTF system is not suitable for Turkey's security requirements, the debates in the Turkish Parliament supports the idea that this legislation enhances Turkey's position on CTF. Similar to the Minister of Finance Mehmet Simsek (*Türkiye Büyük Millet Meclisi Tutanak Dergisi*, 2013a, pp. 634–639), an FIU expert noted that even though some groups and parties evaluate these FATF based CTF measures as dangerous and counter-productive for Turkey's interests, actually these new legal codes and regulations could improve Turkey's position for robust international cooperation, increasing the effectiveness of its CTF. Using these CTF measures, Turkey can ask other countries to freeze the assets of PKK or DHKP/C in line with the requirements of the UNSC Resolution 1373 (2001). If they do not carry out Turkey's request, then the issue can be discussed on legitimate international platforms. Furthermore, given their legal status and the gravity of political power, these international legal instruments can be utilised by Turkey in order to coerce other countries which are reluctant to cooperate on a bilateral basis.[100] It was also claimed by the same interviewee that the new CTF regime has positive effects for the development of Turkey's economy, rather than harming it. With the recent changes on reporting, KYC and regulator measures, the integrity and strength of the Turkish financial sector have been bolstered. Moreover, these regulations are likely to decrease the level of the informal/unrecorded economy in Turkey. Thus, from a financial perspective, the new CTF provisions are useful for Turkey. In this context, Turkey should concentrate on how to utilise these legal tools in order to conduct a more effective CTF in the face of its domestic terrorist threats rather than implementing them on their face value superficially.[101]

In conclusion, it can be asserted that the major drivers for Turkey to enact the CTF legislation were: avoidance of international sanctions, pressure from international organisations and powerful states and protecting the reputation of Turkish state and its economy.

These conclusions are supported by the EU expert interviewee who opined that in order to avoid negative outcomes of non-compliance and to protect the country's reputation and interests, Turkey has adopted the new CTF measures. He further added that the main purpose of adopting this legislation was to de-list

99 This understanding of the issue was stated during the interviews with senior level Judge from Department of Justice No: JD1, senior level CTF practitioner from Law Enforcement Agency No: LE2, senior Level CTF practitioner from Law Enforcement Agency No: LE3 and senior level CTF practitioner from Law Enforcement Agency No: LE7.

100 Interview with a Senior Level CTF Expert from the Turkish FIU – MASAK No: FIU1.

101 *Ibid.*

Turkey from the FATF's grey list. Fighting terrorism and its financial sources was not the primary objective behind this legislation. Even though every political party has a different and limited level of perception and interest on CTF, ultimately, the new CTF legislation is a welcome addition to the statute books.[102]

Another law enforcement practitioner identified the reputational issue being as one of the key factors for compliance and added that "[i]t is important to protect national interests. In this context in order to protect our national interests, we must adopt our legal system in line with those requirements from the UN and the FATF".[103] In addition, the Minister of Finance, Mehmet Şimsek, said that "[. . .] [t]his [CTF] legislation will seriously strengthen our hands and improve Turkey's reputation [. . .]" (*Türkiye Büyük Millet Meclisi Tutanak Dergisi*, 2013b, p. 832). The Turkish Parliament discussions and the accounts from our interviews clearly demonstrate how reputational concerns and national interest influenced the shaping of CTF in Turkey.

An FIU expert answered the question of whether newly passed CTF legislation meets the expectations. According to him, although there are some minor deficiencies, the CTF legal regime meets most of the requirements of the FATF, and it has similar characteristics and provisions to other developed CTF legislation across the world.[104] Another FIU expert argued that Turkey could and should have incorporated freezing mechanisms and other issues the way in which they can be applied domestically via making necessary amendments and regulations in order to speed up the legal process.[105] Even though the FATF did not de-list Turkey from its grey list immediately after the enactment of the CTF law, on 24 October 2014, it recognised Turkey's efforts and amendments in re-shaping its CTF framework and deemed it satisfactory (FATF, 2014d).

While Turkey eventually performed its *jus cogens* responsibilities and brought its CTF regime in line with international standards, a number of Turkish CTF experts argued that there remain various difficulties regarding domestic application of the new CTF provisions, which could have been addressed when the opportunity was there at the drafting stage of this new statute.[106] On the other hand, another expert claimed that "it is a good thing that this CTF legislation does not have domestic usage".[107] Correspondingly, according to a scholar, there are still concerns that government can use this legal tool for eliminating dissent. Ultimately, it was argued that it is not clear if and what kind of supervision or judicial oversight has been taking place regarding the implementation of this CTF regime.[108]

102 Interview with an Expert on EU-Turkey Relations and Terrorism, No: EU1.
103 Interview with a Senior Level CTF practitioner from Law Enforcement Agency No: LE3.
104 Interview with a (former) Senior Level Director from MASAK No: FIU2.
105 Interview with a Senior Level CTF Expert from the Turkish FIU – MASAK No: FIU1.
106 *Ibid.*
107 Interview with an Expert on EU-Turkey Relations and Terrorism, No: EU1.
108 Interview with a Scholar who is an Expert on International Law – Professor at a University No: AC7.

Furthermore, according to a senior level director from a law enforcement agency, the asset freezing mechanism which is conducted solely under an administrative and/or executive decision is problematic. Turkey does not have a Western type of law procedure, such as reverse burden of proof or civil forfeiture orders. While these shortcomings can be seen as a deficiency, the Turkish legal system adheres to the principle of '*in dubio pro reo*'.[109] In addition, law enforcement forces and public prosecution services have the responsibility of proving the crime, not the suspect.[110] This discussion indicates that having an asset freezing mechanism managed by an administrative board without judicial oversight is perceived as a threat to human rights and democracy in Turkey.

In this context, one of the problematic issues emanating from the CTF legislation is the application of Article 7, which regulates the terrorist financing committed within Turkey. If this is the case, according to Article 7, it is not possible to freeze the asset of a Turkish terrorist suspect or a supporter. In order to invoke an asset freezing order, legal authorities must start legal procedures according to the Turkish Criminal Procedure Law, and this process may take a while until an authorisation is given by the courts. However, Turkey can demand that a foreign country freeze the same terrorist's assets located in that country without a court order.

This demonstrates that the CTF legislation overlooks the domestic implementation of asset freezing orders and creates a big gap when prevention of terrorism via asset freezing order needs to be imposed swiftly. For instance, if a PKK terrorist has some amount of money in a bank in the capital city of Ankara which would be used for a terrorist attack in a few days' time, the CTF legislation does not allow this asset to be frozen immediately. Yet Turkey can apply to Belgium for an order freezing the same PKK terrorist's money which is deposited in a Belgium bank and have the assets frozen almost immediately. While it is not our intention to argue here whether administrative/executive asset freezing orders are better than those imposed following a lengthily legal procedure, it is worth pointing out that there is an inconsistency in the application of the same law for the same offence in different jurisdictions. An FIU expert identified the same inconsistency by saying that:

> The missing part of this legislation for addressing our requirements is that we have made this regulation in order to implement UNSCR 1373, to ask foreign countries and to fulfil the demands of other countries for freezing the assets of the terrorists in Turkey. [. . .] With this legislation, we did not provide ourselves an asset freezing mechanism, which can be applied swiftly to the terrorists operating in Turkey who we named following an investigation. Therefore, I would like to say that, if a PKK terrorist has 100 acres of estate beside Ministry of Finance, we could not seize this asset immediately with

109 This is a Latin phrase that roughly translates to 'someone is innocent until proven guilty'.
110 Interview with a Senior Level CTF Practitioner from a Law Enforcement Agency No: LE2.

> this legislation. Whereas for the same terrorist we can ask from Belgium state to seize the terrorist's 100 acres of estate located in Belgium. [. . .] It does not have to be an administrative model, for instance by appointing specially authorised prosecutors or other kind of mechanisms I believe that we should have incorporated into this law a swift and concentrated seizure mechanism for terrorist threats we have.[111]

Furthermore, Article 5 states that "[d]ecisions on freezing of asset under the possession of persons, institutions and organisations designated through the United Nations Security Council Resolutions 1267 (1999), 1988 (2011) and 1989 (2011) shall be executed without delay through the decision of the Council of Ministers published in the Official Gazette" ("Law on the Prevention of Financing of Terrorism", 2013). In other words, the application of this law is constrained by the narrow focus on specific terrorist threats and organisations such as the Taliban, Al Qaeda and its affiliates. Consequently, any future UN Security Council Resolutions on CTF measures for other or new terrorist organisations would not be implemented by the current CTF regime in Turkey until the CTF law is amended by the parliament. Currently, ISIS has been designated as an Al Qaeda affiliated terrorist group, and this organisation and its members have been put into the context of UN Security Council Resolution 1267. However, if the UN decides to change its stance on ISIS, or any other new different terrorist organisation, by accepting it as a separate entity from Al Qaeda and set out new counter measures to be undertaken with a new resolution (apart from UN Security Council Resolution 1267 and others), then Turkey's Prevention of Financing of Terrorism legislation could not be invoked for such new entities. Thus, it can be claimed that the current CTF regime in Turkey has limited application for a broader spectrum of terrorism and its financial activities.

Regarding this criticism, an FIU expert noted that: "[. . .] still the [asset freezing] decisions regarding ISIS is given based on previous decisions on Al Qaeda. In this context if only UN Security Council decides to make a new decision, then it might be possible that it [a new terrorist organisation] will be out of 6415's jurisdiction in terms of financial sanctions, I mean".[112] He also claimed that hypothetically speaking, if the links between ISIS with Al Qaeda totally disappear, then 6415 will not have any implementation area [for ISIS].[113]

As the designation of terrorist entities and what amounts to terrorism change over time, counter-terrorism measures in general and CTF measures in particular can become redundant and ineffective. Accordingly, focusing on particular crimes rather than who commits such crimes ought to drive the application of these measures.

111 Interview with a Senior Level CTF Practitioner from a Law Enforcement Agency No: LE2.
112 *Ibid.*
113 *Ibid.*

Advantages of new legislation and FATF compliance for Turkey

Besides these criticisms, there are positive elements that can be attributed to the CTF legislation which complies with the FATF standards. One of the advantages that has been claimed is that the new law will increase Turkey's capabilities in terms of countering financing of terrorism both internationally and domestically.

According to an FIU expert, before the enactment of this act, Turkey could not formally request asset freezing or blocking orders for terrorist organisations as there was no regulatory framework for it.[114] Now Turkey can apply to other states with its asset freezing mechanism introduced by the new CTF legislation in 2013. It is also believed that this legislation has led to the improvement of Turkey's capabilities against financing of terrorism in terms of drawing other states' attention and assistance towards domestic threats of Turkey.[115] Furthermore, according to another practitioner, "[t]he penalties and our legislation were adequate as I said before [in order to prevent this crime] yet, in this context I assess that this legislation is a good one in terms of [legislation] conforming with the international community".[116] Correspondingly, the former Finance Minister Mehmet Simsek was using a similar approach explaining the rationale behind this legislation by asserting that the new CTF legislation will strengthen Turkey's position in the international platforms, fulfil its duties and responsibilities under international treaties (*Türkiye Büyük Millet Meclisi Tutanak Dergisi*, 2013a, p. 639).

However, such claims can be contested to a certain extend because Turkey did have diplomatic and operational means and connections to reach such goals prior to the CTF regime of 2013. PKK, DHKP/C, the Kurdistan Freedom Falcons (TAK) (PKK affiliated organisation) and IBDA/C had been listed as terrorist organisations according to the EU Terrorist List (COE, 2015) well before 2013. For instance, PKK has been listed as a terrorist organisation by the EU since 2002, and for Turkey, the challenge has never been that it did not have a specific asset freezing request mechanism in its legislation to take action against PKK's financial activities, most of which are conducted in the EU member states. The existing legal, bureaucratic and diplomatic instruments such as mutual legal assistance or extradition demands could have been used pursuant to the UNSCR of 1373 (2001) and in line with the EU terrorist designation list for the purpose of targeting terrorist funds. Beside the UN Security Council Resolutions and EU's terrorist list, the UN Convention Against Transnational Organised Crime and its Protocol Against the Illicit Manufacturing and Trafficking Firearms, Their Parts and Components and Ammunition, Supplementing the United Nations Convention Against Transnational Organised Crime (which were signed by Turkey on 22 July 2002, UNODC, 2004) could also have been employed for both curbing

114 Interview with a Senior Level CTF Expert from the Turkish FIU – MASAK No: FIU4.

115 *Ibid.*

116 Interview with a Senior Level CTF Practitioner from the Department of Justice No: JD2.

the armament of PKK with weapons, and financing activities and financial assets for acquiring these weapons. However, it seems that Turkey was not able to make use of such international law provisions effectively and cooperate with other signatory states (Özgenç, 2013, p. 172) owing to complex factors beyond its control, such as who is designated as a terrorist, or political power balances in the region (e.g. in Syria, Iraq, Iran) which have been dominating the application and enforcement of CTF measures.[117]

Furthermore, according to the MASAK's Activity reports between 2013 and 2015, although the assets of one person in 2014 and seven individuals and seven entities assets have been frozen by Turkey as a result of asset freezing demands made by foreign countries in compliance with the latest terrorist financing legislation, there is no data regarding Turkey's demands from foreign countries for asset freezing of terrorists operating against Turkey (Financial Crimes Investigation Board, 2014, pp. 41–42, 2015, pp. 52–53, 2016, pp. 44–45). This may demonstrate that while Turkey is cooperating with other countries to fulfil their asset freezing demands, at the same time, in light of these reports, it is clear that Turkey has not been using the new CTF legislation for CTF related inquiries and/or requests from its foreign counterparts.

It should be noted here that while the new CTF regime does not have domestic application, as MP Hüseyin Türkoğlu pointed out in parliamentary discussions, "this kind of regulation creates a situation where Turkish national capital and financial system can be manipulated and even destroyed" (Türkiye Büyük Millet Meclisi Tutanak Dergisi, 2013b, p. 818). Indeed, the asset freezing mechanism established in Turkey does not apply to Turkish citizens in Turkey and to crimes committed in the jurisdictions of Turkish courts, whereas this is not the case for the UNSC Sanctions Committee decisions and requests from foreign states. Therefore, even though there is no direct influence of the international CTF regime domestically, there is a possibility that this legislation can have domestic impact.

For instance, the US delegation's visit to Turkey, which took place in August 2010 regarding the US government's sanctions on Iran,[118] was an interesting one confirming the above-mentioned concerns about external influences on Turkish banks and companies and their assets. Regarding this visit, a top executive of a large Turkish bank spoke to *Milliyet* (a Turkish mainstream newspaper) on the condition of anonymity and said that:

> Due to American pressure, a great problem is being experienced in money transfers from Iran to the Turkish banking sector. [. . .] The Americans have

117 For example, PYD and YPG, which are Syrian branches of the PKK terrorist organisation, are supported logistically and financially by the US and some of EU member states in order to fight against another terrorist organisation, ISIS.

118 The US sees Iran as a sponsor of terrorism and detests its nuclear power development programme (U.S. Department of State, 2018).

threatened us with freezing our assets abroad. We may also face a risk of arrest on our trips abroad if we carry out any transfers with those Iranian banks.

(Asbarez, 2010)

Moreover, it was reported that this delegation warned that they would put Turkey's leading public and private energy firms and companies such as TPAO and TÜPRAŞ on their designate lists if they did not terminate their economic relationship with Iran (Çakırözer, 2010, p. 8; Özgenç, 2013, p. 210). Thus, the concerns that the international CTF regime can be used by foreign powers for their political interests via putting pressure on financial and commercial institutions of other countries are real.[119]

5.3.2 Institutional structure

After the examination of the determinants of the legal base and the efficacy of the CTF regime in Turkey, this section considers the institutional structure of CTF and its effectiveness. For this purpose, the interviewees were asked what they think about the existing institutional CTF structure, whether the institutions function adequately for conducting CTF related tasks and if there is a need for establishing a new CTF institution or agency.

The interviews revealed that for some, the current institutional structure in Turkey which comprises law enforcement agencies, financial intelligence units and the customs agency, legal authorities which are adequate and well defined in terms of responsibilities and powers of implementation; therefore, there is no need for a new structure. For example, one of the law enforcement practitioners explained that Turkey has adequate CTF institutions, and the institution he works for and other relevant institutions have the necessary structures to conduct CTF operations, and they are working along with each other in coordination.[120] Reiterating this opinion, a bank manager argued that "the existing institutions in Turkey are adequate whereas in terms of its effectiveness, I think that they are not sufficient".[121] It could be said that existing institutions, which are responsible for CTF, are seen as adequate. However, these institutions need to improve their effectiveness.

119 It is worth noting that such political and diplomatic tensions are not confined to US-Turkish relations. For example, on 17 May 2018 the EU Commission announced its intention to implement the US blocking statute of 1996 (the EU Blocking Statute was originally introduced in 1996 to counteract the US's sanctions on Cuba, Iran, and Libya) to declare the US sanctions against Iran null and void in the EU and to ban European citizens and companies from complying with them. The Commission also instructed the European Investment Bank to facilitate European companies' investments in Iran (EU Commission, 2018a).

120 Interview with a Senior Level CTF Practitioner from a Law Enforcement Agency No: LE2.

121 Interview with a Senior Level Manager of a Bank Branch No: BS1.

On the other hand, a number of interviewees asserted that the current CTF structure in Turkey is not adequate, and there are systemic problems that need to be resolved by re-organisation of the CTF system. In this context, the institutional position of the FIU, MASAK, in the bureaucratic order and its legal powers need to be reformed.

Firstly, according to an FIU practitioner, the centralised organisational structure of the CTF system is problematic for Turkey. He suggested that rather than having a centralised structure, a horizontally organised structure may be more effective. Regarding MASAK, it is noted that while law enforcement agencies (the anti-terrorism police and military units) conduct operations in rural locations and demanding terrain, MASAK is situated in the capital city, Ankara, working as a desk based information centre only with immediate links to tax offices operating in some of the rural areas. Consequently, the assistance provided by MASAK is not beneficial or timely, nor is it of much value in hot pursuit of terrorists and against the guerrilla warfare tactics of terrorist active in Turkey. In order to address this gap, it is suggested that by restructuring the organisational structure whereby MASAK has more regional and local presence is necessary.[122] In other words, it is believed that by empowering MASAK in the bureaucratic order by establishing coordinated units operating at the local level where terrorism and terrorist financing are rife would provide better intelligence and evidence for law enforcement agencies. This would undoubtedly require serious investment in infrastructure, technical and personnel capacity.

Owing to the current position and competences of MASAK in the CTF regime, communication and liaison between MASAK and anti-terrorism units in rural areas are limited, which in turn can hamper the effectiveness of CTF. It is clear that this needs to be adjusted. MASAK does not have any organic links with districts of Turkey (Financial Crimes investigation Board, 2011b) far from Ankara and this shortcoming needs to be addressed perhaps at the first instance, by appointments of personnel who are FIU liaison officers working within the existing enforcement agencies which are well organised all over Turkey. By doing so, coordination, information exchange and transfer and other elements of CTF operations can be improved.

Moreover, according to the first two recommendations of the newly updated FATF Recommendations, states shall prepare their national risk assessment and establishment of a national CTF coordination unit (FATF, 2014e, p. 11).[123] An FIU expert interviewee hoped that during these efforts, Turkey may be compelled to adjust its CTF structure by addressing the current problems mentioned above. But this has not happened yet.

Another problem highlighted by the FIU expert was that owing to the misconception of the legal provisions, MASAK is perceived to be the sole institution

122 Interview with a Senior Level CTF Expert from Turkish FIU – MASAK No: FIU1.

123 These two recommendations are: 1R. Assessing risk and applying a risk based approach, and 2R. National cooperation and coordination (FATF, 2014e).

responsible for CTF in Turkey. According to one FIU expert, this is certainly not the case.[124] These problems may have led to a lack of both ownership of the operational issues and sense of responsibility for problems surrounding CTF by other counter-terrorism agencies and officials. For instance, the words of a legal official reveal the perception about MASAK: "I think that in this [CTF] struggle, MASAK should be used effectively, I assess that MASAK can be very effective in CTF".[125] As it can be seen, there are expectations from MASAK which are impossible for MASAK to deliver in the current legal and bureaucratical structures in Turkey.

It is generally accepted internationally that counter-terrorism and CTF should be conducted by interagency cooperation and strategies (i.e. information and intelligence exchange between various ministries, tax authorities, customs, immigration agencies, police, military, etc.) within the state and with foreign stakeholders.[126] However, our findings during the interviews indicate that MASAK is perceived and accepted as the only responsible and leading agency for CTF efforts in Turkey. Even though MASAK is authorised to conduct research and examination of suspicious activities regarding money laundering and terrorist financing pursuant to the Law on Prevention of Laundering Proceeds of Crime (2006), this does not mean that MASAK was appointed as the main coordinator for CTF or has any superior power over other counter-terrorism agencies to conduct CTF operations.

The AML and CTF legislation do not confer any authority to MASAK to pursue money launderers and terrorists or their supporters; rather, it is responsible for analysing SARs and inform the prosecution service about serious suspicious activities acquired from these reports and/or act on the orders sent from the public prosecution service by researching, examining or providing expertise on AML and CTF related investigations.[127] MASAK reiterates this duty by noting "[i]n its Recommendation 26, FATF requests countries to establish a national and central authority that receives and analyses STRs and sends them to relevant units. Within this framework, as the Turkish Financial Intelligence Unit, MASAK undertakes regulatory, supervisory and training functions as well as basic FIU functions" (Financial Crimes Investigation Board [MASAK], 2015, pp. 11–12).

While it is true that the new CTF legislation 2013, has given MASAK the responsibility as the secretary of asset freezing mechanism and that it has a significant role and responsibility for Turkey's CTF efforts, it was not appointed officially as the leading and sole institution responsible for CTF, contrary to the general perception.

124 Interview with a Senior Level CTF Expert from the Turkish FIU – MASAK No: FIU1.

125 Interview with a Senior Level CTF Practitioner from the Department of Justice No: JD2.

126 The key reason for this is that states no longer face a conventional threat that could be matched by the military might and capabilities of a single state or a unit.

127 MASAK also inspects the private financial sector to ensure compliance with AML/CTF obligations and offers training events.

Another issue is the position and status of MASAK[128] within the Turkish bureaucratic hierarchy.[129] An EU expert opined that:

> From MASAK's perspective, from the beginning, the location of MASAK in the Turkish public management has been wrong. As a subordinate agency of the Ministry of Finance, neither the ministry of Finance or other ministries listen to MASAK and MASAK cannot influence any policy-making effort in its area of responsibility. MASAK does not have enough bureaucratic power in order to reshape the agenda, because of their lower position in the bureaucracy.[130]

It can be said that even though other public and law enforcement institutions and their members recognise MASAK as the main institution responsible for CTF, in reality MASAK does not have enough influence and power thus it cannot instigate any policy or agenda changes as an administrative sub-unit under the Ministry of Finance.

Accordingly, another problem mentioned during the interviews was that MASAK is a weak institution among other agencies, such as law enforcement and intelligence agencies and other legal and military units. In this position, MASAK's influence on these structures is limited. This issue was identified as a key problem by an FIU expert:

> There are problems in regards to MASAK in terms of implementation powers, as well as an administrative institution as we do not have authority to address them. For example, if you are not a law enforcement agency, you cannot influence judicial authorities. However, there are some FIUs and Asset Recovery agencies in the world that are being led by prosecutor/s. This model might be suitable for Turkey.[131]

The law enforcement agencies in Turkey are the biggest and most influential bureaucratic structures in Turkey. Consequently, it is indicated by FIU and EU experts that with such power and influence, they are able to disregard policy and agenda initiatives put forward by MASAK.[132] These arguments point to the existence of a grey area of competency among institutions and agencies, which has important implications for implementation and coordination of CTF efforts.

128 It should be noted that MASAK, Financial Crimes Investigation Board, operating as FIU, has been established as an administrative unit under the Ministry of Finance since 17 February 1997 (Financial Crimes Investigation Board, 2011a, p. 6).

129 For the organisational structure see also Ministry of Finance website (Ministry of Finance, 2011).

130 Interview with an Expert on EU-Turkey Relations and Terrorism, No: EU1.

131 Interview with a Senior Level CTF Expert from the Turkish FIU – MASAK No: FIU4.

132 Interviews with an Expert on EU-Turkey Relations and Terrorism, No: EU1 and (former) Senior Level Director from MASAK No: FIU3.

Moreover, where MASAK sits in the Ministry of Finance is indicated as another problematic issue. As it is already noted, MASAK is an administrative unit, which has duties regarding financial crimes and financing of terrorism under the Ministry of Finance (Financial Crimes Investigation Board, 2011a, p. 6). It can be noted that this administrative nature of MASAK may prevent it from acting independently.

Moreover, in order to make a connection between the freedom of the FIU and effectiveness we should have data that are more empirical on the subject. On the other hand, both FIU experts and senior bank managers believe that MASAK should be placed under a legal authority having legal powers or re-established as an autonomous institution which can act freely, and would be more effective.[133] These accounts suggest that there are concerns regarding the impartiality and the independence and authority of the MASAK. As one EU expert concurred, changing MASAK's place in the bureaucratic hierarchy and empowering it with more powers or placing it as a part of a legal structure rather than an administrative unit might increase the influence and effectiveness of MASAK in the Turkish bureaucracy.[134] While it should be noted that each FIU type[135] has its own pros and cons, it can be asserted that the administrative role and the bureaucratic place of MASAK need to be reviewed.

From a law enforcement point of view, a senior level security service director supported the argument that the MASAK has a bureaucratic weakness by aptly pointing out that:

> For MASAK, I understand from the term of being independent from the law enforcement agencies that it should have been in a type of structure, which could direct and manage the whole process. As you said, if MASAK had been established with adequate technical capacity and expertise by which it could manage and direct the [CTF] process and determine short-term policies for

133 Interviews with a Senior level CTF expert from the Turkish FIU – MASAK No: FIU4 and Senior Level Manager of a Bank Branch No: BS1.

134 Interview with an Expert on EU-Turkey Relations and Terrorism, No: EU1.

135 The Egmont Group classifies FIUs into four types or models: judicial, law enforcement, administrative and hybrid. "The **Judicial Model** is established within the judicial branch of government wherein 'disclosures' of suspicious financial activity are received by the investigative agencies of a country from its financial sector such that the judiciary powers can be brought into play e.g. seizing funds, freezing accounts, conducting interrogations, detaining people, conducting searches, etc. The **Law Enforcement Model** implements anti-money laundering measures alongside already existing law enforcement systems, supporting the efforts of multiple law enforcement or judicial authorities with concurrent or sometimes competing jurisdictional authority to investigate money laundering. The **Administrative Model** is a centralized, independent, administrative authority, which receives and processes information from the financial sector and transmits disclosures to judicial or law enforcement authorities for prosecution. It functions as a 'buffer' between the financial and the law enforcement communities. The **Hybrid Model** serves as a disclosure intermediary and a link to both judicial and law enforcement authorities. It combines elements of at least two of the FIU models." See Egmont (2018).

> law enforcement and others, then we would have achieved the positive outcomes we had desired. However, from the beginning MASAK was established in order to serve the purposes of processing files, checking financial traces and confirming the suspicions; because of this, MASAK is obliged to cooperate with law enforcement agencies. In other words, MASAK was established with the mind-set of a financial auditor. The problem with MASAK, founded with auditor mind-set, despite the fact that it is an organisation [MASAK], which is accustomed to audit formal type organisations, we have expected from it to disclose the behaviours of informal types of organisations. Therefore, it is not realistic to expect from a group of auditors, who even hardly evaluate formal organisations with all the experience they have, to evaluate a traffic [of terrorist finance] which is a very fluid, with a changeable hierarchy, diffuse, and in a changing geography.[136]

As noted above, with its current structure and despite the misconception of its role and competences and ambitious expectations of it, MASAK was not established as an institution that can satisfy these expectations and manage the whole CTF process by providing coordination between units and determining main CTF policy. Moreover, the current structure of MASAK is mainly designed to deal with formal private financial organisations. However, it is expected to find evidence by analysing informal terrorist financing organisations and activities which are often diffused, multi-layered, fluid and conducted in dangerous environments. In the era of globalised threats, notably international terrorism, it is important to ask to what extent MASAK has adapted and oriented itself with the conditions of the continuous security environment and the changing nature of the threats therein. In this framework, by keeping in mind the real terrorist threats Turkey has been facing, it can be claimed there is an urgent need for empowering MASAK so that it can be more flexible, effective and powerful in pursuing terrorist finance and bringing those responsible to justice.

In summary, in this part the legal and the institutional infrastructure of the CTF regime in Turkey were examined critically by considering how able and effective these are for countering the financial activities of terrorists. It can be asserted that both legal provisions are mostly compatible with international and domestic structures. Furthermore, there are specialised institutions and agencies responsible for CTF efforts. However, examination of the legal instruments and our findings through the interviews have revealed that there are problematic areas in both the legal and bureaucratic frameworks in which CTF has been placed.

5.4 The level of CTF implementation in Turkey

For the next stage of the analysis, the CTF implementation processes will be considered in light of the legal and administrative bases explained above. The

136 Interview with a Senior Level CTF practitioner from a Law Enforcement Agency No: LE9.

main purpose of this part is to understand the limits and the effectiveness of CTF implementation in Turkey. In this context, competencies, institutional capacity (e.g. training efforts, calibre of staff, adequacy of technological skills, cooperation and coordination within and between responsible institutions) implementation and effectiveness of Turkey's CTF efforts within the international CTF environment will be examined. In addition to the accounts given by interviewees, international and national official reports, parliamentary records and news items are utilised in our analysis.

5.4.1 Is CTF implementation adequate?

In order to answer this question, we asked our interviewees what they think about the applicability of the CTF measures and efforts and the existing problems regarding this. According to the answers given by CTF experts, practitioners and scholars, it can be asserted that the current CTF regime in Turkey is not adequate. Even though the legal framework provides an internationally aligned set of CTF measures, the implementation of these provisions has proven to be problematic.[137] In other words, while 'law in books' is deemed to be sound, the same cannot be said for 'law in action'. It was said "[. . .] for that reason, by focusing more on implementation [of CTF measures], Turkey needs to improve its intelligence, prevention and monitoring capabilities. We can spend so much time for legislation, but this does not prevent [terrorist financing], the implementation and operation [of laws] are more important".[138] In addition, it is noted by another practitioner that "[h]aving legislation is not important if one cannot address the problems effectively practice. What these [problems] are, coordination, lack of cooperation, training, timidity and on-going envy between institutions".[139] Furthermore, it was asserted by an FIU practitioner that: "[h]onestly, when I look from an effectiveness analysis perspective, I think they [CTF applications] are not at a satisfying level according to our determined targets of confiscation and freezing orders, et cetera".[140]

Similarly, interviewees from law enforcement background stated that Turkey has not been able to conduct an effective CTF strategy. The absence of figures for frozen, blocked or confiscated assets and limited numbers of convictions or court cases demonstrate that Turkey does have an effective implementation problem. In this context it is claimed that there are no or very limited positive outcomes from the current CTF regime; thus it is inadequate.[141] A law enforcement

137 Interviews with Senior Level CTF experts from Turkish FIU – MASAK No: FIU1, (former) Senior Level Director from MASAK No: FIU2 and (former) Senior Level Director from MASAK No: FIU3.

138 Interview with a (former) Senior Level Director from MASAK No: FIU2.

139 Interview with a (former) Senior Level Director from MASAK No: FIU3.

140 Interview with a Senior Level CTF Expert from Turkish FIU – MASAK No: FIU1.

141 Interviews with CTF practitioners from Law Enforcement Agencies, No: LEC0, LE2, LE3, LE6, LE7, LE10, LE11 and LE12.

expert confirmed this trend by stating that "[t]he legislation in Turkey is adequate and provides required authority and competences, there is no problem regarding this, however, in terms of applying these legislations and regulations [in practice] there is a need for making much headway".[142] Another practitioner noted that "in terms of implementation we can say that there has been nothing implemented so far neither by our institution or others".[143] Similarly, another law enforcement practitioner stated that "well, in none of the counter-terrorism operations conducted, have I witnessed that terrorist organisation's assets have been confiscated as being proceeds of crime as a result of targeting and revealing their financial sources and links. It is not even one in ten may be. So, financially, we are able to prevent only very small part of it".[144] Correspondingly, a senior level practitioner noted, "[y]es we have a problem on the implementation part. Why is there a problem? Actually, the problems are not apparently. However, if there are not many outcomes regarding the implementation then you would say there is a problem here, right? Wouldn't you?"[145]

In tandem with these assertions, a senior judge assessed Turkey's implementation of the CTF provisions as being not effective and accepted that these have not been at the intended level.[146] He also noted that counter terrorism is mainly based on arresting or capturing terrorists, and there was little to no attention given to CTF in this strategy. Moreover, he noted that no elaborate and serious work which involves planning or preparation, investigation and court procedures holistically has been done from the perspective of an organised crime prosecutor.[147] From an academic viewpoint, a scholar expressed that "[f]or example, I do not remember any operation conducted by financial branch [of law enforcement agency] for many years. There have been only narcotic operations however, I don't remember any [financial] operations targeting the PKK".[148] An expert from the Customs Office said, "[w]hen it is looked at closely, the PKK continuously develops and/or uses more advanced and expensive weapons and gear and they can buy them. [. . .] So, this sophisticated financial capability demonstrates that the CTF has been ignored in Turkey".[149]

The interviewees' critical views on CTF implementation are important and their answers demonstrate that to them, an effective implementation means solid outcomes such as convictions, asset freezing, confiscations, forfeiture or financial

142 Interview with a Senior Level CTF Practitioner from a Law Enforcement Agency No: LE3.
143 Interview with a Senior Level CTF Practitioner from a Law Enforcement Agency No: LE12.
144 Interview with a Middle Level CTF Practitioner from a Law Enforcement Agency No: LE6.
145 Interview with a Senior Level CTF Practitioner from a Law Enforcement Agency No: LE2.
146 Interview with a Senior Level CTF Practitioner from the Department of Justice No: JD2.
147 *Ibid.*
148 Interview with a Scholar who is an Expert on International Relations – Professor at a University No: AC3.
149 Interview with a Senior Level Expert from the General Directorate of Customs Enforcement No: CO1.

hardship both statistically and ramifications and challenges for terrorist organisations' budgets. However, they emphasised that there has been no evidence of these in CTF practice.

The view that the implementation of CTF in Turkey is not at an expected level is supported by national statistics and international reports. According to the Country Reports on Terrorism 2014, there were no terrorist finance cases which were prosecuted (Bureau of Counterterrorism, 2015, p. 150). In terms of AML and CTF implementation, according to the figures given by the US based International Narcotics Control Strategy Report, there were 15 prosecutions and 3 convictions in Turkey in 2009 (Bureau for International Narcotics and Law Enforcement Affairs, 2014, p. 199). However, it must be noted that these figures are a mixture of both AML and CTF; thus, they may not represent mere CTF related cases. Normally the website of the General Directorate of Criminal Records and Statistics provides the legal statistical data annually (Adalet Bakanlığı, 2016). However, until 2013, the year when the new CTF legislation was enacted, it was not possible to find any explicit data regarding the offence of terrorist finance, prosecution or convictions, especially under Article 8 of Anti-Terrorism Law. The only official figures which are now available come from the statistics of 2013 and 2014, which represent a very limited number of convictions and on-going prosecutions (Adalet Bakanlığı, 2016).[150] While the FATF in its last report on Turkey, Fifteenth Follow-up Report, states that (pursuant to Article 4 – terrorist financing offence – under the new CTF legislation), 41 investigations were conducted, and 18 cases were prosecuted; it concludes that because of the novelty of the CTF legislation, the effectiveness of the CTF regime could not be determined (FATF, 2014a, p. 17).

In addition, although MASAK's annual Activity Reports since 2003 provide statistics regarding suspicious terrorist financing files and the number of cases forwarded to the prosecution service, there is no data presented for evaluating the outcomes of these activities in terms of prosecution, acquittal and/or conviction (Financial Crimes Investigation Board, 2011c). This is possibly because of the status of MASAK as an administrative institution, which separates it from the judicial system and excludes its access to the national legal database, called as UYAP [National Judiciary Informatics System], for acknowledging results of the continuing or concluded terrorist financing cases. This of course, can be overcome easily by requesting such information from UYAP or by UYAP department, which can provide this data to MASAK.

Having identified some of the shortcomings of the CTF regime, it can be argued that these conviction and prosecution numbers albeit very small, can be

150 It must be noted that the statistics are not clear for understanding what the numbers and titles represent. In this context in 2013 for 22 court cases, 63 conviction decisions were given, in 2014 for 21 crimes, 28 conviction and 5 other type decisions were given. In comparison to overall terrorism related crime, around 15,000 occurred in Turkey, so it can be claimed that these figures are limited.

deemed as a positive feature indicating there has been some effort at preventing and addressing financing of terrorism in Turkey. An additional feature has been identified by a judge who asserted that the latest legal amendments and regulations have paved the way for a more robust financial system where financial activities are monitored better.[151] An FIU practitioner evaluated that Turkey is still in its learning phase; in other words, Turkey is learning by trial and error.[152] Correspondingly, a practitioner from a law enforcement background noted that there are on-going efforts and activities in order to fix the problems regarding CTF knowledge, experience, training of staff and technology.[153] These activities are examined below.

5.4.2 *Reasons for insufficient implementation of CTF provisions*

The current implementation of CTF efforts seems to be insufficient and ineffective in terms of satisfying the initial expectations and providing positive results. If this is the case, then it is important to explore what the possible or existing reasons are for this trend.

In regards to ineffective implementation, a practitioner from a judicial background noted that "to some degree [ineffectiveness] is a result of unknowing the issue [CTF]. Well, the legislation stays there, you do not apply it and it stays [in books] like that".[154] A law enforcement practitioner similarly pointed out the lack of awareness and the perception by stating that "it cannot be addressed by only you or with your efforts; other institutions, also, should reach the same level of awareness and the understanding".[155] There seems to be consensus as to the reasons for inadequate CTF implementation: the lack of knowledge and experience of the institutions and their staff regarding how to properly implement CTF measures in practice. In this context, the level of CTF awareness and the perception of related institutions emerge as a significant factor for the implementation.

In relation to the lack of knowledge, inability and hardship experienced by the law enforcement agencies, judges and prosecutors, another factor which hinders the implementation of CTF in Turkey is substantiating the offence of terrorist financing with solid evidence. A senior judge confirmed this by stating that "investigations should be supported with the sufficient evidence, which leads to obtain a result. There are some problems regarding this".[156]

However, a law enforcement practitioner did not accept the lack of awareness as a reason and rather he claimed that the lack of implementation is caused by the

151 Interview with a Senior Level CTF Practitioner from the Department of Justice No: JD1.
152 Interview with a Senior Level CTF Expert from Turkish FIU – MASAK No: FIU1.
153 Interview with a Senior Level CTF Practitioner from a Law Enforcement Agency No: LE1.
154 Interview with a Senior Level CTF Practitioner from the Department of Justice No: JD1.
155 Interview with a Senior Level CTF Practitioner from a Law Enforcement Agency No: LE3.
156 Interview with a Senior Level CTF Practitioner from the Department of Justice No: JD2.

difficulty of coordinating and harmonising the efforts of many institutions, which are part of the CTF eco-system. According to him:

> It [Turkey] is aware of the issue actually but we have problems in terms of applying this awareness into reality. [. . .] Also, you are not the only one implementing the law. In [the Turkish] justice system, there are law enforcement mechanisms, legal mechanisms, and regulations of various ministries, banking system, Council of Bank Audit and Regulation, Capital Market Board, and Secretariat of Treasury. Thus, they all have responsibility, if one of them ignores or do not have care as the others. [. . .] The issue of awareness is old one but there is a discrepancy for [coordinated] implementation.[157]

Similarly, a scholar pointed to issues regarding CTF knowledge, perception, coordination and capacity. According to him, there is much legislation in place, and there are appointed staff for CTF. However, the politicians in Turkey do not have sufficient knowledge of terrorism, there is no synchronisation between institutions, and moreover there is no intellectual capacity for solving these problems. Therefore, the financial activities of terrorists are continuing without any disruption.[158] The problems and difficulties regarding the level of capacity and the coordination between institutions seem to have a direct negative effect on Turkey's implementation efforts. In addition to the difficulties related to capacity, the role of policy makers and the lack of will are expressed as another important element. Regarding this a counterterrorism expert noted that:

> [. . .] [H]ypothetically you may have very good laws on paper. However, in terms of applying these on the field, there may be problems because of inadequacy of institutions or reluctance of politicians or policy makers to implement these decisions taken at the central [parliament] level.[159]

In addition to the lack of political will, limited understanding of counter-terrorism, which tends to overlook the social, cultural and economic dimensions of the issue and only concentrates on the security part, is mentioned as an important factor which decreases the focus on CTF related efforts and hampers their implementation.[160]

There is another criticism of the inadequate level of CTF application. Regarding this, a CTF practitioner noted:

> Even though there is a structure for preventing the financing of terrorism and disclosing its links arising from abroad, there are not any complex big scale

157 Interview with a Senior Level CTF Practitioner from a Law Enforcement Agency No: LE2.
158 Interview with a Terrorism/Counterterrorism Scholar from a University No: AC2.
159 Interview with a Terrorism/Counterterrorism Scholar from a University No: AC2.
160 Correspondence with a Terrorism/Counterterrorism Scholar from a University No: AC5.

> operations conducted against [financing of terrorism] in Turkey; instead, smaller and simple judicial [focusing on criminal activities] operations are undertaken. It is not possible to prevent foreign support with simple operations like that. I think this subject needs to be planned and conducted by the supervision of intelligence agencies, because it is a very hard issue to be addressed legally by law enforcement units alone. [. . .] A limited and small struggle can be conducted locally. In this context, there are no big scale operational activities. Anyway, I do not think that there are adequate efforts for conducting them.[161]

It can be observed that even though there are adequate legal and administrative structures, very simple and low-level local CTF initiatives are conducted. It is true that with these kinds of limited tactical level operations, it is not possible to prevent the financial support of terrorist organisations with international and complex links. For conducting holistic and strategic level operations by targeting all sorts of financial sources and facilitators of terrorists, intelligence services should be included in the planning and implementation processes from the very beginning.

5.4.3 Difficulties regarding the implementation of CTF related laws and regulations

In terms of application of CTF related laws and regulations, law enforcement and legal authorities work together. In the current criminal justice system in Turkey, prosecutors are responsible for conducting an investigation process through law enforcement units. In addition, in order to use any special investigatory powers (e.g. covert operations) in complex CTF cases, courts and judges are the ones who can authorise the use of such measures. In other words, prosecutors and judges are the main decision makers during the process of criminal investigation and the judicial processes.

In this context, how well CTF related investigations and prosecutions are conducted is emerging as an important issue. According to a law enforcement officer:

> Due to the novelty of both subjects [CTF] and the law in Turkey, in terms of application of the law, there can be different interpretations made by [various actors in] the legal mechanism. Normally, a subject under the financing of terrorism law can be interpreted as an offence according to Anti-Terrorism Law (1991) and this may lead to the increase of the penalty. [. . .] The number of CTF investigations, which are conducted as a separate offence under the CTF law, are very limited, because statistically these offences could be interpreted and investigated under different laws or offences. Here, the overlaps between laws and prosecutors and judges can cause this complexity.[162]

161 Interview with a Senior Level CTF Practitioner from the Department of Justice No: JD2.
162 Interview with a Senior Level CTF Practitioner from a Law Enforcement Agency No: LE3.

The same law enforcement practitioner pointed out that in practice prosecutors are often directed by the law enforcement officers with a file they have prepared. Thus, case files prepared with this limited understanding and awareness may affect prosecutors' decision in choosing the right offence.

In a similar vein, an FIU practitioner noted that "although you make a criminal activity reporting involving a CTF offence to the prosecution service in order to open an investigation, the prosecutor may conclude either to instigate an investigation file from the offence of assisting [and abetting] terrorist organisation or not. There are struggles like that".[163] He further added that owing to the slowness of the judicial processes, terrorist/criminal assets which have to be subjected to confiscation might be transferred to other persons or other jurisdictions by suspects/criminals.[164]

In this context, another issue is that there are bureaucratic deficiencies while applying the CTF measures, particularly in the prosecution phase of the CTF. A scholar noted that institutionalism is one of the key problems in Turkey in general, and the same problem is valid in the context of CTF as well. It is a slow process in Turkey to be able to give and receive an official response. He also expressed that the CTF duties are scattered among the responsibilities of so many different institutions. Until recently, this subject has been conceived only from military or security perspectives rather than from an economic and intelligence perspective. Therefore, it is noted that it is not an easy and quick process for an economic CTF struggle to be institutionalised in the Turkish bureaucracy and its CTF practices.[165] It might be suggested that the current CTF struggle in Turkey is not an institutionalised practice yet, and it will need time to reach that optimal implementation level for Turkey.

Regarding the implementation of legal provisions one of the factors is interpretative differences by key stakeholders, whereby prosecutors and judges who are responsible for conducting the investigation, prosecution and sentencing can interpret the new CTF laws differently. For example, the current legal regime allows the possibility that while some prosecutors can assess an offence as assisting and abetting a terrorist organisation, others may conceive the same offence as financing of terrorism.

Another problem in CTF practice is that even though MASAK or the police submit terrorist financing crime files to the prosecutor, these files may be rejected, or the type of crime initially designated by the police may be changed.[166] The

163 Interview with a Senior Level CTF Expert from the Turkish FIU – MASAK No: FIU4.

164 *Ibid.*

165 Interview with a Scholar who is an Expert on International Relations – Professor at a University No: AC3.

166 According to the 2015 Activity Report of MASAK, 74,221 SARs were sent to the MASAK from the financial sector (Financial Crimes Investigation Board, 2016, p. 23). 55 files were opened and the examination of 24 of 55 files was completed by 2015 (Financial Crimes Investigation Board, 2016, p. 37). According to evaluations conducted by MASAK in 2015, the files of 63 people in relation to terrorist offences were sent to the Public

novelty of the 6415 Prevention of Financing of Terrorism legislation may be the reason for this inconsistency, as projected in the IMF report in 2012 that the main challenge for the sophisticated and internationally linked financial system in Turkey would be the implementation of and adaptation to continuously changing international regulations and standards (International Monetary Fund, 2012, p. 30). Given the slow functioning of the legislative system and bureaucracy in Turkey, when law and legal practice are not adapted to international standards swiftly, Turkish prosecutors and/or judges may be behind these new benchmarks and inadvertently enable criminal assets to be transferred to other locations by criminals with ease. Furthermore, in general, law enforcement officers prepare the initial criminal file to be submitted to the prosecution service. The information and evidence in these case files may influence the prosecutor's decision in a negative way. For instance, the lack of awareness and knowledge of the law enforcement officers about CTF may affect the quality of the evidence (which may not be admissible in criminal proceedings) and/or put forward a wrong designation as to the alleged offence. Thus, these kinds of mistakes can affect and mislead prosecutors' decisions. The problems and delays emerging from the bureaucratic system can also prevent swift and flexible implementation of CTF measures in a cross-agency and a coordinated way. Ideally, CTF practitioners and other relevant personnel need to be trained prior to the law becoming effective. However, this has not happened comprehensively in Turkey yet.

5.4.4 Challenges in countering illegitimate and legitimate financial activities

In order to examine the difficulties of implementing an effective and successful CTF regime, the efforts for preventing both legal and illegal financial activities of terrorist organisations should be examined.

Fighting against illegitimate financial activities

As is examined above and acknowledged by various academics (Shelley, 2014 and Ryder, 2018), terrorists both in Turkey and beyond use illegal or criminal activities for raising funds for their longevity and sustainability. While a law enforcement practitioner asserted that "[i]n order to prevent illegitimate sources, there are measures for fighting against smuggling and drugs, and these are implemented. At present, financial sources of terrorist organisations are monitored and we continuously reflect on as to how we can improve our fight",[167] the on-going

Prosecutor's Office (Financial Crimes Investigation Board, 2016, p. 38). However, there is no available data regarding the final decision (whether they were prosecuted and, if so, convicted) on these files by the Public Prosecutor's Office (Financial Crimes Investigation Board, 2016).

167 Interview with a Senior Level CTF Practitioner from a Law Enforcement Agency No: LE3.

high terrorist threat level in Turkey indicates that there are inherent challenges in terms of stopping such terrorist activities.

Prevention of crime and public security are two of the key priorities of law enforcement agencies, yet there seems to be an increasing appreciation that drivers and enabling elements for crimes (e.g. illicit financial sources of terrorism) need to be addressed also. This was confirmed by a number of interviewees including a law enforcement practitioner who expressed that even though they take steps at the tactical level, their efforts and capabilities can produce limited outcomes. He explained that the law enforcement agencies have been undertaking required steps for preventing illegal activities such as preventing smuggling or destroying drug yielding crops.[168] While these efforts can be undertaken at the tactical level against such crimes (for which institutional expertise and capacity have been developed over time), more complex actions such as following money or other technology related measures could not be conducted with the tactical level units as they lacked both the expert personnel and the technical tools to do it.

Another issue for law enforcement agencies is how and what crimes to prioritise. One practitioner said that "[o]ur priority is terror. When there is terror, combating against drugs and/or its financing take the second place in the [priority] list".[169] Because countering terrorism or capturing individual terrorists is the main perceived priority amongst almost all political circles within and outside Turkey, and given the fact that law enforcement agencies have been among the key victims of terror attacks with thousands of casualties, for the law enforcement units, hot pursuit and termination of terrorist cells naturally become priorities among other crimes which may be related to terrorism.

In respect to this trend, another view is that even though there is an on-going active terrorism problem, Turkey's efforts against drug trafficking and smuggling[170] are very successful. In this regard, besides the domestic reports, the UNODC and other international reports and statistics demonstrate that Turkey is successful at and a significant partner in tackling organised crime effectively (Europol & European Monitoring Centre For Drugs and Drug Addiction, 2016, pp. 55, 65, 74) and the UNODC (2015, pp. 31–32). It is also stated that it is not an easy task dealing with crime in environments where terrorism is rife. Moreover, the instability of the neighbouring states such as Syria and Iraq makes things more complex and difficult for Turkey.[171] This may indicate that Turkey's efforts against organised criminal activities of both criminals and terrorists are above

168 Interview with a Middle Level CTF Practitioner from a Law Enforcement Agency No: LE8.

169 Interview with a Senior Level CTF Practitioner from a Law Enforcement Agency No: LE10.

170 During the interviews although it is known that many criminal activities are committed by terrorist organisations, problems related to countering smuggling and drug trafficking were singled out as key priorities by most of the practitioners.

171 Interview with a Senior Level CTF Practitioner from a Law Enforcement Agency No: LE2.

the standards though the existence of terrorism and its financing undoubtedly continue. This is one of the unique and puzzling features of Turkey's security environment.

Another issue worth noting is the fact that there are problems regarding the quality of the legal provisions including their deterrence against smuggling and other types of organised crimes and the law enforcement forces' ability to prove crime with admissible evidence. According to the practitioners interviewed, these problems need to be addressed in order to improve Turkey's effectiveness and limit terrorists' coffers.

According to a senior level FIU director, the lack of effective enforcement of laws encourages criminals to continue their activities in Turkey. In addition, it is noted that law enforcement units do not always act diligently to obtain substantive and admissible evidence which can be used to secure a conviction. Even though a law enforcement unit or border guards may catch a drug smuggler, s/he can be freed in a very short time either due to a lack of elaborately collected evidence or owing to current lenient sentencing rules.[172]

Another practitioner from a customs agency highlighted the issue of smuggled goods for terrorist financing. He noted that these smuggled goods are sold in the city centres, even in the capital city of Turkey. For instance, although there are legal provisions which prohibit selling contraband cigarettes, these cigarettes can be bought easily and openly.[173] This point may indicate that the level of awareness amongst officials and the knowledge of how to deal with this kind of underground trade which has its links with terrorist finance are not sufficient, and subsequently these activities continue to finance terrorist organisations.

Another dimension from a broader perspective of CTF is the eco-system which offers suitable conditions for smuggling and other illegal activities to thrive. A scholar indicated that the economic and political aspects of smuggling are other factors which may impede the effectiveness of the CTF regime: Firstly, economic competition between states or domestic political interests and balances can affect state's policies regarding dealing with smuggling. Secondly, reluctance of local political actors to implement the rules imposed by the central government may impact their implementation. Thirdly, political expectations or other personal goals of politicians may result in government turning a blind eye to certain criminal activities. As is the case in Turkey with its border regions and vast coastline, illegal eco-systems with far-reaching networks and based on *inter alia* smuggling of immigrants, animals, petrol/fuel, drugs, cigarettes or various raw materials, it can be challenging for states to prevent or disrupt this system completely.[174]

Additionally, when terrorists see this well-established and/or emerging eco-system as an opportunity on the other side of the border, they immediately try

172 Interview with a (former) Senior Level Director from MASAK – FIU No: FIU3.
173 Interview with a Senior Level Expert from the General Directorate of Customs Enforcement No: CO1.
174 Interview with a Terrorism/Counterterrorism Scholar from a University No: AC2.

to be a part of it. From that moment on it is not possible to address this issue only with traditional local crime prevention methods as it is now a transnational activity with new dynamics. Therefore, the same scholar rightly noted that "now if you see the case from this perspective you cannot address this problem with traditional methods because dealing with this issue [smuggling] is not a local police problem anymore".[175] Regarding the same issue, a customs office practitioner emphasised that one possible reason for smuggling is the differences in prices for the same product. Such price differences make smuggling attractive and profitable for the criminals. For example, smuggled diesel on the black market in Turkey is sold at a fraction of the price for legal diesel. It is stated that due either to the fact that the prices and taxes on goods are very high or to the fact that the buying power of people is weak and unemployment is high in certain parts of Turkey, smuggling becomes a very attractive business for criminals as the activity is sustained and supported by regular demand from the local people.[176] This demonstrates that economy has its own rules; ignoring these rules and implementing policing tactics against smugglers alone are not enough to prevent crime. Economic measures should be part of the strategy against both terrorist financing and smuggling.

In contrast, a law enforcement practitioner opposed the argument that smuggling is the only way for people to live just because there are no jobs or opportunities for people. He argued that:

> Why is smuggling committed in the region [South East and East Anatolia regions], [because] there is no job and work. I say to the people who think like this; [if they want] they can look at the records of agricultural support credits given by banks between 1970 and 1980, even until the 1990s. The amount of unpaid loan is very few. Moreover, throughout Turkey 60 percent of these credits in the field of stockbreeding were given to the people from this region of the country. The rumour that people from this region are not productive and thus inclined to smuggling is only an urban legend in this sense. [. . .] There is a terror economy here. Before, there was a healthy economy here actually but there is no research on it. No one asks how these people were making a living there in the 1980s.[177]

It seems that the CTF stakeholders in Turkey have contrasting views on the ecosystem of criminal activities that feed terrorism. While some argue that economic policies should be in place to minimise the profit thus incentives for crime, others argue that Turkey has provided various economic measures and investment in regions where terrorism is acute.

175 *Ibid.*
176 Interview with a Senior Level Expert from the General Directorate of Customs Enforcement No: CO1.
177 Interview with a Senior Level CTF Practitioner from a Law Enforcement Agency No: LE9.

In the context of cross-border criminal enterprises and activities which finance terrorism, providing border security and cooperation with bordering countries emerge as military elements of the issue. One of the CTF practitioners who is experienced in border security stated that the tough physical characteristics of the terrain along the border areas of Turkey is another difficulty for securing borders and preventing illegal activities such as smuggling.[178]

The current level of border security (monitoring and control) and geographical limitations have a direct effect on the effectiveness of the CTF. Thus having a strong border regime and cooperation with other countries emerges as a critical issue, and the interviews reveal that Turkey has been experiencing problems on this issue. When one takes into account the harshness of the terrain on the border areas, the unstable situation caused by the lack of governance and control on the other side of Turkey's border in the South West, as a result of on-going conflicts in Iraq and Syria and activities and attacks by PKK and several other terrorist organisations, it is not surprising that the task is enormous.

Smuggling activities and their terrorist financing links in Turkey are significant problems, which need to be addressed elaborately and holistically. Not only legal and enforcement activities but also the prevailing conditions of the criminal eco-system and exploitable weak areas (including economic, socio-political, geographical factors) should be taken into account when developing a strategy towards it. As one of the interviewees mentioned, there is not the culture of initiating an elaborately planned and strategic CTF operation in Turkey. However, the recent legislative developments regarding CTF actually allow for such action.

Fighting terrorist financing from legal sources

In addition to the proceeds from their criminal activities (e.g. drug trafficking), terrorists also have financial resources which come from legitimate enterprises. This makes CTF in general and identifying and preventing such assets in particular an exceedingly difficult task. In this context, it is important to focus on how the CTF community is dealing with legal financial sources of terrorist organisations and the methods terrorists employ to raise funds within and through these seemingly legitimate activities.

A law enforcement practitioner stated that, "I know that the voluntary donations given to terrorists constitutes the biggest amount for financing terrorism, whereas I am aware of that preventing it is also difficult because people donate knowingly and wilfully, moreover they can do this by hand if necessary. [. . .] The steps which can be taken against on this issue are very limited".[179] This kind of financing activity can be committed with ease and it is very difficult to spot.

178 Interview with a Senior Level CTF Practitioner from a Law Enforcement Agency No: LE10.

179 Interview with a Middle Level CTF Practitioner from a Law Enforcement Agency No: LE6.

Consequently, the counter measures, which can be used for preventing them, are very limited in this context. This aspect of terrorist finance reminds us that counter-terrorism strategy needs to combine elements, beyond military and policing operations, which address why people support terrorism and how we can determine and deal with the root causes of terrorism.

Another challenge posed by legitimate financing activities for terrorist purposes is that proving the offence of financing terrorism becomes an arduous task as it is the final destination of the assets and support that would be criminal, not the source itself. According to a judge:

> Dealing with legal sources is very hard because proving this crime is very difficult. Moreover, terrorist organisations use this type of sources mostly. A prosecutor cannot be successful on this issue alone, without using the tactics and techniques, as we call them special measures, I assess that they might be helpful.[180]

Moreover, as one of law enforcement practitioners noted:

> Well, I do not think laws can solve this [issue of legitimate financial resources of terrorism]. I believe that enacting laws which prevent people to give their legitimately earned money to someone may cause serious constitutional problems. Rather than inadequacy both in our country and the world detecting, understanding and addressing this crime are very hard whereas for people committing it, it is very easy to come up with [alternative] excuses to avoid culpability. For example, under the disguise of a charity, the money may be collected for Al Qaeda camps and acquiring weapons in Iraq, which can be justified easily by saying that they would buy food and medicine for the starving children in Afghanistan. We do not have capability to prove and say 'No, you will not buy these'.[181]

In addition, it was added by the same practitioner that it is hard to prove a terrorist financing offence when the resources and money are kept by law-abiding (non-suspect) citizens or businesses on behalf of terrorists. In order to avoid law enforcement agencies and detection by intelligence services, terrorist organisations indeed use such entities for storing money.[182]

A scholar highlighted the same problem, noting that personal bank accounts are used to store money destined for terrorism, whereby it is difficult to prove the link between terrorists and the owner of that account.[183] According to an

180 Interview with a Senior Level CTF Practitioner from the Department of Justice No: JD2.

181 Interview with a Middle Level CTF Practitioner from a Law Enforcement Agency No: LE6.

182 *Ibid.*

183 Interview with a Scholar who is an Expert on security studies – Professor at a University No: AC4.

FIU expert, "proving that terrorist financing crime was committed willingly and knowingly" is another difficulty in Turkish legal system CTF practitioners' encounters.[184] In this regard, it can be noted that detecting these individual bank accounts as suspicious and investigating the potential links of account holders with terrorist organisations and proving that the real owners of this money are the terrorists is extremely difficult for CTF practitioners. Besides finding sufficient evidence, reluctance of people to share information on this subject disrupts law enforcement and implementation of other CTF efforts. As one CTF practitioner opined:

> Because there is no way of proving this and investigate, now if you go to prosecutor and say that we have intelligence that someone from this village or company gave money to this [terrorist] organisation. Then prosecutor will ask you: 'so what do you have? Do you have any proof for this?' Does the man in question come and give a statement regarding the case? No, he does not, because when you talk with him in private, he says [terrorist] organisation is threatening me. You say come and give your statement; he does not, because he has a perception that nothing will happen in the end. Then, why should he? There will be something in the end or not but he has a concern that if he does, there is a possibility that someone working in the court can leak this information to terrorists, and then he will be again in trouble. So, he fears and does not give any statement. [. . .] Even though all prosecutors, judges, law enforcement, governor and district governors they have all legal and preventive responsibilities, however this crime is committed in front of everyone's eyes. [. . .] Nothing can be done legally because there is no evidence, there is nothing in terms of prevention because there is no coordinator either.[185]

It is very difficult, if not impossible, countering these legal activities of terrorist financing without any proof. In addition, people who might be witnesses or give money to terrorists willingly or under duress might be reluctant to share information because they do not believe that the security forces could protect them. Even though most of the CTF officials are aware of various PKK financing activities in their respective jurisdictions, due to the lack of evidence and lack of a coordinator, efforts can be undertaken only on a limited scale for preventing terrorist finance.

In addition, the supervision of donations and non-profit organisations and charities is another important aspect of legal sources of terrorist financing. It was

184 Interview with a Senior Level CTF Expert from the Turkish FIU – MASAK No: FIU1.

185 Interview with a Middle Level CTF Practitioner from a Law Enforcement Agency No: LE4.

stated in the interviews that the supervision mechanism on these entities is not working properly. A judge expressed that:

> We have to determine how this money is going to terrorists. That's why we should ask for example that for what purposes did you collect money from this or that charity music concerts via this association? This issue and its supervision should be expressed in the laws clearly. When you find out that the money did not go to the right place what one should do. I have to ask you what you did with the money you have collected. Reverse responsibility, you have to explain where the money is. But firstly, if I have this supervision mechanism and the authority then I can ask you these questions. If I do not have it, I will not be able to ask you anyway. This is the problem in Turkey, there is no supervision mechanism. [. . .] [W]hen you look at the money collected in South Eastern parts of Turkey by terrorist organisation [PKK] you can see that there is no supervision mechanism there. You did not audit, whereas if you had checked where the money was going then you might have prevented their activities as well. There is no supervision, so we have deficiencies regarding our supervision system.[186]

It is claimed above that the existing regulatory framework and supervisory mechanism for monitoring whether money collected or gained from legal activities has been delivered to the right hands are not adequately functioning. The authorities do examine or investigate the purposes for which the money was collected or used. Thus, in order to ensure that money and other property collected for legal or philanthropist goals (rather than for terrorist financing) Turkey needs to establish robust monitoring and control mechanisms.

This is sometimes not easy at all, even if there was a good monitoring system, for example one that is based on sound auditing and accounting practices. It is known that municipalities, sport clubs and various other social and public service organisations collect taxes or fees (in the form of donations) in Turkey, and these entities are popular venues used by terrorists. One of the law enforcement practitioners claimed that some municipalities in Turkey have been funding PKK terrorism. He asserted that both financial assets belonging to the municipality itself and part of the salaries of employees of the municipality have been diverted to PKK.[187] According to a senior judge, sport clubs are also used for funnelling money to terrorists in Turkey. Donations made to any sport club for supporting terrorism may be difficult to prevent; however, it can be checked easily where these donations go or for what purposes they are used by the existing tax

186 Interview with a Senior Level CTF Practitioner from the Department of Justice No: JD1.

187 Interviews with Middle Level Law Enforcement Agency No: LE4; Senior Level FIU members No: FIU3, FIU4 and EU Expert No: EU1.

legislation.[188] These accounts indicate that terrorist organisations not only use private legitimate business for income but are also able to manipulate and exploit public entities and local governments.

In connection to the problems is the limited capacity of the state to monitor the financial activities of its subsidiary organs (e.g. local authorities and municipalities). This was confirmed by an EU expert who stipulated that financial audit of public agencies such as municipalities by the Turkish Court of Accounts is very limited.[189] He claimed that although municipalities in Turkey can establish their independent enterprises, the capacity of this court only allows for supervision of no more than 20 percent of all the 1,397 municipalities in Turkey. He argued that effective CTF goes hand in hand with good governance and transparency in all aspects of economy and financial reporting; hence, these factors should be taken into consideration as important elements of CTF strategy. Accordingly, it was argued that firstly, Turkey should address its basic governance problems in its public institutions. Regarding the audits of public entities, it is clear that not enough has been done. For example, out of the 1,397 municipalities in total (T. C. İçişleri Bakanlığı [Republic of Turkey Ministry of Interior], 2011), only 121 of them in 2014 and 172 of them in 2015 were audited by the Court of Accounts (Sayıştay Başkanlığı [Supreme Court of Accounts], 2013 and 2015).[190] These numbers indicate that supervision and audit mechanisms need to be activated and aligned with CTF related tasks.

Another challenging issue in the context of proceeds from legitimate businesses which end up in the hands of terrorists is extortion or racketeering.[191] For example, contractors with construction businesses in the regions where PKK has a stronghold have to yield to the demands of terrorists, often under duress. According to a law enforcement practitioner, nearly all the contractors who have

188 Interview with a Senior Level CTF Practitioner from the Department of Justice No: JD1.

189 The Turkish Court of Accounts is the supreme audit institution in charge of auditing all accounts related to revenues, expenditures and property of government departments financed by general and subsidiary budgets (Turkish Court of Accounts, 2018).

190 The numbers of municipalities counted manually from the records of the audits is presented on its website.

191 The phenomenon of racketeering extortion in the context of terrorist finance has also been acknowledged by the EU and US. For example, the European Economic and Social Committee on Civil Society participation in the fight against organised crime and terrorism (2006/C 318/26) expressed that terrorist groups have often acted like mafia-style organisations which finance their actions through criminal activity: trafficking of narcotics, weapons and human beings, credit card fraud, hold- ups, robberies and extortion of professionals and businessmen, illegal gambling and other crimes. The Communication from the Commission to the Council and the European Parliament on measures to be taken to combat terrorism and other forms of serious crime, in particular to improve exchanges of information / COM/2004/0221 final stated that "When seeking financing, terrorist organisations often also use methods similar to those of criminal organisations, such as extortion, kidnapping with ransom demands and all kinds of trafficking and fraud". The US has expanded the use of the Racketeer Influenced and Corrupt Organizations Act, 1970 ('RICO') in the context of CTF as early as the 1980s (Joseph, 1990).

won a public tender to build dams, roads, schools or hospitals in the southeastern regions of Turkey have to pay the so-called 'revolutionary tax' determined by the PKK. If they do not pay, they all know that the terrorists will not allow them to finish their jobs by burning their vehicles and kidnapping workers. In order to avoid such negative ramifications, it was alleged that nearly 90 percent of contractors pay up whether they support PKK or not.[192] The following example was provided by a law enforcement agency director:

> A company which was constructing roads between two cities, Siirt to Şırnak, was raided and their equipment and the vehicles were burned many times due to the fact that the contractor refused to pay the tax to the terrorists. Ultimately the contractor obliged to pay the money to terrorists and officials knew about this. All the contractors who are constructing dams, schools and electricity lines have been paying the tax to these men [terrorists].[193]

He added that in the case of PKK, the number of legitimate sources it can harness seems to surpass the illegal sources. In this environment, business contractors play an important role for PKK's financial support. Contractors pay money to protect their assets and businesses from PKK threats and therefore continue their activities safely. It was asserted that the money collected from many contractors working in the region is more than enough for PKK. In addition, these people do not use the banking system; rather, cash or other alternative ways are used for payment. Therefore, without any suitable tool for investigating legal financial activities, law enforcement remains limited.[194]

Another significant aspect to consider is that there is a direct link between the state authority/security and the terrorist financing. Many practitioners and experts agreed that because Turkey cannot provide its people a secure and safe environment in the southeastern parts of the country, PKK fills this authority gap and organises its financial activities more easily than other parts of Turkey. People who are living in these places support PKK terrorism financially because PKK has the control of the area, and these people do not have any other option but to provide financial support to PKK. Pragmatically, people obey the rules of the strongest faction in the region. This gives PKK a legitimisation in the eyes of the society, because PKK is the one who can provide security and safety for them, rather than the state.[195]

It is clear that in certain parts of Turkey, investment in infrastructure and development goes to the PKK coffers because of the fact that contractors and investors

192 Interview with a Senior Level (retired) Director from a Law Enforcement Agency No: LE5.

193 *Ibid.*

194 Interview with a Senior Level (retired) Director from a Law Enforcement Agency No: LE5.

195 Interviews with practitioners from law enforcement background No: LE4, LE5, LE7, LE10 and a Terrorism/Counterterrorism Scholar from University No: AC2.

do not feel safe and secure. Therefore, it might be asserted that Turkey's lack of authority in this region indirectly and unintentionally finances PKK terrorism. As Freeman (2011) notes, financial success has positive impact on the terrorist organisations' legitimacy. Therefore, the security and safety of the society provided by the state has a direct effect on the prevention of financing of terrorism. In other words, it is difficult to implement an effective CTF regime in an environment where security and safety are not provided by state. Unfortunately, this is the conundrum which Turkey faces when it comes to implementing its CTF regime.

Conducting an effective fight against legitimate sources of terrorist financing is a difficult task for CTF practitioners. Proving the crime and ineffective supervision mechanism are some of the key challenges. In this context, terrorist organisations operating in Turkey can easily raise funds via legitimate sources. Turkey's record indicates that the fight against legitimate financial sources has been less effective than efforts against illegitimate financial sources of terrorism. Regarding this, comments by an experienced law enforcement practitioner are fitting:

> Turkey is very successful and competent in dealing with criminal activities (e.g. smuggling, drug trafficking) because there has been an existing established perception and praxis on this subject in Turkey. However, Turkey is not competent in addressing legal or pseudo-legal financial activities and sources of terrorists unlike addressing illegal activities. The problem with legal sources is that law enforcement forces in Turkey cannot determine clearly when exactly a legal financial activity should be named as an illegal one. Turkish CTF officials do not have adequate understanding of the subject due to lack of knowledge and experience.[196]

Comparing effectiveness of CTF against the two main sources employed for terrorist financing – legitimate and illegitimate sources – addressing criminal activities seems to be easier for security forces, because they have the intuition, knowledge, experience and lessons learned over time. However, in the case of legitimate financial sources of terrorism, it is the opposite. The lack of knowledge, experience and awareness for how to deal with these types of activities is a major factor hurdle for CTF practitioners. In terms of cutting of the legitimate sources of terrorists in Turkey, the authority of the state and security should be established by the state in key strategic regions of the country in the first instance.

5.4.5 *The adequacy of cash controls*

Cash money transfers by different methods are widely used by terrorists. The use of cash places terrorists one step ahead of law enforcement agencies and other related institutions because when cash passes from hand to hand, it virtually leaves

196 Interview with a Senior Level CTF Practitioner from a Law Enforcement Agency No: LE9.

no trace. Hence, in the context of CTF, controlling and monitoring cash transfers are important issues for both Turkey and the international community. As one FIU director noted "[f]irst of all, cash money must be controlled in Turkey because both terrorists and organised crime organisations are using this money. According to the Turkish legal system, people do not have to report their cash unless there is a demand made by the officials, whereas reporting cash should be an obligation similar to other countries".[197]

According to the current legal framework in Turkey, submitting cash flow statements or cash transfer or payment reports by travellers is not compulsory, which is undoubtedly not an ideal situation from a CTF perspective. If a customs officer demands such from a traveller, only then does that individual have to report his/her cash. Therefore, for an effective CTF, this reporting element should be compulsory for everyone who has cash money. On the other hand, it was noted by a law enforcement practitioner that there have been some working groups composed of law enforcement agencies, MASAK – FIU and other institutions finding ways of increasing their capability to deal with cash transfers, alternative money transfer methods and new technological developments such as the usage of digital coins, cryptocurrencies and cyberspace more effectively.[198] While the current situation was assessed by an FIU director as not being adequate, a scholar claimed that current developments and regulations in the Turkish economic and financial system led to an increase in the state's control of the money movements, and as a result, the ratio of unrecorded economy decreased.[199] Although the economic and financial systems have been improved and regulated, if and to what extend these improved the monitoring of cash traffic are not yet clear.

The Turkish economy has been static, and its currency has declined significantly in recent years.[200] As a result, in order to attract investment and foreign currency, the Turkish government has provided numerous incentives. However, some of these measures create risks for CTF and combating other serious organised crimes. For example, the recent changes introduced by a circular issued by the General Directorate of Customs Guards on 15 April 2015 (Uçarmak, 2015) paved the way for allowing cash transfers from outside of the country to enter the Turkish economy without a cash transfer report at customs and omitted the prosecution in case of any suspicion regarding financing terrorism, money laundering and violation of other related laws which were mentioned in the previous circular issued in 2013 (Altunyaldız, 2013). In other words, with the recent changes, bringing cash from abroad is not subjected to any reporting mechanism

197 Interview with a Former Senior Level Director from MASAK No: FIU3.
198 Interview with a Senior Level CTF Practitioner from a Law Enforcement Agency No: LE3.
199 Interview with a Scholar who is an Expert on International Relations – Professor at a University No: AC3.
200 In 2009, one Turkish Lira was 2.19 to one GBP. In October 2018, it was trading at 8.87 to one GBP. For a 10-year performance of the Turkish Lira, see XE (2018).

at customs unless the passenger chooses to declare this.[201] According to an anonymous customs comptroller who was interviewed by the *Hürriyet* newspaper:

> Before 2004, it was mandatory for the passengers to report every type of cash they carried with them when they entered the country. In the following years, cash controls have been softened with the issued circulars. With the introduction of the last circular, the control on the source and the amount of the cash limit seems to be removed. [. . .] With this circular AML legislation might even be circumvented.
>
> (Dağlar, 2015)

An FIU practitioner expert explained the logic behind issuing this circular, which seems to be against international AML and CTF norms. In this regard, he noted that:

> This circular does not and cannot influence and change the application of legislations against money laundering and terrorist financing because these laws are still in use and hierarchically superior than circulars. However, as I heard, the main goal of this circular is to soften the cash controls because of so many Syrians who are fleeing to Turkey with their assets and money. Actually, it is said that this is an initiative in order to assist Syrians entrance to Turkey with their cash easily. Nevertheless, when it is proceeded so much in terms of internationally and FATF standards, this [circular] took the attention of international community unnecessarily. There is only one little issue there says no one can be coerced to report whereas this does not change the existing law. Other than that, this [circular] unnecessarily puts Turkey in a difficult position and it does not have any practical application. I believe that the customs did not contact us before preparing this circular, otherwise we would know about it.[202]

This detail is yet another example of the lack of coordination and communication between various departments with responsibility for CTF. It also indicates that there are weaknesses in law making as the detail and purpose of secondary

201 It is worth noting that a cash repatriation law enacted in August 2016 as part of a general economic stimulus package allowed Turkish citizens and corporations to freely transfer and use currency, gold and other capital market instruments, declaring the source of funds. The law immunised declared funds from investigation and prosecution, which may have created a money laundering vulnerability. While this law expired on June 30, 2017, it allowed for a considerable period of time, for any form of assets (gold, cash, etc.) to enter the country without any background checks as to legitimacy and beneficial ownership of these (Norton Rose Fulbright, 2017).

202 Telephone conversation with a Senior Level CTF Expert from the Turkish FIU – MASAK No: FIU1.

legal instruments (in this case a circular) are not holistic and contradict the aims of other superior laws (e.g. CTF and AML statutes). According to the hierarchy of norms and laws in the Turkish legal system, this circular does not officially change the requirements of the laws on AML and CTF. However, such inconsistent rules may cause confusion for the officials, and consequently, this gap may be exploited by terrorists and money launderers to finance their activities. Moreover, such laws dent the credibility of the country in terms of its commitment to fighting terrorist finance. Thus, the quality and implementation of cash monitoring and controls are in urgent need of improvement in Turkey.

5.4.6 The level of implementation by private financial sector

As already mentioned in the previous chapters, along with public institutions involved in CTF, the efforts taken by the financial sector, especially the banking sector, are equally important. Thus, the level of implementation and the challenges encountered in this part of the CTF system in Turkey need to be examined.

The expectations of the formal financial sector are very high in terms of catching terrorists, disrupting or foiling terrorist attacks and ending terrorist organisations. However, as mentioned in Chapter 3 and earlier in this chapter, there are inherent problems pertaining to the CTF law in books as well as problems with the CTF law in action. For instance, the problem of information exchange between the private financial sector and intelligence and security agencies is a present obstacle in Turkey's CTF efforts. According to an FIU practitioner, these expectations do not reflect realities. According to him:

> However, you are missing a difficulty here; a terrorist cell sent $5,000 to an unrelated man and next day this man was bombing a synagogue. You cannot expect from financial sector to pick this like tweezers, or if there is no sensitive information, you cannot expect from the FIU to find him although his $5,000 recorded in its database. There is a need for an interactive network between intelligence agencies and the financial sector.[203]

As noted, it is not realistic to expect a bank to determine accurately a very small amount of terrorist financing activity without real-time information exchanges between them and the intelligence units and law enforcement agencies. In the current CTF regime in Turkey, there is not such an information exchange platform or a structure for effective information flows. As the example provided by an FIU practitioner demonstrates, a terrorist cell can easily transfer $5,000 to a terrorist, and this person can use the money for a terrorist attack.

203 Interview with a Senior Level CTF expert from Turkish FIU – MASAK No: FIU1.

Another issue worth considering is how important it is for the banking sector to implement the CTF measures effectively. Regarding this, a bank manager noted that:

> For me, there are only series of rules and regulations which are not effectively applied. The most effectively applied part [of CTF regime] in the banks, apart from SARs, is the customer due diligence processes such as identification requirements for knowing the customer. [. . .] Financial sector in Turkey is rather focusing on the instalment and provision of the continuity of the [fintech] systems in order not to violate any CTF measures and regulations. It could be said that the financial sector in Turkey is not fully aware of the importance of proper implementation of CTF regulations.[204]

Moreover, the same senior level bank manager adds that for the banking sector in Turkey, CTF measures and applications are accepted as a mere list of rules to be followed and implemented. Consequently, the financial sector tends to comply with any regulations and measures put in front of it without much resistance. He also claims that the main driver for the banking sector for implementing these measures is not the sanctions or criticism by official comptrollers. The key factor is the protection of the reputation, brand and profit.[205] In this framework, it can be said that AML/CTF measures such as SARs, due diligence (e.g. know your customer applications) are the ones which are implemented effectively by banks. However, it should be noted that these measures, which were originally designed for anti-money laundering purposes, are not compatible with CTF.

Regarding this issue, a law enforcement official stated that "well, on the one hand you will say [to banks], report suspicious transactions, on the other you will say: be more selective. Then the rule [regarding reporting suspicious activities] should be identified more clearly. Because, otherwise the staff might not be able to analyse the financial risk in order to avoid taking any responsibility".[206] It is true for the banking sector that there is need for more accurate, clear identification and the description of the threats and indications of how to detect terrorists and their financial activities. In addition, a banking manager expressed that there is no feedback mechanism or any statistical information shared with the banks by the government regarding the results of the SARs sent from banks.[207] This demonstrates that due to lack of a feedback mechanism, banks try to fulfil their CTF obligations blindfolded and/or on autopilot without paying much attention to the quality or the detail of the products of their AML/CTF practices.

An FIU expert stated that there is an asymmetric information problem within the financial sector: the financial sector does not have any information regarding

204 Interview with a Senior Level Manager of a Bank Branch No: BS1.
205 Interview with a Senior Level Manager of a Bank Branch No: BS1.
206 Interview with a Senior Level CTF Practitioner from a Law Enforcement Agency No: LE2.
207 Interview with a Senior Level Manager of a Bank Branch No: BS1.

who the suspects or actual terrorists are and what they are doing. Moreover, they do not know how to detect them and their potential and actual financial activities.[208] However, they are required to fulfil their obligations in terms of CTF and AML. Due to existing defined risk parameters for issuing terrorist financing, SARs are neither clear nor relevant for CTF purposes,[209] and MASAK – FIU is inundated with so many SARs, which results in an overwhelming amount of work and information pollution for the analysis units. A lack of direction to the financial sector by key CTF agencies adds another layer of challenge for an effective CTF in Turkey. To address this problem, MASAK – FIU should provide more accurate risk parameters for the financial sector, which would direct and assist them for reporting suspicious activity or transactions. There should be a feedback mechanism for the financial sector where MASAK – FIU can act as an interface unit between intelligence, security forces, judiciary and financial sector. In this regard, MASAK – FIU may direct the financial sector by providing feedback and warning about high-risk customers, institutions, regions and places.[210] It can be suggested that this kind of approach would solve the problem of exchanging CTF related sensitive information between the public and private sectors; thus the tension which negatively affects the cooperation and coordination between these institutions can be mitigated.

In addition, as an FIU practitioner noted, submitting SARs on their clients is a serious concern for banks and they are reluctant to do so because of the real possibility that they may lose their business and money.[211] These concerns and fears are acute particularly because, in Turkey, prosecution and conviction rates for money laundering and terrorist financing are extremely low (Turksen et al., 2011); thus submitting SARs becomes a fruitless effort. Thus, following up SARs, improving success rates of prosecution and convictions along with providing a clear picture and orientation for the private financial sector are the necessary components which need be realised in Turkey's CTF regime.

Blacklisting and asset freezing

Another issue which was raised during our interviews is the effect of blacklisting and asset freezing orders. In tandem with the common shortcomings of the international CTF regime, which were reviewed in the previous chapters, problems pertaining to these two areas are also present in Turkey. Firstly, an FIU practitioner expressed that the names listed by the UNSC Resolutions (e.g. UNSC

208 Interview with a Senior Level CTF Expert from the Turkish FIU – MASAK No: FIU1.

209 According to the same FIU expert, it is deliberate that the parameters which are given to the private financial sector for issuing SARs are generic rather than accurate and clear. It is feared that providing more accurate and very clear SAR parameters to the private financial sector might result in compromise of sensitive information and expose security institutions' secret *modus operandi* in terms of undertaking CTF efforts.

210 Interview with a Senior Level CTF Expert from the Turkish FIU – MASAK No: FIU1.

211 Interview with a Senior Level CTF Expert from the Turkish FIU – MASAK No: FIU4.

Resolution 1267 and others) are not clear, and it is problematic for financial institutions to know whether these people are on the sanction list. As there are so many 'AKA – also known as' names for the same person in these lists, both private financial and public sectors do not accurately know to whom such measures apply. In the current system, in order to confirm someone's identity in case of any name resemblance and suspicion, a bank employee should communicate with MASAK – FIU first and then via Ministry of Foreign Affairs reach the UN Sanctions Committee. This lengthy process clearly is not viable way of confirming the identity of a person. It is noted that most probably, the UN Sanctions Committee will not be able to give clear information regarding the identities either, because they do not have accurate information in the first place. The second problem stated by an FIU practitioner is that some of the terrorist organisations, such as Al Nusra Front, are listed only by the names of the organisations without other details such as the names of their members and affiliates. Listing merely the names of the terrorist organisations does not give any clue to a bank employee regarding who has links with terrorist organisations or who is really a suspect. This limited scope can be interpreted either as over or under inclusive. In any event, as banks are not intelligence or law enforcement agencies, their employees' perceptions and knowledge of terrorist organisations are limited. This causes problems in terms of targeted and smart application of the CTF regime.

Pursuant to the recent Legislation No. 6415 on counter terrorism, Turkey updates the names on the UNSC 1267 list, yet there has not been any match or identification of a person on this list by a Turkish bank. Even if there is a match, a customer can reject or appeal such designation by the bank because there is often not adequate or substantive information to confirm this designation.[212] On the other hand, as another FIU expert optimistically noted, the fact that there has not been any matches shows that Turkey is not a source country for terrorist financing for the listed organisations, individuals and other entities.[213] Regardless of the implications of these lists, the key guiding principle is that the names ought to be more accurate and verifiable by evidence. This would enhance the legitimacy and integrity of the lists and would ensure better compliance and CTF operations.

It can be said that in terms of the Sanctions Committee lists and asset freezing orders, there have been genuine efforts by the Turkish government to comply with international obligations, yet there have not been any positive results or outcomes as a result. Although all the necessary mechanisms and legislation are pretty much in place in Turkey (in line with UNSC Resolutions and FATF Recommendations), due to the limited information provided for the identification of the possible suspects, terrorists or sponsors within these lists, the financial sector finds it hard to detect anyone in practice. Consequently, without providing adequate information to detect and identify suspects, implementing international CTF measures to listed organisations by national CTF statutes seems symbolic

212 Interview with a Senior Level CTF Expert from the Turkish FIU – MASAK No: FIU1.
213 Interview with a Senior Level CTF Expert from the Turkish FIU – MASAK No: FIU4.

or a mere diplomatic gesture. The FIU experts[214] think blacklisting and related asset freezing methods are not effective for ideal implementation and effective CTF struggle.

Banks and other responsible financial institutions should appoint compliance officers and compliance units according to their size and capacity. Basically, compliance officers supervise the implementation of AML and CTF policy and take necessary precautions and report directly to MASAK about the problems or violations as independent experts from each bank. According to the current AML/CTF regulation, the compliance officers are expected to be independent, impartial and honest, and similarly, the board of directors for the bank are expected to create a suitable environment for compliance officers to conduct their tasks and responsibilities.[215] However, it is questionable if and to what extent the compliance officers are able to influence the implementation of CTF measures and act independently. According to a bank manager, most of the compliance officers cannot act independently:

> I do not think that all of them are capable of doing this task [independently], most of them depend on their institutions thus they cannot move out of the decision circle of their institutions. I think that their organisations selected them because they are the ones who would not be able act independently. I do not find them independent, because ultimately they have to serve the interests of the organisation. [. . .] For that reason they should be positioned very independently, otherwise they cannot move out of organisation policy and influence. I think regulating their situation by better legal provisions can be useful.[216]

According to this claim, compliance officers, who are responsible to supervise, direct their banks and report suspicion and/or violations of CTF regulations to the FIU and other legal units, cannot act against the policy of their banks independently, such as reporting their institution to the public prosecutor or MASAK in case of a violation within the bank. This account gives us a clue that there are concerns regarding the independence of compliance officers for reporting their banks or institutions, which might cause economic and legal ramifications for this reporting act. As suggested above, a legal amendment or regulation which will change compliance officers' positions or increase their protection against their financial institutions may let them act more independently.[217] Rather than being

214 Interviews with Senior Level CTF Experts from the Turkish FIU – MASAK No: FIU1 and FIU4.

215 For more information, see the Regulation on Program of Compliance with Obligations of Anti-Money Laundering and Combating the Financing of Terrorism (Ministry of Finance, 2008).

216 Interview with a Senior Level Manager of a Bank Branch No: BS1.

217 It is beyond the scope of this monograph to analyse and comment on independent reporting, whistle-blowing or public disclosures in detail. However, the importance of these

employed solely by banks, these compliance officers can be aligned to an independent body or professional organisation (i.e. similar to an auditors' association, or a bar for lawyers) established by law and accredited by financial sector regulators.

Preferences by terrorists – Banks are not the one

Even though there is limited empirical data on how effective CTF measures are in the Turkish banking sector, it can be claimed that banks in Turkey are equipped well against terrorist financing in terms of fulfilling their obligations in line with international and regional (the EU) AML/CTF standards (Turksen et al., 2011). Turkey's CTF regime and environment have been monitored and assessed not only by the FATF, but also by the terrorists as well because terrorists would like to exploit any weaknesses in that system.

At this point, in order to understand and evaluate the efficacy of the CTF measures in the banking sector, it is important inquire as to how frequently or to what extent the formal banking or the financial system is used by terrorists. Regarding this issue, an FIU expert stated that most of the terrorist financing case files are compiled and prepared by the prosecutors, and these are not initiated following an SAR.[218] Annual reports by MASAK – FIU also indicate that there are terrorist financing cases following an SAR. Even though the existing SAR process can be used to track suspicious money transfers, a mechanism designed for AML purposes, these measures are not useful or fit for detecting and preventing financing of terrorism especially in Turkey. The same FIU expert explained that "[m]aybe we can clearly say that actually they [terrorists] are not using the banking system directly; hence it is not easy to track them in this environment [. . .]". It was also claimed that terrorist organisations, particularly those which operate in Turkey, do not use the formal financial system for their fund transfers.[219] Osman Öcalan, the brother of the incarcerated leader of PKK, Abdullah Öcalan, correspondingly stated that PKK has not been using banks in order to funnel their funds (Rudaw, 2015).

In light of these findings, there are two possible conclusions which are connected:

It can be claimed the current CTF environment and measures such as reporting, due diligence and KYC applied by the banking sector are not effective for detecting and disrupting terrorist organisations. This is because the banks do not receive adequate information from the authorities and/or fear losing customers and/or do not trust the current AML/CTF regime to deliver any tangible results. Furthermore, the bank professionals (e.g. compliance officers)

elements in any AML/CTF regime has been acknowledge by many scholars (Turksen, 2018; Dow & Turksen, 2017, Srividhya and Shelly, 2012 and Glazer & Glazer, 1989).

218 Interview with a Senior Level CTF Expert from the Turkish FIU – MASAK No: FIU4.

219 *Ibid.*

responsible for reporting and monitoring compliance are not able to operate in an enabling environment to perform their duties independently. In addition, it seems to be the case that most terrorists in Turkey do not use the banking sector for their money transfers and other activities; thus, there is no paper trail to even contemplate suspicious activity and report it. Rather, terrorists prefer alternative (informal) money transfer methods to evade these strictly implemented due diligence measures in Turkey.[220] These trends demonstrate that every jurisdiction, terrorist organisation or type of financial source and methods needs to be addressed by a tailored approach, taking into account the peculiarities and unique operational challenges of that system. The one-for-all type approach does not seem to be working where formal financial systems are avoided and/or not used by terrorists.

5.4.7 Using AML methods for CTF

When the governments around the world decided to target the financial capabilities and sources of terrorist organisations with significant intensity after 9/11, this process was patched onto the existing AML measures and frameworks such as the FATF Recommendations. However, the efficacy and effectiveness of AML provisions and standards dealing with terrorist financing are still a contested topic, as explained in previous chapters. Terrorist finance derives from both illegal and legal sources and thus is fundamentally different than the laundering of proceeds of crime. From a financial sector manager's perspective, the effectiveness of AML for CTF is also seen as a problematic issue. According to him:

> Well, the measures developed for dealing with money laundering can be used for countering terrorist financing, but this may not cause to improve my decision-making capacity independently for issuing an SAR or countering financing of terrorism in the first instance [. . .] I can detect a money laundering process whereas I cannot detect financing of terrorism. I think that the bank staff need to have this knowledge directly. [. . .] It cannot be said that the systems developed for anti-money laundering are well integrated with [countering] financing of terrorism.[221]

On the same topic, an FIU expert had a somewhat different perspective and asserted the following:

> Therefore, as an expert I find it logical to use the measures and tools developed mainly by FATF Recommendations and UN Resolutions for the financing of terrorism as well. But the illogical part is that you can suspect from the high amount of money or depositing money after splitting up to 50

220 Interview with a Senior Level CTF Expert from the Turkish FIU – MASAK No: FIU4.
221 Interview with Senior Level Manager of a Bank Branch No: BS1.

> parts as a result of the typology you have, however these typologies may not be suitable for terrorist financing. For example, in MASAK – FIU we have separated typologies and developed suspicious transaction typologies only exclusive for terrorist financing. [. . .] Yet the only thing can be added related to financing of terrorism is that both on the international and domestic level you have to demonstrate and indicate clearly to the financial sector that who is or who can be a terrorist.[222]

According to these accounts, it is hard for the banking sector to decide whether any suspicious activity can be classified as money laundering or terrorist financing. It is not clear how to decide whether any bank transaction is a subject of money laundering or terrorist financing in terms of existing typologies. Due to lack of experience and knowledge, identifying a suspicious transaction as a money laundering activity is easier for them than deciding that it is a terrorist financing activity. Thus, the financial sector should be informed about both international and domestic terrorism threats and terrorists regularly and in more detail. AML measures can be used for some terrorist financing cases to a certain extent but not all. As MASAK already did, AML and CTF typologies should be designed and applied differently. However, without informing the financial sector about current terrorist threats and related accurate typologies for detecting suspicious terrorist financing activities, there is less chance to produce effective outcomes. It seems that the problems regarding the application of AML measures for CTF purposes are valid in the context of CTF effectiveness in Turkey. Moreover, it should be noted that MASAK's efforts on developing CTF oriented typologies are important for addressing deficiencies in detecting potential terrorist financing cases. Moreover, these efforts need to be backed by accurate criteria and better information sharing for supporting the financial sector.

5.4.8 Arrest centric law enforcement

Another significant factor influencing the effective implementation of CTF efforts is the arrest centric approach adopted by CTF practitioners, which is not only superficial but also inadequate as it focuses on arresting and convicting low-level criminals. During the interviews, nearly all the parties touched upon this topic. It was noted that for law enforcement and legal authorities, it is more important to arrest and convict terrorist financiers than to disclose the main financial network in which more than one terrorist is active.

According to a law enforcement practitioner, because of the existing priorities and limited capacity of law enforcement units, they tend to focus on capturing criminal assets such as drugs or smuggled goods and arresting criminals. However, they are not inclined to dismantle the main criminal and financial mechanisms which raise money for terrorist organisations and organised criminal activities.

222 Interview with Senior Level CTF Expert from Turkish FIU – MASAK No: FIU1.

Rather than investigating who the leader or leaders are of this organisation, what links they have and where their sources come from, arresting and sentencing low-level criminals, foot soldiers or financiers is perceived to be an easier and preferred option. Every law enforcement agency with CTF responsibilities seems to be content with this limited implementation.[223] A director from the MFA supporting the above asserted that it is because this type of application is much easier for practitioners. She noted that "[r]ather than, for instance, sentencing someone for the offence of financing terrorism, which needs extra work and efforts to prove, it is much easier to punish someone for the crime of being a member of terrorist organisation, in Turkey. This is the easiest and guaranteed way for convictions of terrorist offences in Turkey".[224]

Another law enforcement practitioner asserted that the main problem emanates from the lack of awareness and knowledge of law enforcement and legal practitioners. He argued that:

> More importantly, I see that this issue [CTF] is not known well and existing legal provisions are not understood well either. For instance, I see that when a drug seized from a drug trafficking organisation, the assets of their members, whose only job is drug trafficking, are not touched, moreover there is no investigation on them. In my opinion although existing legislation is adequate, these are not considered due to lack of awareness. Especially if the awareness of prosecutors can be increased and the importance of this issue is understood then I believe there will be more comprehensive success on this issue. [. . .] Low-level law enforcement officers immediately focus on the subject of crime [such as drug, weapon, smuggled commodity et cetera] rather than bank accounts, private assets and incomes from their families. Lack of awareness on this issue [components of terrorist financing] is the main problem.[225]

During the investigation phase of terrorism related offences, the financial aspect seems to be ignored due to lack of knowledge and awareness. The investigations conducted are focused on the material evidence on terrorist act/s rather than the financial background of that crime. As one scholar noted:

> When we examine records of statements [of terrorists], I have read hundreds and thousands [of] statements, I did not see any question posed to a terrorist who is captured with a weapon that how s/he acquired the weapon, or to a man arrested in a terror cell, it was not asked how s/he pays the rent for the house. Because we always, as classical terms, ask where is the weapon, did you find the weapon, yes, oh ok, it is done. Because it [the weapon] is the

223 Interview with a Middle Level CTF Practitioner from a Law Enforcement Agency No: LE11.

224 Interview with a Senior Level Director from the Ministry of Foreign Affairs No: MFA1.

225 Interview with a Middle Level CTF Practitioner from Law Enforcement Agency: LE6.

> material evidence [which suffices for conviction], we ignore peripheral elements of the crime such as financing of that crime; this is one of our biggest weaknesses.[226]

Correspondingly, a judge stated that well-planned, detailed investigations have not been undertaken for the financial activities of terrorists. He stated that:

> We will arrest a terrorist or a suspect, put in custody, take him to court, judge him then convict him to 10 or 15 years of prison sentence, ok. What about the rest? Actually, the rest was the important part of it, can I explain? In other words, as I understand there has not been a lawsuit process and deep examination in total on the points of where do these sources come from, where do these men go, what do they eat and drink, where does the weapon come from. [. . .] There has not been any initiative not only for PKK, but also for other terrorist organisations such as DHKP/C, Hizbullah, Al Qaeda.[227]

It might be claimed that sentencing those who are believed to finance terrorism is a secondary goal of the Turkish law enforcement and legal authorities, and very little (if any) priority is given to decreasing the amount of terrorist finance. Arresting and punishing terrorists are seen as more important and subsequently exercised with a good degree of success regularly. However, inquiring about the financial background of terrorist organisations and their terrorist activities needs more effort, and at the end, there may not be a tangible outcome to showcase to the public. Thus, both law enforcement and legal practitioners tend to ignore the financial aspects of terrorism. As mentioned above, the organisational habits of practitioners and the level of their training and awareness are important factors affecting the CTF dimension of the financing of organised crime in general. A recent circular issued on 20 February 2015 by the Ministry of Justice on Prevention of Laundering Proceeds of Crime and Financing of Terrorism aims to increase cooperation in and sensitivity towards CTF and stipulates clearly the steps and processes for undertaking a financial investigation for both terrorist financing and money laundering cases (Bozdağ, 2015). This circular clearly demonstrates that Turkey's authorities are aware of terrorist financing problem and have recently begun to address it by encouraging and concentrating legal and law enforcement efforts on money laundering and terrorist financing.

Furthermore, it was also mentioned during the interviews that the reward system applied by the criminal justice system in Turkey might have influence on the arrest-oriented approach.[228] It was noted by an FIU expert that the effects

226 Interview with a Scholar working as CTF Practitioner Expert on counter-terrorism and radicalisation No: AC6.

227 Interview with a Senior Level CTF Practitioner from Department of Justice No: JD1.

228 According to this system when drugs and related material are seized or captured by law enforcement forces or other agencies, the personnel involved in this operation are awarded the money according the market price of the seized material. This is the public application

of using rewards on both public and private sectors are different. For the public sector, where officials can be rewarded for their success in seizing drugs or other related illegal materials, this application may decrease the effectiveness of CTF efforts. For instance, rather than applying a controlled delivery operation till the last stop of the drug transfer in order to disclose and arrest whole drug trafficking networks, law enforcement agencies might have been choosing to intervene before drug traffickers leave the country so as not to have to share the reward and success with other agencies within or outside Turkey. On the other hand, using rewards for dealing with financial crimes in the private sector seems to be more effective. People are keen to share sensitive information, which might be used to disclose financial crimes in companies, with officials in order to get the reward provided by the Ministry of Finance. However, in the case of financing of terrorism, there is no such application, which may be useful for an effective struggle.[229] Offering a reward for providing information in order to disclose financial crimes seems to be effective. The use of reward based reporting seems to even overcome the strongest relations and alliances; an FIU expert stated that he witnessed that a father was reported by his son in order to take the reward.[230] Even though a new regulation on rewarding citizens who assist security forces to arrest terrorists was introduced by the Ministry of Interior in August 2015 (T. C. İçişleri Bakanlığı, 2015), there is no provision regarding rewards available for providing information which can be used for unveiling terrorist financing. It can be asserted that there is no rewarding system for disclosing financial activities of terrorists and their supporters, and there is no effort to establish such a system in the near future. This can be another recommendation for the CTF regime Turkey: by using a reward mechanism, the information collected from society can be increased, and subsequently, the effectiveness of the CTF could be improved.

5.4.9 The level of financial investigation and intelligence efforts

The importance of financial investigation and intelligence activities has increased in the aftermath of 9/11, especially in the US (Clunan, 2006; Roth et al., 2004; Parker & Taylor, 2010). In collecting information regarding the past, present and future activities of terrorist organisations, it has been conceived that both financial investigation and intelligence methods are producing positive outcomes (HM Treasury, 2007; Levitt & Jacobson, 2008). In this context, during the interviews, the current situation of the application of financial investigations and intelligence activities in Turkey was discussed.

---

of award system in Turkey. Similarly, in the private sector, there is another awarding system. In this case if citizens give or provide accurate information about specific crimes such as terrorism or financial crimes, they are paid money according to the importance of their assistance for disclosing or solving the crime.

229 Interview with a Senior Level CTF Expert from the Turkish FIU – MASAK No: FIU1.

230 *Ibid.*

As one FIU expert expressed, the financial investigation component of both money laundering and terrorist financing cases is conducted at the very late stages of the investigation. He also noted that the premature arrests or knee-jerk operations before all the potential criminal and financing links are established may be the reason for this trend. Consequently, many opportunities for finding clues and evidence during the investigation phase could be lost because of this reactionary, early interference. In addition, it was stated that even though the FATF recommends carrying on both criminal and financial investigations simultaneously, most of the criminal investigations in Turkey are not undertaken in the way recommended by the FATF.[231]

Another problem stated by a law enforcement practitioner regarding financial investigation was that:

> Financial investigations, this is a problematic issue. How problematic is it? Because the law enforcement structure is different [in Turkey]. For instance, there are no similar organisations in Turkey such as [. . .] new NCA [National Crime Agency] in the UK [which hosts diverse expertise]. How is this [financial investigation] conducted in Turkey? In Turkey after the investigation is started, with the authority and the request of the prosecutor, specialists from other areas [of the criminal justice system – such as forensic accountancy team] are called upon to participate in the investigation. But this not done on a permanent basis, thus there is no continuity for them to be involved in the case from the very start to the end. Most probably this person [specialist] may know about the financial aspects of a particular crime very well whereas it would be better if he had been involved in the criminal investigation as a member from the start. Currently, [for instance] we already have people with expertise in traditional criminal matters. Now, I believe that the financial investigations would be more detailed and comprehensive, if we could hire civil servants who are experts on financial investigations. [. . .] May be the only thing that should be done regarding the law enforcement is that financial investigators should be a part of law enforcement agency.[232]

It was acknowledged that there is a need for joint investigations whereby financial experts who are competent in financial audits participate in criminal/terrorism related investigations. At the same time, it was identified that such financial experts know little about criminal investigations in comparison to law enforcement officials. In addition, financial experts often have a temporary role and presence in these investigations. Therefore, it may be better to have financial experts who are also trained well in criminal investigation techniques in the law enforcement agencies and have their involvement throughout the investigations and operations. Currently, law enforcement agencies do not have permanent financial

231 Interview with a Senior Level CTF Expert from the Turkish FIU-MASAK No: FIU1.
232 Interview with a Senior Level CTF Practitioner from Law Enforcement Agency No: LE2.

specialists; rather, they may be seconded from other departments if requested by the prosecutor. Consequently, it is clear that there is a need for integrated capability which addresses both financial and criminal aspects of the investigations. And the arrest centric tendency mentioned previously results in a narrow focus and clouds the whole picture of terrorist networks and their financing activities.

Regarding financial intelligence activities, a senior level FIU director noted that financial intelligence has similar phases and processes as other types of intelligence activities.[233] Financial intelligence is accepted as one of the most important parts of CTF efforts. However, there are problems regarding financial intelligence usage and production in Turkey. Regarding this, the FIU director stressed that while law enforcement agencies try to prevent the financial activities of terrorists, MASAK – FIU should find out the source of this financial activity by mapping its network structure using financial intelligence effectively. Yet owing to the limited powers and capacity of the Turkish FIU, it was noted that currently Turkey is far from achieving this.[234] This may show that the level of financial intelligence utilisation as part and parcel of CTF is not at the expected level according to the CTF practitioners.

Another important issue noted by the same director was that MASAK as an intelligence unit should be composed of personnel who are from different backgrounds comprising both criminal, terrorism and financial investigation expertise. He explained that MASAK – FIU, operating as one of the intelligence units, comprises employees who come from similar backgrounds, such as finance and economics. However, in order to conduct financial intelligence tasks effectively, he was of the opinion that MASAK should employ personnel with eclectic expertise such as legal, law enforcement, academic and research. Employees with financial expertise can analyse financial records easily, whereas they may not analyse and interpret this data within a terrorism framework as a counter-terrorism expert would. It was also pointed out that this limited scope of expertise in MASAK was criticised by the FATF. Similar to the suggestions of a law enforcement practitioner who opined that financial experts should be embedded in the organic structure of law enforcement in general, it was stated by the FIU practitioner that the current FIU organisation, MASAK, needs experts with different backgrounds such as terrorism, legal, criminal and law enforcement in order to complement the existing expertise.[235]

For MASAK, as a financial intelligence unit, it is correct to say that production of intelligence and evaluation of financial intelligence are important issues, which undoubtedly need input from and cooperation with private and public

233 Although there are various classifications, according to the Turkish National Intelligence Agency (2016), the main accepted intelligence production process is called 'Intelligence Cycle' which is classified in four steps: 1. Determining the Intelligence Requirements and the Orienting the Collection Activity; 2. Collecting Information; 3. Processing Information (Evaluation); 4. Disseminating and Using the Intelligence.

234 Interview with a (former) Senior Level Director from MASAK – FIU No: FIU2.

235 Interview with a (former) Senior Level Director from MASAK – FIU No: FIU2.

stakeholders. Otherwise, the intelligence may be deficient or misleading or, at best, will not produce concrete achievements against terrorists. Nevertheless, the current structure of MASAK is not fully conducive to producing evidence admissible in criminal courts due to a lack of diverse backgrounds among its staff, which can limit its understating of how the criminal justice system operates. Without accurate intelligence, it is hard to sustain a successful CTF strategy. In this context, by assembling experts from different disciplines, these structural and capacity gaps could be addressed, and the effectiveness and the quality of the intelligence can be improved.

It is clear that counter-terrorism requires diverse elements of evidence and expertise. Roberge (2007, p. 201) highlights the importance of combining different types of intelligence for a better CTF implementation. Regarding this, a senior director from FIU stated that "[w]e need information acquired from the field, because, while we can advance the investigation to a certain degree with financial evidence, we are often stuck because of lack of information [for the substantive terrorist activity itself]".[236] In this regard, beside financial intelligence, the intelligence collected from the field and especially human intelligence are very important for concluding and achieving solid outcomes in financial investigations. Thus, MASAK cannot finalise its terrorist financing files examinations without intelligence collected from the field, and subsequently the prosecutors, due to this shortcoming, cannot start judicial proceedings. In addition, it is noted that, due to the ill-structured administrative position of MASAK – FIU in the Turkish bureaucratic hierarchy, other law enforcement institutions position themselves above MASAK and claim superiority, and subsequently, they are reluctant to share information with it. Even though all state institutions are under a legal duty to meet MASAK's information demands, these institutions continue their reluctance to share their information with MASAK.[237] Thus, using mere financial intelligence collected from financial documents without having related intelligence collected from other sources, it is not easy for FIU analysts to produce eloquent intelligence for initiating comprehensive operations against terrorist financing. This shows that the analysis conducted by MASAK depends mainly on the financial information it can gather; the lack of cooperation and its inability to collect information beyond financial intelligence are the missing parts in the CTF regime in Turkey, which need to be fixed.

In this framework, it is important to examine the sufficiency of on-going intelligence efforts in terms of CTF. A senior director from the Ministry of Foreign Affairs emphasised the importance of holistic intelligence gathering and added that detecting the terrorist related activities, members, links, and financial activities should be determined and monitored closely. Discovery and determining individuals' role/s in the terrorist organisation are especially important in order to combat the financial operations. It is suggested that profiling and information

236 Interview with a (former) Senior Level Director from MASAK – FIU No: FIU3.
237 Interview with a (former) Senior Level Director from MASAK – FIU No: FIU3.

repository tools can be used effectively for this purpose, adding that "[w]ell, all these capabilities are available in Turkey but how effectively are they used? In practice, they are not used effectively, whereas I think that Turkey should use these tools more effectively".[238] These findings indicate that even though the role of intelligence efforts addressing financing of terrorism is accepted as a significant and essential element of effective CTF, the adequacy of the applications of intelligence tools for CTF is not assessed as sufficient or effective.

Similarly, an FIU practitioner did not think that the intelligence is adequate in the context of CTF in Turkey. It was argued that there is no clear information regarding the amount of money owned [by terrorists] and how much of it is acquired from legal or illegal activities. Even though there are many different speculations regarding the domestic and international financial sources of PKK, an accurate amount of PKK's financial capacity and size is anyone's guess.[239] According to another law enforcement practitioner, because of the lack of comprehensive intelligence, the financial links and their role in combating terrorism are underestimated or not prioritised. In addition, the quality of the intelligence provided is not sufficient.[240] In a similar line of thought, a scholar emphasised the importance of intelligence in counter-terrorism and noted that:

> If you do not know [the details of criminal activity] you cannot do anything [to counter it] . . . [f]or that reason, you need to have very deep intelligence source. Actually, you need to know what is critical, where the money is coming from. I do not think that these are known fully in Turkey. Where does this [terrorist] money come from, I have never heard and seen any information answering that question: what is the monthly cost of a single terrorist for the terrorist organisation. [. . .] If you cannot understand something then it cannot be critical element for you. It is critical but we cannot understand it because we do not know magnitude of it. [. . .][241]

These accounts provide further evidence that Turkey's financial intelligence activities undertaken by law enforcement and intelligence agencies are limited. Thus, it can be claimed there is no established financial intelligence network or framework, which is operated by all intelligence agencies in Turkey. Consequently, it may be asserted that both financial investigation and intelligence applications, which are critical for both counter-terrorism and CTF, are not at a desired level. Institutional, organisational and operational problems dent the quality and effectiveness of investigation and intelligence efforts for CTF.

238 Interview with a Senior Level Director from the Ministry of Foreign Affairs No: MFA1.

239 Interview with a Senior Level CTF Expert from Turkish FIU – MASAK No: FIU4.

240 Interview with a Middle Level CTF Practitioner from a Law Enforcement Agency No: LE4.

241 Interview with a Scholar Expert on International Relations – Professor at a University No: AC3.

Even though the current intelligence gathering and operations for CTF are not at an expected level, there have been some initiatives to improve these. For example, the Law on the State Intelligence Services and the Turkish National Intelligence Organisation ("Devlet İstihbarat Hizmetleri ve Milli İstihbarat Teşkilatı Kanunu", 1983) which regulates intelligence activities and responsibilities, was amended by in 2014. With these amendments, one of the main purposes is to increase the National Intelligence Agency's capabilities and powers for CTF. In this regard, the National Intelligence Agency (MIT) has been given the authority to access all kind of financial records and documents which may be written or stored in a database digitally. Although a number of concerns have been raised, particularly in relation to the right to privacy (Human Rights Watch, 2014), with the introduction of this amendment, it may be claimed that the gap regarding financial intelligence gathering may have been filled. It is not wrong to assert that these efforts may be evaluated as positive steps towards a better CTF environment. Furthermore, it may be noted that in contrast to the limited intelligence capability of MASAK, the National Intelligence Agency (MIT), would have a better opportunity to conflate both information collected from field and the financial sector and produce better intelligence outcomes for counter-terrorism units and prosecutors. However, due to the secrecy of the institution and limited information available publicly, it is hard to comment on whether and to what extend the MIT has the capacity to analyse these different types of information and gather quality intelligence.

In this section of our analysis, the reasons for the limited implementation and effectiveness of CTF in Turkey were identified and discussed. In doing so a number of issues pertaining to legal provisions, challenges for law enforcement and judicial agencies combating legal and illegal sources of terrorist financing, implications these rules for the financial sector and, last but not the least, the adequacy of financial intelligence and financial investigations in Turkey were examined. Next, we consider the capacity of the relevant agencies endowed with the responsibility to combat financing of terrorism.

5.5 The level of CTF capacity

In terms of the level of capacity of CTF institutions and the capability and competence of their staff, the training efforts, specialisation on CTF and technological tools they can employ are analysed by using personal accounts and related documents and reports. Undoubtedly, Turkey has a CTF system based on legal and administrative infrastructures (which are informed by international standards) and relevant departments with personnel who are supposed to be experts on this subject area. However, for a critical understanding of the dynamics therein and to provide granular detail as to the effectiveness and the success level of CTF implementation, it is necessary to examine areas beyond the law in books and legislative arrangements. Hence, we examine to what extent these institutions and their staffs are capable of conducting a CTF campaign.

In terms of examining the competency of institutional capacity, our interviewees were asked what they think about the capacity of the institutions responsible for CTF. Here the concept of 'capacity' needs to be clarified. In the context of this study, 'capacity' refers to the level of autonomy and authority of CTF institutions to carry out responsibilities arising from the CTF legislation. More specifically, this term has two dimensions: the first is the institutional capacity; the second one indicates the individual level of capacity. In regards to institutional capacity, capacity denotes the level to which an institution has sufficient resources, such as personnel, budget, tools, vehicles and technology, for CTF operations nationally and internationally. Secondly, at the individual level, the term refers to the level of competency of the agents of the CTF institutions in terms of their awareness, training, ability to apply their skills and how sufficiently technology and related instruments can be used by the CTF practitioners. However, it should be borne in mind that distinguishing these two realms to define capacity is not a simple task, particularly because of the inherent entangled structure of the concept. Within this framework, the level of capacity is examined, and in general, it can be claimed that while the institutional CTF capacity of the related organisations and agencies is at a satisfactory level, the individual level capacity is problematic. However, there have been some efforts to improve individual capacity, which needs time to achieve the desired levels.

Regarding the capacity of institutions, a senior level practitioner noted that:

> Theoretically, the capacity that has been acquired by the institutions is sufficient, however, the biological part is weak. In other words, employees are inadequate, whereas in theory or according to law or training, they all are competent. However, when it comes to practice, due to the degenerated organisation culture, they are incompetent actually.[242]

In contrast, a scholar asserted that, "I believe Turkey has everything it needs. [. . .] There is a highly developed human potential on counter-terrorism and terrorist financing recently in Turkey. Thus, I think that the state has everything in abundance in terms of money and human resources".[243] Although another scholar similarly agreed with the idea that there is no problem in terms of finding personnel and financial sources [in Turkey] to counter terrorist finance, he distinguished his stance on the question of whether or not these people are qualified for CTF purposes. In his opinion, the appointments for CTF positions have been made by looking at qualifications of applicants rather than field work experience; "in other words, the qualification is more important than the capacity".[244]

242 Interview with a Senior Level CTF Practitioner from a Law Enforcement Agency No: LE9.
243 Interview with a Scholar who is an Expert on Security Studies – Professor at a University No: AC4.
244 Interview with a Scholar who is anExpert on International Relations – Professor at a University No: AC3.

On this point, another FIU practitioner approached the subject from a more fundamental perspective. He pointed out that there is an urgent need for a comprehensive examination of the current CTF system:

> Of course, you need new capacity, new human [resources]. In my opinion, before saying anything such as I need this and that, it should be determined what you actually need regarding the capacity [. . .] that's why the national risk assessment should be done elaborately, in other words firstly, the requirements and problems should be identified and later [it can be decided] what should be done about it.[245]

Here it was also noted that even though technological, personnel and financial capacity seem adequate, the competences of employees are not sufficient to produce effective outcomes in terms of CTF.[246] There is no argument that Turkey has the ability to provide every kind of capacity related resource; however, the competency and the effectiveness of the human factor are the key concerns. In order to change this situation, firstly there is a need for a 360 review and analysis of the CTF system for determining requirements and problems. Rightly, as it was pointed out, without doing this risk assessment and critique, any effort for improving capacity would be a fruitless activity. Thus, it is suggested that CTF institutions should define their aim and vision and consequently re-examine their requirements and build their capacity in the light of this analysis. It can be claimed according to the accounts from our interviews that Turkey has every material source needed for CTF; however, current capacity of all CTF institutions are not suitable for effective implementation. Therefore, Turkey should determine its CTF capacity requirements in light of its CTF risk analysis, and it should rebuild its capacity in order to address these findings.

5.5.1 The level of CTF training

The quality and efficacy of CTF training is another significant variable affecting the effectiveness of the CTF regime in Turkey. Examination of the application of CTF measures and the outcomes (or the lack of positive outcomes as the case is in Turkey) may indicate the current level of training. In this context, it could be claimed that CTF implementation in Turkey is insufficient. This shortcoming is partly due to the lack of personnel who are well trained and experienced enough to provide training to others; furthermore, there is a shortage of personnel who know how to enforce current legal instruments pertaining to CTF. Regarding this issue, a law enforcement officer highlighted that, "Most of the personnel are uninformed on this [CTF] subject. Currently, we have been

245 Interview with a Senior Level CTF Expert from the Turkish FIU – MASAK No: FIU1.
246 *Ibid.*

conducting training events in order to address this gap".[247] Another law enforcement practitioner was of the opinion that "there are many well-trained personnel [on terrorist financing]".[248] It may be true that there are well-trained personnel, as is mentioned by one of the law enforcement practitioners; however, the limited prosecution and conviction numbers indicate that there might be problems regarding simulating terrorist financing scenarios so that the CTF agents are able to cope with and work in real cases. Moreover, an FIU senior director and two law enforcement practitioners noted that institutions and responsible officials are not qualified enough; as key actors, prosecutors and law enforcement units are not sufficiently informed on the issues surrounding CTF, and the level of training varies among agencies.[249]

Even though some of the interviewees claimed that Turkey has well-trained CTF staff, the very limited number of investigations, court cases and convictions of persons involved in terrorist financing demonstrates that the ability of the CTF agents to apply this knowledge in law enforcement is weak. Furthermore, it is clear that law enforcement officials and judicial personnel such as judges and prosecutors especially need well-defined and fit for purpose CTF training. As some practitioners pointed out, CTF training regarding the powers and duties of law enforcement agencies pursuant to the new CTF legislation, trainings aimed at increasing awareness of terrorist financing methods in both the public and private sectors are urgently needed.[250]

As a CTF practitioner noted: "the effectiveness of [CTF] training can be debated however, we are not outsourcing training".[251] Another practitioner pointed that because of the novelty of CTF, the level of training might be insufficient or too generic for all institutions. Thus, it will take time for these trainings to be fine-tuned, understood and applied in practice by practitioners. Additionally, it was stated that currently, CTF training is not a priority for law enforcement staff nor is it pressed upon them by senior level officers. Bearing in mind the heavy workload they already have, there is a need for careful thinking about how CTF training is designed and delivered. If and when this is done, it will undoubtedly improve the level of effectiveness in practice.[252] An EU expert stated that "[. . .] the competency of the officials working in these institutions on both national and international legislations is super". However, they are not good at

247 Interview with a Senior Level CTF Practitioner from a Law Enforcement Agency No: LE12.

248 Interview with Middle Level CTF Practitioner from a Law Enforcement Agency No: LE11.

249 Interviews with a (former) Senior Level Director from MASAK No: FIU3, Senior Level CTF Practitioners from Law Enforcement Agencies No: LE2 and LE3.

250 Interviews with Senior and Middle Level CTF Practitioners from Law Enforcement Agencies: LE3, LE6; a Senior Level Manager of a Bank Branch No: BS1 and a Senior Level Expert from the General Directorate of Customs Enforcement No: CO1.

251 Interview with Senior Level CTF Expert from Turkish FIU-MASAK No: FIU4

252 Interview with Senior Level CTF Practitioner from a Law Enforcement Agency No: LE3.

applying this in real life.[253] In other words, CTF training and the CTF regime in Turkey need time to mature.

According to our interviews with stakeholders, the level of specialisation on the CTF is inadequate in Turkey. As a CTF practitioner and FIU expert noted, the current career planning system does not let the members of law enforcement agencies specialise in CTF because mostly, after their graduation and qualification, these personnel are appointed to different tasks during their careers without being allowed to gain experience in CTF. Correspondingly, most of the prosecutors and judges are not specialists on terrorist financing either; only a handful of them know the subject.[254]

As a scholar emphasised, every institution's priority is different, and CTF may not be perceived as a priority task in some of the law enforcement agencies; in this context, specialised units need to be established.[255] This indicates that Turkey needs to address specialisation on CTF via reorganising its CTF system along with specialised CTF training therein. Furthermore, as a law enforcement practitioner pointed out, "neither the police nor the gendarmerie are specialised on this subject [of CTF] adequately"; thus it would be wrong to expect many success stories due to the fact that these subjects have secondary or tertiary importance in their eyes.[256] And he added that "their priority is on different cases which may have more publicity, such as seizing large amounts of heroin or solving an important murder".[257] The situation of the legal practitioners and the judiciary is similar. Regarding this, a judge stated that "[n]ow the problem is shortage of specialists on this subject [CTF]. The number of judges and prosecutors who are expert on this subject is very few. [. . .] Honestly speaking, the number of trained specialists on this topic is not sufficient in Turkey".[258]

A director from the financial sector noted that even though MASAK – FIU staff have started to specialise in CTF and AML issues, many of the auditors who are tasked, often by secondment, from different public financial institutions such as tax comptrollers for conducting CTF and AML audits in the financial sector on behalf of MASAK, are not experts on these issues. Because they have different backgrounds and expertise on tax or other financial activities, it is difficult for them to interpret their findings in terrorism related organised crime activities.[259]

It was also noted that in order to conduct an effective CTF and disrupt transnational financial activities of terrorist organisations, Turkey needs to improve

253 Interview with an Expert on EU-Turkey relations and terrorism, No: EU1.
254 Interviews with CTF Practitioner-Civil Servant from a Law Enforcement Agency No: LEC0 and former Senior Level director from MASAK No: FIU2.
255 Interview with a Scholar working as a CTF Practitioner Expert on Counter-terrorism and Radicalisation No: AC6.
256 Interview with a Middle Level CTF Practitioner from a Law Enforcement Agency No: LE4.
257 *Ibid.*
258 Interview with a Senior Level Judge from the Department of Justice No: JD1.
259 Interview with a Senior Level Manager of a Bank Branch No: BS1.

the competency of CTF personnel, especially on the international law aspects of terrorism and terrorist financing. According to an international law expert:

> This [CTF] is not an easy field, look, FATF is OK, when we look at the OFAC example we can see that we need to construct a very serious body of expertise, you must know how to track money and monitor money transactions. You need to know where to put pressure and to see where you can catch it. Thus, you need to establish the bureaucracy for this.[260]

While it is important to consider the national aspects of the CTF regime, given the fact that most of the terrorist organisations operating in Turkey have international links and terrorism is seen as a universal crime, it would be wrong to disregard the international dimension of CTF. As the increasing importance of and the threat posed by transnational terrorism have led to growing investment by the international community and created numerous legal instruments which are designed to counter terrorism internationally and nationally, Turkey needs to use these as an opportunity to renew its CTF environment. In order to utilise these international tools effectively and in a meaningful way, Turkey needs to have well-trained international law specialists who know how to operate its CTF mechanism in collaboration and cooperation with other CTF agencies across the globe. However, as one judge indicated, Turkey does not have a specialised bureaucracy dealing with CTF internationally; consequently, it can be said that establishing a CTF bureaucracy that can operate inter-agency in Turkey and internationally is undoubtedly going to improve Turkey's CTF capabilities.[261]

In addition, there is a need for a multidisciplinary approach in which experts from different backgrounds can work together. While auditors can read financial records and detect the anomalies therein, they may not be able to interpret this financial data adequately in the context of the current terrorist threats. Thus, bringing in experts from different backgrounds, such as law enforcement, finance, intelligence, legal and academic fields, community leaders and workers would improve the current capacity of Turkey's efforts. Furthermore, the specialisation on terrorist financing should be planned elaborately based on the type of terrorist organisations, their respective financial sources and activities, target countries and sectors.

Regarding specialisation on CTF, a number of CTF practitioners provided suggestions. A law enforcement practitioner suggested that a new financial law enforcement agency ought to be established as the existing agencies have different priorities, institutional history and experience in other types of crimes. According to him, neither the law enforcement agencies nor the judiciary can read and interpret financial records. In order to investigate and deal with CTF, AML and

260 Interview with a Scholar who is an Expert on International Law – Assistant Professor at a University No: AC1.

261 Interview with a Senior Level Judge from the Department of Justice No: JD1.

other financial crimes, an independent financial law enforcement agency which specialises in CTF and AML methods and which understands the international dimensions of these phenomenon and is empowered with an authority to impose sanctions is needed.[262] A judge supporting this idea noted that law enforcement agencies in Turkey have problems when it comes to financial crime/s because they are not good at finding evidence and preparing detailed files for these types of crimes.[263] In this context, the financial field and crimes therein are quite new concepts for law enforcement agencies in Turkey who are used to dealing with different types of crimes. Moreover, when this new field is combined with a contested and contentious subject such as terrorism, then the situation becomes more confusing and misleading for them. They try to solve the problems with conventional methods, which do not have any influence on the problem. Another suggestion, as mentioned before, is the involvement of financial investigators with forensic accountancy and investigation expertise. Law enforcement agencies do not accommodate such specialists in their organisations. It is believed that the employment of financial investigators inside law enforcement agencies or counter-terrorism units would improve the effectiveness of CTF and fighting other types of financial crimes.[264]

An FIU director noted that there is also a need for financial intelligence analysts who can conflate financial clues with the activities of terrorist organisations:

> Especially, as far as I can see, the only problematic field is that, we do not have enough human resources of financial intelligence analysts who can evaluate financial transactions eloquently taking into account the peculiarities of different terrorist organisations. So, having only intelligence officers is not enough.[265]

While the members of law enforcement agencies may find analysing financial records challenging, financial intelligence analysts may struggle establishing a strong case against terrorists by only looking at financial records. Thus, a financial intelligence analyst would need to think comprehensively by cooperating with traditional counter-terrorism units and incorporating their findings and intelligence in their analysis.[266]

Establishing a Specialised Court for Terrorist Financing is another idea which was put forward by the CTF experts. A judge stated that:

> Appointing a financial expert as a councillor to the prosecution [as a permanent position] will be very welcome, because we do not know how to

262 Interview with a Middle Level CTF Practitioner from a Law Enforcement Agency No: LE4.

263 Interview with a Senior Level CTF Practitioner from the Department of Justice No: JD2.

264 Interviews with Senior Level CTF Practitioners from Law Enforcement Agencies No: LE2 and LE6.

265 *Ibid.*

266 Interview with a (former) Senior Level Director from MASAK No: FIU2.

> read financial tables and do not have any training in this regard. Whatever law enforcement agency brings to us or whatever court expert says we tend to follow them. Therefore, if there is a financial expert working with prosecutors then I believe this would be good feature for addressing financial crimes.[267]

Similarly, as a senior FIU director noted, "[. . .] there are even specialised courts for intellectual property rights, so a specialised court on financing of terrorism should be established. MASAK can provide experts for the court and other institutions. [. . .] This kind of CTF application can be very beneficial".[268] A judge stated that "[. . .] there is a need for specialised courts, specialised prosecutors [for CTF]".[269]

It is clear that the prosecutors and judges in Turkey are not inherently experts or trained in financing of terrorism; they depend on the evidence provided by law enforcement agencies or expert witnesses when dealing with these crimes. Establishing a specialised court dealing with terrorist financing is believed to be necessary for improving the CTF regime. A centralised and specialised court, which has experts on CTF, can also improve the competence and effectiveness of judicial practitioners in lower courts. In the existing system, no judge, prosecutor or law enforcement agency is an expert on reading financial records or interpreting terrorist money transfers and flows; some may not have even read the related CTF legislation. Thus, the number of convictions and cases of terrorist financing is very low.

As one scholar rightly pointed out, there is not an established white-collar or financial crime bureaucracy in Turkey[270] and added that:

> There is an economic bureaucracy side of this issue or economic security bureaucracy in which one should know the requirements and the language used there. So, there is a new regime in which OFAC and FATF exist. In order to be successful, one should have competent personnel who can speak the language of this new bureaucracy. However, we do not have these staff. This bureaucracy needs to be improved.[271]

It is clear that the current CTF system needs investment in professional training so that CTF expertise and specialisation can be imbedded. There is consensus among the CTF practitioners whom we interviewed that the CTF agencies need to be reformed with a view toward building CTF specialisation by combining and integrating skills from financial and traditional law enforcement practices.

267 Interview with a Senior Level Judge from the Department of Justice No: JD3.
268 Interview with a (former) Senior Level Director from MASAK No: FIU3.
269 Interview with a Senior Level Judge from the Department of Justice No: JD1.
270 Interview with a Scholar who is an Expert on International Law – Assistant Professor at a University No: AC1.
271 *Ibid.*

5.5.2 *The level of technological capacity*

Another component of capacity is the technological tools and capabilities and the level of utilisation of these for CTF purposes. Regarding the technological capacity of CTF institutions, we asked the interviewees whether there are adequate technological instruments, programs and staff capable of using them. In light of the responses, it can be stated that in general, the technological capacity of institutions conducting CTF related tasks seems adequate. Recently, new technological tools and programs have been acquired and used by law enforcement and FIU for CTF purposes. A CTF expert stated that "as far as I can see, all of our institutions, not just MASAK – FIU, are improving their abilities in this area and they have staff who can use these tools and provide training about them".[272] However, it is important how effectively these technological abilities and tools are used by the staff. Regarding the personnel who use these tools, another expert noted that "there are competent personnel who can conduct profiling, link analysis, social network analysis in Turkey".[273] Another point stated by a practitioner is that:

> We are going so fast; I mean if there is a new program released abroad, it is acquired immediately here. There is no problem regarding human resources, technology, or physically, however it is important how you use the computer, which parameters you have entered. If you do not enter right parameters, computer will not give you [the right] information.[274]

It is asserted here that the responsible personnel who are using these programs are well trained and capable of effective investigations. It should be noted, however, that the accuracy of variables entered and the questions asked determine the quality of outcomes produced by these highly developed programs and tools. In general, during the interviews, it was observed that the institutions are seriously caring for the importance and utilisation of technology both for conducting analysis and information sharing. In this context, the expert from the Customs Office stated that the technological level has been improved very much lately. Cash statements made at borders can be monitored online, and a very robust risk analysis system has been established. All required technological devices and programs have been provided and used. Due to an advanced network and technological base, PNR information is received from airlines and other travel services.[275]

The technological level of MASAK is noted as very advanced by the experts as well. In recent years MASAK has completed several technology-based projects and started to use them. MASAK has created its national intelligence analysis

272 Interview with a Senior Level CTF Expert from the Turkish FIU – MASAK, No: FIU1.

273 Interview with a Scholar working as a CTF Practitioner Expert on Counter-terrorism and Radicalisation No: AC6.

274 Interview with a (former) Senior Level Director from FIU – MASAK, No: FIU2.

275 Interview with a Senior Level Expert from the General Directorate of Customs Enforcement No:CO1.

program, which was designed according to the requirements of MASAK and Turkey. In the current situation, MASAK can monitor most of the financial sector's activities on online.[276]

All other law enforcement agencies also have required technological tools and software in order to collect intelligence and conduct investigations. Moreover, they have personnel trained in using these instruments effectively. It is noted as a problem, however, that even though there are different analysis programs and tools, the reluctance of the judiciary to warrant/authorise accessing databases is one of the problems experienced by law enforcement agencies.[277] While these programs can provide very good analysis of data for conducting effective investigations, without legal authority, these programs and users can become redundant. Moreover, with the system called UYAP (National Judiciary Informatics System), the judicial authorities can share information on suspects or arrest orders with the law enforcement agencies in an online environment, which can improve their success against criminals. In other words, the technological infrastructure for sharing information online with speed is available for judicial and law enforcement agencies.[278] Once again, it is clear that given the lack of positive results (in terms of prosecution and conviction numbers of terrorist financing offences), the use of these available technological tools and systems may be inadequate.

The private financial sector is another important domain where technology has been beneficial. As an FIU expert noted, due to its legal obligations, the Turkish banking sector has a very advanced technological infrastructure for detection, monitoring, profiling and reporting. Before MASAK announced the names added to UNSC Sanctions list, banks in Turkey had these names in their systems already. Moreover, not only do they follow UNSC Resolutions because of their global activities, they also follow the lists and updates by the US Treasury Department, OFAC and the EU as well.[279] A professional from the banking sector stated that the CTF systems in banks mainly focus on suspicious activities and possible scenarios for CTF and AML.[280] Banks can create and use their own scenarios for CTF and AML goals, and the banking sector in general has well-trained experts for using these programs and tools to identify and mitigate risks. However, he had concerns as to how accurately these scenarios and risks are analysed by the experts and provide value for CTF.[281] One of the issues relates to the information flows coming through and going to the branches from the headquarters. It was noted that the information was accumulated and collated at the head office, and the people who work there cannot directly reach the information from the

276 Interviews with Senior Level CTF Experts from the Turkish FIU – MASAK No: FIU1, FIU2, FIU3 and FIU4.

277 Interviews with a Senior Level CTF Practitioners from Law Enforcement Agencies No: LE2, LE3, LE6, LE7 and LE11.

278 Interview with a Senior Level Judge from the Department of Justice No: JD1.

279 Interview with a Senior Level CTF Expert from the Turkish FIU – MASAK No: FIU4.

280 Interview with a Senior Level Manager of a Bank Branch No: BS1.

281 *Ibid.*

field gathered by personnel who have face to face contact with the clients. It is acknowledged that it is critical to create databases where information can be gathered and analysed, but it is also important to empower the contact points that have direct access to information and interaction with the clients.

Overall, the level and availability of technological instruments seem to be adequate, albeit the utilisation of their scope can be limited at times. Technological infrastructure and physical requirements (hardware and software) have been provided as analytical tools, and it can be claimed that the proficiency level of the staff that are operating these tools is also adequate. Despite the high level of technological engagement provided, all these tools and programmes need optimal variables and parameters designated by human intellect, and at this critical juncture, the accuracy of these values determines the success of CTF related tasks. It can be argued here that besides having appropriate technological means and trained staff, developing and determining correct or near correct optimal variables revealing terrorist financing is a key aspect for improving the effectiveness of CTF.

Moreover, in order to improve this capability, there should be separate yet interconnected parameters which are country and financial source focused and/or terrorist organisation specific. In this context, MASAK's national intelligence analysis program can be given as a good example. The private sector is the forerunner in embracing technological developments in this field, mostly because of the high costs of making a mistake or a failure and the legal and commercial consequences of that. In addition, it is striking that even though for the banks in Turkey there are no official or legal sanctions for applying foreign states' blacklists, the global links they have and the negative ramifications of not applying them seem to force them to embrace these as obligations. There are so many critics and inconsistencies from legal and human rights perspectives for the blacklists created by other countries as was discussed before. If one Turkish citizen would like to have any banking relation with any of those names listed, although there are no legal or administrative constraints, they may have problems conducting their transactions. Here it can be seen that other countries' national financial sanctions can become *de facto* sanctions in other countries 'unofficially'.

In concluding the analysis on CTF capacity, it can be asserted that in terms of money, human resources or technological tools, the Turkish CTF regime is satisfactory.[282] However, in terms of training and competency of CTF practitioners, despite the many training programmes, the levels of attainment and the competences (in light of limited results), the capacity is not at a desired level. Due to the particulars of the CTF in Turkey, it can be claimed that improving CTF training

282 From law enforcement agencies to FIU, customs, legal authorities and the private sector, they all have sophisticated technological applications used for information sharing, analysis, detection and monitoring purposes. In short, it can be said that Turkey's physical capacity for CTF is adequate, whereas the biological part needs to be improved. There are efforts for improving this part; however, this needs time.

capacity which then produces tangible results may take some time. It was suggested that the lack of both specialisation and an enabling environment (which is examined further in the next section) where these specialists can work together are the most important reasons for not having an effective CTF implementation. Therefore, it emerges that Turkey needs to redefine its CTF training structure and methods and reconstruct these by establishing a financial bureaucracy comprising experts in finance, terrorism, international law and other related criminal law and criminology disciplines. Subsequently, it is also possible to assert that the efficacy of the CTF legal framework which underpins the above shortcomings is not satisfactory either.

5.6 Coordination and cooperation levels

Another important part of CTF implementation is the level of coordination and cooperation among responsible CTF agencies and institutions and between states and international organisations. Although there may be many similarities between terrorist organisations, they are not the same, and all of them evolve over time. Having domestic and international cooperation and coordination is a must for fighting against both terrorism and its financing, owing to the fact that it is relatively easy for terrorists to adapt and find new ways to fund and sustain their activities. For instance, if the authorities in one state can manage to constrain the resources or activities of some terrorist groups, then these terrorists can easily move their activities to other jurisdictions where they can continue their activities and evade the law enforcement agencies of that initial country. In this context, it is important to examine and monitor the ability of terrorist organisations to transform and reform themselves. It is critical therefore to establish adaptive and flexible coordination and cooperation mechanisms for CTF at the domestic and international levels. Hence, we also examine the implementation of CTF in terms of coordination and cooperation among law enforcement agencies. CTF practitioners and members of the Turkish academia were asked what they think about the level of cooperation and coordination among the private and public sectors responsible for CTF and if it is possible to improve the existing situation.

Regarding the current situation of coordination and cooperation in Turkey, a law enforcement director stated that the coordination and cooperation between institutions in terms of CTF is adequate and functioning well, particularly in regards to collecting and exchanging information. He provided an example of a successful joint cash monitoring operation in which the law enforcement agency, customs and MASAK have all been involved. According to him, "there is a very good harmony among the institutions in terms of information exchange and expert support".[283] The successful cash control operation mentioned here with the cooperation of the Turkish National Police Agency, MASAK and Customs

283 Interview with a Senior Level CTF Practitioner from a Law Enforcement Agency No: LE3.

Agency indicates and proves that having a good cooperation and coordination between institutions can produce effective outcomes.

However, it should be noted that the above example might be an isolated case or an exception as the statements from other CTF practitioners were not equally positive. In contrast to the claims of this practitioner, other practitioners and academics claimed that coordination and cooperation between CTF institutions are not at an expected level. A scholar stated that "officials may claim that coordination and cooperation between responsible organisations are perfect; however, I do not think this reflects the reality".[284] Another law enforcement practitioner similarly noted that, "[a]ctually I do not think that it [coordination] is at the desired level".[285] It was pointed out by an FIU practitioner clearly that "there are some shortcomings in terms of cooperation among institutions".[286] A CTF expert agreed by stating that "in terms of financing of terrorism there is no coordination, however this problem is not confined to counter-terrorism or CTF".[287] Given the fact that the majority of the responses pointed out the systemic failure of effective communication and coordination between CTF agencies, it can be concluded that these are areas in need of improvement.

When pressed as to why the CTF regime suffers from poor communication and cooperation, it was noted that every institution in Turkey wants to be successful and act alone in the framework of its area of responsibility, and they do not want to share their success and publicity with others. It can be said that institutional ambitions and possible turf wars between law enforcement agencies play an important role in hindering the coherence between CTF units. The below example given below by a senior level FIU director aptly illustrates the current state of affairs:

> A counterfeit cigarettes operation was conducted and we [MASAK] told the law enforcement agency that we would like to provide personnel [Financial Expert] for assistance but they said no, 'we do not want it'. Why because they want to collect the entire trophy for themselves and not to share [it with others]. But what happened later, all the people who got arrested were either acquitted or got out of jail easily. At the end, police made a publicity stunt and showcased their success. That is why, even though they have arrested the smugglers but they freed again. Why? Because, they could not substantiate the case with substantive evidence and enforcement is weak.[288]

In contrast to the claim made by law enforcement officers that all CTF units are working in coordination, this example shows that turf wars still can happen, and

284 Interview with a Scholar who is an Expert on International Law – Professor at a University No: AC7.

285 Interview with a Middle Level CTF Practitioner from a Law Enforcement Agency No: LE8.

286 Interview with a Senior Level CTF Expert from the Turkish FIU – MASAK No: FIU4.

287 Interview with an Expert on EU-Turkey Relations and Terrorism, No: EU1.

288 Interview with a (former) Senior Level Director from MASAK – FIU No: FIU3.

cooperation may not be at a desired level. If the police had accepted the financial expert offer from the FIU, then they could have found the required evidence using financial investigation tools and expertise to constitute a robust court file which could have secured a conviction and been a good deterrent for future potential offences. This is a good example of how ambitions and competition as well as too much focus on quick gains can lead to poor coordination and cooperation between law enforcement agencies.

As another CTF expert noted, there is no established coordination unit or organisation which fulfils the responsibility of providing coordination between responsible institutions and agencies. Moreover, in the present CTF system, every organisation looks at an issue from its area of expertise and tries to fulfil its responsibility by a narrow approach without collaborating with agencies which can complement the work they do. This approach, although it provides some advantages, prevents all the actors from seeing the big picture in terms of implementing a broad and coordinated CTF campaign.[289]

The interviews have allowed us to identify yet another inherent problem in the CTF regime in Turkey: not only is there no designated unit or institution which is responsible for coordination of CTF operations, but also there is no agency to provide leadership and coordination in tactical and prevention strategies in regard to CTF. According to a scholar, "[w]e cannot provide neither coordination for financing of terrorism nor the coordination for counter-terrorism".[290] This should be perceived from a broader perspective because on the tactical or practice levels, prosecutors are designated and authorised as the main coordinators of conducting criminal investigations; however, it is still unclear who is the coordinator for the prevention aspects of the financing of terrorism offence at the tactical level. It is noted at the strategic level that there is a need for an overarching structure, which will coordinate and regulate CTF activities in accordance with all the responsible parties[291] and raise public awareness of suspicious activities.[292]

Having said that, it should be noted that there have been various coordination committees in place for financial crimes and counter-terrorism in general. In order to fulfil the duty of coordination and cooperation in these spheres, the 'Fight against Financial Crimes Coordination Committee', the 'Counter-Terrorism Coordination Committee', and the 'Counter-Terrorism High Commission' and 'National Security Council' meetings are undertaken by responsible

289 Interview with an Expert on EU-Turkey Relations and Terrorism, No: EU1.

290 Interview with a Scholar who is an Expert on International Relations – Professor at a University No: AC3.

291 Interview with a Middle Level CTF Practitioner from a Law Enforcement Agency No: LE4.

292 It should be stated that the lack of CTF coordination is not unique to Turkey; there are shortcomings in the other countries as well, as mentioned in the previous chapters, Clunan's (2006) analysis of the US CTF system and the weaknesses therein are good examples in point.

institutions at different bureaucratic levels. One noteworthy and key criticism of these committees is the ambiguity of the decisions made by these committees, which need to be implemented and enforced by the practitioners. A law enforcement practitioner directly addressed this issue by stating that:

> I think that cooperation in Turkey is sufficient theoretically. Why? There is MASAK, above MASAK there is Counter-Terrorism Coordination Committee, and above it there is Counter-Terrorism High Commission and there is ultimately National Security Council. Moreover, there are regular meetings and we have the problem of how to apply the measures taken as a result of these meetings [. . .] in other words there are problems regarding how to realise these decisions taken. [. . .][293]

Another practitioner said that "[i]t does not mean that there is coordination whereby a committee meets only one or two times a year, there is a serious disconnection between institutions".[294] Correspondingly, an FIU senior director who had participated in many of the Fight against Financial Crimes Coordination Committee meetings expressed that:

> We all are talking about the problem of coordination; I simply laugh at this. You coordinate OK, then who will coordinate the coordinator; there is another coordination commission [Fight against Financial Crimes Coordination Committee] you know, in terms of legislation. However, what does this coordination commission do? They gather every one or three months whereas they do not produce solid outcomes in terms of coordination. Moreover, most of the people participating in these committee meetings do not have an idea of what they actually do there. Therefore, coordination is OK, whereas the more important issue is whether the support would be provided to subordinate bodies [in practice].[295]

Regarding the activities undertaken by the Fight against Financial Crimes Coordination Committee, another FIU expert stated that this committee does not have specifically defined operational powers in terms of countering financing of terrorism at an operational level.[296] Therefore, it cannot fulfil the responsibility of providing coordination and other duties expected from it. It should be noted that according to the legislation of Prevention of Laundering Proceeds of Crime (2006), this committee has limited powers and does not have any authority as mentioned above; it merely demonstrates that there is political will to fight terrorism at the government level.

293 Interview with a Senior Level CTF Practitioner from a Law Enforcement Agency No: LE9.
294 Interview with a Middle Level CTF practitioner from a Law Enforcement Agency No: LE4.
295 Interview with a (former) Senior Level Director from MASAK-FIU No: FIU2.
296 Interview with a Senior Level CTF Expert from Turkish FIU – MASAK No: FIU1.

Until 9 July 2018,[297] the Counter-Terrorism Coordination Committee was one of the places where the decisions and coordination efforts in order to address terrorism could be taken with the participation of state departments and responsible institutions.[298] However, it is surprising that the head of MASAK was not a natural member of this committee according to the law on Organisation and Tasks of Under Secretariat of Public Order and Security (KDGM) ("Kamu Düzeni ve Güvenliği Müsteşarlığının Teşkilat ve Görevleri Hakkında Kanun [The Law on Organisation and Tasks of Undersecretariat of Public Order and Security]" 2010), which was and still is a respectively new institution established "to ensure productivity and effectiveness in the field of counterterrorism while in coordination with other institutions and also to determine and meet multifaceted needs" (Kamu Düzeni ve Güvenliği Müsteşarlığı [Undersecretariat of Public Order and Security], 2013). The side-lining or exclusion of a key intelligence agency from this committee has had serious implications for the effectiveness of CTF.

A CTF expert noted that even though it was suggested to the National Assembly that they ought to amend the law for the involvement of the head of MASAK to this committee by a motion, the idea was rejected. It is curious as to why the head of the FIU – MASAK, who could provide helpful information regarding the financial aspect of terrorism, is not a member of this committee which decides on the nation-wide counter-terrorism efforts and how they are coordinated. In addition, even though KDGM has been given the task of coordination of counterterrorism efforts, in its responsibilities, there is no explicit mention of a task regarding coordination of measures against financing of terrorism. For a newly established institution, KDGM, in 2010, with the main responsibility of providing coordination, not to mention coordination of efforts against the financial aspects of terrorism anywhere in its responsibilities is another weakness. These examples may indicate that the role of the FIU – MASAK and coordination of CTF efforts are not seen as significant topics for Turkey's counter-terrorism strategy by either the Counter-Terrorism Coordination Committee or its secretariat KDGM.

297 On 13 September 2018 with Presidential Degree No 17 (2018), the Department of Internal Security Strategies was established under the Ministry of Interior in order to carry out the tasks and missions of KDGM, which was closed down on 9 July 2018 with Presidential Decree No 1 (2018). As there is no information available about this new organisation, the Department of Internal Security Strategies, it is not possible to provide any insight in terms of its CTF role and functions.

298 Members of this committee under the chairmanship of the Minister of Interior are, the Deputy Chief of General Staff, the Gendarmerie General Commander, the National Intelligence Organization (MIT) Undersecretary, the Justice Ministry Undersecretary, the Interior Ministry Undersecretary, the Foreign Ministry Undersecretary, the Public Order and Security Undersecretary, the General Director for Security and the Coast Guard Commander ("Kamu Düzeni ve Güvenliği Müsteşarlığının Teşkilat ve Görevleri Hakkında Kanun" [The Law on Organisation and Tasks of Undersecretariat of Public Order and Security], 2010).

Furthermore, there are problems pertaining to other committees. For instance, the National Security Council, the top Security Council in Turkey, issues a press release after every council meeting in which decisions and suggestions are made public. The press release which was published after the meeting on 27 October 2010 was the first time Turkey explicitly warned foreign states about increasing their efforts for investigating, analysing, deterring and preventing the financial resources of PKK (MGK Genel Sekreterliği [Secretariat General of National Security Council], 2010). It is surprising that the financial aspects of terrorism have been mentioned only once by the National Security Council which is the highest coordination authority where security related matters are discussed and decided. Moreover, on its website, the National Security Council provides information and various research findings on a number of international and national security related issues such as the transatlantic slave trade and drug trafficking, yet there is no information on or mention of financing of terrorism or financial aspects of terrorism (MGK Genel Sekreterliği [Secretariat General of National Security Council], 2013). These examples may represent the lack of awareness about and importance given to financial activities of terrorists in terms of the coordination aspect of the CTF system in Turkey.

As mentioned before, there are different coordination committees at different levels which are supposed to lead counter-terrorism and CTF strategy. These bodies or political elites do make decisions; however, the problem is that responsible institutions cannot apply these decisions in practice. In other words, there are problems regarding institutions in that they are not able to adapt their policies according to decisions made by these committees.

In theory, Turkey has coordination mechanisms which are seen by some to provide this function effectively. In reality, there is a lack of sufficient cooperation and coordination between institutions. These shortcomings may well originate from negligence and/or lack of awareness of terrorist financing addressing at the top level of the bureaucracy which has inevitably impacted the CTF success.

5.6.1 Establishing a coherent and holistic structure

Limited CTF coordination and cooperation lead to an ineffective CTF regime whereby the legal provisions cannot be applied, intelligence from and between agencies cannot be shared in a timely manner, CTF operations cannot be synchronised, and any holistic prevention strategy cannot be implemented or optimised. As confirmed by our interviewees, the law enforcement agencies do not seem to share a common culture, values or priorities, and their willingness to integrate their capabilities and expertise with others seems to be rare.

As one practitioner stated, the different backgrounds of institutions might be one of the reasons for their varying and at times diverging approaches to CTF. For instance, when the phenomenon and problem of terrorism is defined by and approached from a military framework, the enemy, war concepts and use of force emerge and dominate the potential solutions. Whereas, when an agency with a duty to counter financial or economic crimes looks at the same issue, they interpret the problem from a different perspective, such as using financial figures, monitoring money transfers, reporting et cetera.[299] Therefore, a multidisciplinary approach, which includes specialists from complementing disciplines, may be able to analyse the issue from different angles and provide a much better picture in order to produce effective responses. Individual approaches of institutions unsurprisingly decrease the total outcome; thus, an interagency model, in which all institutions share the same values and use all their unique abilities collectively, can carry out a harmonised and successful CTF operation in Turkey.

As the CTF regime lacks an overarching coordination authority,[300] it is difficult to bring various law enforcement agencies under common goals and conduct multi-agency operations. Furthermore, existing coordination committee meetings have not been producing intended results. Even though MASAK seems to be accepted as the main organisation for ensuring CTF coordination, it can be claimed that its limited capacity and exclusion from the key coordination organs (e.g. the National Security Council) make this task a futile effort.

Terrorist financing has many facets. While several agencies in Turkey have overlapping responsibilities in countering terrorism and CTF, they tend to push in disparate directions which are driven by their respective expertise and backgrounds. Accordingly, a coordination mechanism should be established so that all the responsible stakeholders can contribute towards the same objectives.[301] For that purpose, a CTF network should be formed at both the domestic and international levels. Every institution should participate and perform its responsibilities seriously without leaving the issue to be dealt with by the police and the military.[302]

In order to conduct an effective CTF, a multidisciplinary interagency organisation can be established combining expertise. According to practitioners' suggestions, this structure can be formed as an ad hoc committee model or as a new separate organisation. Moreover, it is believed that if all organisations have a liaison officer stationed at this organisation in order to reach and exchange information easily and quickly, it would improve the effectiveness and speed of information exchange and access. Correspondingly, as a practitioner and a scholar noted, a similar structure should be formed abroad in order to investigate and follow international terrorist activities because the international links of terrorists are equally, if not more, important.[303]

Furthermore, the literature (Passas, 2006b; Roberge, 2007; Levi, 2010; Bures, 2012; Barrett, 2012) on financing of terrorism looks at the role of private and public partnership in terms of increasing coordination and cooperation; however, it can be claimed that the inclusion of society at large as a key partner is missing.

299 Interview with a (former) Senior Level Director from MASAK – FIU No: FIU2.
300 Interviews with a Senior Level Director from the Ministry of Foreign Affairs No: MFA1.
301 Interview with a Terrorism/Counterterrorism Scholar from a University No: AC2.
302 Interview with a Senior Level CTF Practitioner from a Law Enforcement Agency No: LE3.
303 Interviews with a Senior Level Judge from the Department of Justice No: JD1 and a Scholar who is an Expert on Security Studies – Professor at a University No: AC4.

In this regard, as one practitioner noted, the citizens should be included in the on-going CTF efforts by providing information and contributing towards de-radicalisation initiatives. Public information on responsible donations or buying counterfeit or smuggled goods can also contribute to CTF efforts.[304] However, in order to achieve this goal, security and other institutions must gain the trust of the people,[305] and a serious public relations campaign which would raise awareness regarding terrorist financing should be conducted.

The idea of creating a societal awareness among the people and gaining their material and emotional support is one of the important pillars of fighting against terrorism and financing of terrorism. In this framework, public awareness should be created among the citizens in order to convey the message that the money they spend buying smuggled cheap oil or cigarettes or counterfeit commodities may go indirectly into the hands of terrorist organisations. Citizens should be informed about how they can assist security forces, and clear communication lines should be established to that effect. In addition, the efforts of citizens should be supported by a reward scheme.

Currently, there are hundreds of public service announcements/videos for raising awareness about a variety of public security related issues. However, out of 404 public service announcement videos, there is only one which addresses financing of terrorism. This was produced on 19 July 2012 and is about smuggled commodities and their links with terrorist funding (Emniyet Genel Müdürlüğü [Turkish National Police], 2012). Since then, there has been no other initiative which mentions other aspects of financing of terrorism or alerts people to potential abuses. Besides policing and applying legal measures, informing the public and mobilisation of society can be indicated as other significant factors for quality CTF implementation.[306] This is another aspect of the Turkish CTF regime which needs to be addressed.

The level of CTF coordination and cooperation at the national level was examined in this section. Since terrorism and financing of terrorism have cross-border elements and are seen as universal crimes, the international aspects of CTF efforts in Turkey need to be examined. The following section does this.

5.6.2 International level coordination and cooperation

The latest report of FATF on Turkey states that both national and international cooperation on non-profit organisations (2014a, p. 39) and establishing an

304 Interview with a Senior Level CTF Practitioner from a Law Enforcement Agency No: LE3.

305 Interview with a Scholar who is an Expert on International Law – Professor at a University No: AC7.

306 Because of possible differences and sensitivities across communities within a society, these kinds of public relations campaigns should be undertaken carefully and without offending or stigmatising any particular section of that society. For instance, following 9/11 suspect communities were created as a result of branding all Muslims as terrorists (Breen-Smyth, 2014, p. 229).

international coordination mechanism for the seized or confiscated assets are still not strong (2014a, p. 38). It is clear that not only the domestic efforts of Turkey regarding CTF but also cooperation and coordination capability at the international level are equally important. Firstly, Turkey's ability to mobilise other countries in its CTF struggle is examined. Secondly, the level of utilisation of both national and international legal instruments and agreements regarding CTF are considered. Thirdly, the level of soft power applications, such as political, diplomatic or economic incentives for inducing other actors to participate in or support Turkey's CTF campaign, are identified. Lastly, the obstacles and inconsistencies which hinder the above initiatives are examined.

Turkey's CTF efforts in terms of coordination and cooperation at the international level have not been satisfactory according to our interviewees. A senior level director from the MFA stated that "[o]n this issue [international CTF efforts] Turkey can be more active. Moreover, specialist prosecutors should be trained and we should be more competent on international subjects and investigations".[307] She also highlighted the inadequacies regarding the international and legal dimensions of the issue and Turkey's efforts in this realm being below the expected level. Another practitioner noted that it is not sufficient merely to be in coordination with everyone on paper. He emphasised that there should be concrete action in the field and at the operational level.[308] Consequently, Turkey's international level of coordination and cooperation efforts is not evaluated as effective due to lack of solid actions both in terms of joint operations and the very limited number of prosecutions.

As explained earlier, Turkey is an important and committed member of the international community, actively participating in and supporting all kinds of initiatives, organisations and legal agreements pertaining to CTF. However, reflections of these international efforts do not seem to have delivered reciprocal benefits for addressing the security and terrorism threats in Turkey. Moreover, Turkey's ability to reverse this situation seems to be limited. It is argued that Turkey should do more internationally to ensure that support from countries goes beyond paying lip service and actually starves terrorist organisations operating against Turkey (such as PKK and DHKP/C) of their funds.

Turkey has signed up to and incorporated international (soft and hard) legal instruments on CTF in good faith. Even though Turkey has been cooperating with other countries, its international level efforts in CTF seem to be inadequate. Recent CTF laws in Turkey have provided the opportunity for Turkey to ask other countries for freezing and confiscation orders for terrorist assets. However, this mechanism has not been used effectively by Turkish authorities against terrorist organisations which are direct threats to Turkey. It can be argued that Turkey should concentrate on how to use UNSCRs and other international legal tools (FATF Recommendations, regional policies (e.g. the EU) and national laws

307 Interview with a Senior Level Director from the Ministry of Foreign Affairs No: MFA1.
308 Interview with a Senior Level Judge from the Department of Justice No: JD1.

of other countries) for addressing its financing of terrorism problem by gaining the support of countries and international organisations and institutions. In order to do this, Turkey needs to invest in personnel who are well versed in invoking legal instruments in these platforms. In addition to judicial and law enforcement measures, Turkey should be more active in raising awareness at the international level and find ways to encourage other countries for effective cooperation and coordination.

In this context, an FIU expert expressed that the recently adopted international and national legal and administrative tools against terrorist financing have improved Turkey's ability by providing diplomatic and legal mechanisms for addressing CTF. Moreover, he added that, "[. . .] these are very important developments; however, they [CTF tools] have not been used yet, but it does not mean [they will not]".[309] These abilities are important, but it seems that their application such as freezing, seizing or confiscating assets of terrorist entities are still limited and far from achieving the expected goals. Similarly, as another FIU expert stated, "by [u]sing law No: 6415 [Prevention of Financing of Terrorism] and UNSC Resolution 1373, we [Turkey] should ask from other countries for freezing and confiscation orders for terrorist assets; we should do this".[310] He added that:

> I think that certainly; Turkey must be more active. Plans for cross border operations should be prepared and by conducting such operations, terrorist assets should be acquired back [to country]. For this goal, I think that there should be bilateral agreements with other countries, and there should be more focus on international cooperation. In comparison to the size of Turkey and [its security problems], I think that the proportion of Turkey's international efforts is incoherent. Turkey should take more active role on this.[311]

Even though these international CTF instruments give a wide array of opportunities, which can be utilised by Turkey for reaching the aim of disrupting the financial abilities of terrorist organisations, there have not been many success stories. From a Turkish perspective, one of the possible reasons may be that, due to the novelty of the issue for Turkey, it has not been able to apply these tools for mobilising other countries that are obliged to move in line with the UN and other FATF requirements. In terms of international cooperation, UNSC Resolutions, international conventions and domestic legislation would all support the legitimacy of Turkey's pledge for better cooperation; however, Turkey needs to develop the tools and mobilise others in the international community by engaging them in specific CTF initiatives (e.g. cross-border operations).

309 Interview with a Senior Level CTF expert from the Turkish FIU – MASAK No: FIU4.
310 Interview with a Senior Level CTF expert from the Turkish FIU – MASAK No: FIU1.
311 Interview with a Senior Level CTF expert from the Turkish FIU – MASAK No: FIU1.

A CTF expert pointed to the advantages of international efforts on CTF by saying, "[o]pening investigation files and following them at the international level for financing of terrorism provide fringe benefits as well. Through this effort, one can crack down [terrorist] organisations".[312]

There is no doubt that Turkey's efforts on international CTF front need to be improved. At the same time, it also clear that the legal and security bureaucracy in Turkey is not very competent at engaging with other foreign countries' legal systems and meeting their standards. Our findings point to the same weaknesses which we have identified earlier, in the context of competencies of the law enforcement agencies.

A CTF expert in applications of mutual legal assistance, extradition and other types of legal actions expressed that "[. . .] one of the mostly repeated complaints made [by our international partners] is that the investigation files prepared [by the Turkish authorities] are deficient and insufficient [for convincing other parties]".[313] He added that:

> They [foreign legal authorities] are saying to us convince me whether this man is a terrorist or member of a terrorist organisation. If you cannot put any evidence in front of them in order to convince, then they say that sorry but this man is your [political] opponent. Firstly, you did not ask to these men appropriate questions. Secondly, you do not have specialised units on this issue and thirdly we have serious problems documenting the facts.[314]

Correspondingly, a senior level judge iterated similar claims:

> We have required infrastructure in terms of international cooperation such as in international conventions for prevention of terrorist financing, again we have conventions regarding extradition, and we have bilateral agreements with other countries. [. . .] [F]rom the beginning of the process, it is obvious that there are big problems with the files prepared for extradition; I am saying from the beginning because if you do not work with the specialists or who knows this job very well; if you cannot put the evidence on the table, normally you cannot be angry with your counterparts who live and work in countries where rule of law is more developed.[315]

As a senior FIU director claimed, "[m]oreover, judges and prosecutor are unaware of the issue, most of them are not aware of the provisions of the Law No: 5549 (Prevention of Laundering Proceeds of Crime (2006) and No: 6415

312 Interview with a Senior Level Director from the Ministry of Foreign Affairs No: MFA1.
313 Interview with a Scholar working as a CTF Practitioner Expert on Counter-terrorism and Radicalisation No: AC6.
314 Interview with a Scholar working as a CTF Practitioner Expert on Counter-terrorism and Radicalisation No: AC6.
315 Interview with a Senior Level Judge from the Department of Justice No: JD1.

[Prevention of Financing of Terrorism) and have not even read these once".[316] Similar observations have been made in the FATF's Third Mutual Evaluation Report, which states that "[p]rosecutors and judges [interviewed] do seem however to have limited awareness of AML/CFT issues" (2007, pp. ii, 48, 51).

Moreover, the inappropriate and inadequate investigation or extradition files on terrorism or CTF offences may cause negative perceptions in the minds of foreign officials that files coming from Turkey are the result of a 'too broad' interpretation of terrorism and do not meet the minimum standards of due diligence, principles of criminal investigation and process. An EU expert noted that "according to a study done here [The EU Delegation of Turkey] on this topic, 85 percent of demands sent from Turkey to [EU] Member States in the last decade are not well-prepared [. . .] in some of the files sent there is not even a mention of clear offence!".[317]!"

This demonstrates that Turkey needs to improve its competence and standards in terms of international mutual legal assistance applications and demands. Due to lack of well-prepared criminal files, Turkey is less likely to have positive results from these initiatives. However, Turkey has started improving its capacity in this area, and furthermore, the recent closing of the ROJ TV (the main TV station sponsored by PKK which broadcasted from Denmark and Belgium) case can be given as a successful example of Turkish efforts against PKK terrorism in the international arena. As one senior level director noted, during the Operation 'Sputnik'[318] in 1996 there was no international cooperation, and Turkey did not know how to deal with a terrorist financing case which took place in several foreign states, such as Belgium and Luxemburg. It was stated by the same expert that Turkey has not been successful managing this case from the very beginning. However, after these unsuccessful experiences, it was argued that Turkey has learned how to deal with these kinds of issues, especially on the ROJ TV case. An interviewee stated that:

> On the contrary, [of previous negative results] ROJ TV case is the joint work with the participation of all Turkish institutions. ROJ TV case is not only about propaganda but also a terrorist financing case. For this case, evidence was collected very professionally and the context of the case was explained very clearly. In this context, we can say that Turkey did a very good job here.

316 Interview with a (former) Senior Level Director from MASAK – FIU No: FIU3.

317 Interview with an Expert on EU-Turkey Relations and Terrorism, No: EU1.

318 The MED-TV station was being used as the main TV channel for the dissemination of PKK news and propaganda between 1995 and 1999. MED-TV studios near Brussels were raided by Belgian police regarding the PKK/KONGRA-GEL terrorist organization's money laundering with drug and arms smuggling through MED TV on 18 September 1996. The code name of the operation was 'Sputnik'. In this operation five persons were arrested and many documents and much film footage were seized (Mango, 2005, p. 82). The legal case was dropped due to the statutory limit by 8 September 2007. However, Turkey's efforts regarding the appeal process are continuing (Ministry of Foreign Affairs, 2007).

> [. . .] Turkey learned this subject very well due to the fact that mostly it has had to deal with the abroad financial activities of terrorists.[319]

While it is rare, Turkey's effort in closing ROJ TV was a clear success story. As a result of the case file prepared by the Turkish officials, the Danish Supreme Court found ROJ TV guilty of promoting terrorism and disqualified it from broadcasting (Danish Supreme Court, 2014). The Turkish Ministry of Foreign Affairs (2014) welcomed this decision by stating that "[it is] confirmed by this decision [Danish Supreme Court] once more that PKK is a terrorist organisation, ROJ TV is financed by PKK; ROJ TV broadcasts programmes which promote terrorism through disseminating the PKK propaganda [. . .]". However, the case also revealed that although ROJ TV and its parent company Mesopotamia Broadcast has been designated as involved in financing of terrorism, and though another linked case found that 140 million Danish kroner was collected and transferred to PKK through these companies, no one was found guilty of a CTF offence, and there was not a single confiscation order given regarding the assets of these entities apart from fines imposed on these companies (*Hurriyet Daily News*, 2014a). In other words, there was not any measure taken against the financial aspects of terrorism or the persons involved in these court cases.[320] So it can be claimed that the success was limited. This case demonstrates that Turkey is developing its capabilities and learning how to deal with financing of terrorism on the international level. However, the limited number and scale of successful cases indicate that Turkey needs to improve its criminal procedure standards so that these can meet the standards of courts in foreign jurisdictions.

Furthermore, as a senior FIU director suggested, international CTF based intelligence capacity needs to be developed, and international media and other public relations tools should be used more effectively to create pressure on terrorist sponsors or on those who provide safe haven to terrorists. According to him, Turkey is not using these tools in order to gain other countries' support.[321] Thus, the role of public relations at the international level is increasingly seen as an important element for Turkey's CTF success.

Another problematic issue is the legal status of personal data protection in Turkey which hinders the possibility for Turkish officials to undertake joint operations and information exchanges with international CTF counterparts. The draft of the Personal Data Protection Law of Turkey was prepared ten years ago, and Turkey did not enact statute until 2016. The absence of this legislation has created a serious obstacle for operational cooperation with international partners in general and with the EU in particular and eliminated any chance of intelligence

319 Interviews with a Senior Level Director from the Ministry of Foreign Affairs No: MFA1.

320 This is probably because of the lack of evidence linking persons to the company.

321 Interview with a Senior Level (retired) Director from a Law Enforcement Agency No: LE5.

exchange and joint investigation opportunities between EU and Turkish CTF agencies.

Although Turkey enacted its first Personal Data Protection Law on 24 March 2016, according to the EU, this new legislation is far from guaranteeing the protection of personal data and was not found to be compliant with the EU data protection standards (Özalp, 2016).[322] The EU's Progress Report on Turkey (EU Commission, 2016a, p. 7) stated that, "[m]oreover, Turkey ratified the COE [Council of Europe] Convention on the Processing of Personal Data and its protocol, and adopted a law on personal data protection which, however, is not fully in line with the EU *acquis*". While Turkey has sent a letter to EUROPOL for signing an operational cooperation agreement between two parties (Özalp, 2016), it is unlikely that Turkey will be able to cooperate and coordinate with the EU on the operational level until it is fully compliant with the EU standards.

It can be concluded that Turkey's CTF capacity and efforts at the international level are weak. Turkey has had limited success in convincing or inducing other parties to move against financing activities of terrorist organisations targeting Turkey. Furthermore, there has been a minimal number (if any) of joint CTF operations. These shortcomings stem from a combination of factors: Firstly, Turkey's laws and criminal justice practices are not in line with the legal principles and practices found in potential partner countries (e.g. the EU Member States and its agencies such as EUROPOL). Secondly, Turkey has not managed to build strategic partnerships at the institutional level with other CTF agencies of the world.

As one practitioner noted, the economic, political, military and diplomatic strengths of a country determines its influence on the other countries' decisions. In this context, Turkey is not believed to be as effective in influencing other countries' actions on terrorist financing threats which it faces (e.g. PKK and DHKP-C).[323] International law is important; however, finding common interests and persuading others to act jointly against Turkey's terrorism threats and its financing dimension are another significant part of the issue. According to one senior level practitioner, the terrorism problem of Turkey should be explained to other countries where terrorists operate by taking into account their culture, legal norms, social structure and political culture.[324] Although diplomatic affairs are based on mutual and dual relations, it can be argued that Turkey needs to improve its influence on other countries in order to gather support for its counter-terrorism priorities.

322 The data protection standards and principles in the EU are provided by the General Data Protection Regulation: (EU) 2016/679 of the European Parliament and of the Council of 27 April 2016 on the protection of natural persons with regard to the processing of personal data and on the free movement of such data, and repealing Directive 95/46/EC (General Data Protection Regulation).

323 Interview with a (former) Senior Level Director from MASAK – FIU No: FIU2.

324 Interview with a Senior Level CTF Practitioner from a Law Enforcement Agency No: LE9.

Another important point to revisit at this juncture is the differing perceptions, interpretations and priorities as to who is a terrorist or a terrorist organisation. While international bodies such as the UN, FATF, or Western countries such as the US and the UK have been interpreting financing of terrorism as a serious problem stemming from religiously motivated organisations or from a Jihadist terrorist organisations framework, for the Turkish government, the key threats to its national security come from very different types of terrorist organisations which are funded by equally different methods. In short, it can be argued that the perceptions and concerns of Turkey and international actors are different; consequently, this differentiation and other related political, cultural, national interests and goals might result in frictions regarding establishing a common ground for cooperation and coordination against financing of terrorism.

Most of the practitioners and experts we interviewed stated that they do not believe and see the sincerity of other states in fighting terrorism in Turkey. It is believed that other states have not been acting honestly and do not want to cooperate against terrorism threats in Turkey as long as these do not pose any serious threat to their own security. Such negative sentiments and experiences by CTF agencies and the Turkish public at large have significant consequences for CTF implementation, cooperation and success.[325] It should be noted here that Turkey's disappointment in this regard is based on real cases (highlighted earlier) which relate to the European structures of PKK and the DHKP/C terrorist organisations which to this day have been able operate at will in these jurisdictions without any real consequences. As one practitioner stated, such factors may lead officials in Turkey to think in a reactive manner and "to feel that nothing will change and thus they may say why should they cooperate and help other states while they do not help them in terms of cooperation, and information exchange".[326]

In addition, the experts and practitioners noted that even though PKK and DHKP-C have been listed as terrorist organisations by the EU and other states, there has not been solid action for preventing or punishing their financial activities. Despite the fact that countries such as France and Germany have conducted a couple of operations against PKK and its financing activities, the outcomes of these were so minimal and to some extent "ostensible" according to a CTF practitioner.[327] Another CTF practitioner agreed that the efforts of foreign countries against terrorist organisations operating against Turkey are superficial and noted that:

> Counter terrorist financing operations are conducted against the PKK in the EU. However, generally these are ostensible operations in order to show that they are doing something. Germany arrested 10 people, however, charities,

325 Interview with a Senior Level CTF Practitioner from a Law Enforcement Agency No: LE2.
326 Interview with a Senior Level CTF Expert from the Turkish FIU – MASAK No: FIU1.
327 Interview with a Middle Level CTF Practitioner from a Law Enforcement Agency No: LE4.

> foundations, health-centres belonging to this terrorist organisation or other activities of them are still running. You know, ROJ TV has been closed after so many years. . . [What has happened later?] immediately after its closure the station was named as Sterk TV which started to broadcast in Norway. I am wondering, if this would have been the same if an Al Qaeda or ISIS television had done the same there [in Europe]? Therefore, we can say that there are some initiatives taken by Europe; however, they are not so sincere.[328]

Even though, in Europol's official annual terrorism report, PKK and its quasi-legitimate organisations have been listed and their links with PKK are explicitly stated, it is surprising to see that there is no mention of any action taken against them. Europol states that:

> The PKK is still regarded as a terrorist organisation in EU Member States, despite appeals by activists for its removal from the EU list of terrorist groups. The organisation has renamed some of its institutions in Europe: KON-KURD (the Confederation of Kurdish Associations in Europe) changed to the Congress of the Kurdish-democratic association in Europe, KCD-E; and YEK-KOM (the Federation of Kurdish associations in Germany) to Kurdish-democratic association centre of Germany (NAV-DEM). However, these changes have had little impact on their structure and functionalities.
>
> (Europol, 2015, p. 28)

It is obvious that the EU has ample information on these terrorist organisations and their affiliates. However, at present, these entities continue to operate in the EU. It is accepted that both PKK and DHKP-C have been designated as terrorists by the EU in several terrorism reports where it is stated that "[t]he EU continues to serve as an area for financing, logistics, refuge and procurement for terrorist groups that conduct their main activities outside Europe. This applies in particular, but not exclusively, to the Turkish terrorist groups, PKK and DHKP/C [. . .]" (Europol, 2014, p. 9). The continuation of these activities and the lack of law enforcement against them may indicate that the efforts at disrupting financial and logistical networks and activities of these terrorist organisations in the EU are not adequate. Except for a couple of operations conducted by some of EU members against the financial activities of PKK and DHKP-C, there seems to have been minimal success in disrupting their financial activities.[329]

328 Interview with a Senior Level CTF Practitioner from a Law Enforcement Agency No: LE3.

329 When looking at the amount of seized and confiscated assets, numbers of arrests, and sentenced terrorists and their supporters, they seem not as significant as the practitioner states above. This can be seen from the following EU TE-SAT reports: While there was no CTF operation against the PKK, there was one in the Greece against DHKP-C (11 suspects arrested) in 2014 (Europol, 2014). In 2013 France and Spain for PKK (23 suspects arrested and €25.000 seized), Austria, Greece, Germany, Italy and Spain conducted operations against DHKP-C (16 suspects arrested) (Europol, 2013). In 2012 only in Denmark,

Another interesting case is the murders of three PKK members in Paris on 9 January 2013 (BBC World, 2013).[330] Regarding the killings, the EU TE-SAT report states that:

> On 9 January 2013, three Kurdish women were murdered in the Kurdish Institute of Paris (France). Two of the victims were senior members of the PKK's European structures and were actively involved in the financing of the organisation's activities.
>
> (Europol, 2014, p. 31)

To an inquiring mind, by reading this excerpt, it may be clear that the information regarding PKK's financial activities carried out by these members and their affiliation was not new information for the French authorities and/or Europol. Although PKK is designated as a terrorist organisation by the EU, and these were known PKK members, it is important to find out why nothing was done to arrest these people who were actively engaged in terrorist activities in the European Union until these murders were committed. It is important to ask, also, if these people were collecting and organising fundraising activities as members of Al Qaeda or the so-called Islamic State instead of PKK, could the responsible agencies and officials still ignore their existence in their country? It can be argued, as interviewed experts and practitioners also expressed, that there is clearly an issue of lack of sincerity or application of double standards here, which does not orientate towards the very much needed principle of solidarity against terrorism – a narrative which has been re-sounded time after time following deadly terrorist attacks against Western countries and EU citizens in recent years. Moreover, another confusing part of this report is that, as stated in the first paragraph under the title "Terrorist Attacks and Arrested Suspects":

> In 2013 seven people were killed in terrorist attacks in the European Union (EU): one British Army soldier in London (UK), one elderly Muslim male

---

an operation conducted against the PKK relating to the ROJ TV case (8 suspects arrested for collecting 140 million Danish kroner for the PKK then freed by the court in 2014) (Europol, 2013, p. 28). France, Germany and Romania conducted operations against the PKK in 2011 (Europol, 2012, p. 24). In 2010 Belgium, France, Nederland, Italy, Romania and Slovenia conducted operations against the PKK (Europol, 2011, p. 22). The PKK's financial records and donation receipt books were acquired in an operation in Austria in 2009 (Europol, 2010, p. 69). In 2008 Italy (a PKK cash courier arrested), Slovakia (a suspect arrested for supporting the PKK at the operations against PKK and a joint operation against DHKP-C (8 suspects arrested for financing of terrorism) in the same year conducted by France and Germany (Europol, 2009, pp. 29, 33, 62)

330 The victims of these murders: the first senior member was Sakine Cansız, one of the founding members of the PKK terrorist organisation and the first female senior level member of the PKK. Fidan Doğan was the Paris representative of the Kurdistan National Congress (KNC), who was lobbying on behalf of the PKK with the EU diplomats. The third low-level member was Leyla Söylemez, who was a woman representative of the PKK (Yıldız, 2013).

> in the West Midlands (UK), two members of a right-wing extremist party in Athens (Greece) and three high-ranking Partiya Karkerên Kurdistan (PKK, Kurdistan Workers' Party) members in Paris (France)
>
> (Europol, 2014).

Classifying the murders of three terrorist members as terrorism is confusing. It can be easily said that this is a criminal case which needs to be inquired under criminal justice standards. However, it is hard to understand the logic of naming the murders of three terrorists as a terrorist attack in a serious official EU document. It can be asked if, according to the definition of terrorism inferred in this report, it would be a terrorist attack if Osama Bin Laden had been killed by a simple criminal because of a dispute rather than as the result of an operation conducted by US forces in Abbottabad, Pakistan. Obviously, Europol's terrorism report ought to explain this new interpretation of terrorism or correct its fault. What is also worth noting is that the victims of this deadly attack (one of whom, Sakine Cansiz, was a founding member of PKK) are presented as activists by the media rather than members of a designated terrorist organisation (the Guardian, 2013; Reuters, 2013; Spiegel, 2013; and France24, 2016).

In addition, terrorist lists established by other states are another part of the international level of cooperation whereby, according to the practitioners and scholars, these efforts have only symbolic effect regarding prevention of activities of terrorist organisations operating against Turkey. As an FIU expert stated:

> For instance, some countries in order to demonstrate their orientation to the international community objectives, say that they have a 'terrorists list'. Then when you open and look at this list you see only the name of the terrorist organisation is written, for example putting the PKK's name into the list as 'PKK' such as the US and some European countries did. Consequently, it is not possible for a legal entity as the PKK to own any assets. Thus, listing it [PKK] does not have any meaning in practice. [. . .] Then this is an ostensible act. Therefore, if you will use lists, if you want it to be effective then the names of individuals not only the name of organisations need to be listed as well.[331]

Following diplomatic efforts of Turkey, PKK and DHKP/C are listed both in the US and the EU as terrorist organisations. However, similar to the opinion above, another CTF expert noted that "[w]ell, even though there are lists, they [states] behave according to their interests, and we or you see that these lists do not have influence in terms of implementation and practice [on the ground]".[332] Correspondingly, Özgenç (2013, p. 170) finds the lists and designations, in which

331 Interview with a Senior Level CTF Expert from the Turkish FIU – MASAK No: FIU1.

332 Interview with a Scholar working as a CTF Practitioner Expert on Counter-terrorism and Radicalisation No: AC6.

PKK and linked organisations were involved, made by the US and some Western countries act only as a simple gesture for Turkey.[333] Ultimately, these trends render the Turkish CTF effort ineffective.

Another interesting situation should be mentioned which has become a hot topic for Turkey recently with the rise of the Syrian crisis and the Islamic State problem in the Middle East and further afield. There are many groups and parties fighting against the Islamic State, and these groups vary from Al Qaeda affiliated Al Nusra Front (Amoroso, 2016, p. 219) to PKK affiliated Kurdish Democratic Union Party (PYD) in Syria and its armed front People's Protection Units (YPG) (Krahenmann, 2016, p. 239). In this context, for the Turkish Ministry of Foreign Affairs, PYD and YPG are affiliated with the PKK terrorist organisation; thus, they are considered as terrorist organisations as well (Ministry of Foreign Affairs, 2016).[334]

In this framework, even though Turkish political and official authorities declare that both PYD and YPG are terrorist organisations as the Syrian branch of the PKK terrorist organisation, and they are affiliated and coordinating their terrorist acts together (Ministry of Foreign Affairs, 2016), according to US officials, both PYD and YPG are accepted and supported as legitimate entities which are effective combat forces against Islamic State terrorism on the ground (*Hurriyet Daily News*, 2015). In this situation PYD and YPG are supported with sophisticated weapons and logistically by the US government. Moreover, as the US state department spokesperson states, these organisations are not accepted as terrorist organisations because they are not on their lists. However, according to the official website of the US National Counterterrorism Center, which was established by Presidential Executive Order in 2004, in order to make joint operational planning and joint intelligence, PYD is represented as the Syrian affiliate of PKK, also known as Kongra-Gel (KGK):

> In addition to its stronghold in Northern Iraq, to which KGK [PKK] fighters probably are withdrawing according to the peace settlement [with Turkish Government], the KGK's Syrian affiliate, the Democratic Union Party

333 The president of the US identified PKK as a significant foreign narcotics trafficker under the Kingpin Act in May 2008, and on October 14, 2009, and April 20, 2011, the Treasury designated a total of eight PKK leaders pursuant to the Kingpin Act (U.S. Department of Treasury, 2012). However, it can be said that this listing has not been producing any solid action against PKK and its financial activities until now, apart from the symbolic support of the US.

334 PKK also has offshoots and affiliates in Iran, Syria and Iraq. KCK, headed by the imprisoned Öcalan, is the same organisation as PKK. "KCK" is "PJAK" in IRAN, "Tawgari Azadi" in Iraq and "PYD/YPG" in Syria. PYD/YPG's affiliation with PKK is clear. PYD/YPG was set up under the control of the PKK terrorist organisation in 2003. They share the same leadership cadres, organisational structure, strategies and tactics, military structure, propaganda tools, financial resources and training camps (Ministry of Foreign Affairs, 2016).

> [PYD], has increased its presence in northern Syria by establishing control in Kurdish areas.
>
> (The National Counterterrorism Center, 2014)[335]

In addition, according to Soylu (2016), there is serious evidence which supports the organic link between PKK and PYD, PYG terrorist organisations. Soylu (2016) substantiates his claims by showing the existing links between PKK and the PYD and YPG, by citing evidence from PKK's official documents and websites and PKK and PYD leaders' statements and by references to the US diplomatic cables revealed via WikiLeaks. Furthermore, as a prominent expert on Kurds, Gunter (2014) confirms that PYD was established by PKK in 2003, and it is still affiliated with PKK.

Moreover, in the annual terrorism reports of Europol, PYD is defined similarly to the above context. While the 2014 EU's TE-SAT report states that "PKK and its Syrian equivalent, the Partiya Yekitîya Demokrat (PYD, Democratic Union Party), were involved in the Syrian conflict in 2013" (Europol, 2014, p. 32), in the 2015 report, it is stated that "[. . .] demonstrations occurred across many EU Member States in support of the Kurdish resistance against IS. Sympathisers of the PKK and of their Syrian Kurdish counterpart, PYD (Kurdish Democratic Union Party), were observed among the participants" (Europol, 2015). In these official terrorism reports of Europol, PYD is represented and accepted as the Syrian faction and counterpart of PKK under the section where PKK is explained. However, in addition to their office in Moscow, Russia, PYD and its armed wing YPG have opened official representation offices in some of the EU countries such as Prague, Czech Republic; Stockholm, Sweden; Berlin, Germany and Paris, France (Aydoğan, 2016; Taştekin, 2016). Consequently, it can be argued that the success and the effectiveness of coordination and cooperation at the international level not only depend on how countries are fulfilling their responsibilities, but also depends on to what extent other countries' interests and foreign policy priorities are lined up against these efforts. As in the case of Turkey, although Turkey is part of many international and bilateral agreements and fully compliant with the international CTF and AML regimes, terrorist organisations and their affiliates which threaten Turkey can easily find safe havens in the midst of the EU. Moreover, they are supported financially and logistically by the US and some of the EU countries which are also pioneers of building the international regime and standards against financing of terrorism. Without international support, it is not an easy task for any country to deal

335 In the following days, this website and its content were mentioned both in the social and normal media for debunking US claims, and the webpage cited above became inaccessible. It is no longer possible to access the mentioned webpage. In addition, this webpage is cited officially by the Directorate General of Press and Information in Turkey (Republic of Turkey Office of the Prime Minister Directorate General of Press and Information, 2016).

with the financial and other aspects of terrorism particularly if terrorists can find support and money from states which also provide them safe haven and active support. Therefore, a critical analysis of the effectiveness of CTF in Turkey or any other country for that matter, must be considered and balanced against these elements.

As observed above, international cooperation and coordination depend on various factors, and some of these are not under the sole control of a single state; thus, they can create unsurmountable obstacles for the CTF regime therein. It is fair to say that Turkey needs to improve its diplomatic efforts and international law related expertise and focus on applying international conventions more effectively and in line with universally accepted principles and standards of criminal justice. However, cooperation and coordination cannot be done by the efforts of a single state. Even though Turkey has done its part in line with its commitments under international legal instruments, different interests and threat perceptions by other states have resulted in inconsistent and inadequate coordination and cooperation and at times no willingness to aid its CTF priorities and operations. While it has been emphasised that the 'one man's terrorist is another's freedom fighter' approach would not enhance solidarity in countering terrorism, PKK and other terrorist organisations have been carrying out their financial activities in a number of EU member states explicitly, and hardly anything has done by these countries stop such terrorist organisations. Thus, the opinions expressed by CTF practitioners and the scholars that some of the approaches by the EU countries are not sincere in terms of combating against terrorism have a degree of validity.

It can be asserted that national interests of states play an important role in determining their cooperation with Turkey against PKK and other terrorist organisations and their financial affairs. The money collected by PKK in Europe has not been perceived as a security issue to be handled urgently as long as they do not cause any harm for their homeland security and domestic and overseas interests. In addition, PYD and YPG, which are Syrian branches of PKK, are supported logistically and financially by the US and some of the EU member states in order to fight against another terrorist organisation, namely the so-called Islamic State. This demonstrates an interesting, contested, and maybe unprecedented situation. Especially during the Cold War, terrorist organisations were used against hostile states by other states as proxies rather than conventional war; at present, once again, states are using and supporting terrorist organisation/s in order to wage war against other 'more' dangerous terrorist organisation/s.

It can be argued that the individual approaches of states and their varying terrorist and terrorism definitions create serious obstacles for sincere international cooperation and coordination between countries. In this environment, it seems that even though Turkey has fulfilled its international responsibilities, having no due regard for Turkey's specific security and terrorist threats by its neighbours and Western allies has created significant and negative consequences for its counter-terrorism and CTF regimes.

5.7 The level of impact on terrorism and success of CTF system in Turkey

In this part of the analysis, the impact on terrorist organisations and the overall success of the existing CTF system are examined. In order to find out the impact and success of the CTF system and its applications, the following questions were posed to the interviewees:

- What do you think about the impact of the CTF efforts, applied by Turkey, on terrorist organisations?
- How do you evaluate the success of the current CTF applications in the overall counter-terrorism framework?
- If it is successful, then how do you explain this success? If it is not successful, then what are the reasons behind this situation?

In this framework, firstly, the effects and the impacts of existing CTF efforts and applications and secondly, the success of CTF system in Turkey will be examined.

5.7.1 The CTF impact on terrorist organisations

In this part, the impact of the CTF law and practice on terrorist organisations, especially those attacking Turkey, are analysed. The term 'impact' is perceived as the concrete results which lead or force terrorist organisations towards negative behavioural changes in terms of their operational, strategic and organisational environments, and also the success of the existing CTF measures and their implementation through SARs, know your customer, due diligence applications and financial investigations. A terrorist organisation's decision to postpone some of its attacks or to negotiate with their target country due to lack of funds caused by effective CTF efforts can also be given as cases in point for the understanding of 'impact' in this part of the analysis. In the interviews two different answers emerged (yes and no) as to whether there is an impact on terrorist organisations and their terrorist acts. These are examined in turn:

CTF has no impact

According to the interviewees, the current CTF regime in Turkey does not have an impact on terrorist organisations. Most of the assertions converged on the conclusion that the main reason for this limited effectiveness is the inadequate implementation conducted at the ground level which if conducted appropriately, would harm terrorist organisations. In other words, the level of implementation is not adequate to create any impact.

As one law enforcement practitioner noted, in order to evaluate the level of the impact of CTF measures on terrorist organisations, firstly, outcomes of the CTF implementation need to be seen, and then the impact of CTF applications can be assessed against these results – he has not seen such result thus deemed the CTF regime as ineffective.[336] Another practitioner similarly stated that "due to the fact that there is no [CTF] action against [terrorists], there is no [observable] impact upon [terrorist organisations]".[337]

Terrorist organisations are not affected by the CTF efforts because they continue with their activities as usual. It is hard to prevent terrorists because as was mentioned previously, they are adaptable and do find different ways to evade law enforcement even if there is a robust CTF regime. As an EU expert observed:

> There is no impact, I think zero impact. Because in Turkey everyone thinks PKK as the only terrorist organisation and the PKK is financed by the municipalities already ok? [. . .] Hizbullah brings money thorough Iran border in suitcases. [. . .] I think they [CTF measures] do not have any impact in Turkey because one of its dimensions is banking sector and banking sector in Turkey is at a very advanced level. [. . .] So the methods they used are different [meaning that they do not use the banking system] than we focus on and honestly, I do not think that the CTF measures have impact domestically.[338]

Beside the problems regarding capacity, training, coordination and cooperation between institutions, terrorist organisations are not using methods and tactics which are monitored by Turkish CTF practitioners. They often find ways to circumvent CTF measures and carry on their activities in areas and sectors where the authorities are not looking. The continuing operational scope and success of terrorist organisations in Turkey are a testament to their success as well as the level of ineffectiveness of the CTF regime.

Regarding terrorist finance in general and PKK's financial activities in particular, it was stated by a scholar that "I do not think they [CTF efforts] have determining and long lasting impact on them. For instance, I am not sure and I do not know whether there was a time when we said OK, we cut PKK's funds, and therefore PKK as an organisation was weakened".[339] It was further asserted that it would be more effective and successful to destruct PKK's supply channels than to interdict PKK's financial sources. According to this scholar, the role of cash/money is exaggerated, and terrorists may not depend so much on money. For example, in the case of PKK, terrorists ask villagers to grow produce (e.g. potatoes or tomatoes) in designated and remote places for their survival. In this framework it is argued that preventing this logistical support may cause more impact on terrorist groups than preventing cash flows. He also noted that "[. . .] it is not possible to claim that terrorists are influenced negatively because

336 Interview with a Middle Level CTF Practitioner from a Law Enforcement Agency No: LE11.

337 Interview with a Senior Level CTF Practitioner from a Law Enforcement Agency No: LE7.

338 Interview with an Expert on EU-Turkey Relations and Terrorism, No: EU1.

339 Interview with a Scholar who is an Expert on International Relations – Professor at a University No: AC3.

of Turkey's CTF efforts".[340] Another expert on terrorism similarly claimed that "CTF is not a determinant factor on terrorist organisations among other counterterrorism methods".[341] A practitioner from customs stated that "for all the things done, there is no deterrence and impact nor are there any lessons learned and expertise which emerge from these efforts. Thus there is no impact nor success".[342]

A (former) senior level FIU director highlighted the peace process period between the Turkish government and the PKK terrorist organisation and opined that:

> Turkey has just recently started its fight against terrorist financing and because of the peace process, not much has been done for this purpose. What is available stays as it is and new things, which need to be introduced, are not introduced on the field against PKK. In this context, we can claim now that there is not any fight against financing of terrorism. Consequently, we could not come to the stage to evaluate the impact of our new efforts on terrorist organisations due to the fact that there is no real CTF. In order to come to a stage where we can claim to have positive impact, there needs to be field work, coordination and cooperation among institutions and lots of courage.[343]

Another particular detail that emerged from the interviews is that after fulfilling the international CTF requirements and delisting itself from the FATF's grey list, Turkey has stopped focusing on CTF. In addition to the above statement, another (former) senior level director stated that "[. . .] currently, I cannot see confiscation of much terrorist money".[344] From these accounts, it is conceived that although Turkey has put CTF as a new instrument into its statute books, in order not to instigate a conflict between PKK and security forces and not to stall the Peace Process negotiations, Turkey did not use its CTF tools against terrorist organisations.

Coupled with the lack of serious and systematic CTF implementation against terrorist financing in Turkey, it can be argued that no impact can be seen on terrorist organisations. Thus, Turkey's CTF efforts and applications against terrorist organisations seem not to have caused any behavioural change on their general strategy and capabilities.

One of the reasons for the very limited or no impact on terrorist organisations may be because CTF is a new concept in Turkey. As one FIU expert noted, "it is too early to assess whether new CTF regulations and their application are

340 *Ibid.*
341 Correspondence with a Terrorism/Counterterrorism Scholar from a University No: AC5.
342 Interview with a Senior Level Expert from the General Directorate of Customs Enforcement No: CO1.
343 Interview with a (former) Senior Level Director from MASAK-FIU No: FIU3.
344 Interview with a (former) Senior Level Director from MASAK – FIU No: FIU2.

successful or not. We need time to assess these". On this topic, an FIU expert correspondingly expressed that:

> Not until today but from this point forward, I think especially the Law No. 6415 is the first step and I believe it is examined by terrorist organisations very elaborately more than we would guess. Later on, when we start to apply this in practice, its deterrence will increase against the threat. I believe that there is a strong consensus and determination within the public sector [. . .] however, it is important to put this into practice where we can see its ultimate outcome. [. . .] Yet, I do not think that we are at this stage.[345]

In this context, the introduction of new CTF legislation, trainings, capacity buildings and other efforts are all at an initial stage. Reaching a level where an effective CTF implementation is conducted will take time for Turkey and its CTF institutions. It can be said that Turkey is still learning how to use these new legal provisions and financial tools effectively. Moreover, Turkey focuses its efforts for fulfilling international requirements and responsibilities at the international community while having a relatively weak and ineffective domestic CTF application which produced no impact on terrorist organisations. As some practitioners previously indicated, this trend is a result of the pressure by the FATF.[346] Thus, it can be argued that Turkey's domestic CTF efforts in this sense are weak and ineffective, in comparison to its efforts at the international level.

In addition, as previously mentioned, countering financing of terrorism did not emerge as a direct and natural necessity of responding to PKK and other terrorist organisations' financial activities. It was the result of international demands and pressure on Turkey. For a long time, the financial resources and activities of PKK were not targeted systematically. Consequently, as some experts rightly expressed, PKK has never experienced a financial difficulty until recently.[347] This may be used as an indicator to understand the impact of the current CTF applications on the PKK terrorist organisation. Furthermore, as another scholar noted, in order to meet the daily vital requirements of its members, PKK has managed to integrate itself economically and to some degree create its own financial ecosystem in Northern Iraq and the Qandil Mountains, where they use this region as a safe haven. Therefore, an economic market and opportunity were created for meeting PKK's needs.[348] Furthermore, PKK has a complex economic structure, which has fed and managed its budget from various financial sources and different countries successfully since the early 1980s. Given the limited action against

345 Interview with a Senior Level CTF Expert from the Turkish FIU – MASAK No: FIU1.

346 Interviews with a Senior Level Manager of a Bank Branch No: BS1 and a Middle Level CTF Practitioner from a Law Enforcement Agency No: LE4.

347 Interviews with a Terrorism/Counterterrorism Scholar from a University No: AC2 and a Scholar who is an Expert on International Relations – Professor at a University No: AC3.

348 Interview with a Scholar working as CTF Practitioner Expert on Counter-terrorism and Radicalisation No: AC6.

this complex and transnational network of financing and the continuing threat posed by this terrorist organisation, the ramifications of Turkey's CTF efforts on PKK has not led to any change in terms of operational, organisational and financial capabilities. As Vittori (2009) opined, it can be asserted that the level of economic strength and freedom that a terrorist organisation reached emerges as an important independent variable for terrorist organisations' resistance towards the impacts of CTF efforts. Even though it might have been possible to limit its financial resources to some extent at the initial stage of PKK's foundation, this is now huge challenge. As an EU expert stated:

> In our story with the PKK, it is not important whether these men have money or not now, the real issue is that, still they have been able to recruit people for their ranks for thirty years. Still this is the issue on the table and it is not possible to say that they cannot raise funds in these conditions.[349]

The social and ideological support provided by the populace are also important for terrorist organisation's financial activities. As Shapiro and Siegel's (2007) study illustrated, restraining terrorist funds may start to be effective for cracking down on a terrorist organisation after reaching a critical threshold. After passing this stage, following efforts undertaken by governments may cause larger impact on them whereas if they cannot reach that threshold, CTF efforts will not cause any impact on terrorist organisations. However, in the case of PKK, considering its impressive financial budget and organisational sophistication, it can be claimed that for CTF practitioners to reach that critical threshold, Turkey needs to do a lot more and adopt a long-term strategy. Given these conditions, policy makers ought to reassess whether it is the right decision to concentrate their efforts on preventing financial sources and financial activities of PKK. As one scholar argued, the level of the violence produced by terrorist organisations can increase the amount of funds raised. In this context, he argued that it is not possible to finish a terrorist organisation which could manage to create its own financial system.[350] Consequently, the economic capacity a terrorist organisation has is another variable affecting the level of impact.

CTF has impact

In contrast to the views expressed above, some practitioners are of the opinion that current CTF measures and their application might have had a degree of impact on terrorist organisations in Turkey. One of the aspects of this impact is the limitation of terrorist organisations' capabilities. According to a senior level CTF practitioner, terrorist organisations change their overt financial activities

349 Interview with an Expert on EU-Turkey Relations and Terrorism, No: EU1.

350 Interview with a Scholar who is an Expert on International Law – Professor at a University No: AC7.

to covert ones in order not to compromise their operational safety. For example, he argued that PKK has been coerced into changing its financial behaviour: rather than transferring larger amounts of money, they transfer funds in smaller dividends, and rather than using formal banking system, they use cash couriers who can be disclosed easily by the law enforcement forces. In addition, it was claimed that this stringent environment not only limits their financial opportunities, but also increases the costs of their financial activities from an operational safety perspective.[351] Similarly, another senior level practitioner noted optimistically that the CTF measures will start to have influence on terrorist organisations gradually, and terrorist organisations will not be able to act freely anymore.[352]

Another claim is that the CTF implementation has reduced public support for PKK. It was claimed that PKK has started using extortion and collecting forced donations from the constituency where it operates as a direct result of CTF measures. It is claimed PKK's struggle has been continuing for more than 30 years without realising its key aim – establishing an independent Kurdish State – whereas it has been continuing to collect money from people using threats and other means. In this framework, it is believed that the legitimacy and the reputation of PKK are decreasing among the people living in terror affected areas in Turkey.[353]

To some of the law enforcement practitioners, limiting the capability and capacity of terrorist organisations and decreasing their societal support are some of the main goals of Turkey's CTF strategy. It can be claimed that some of these goals might have been achieved. However, as other practitioners and experts noted, terrorist organisations, especially PKK, continue their terrorist campaigns without any major disruption or without shifting tactics despite the CTF efforts. It can also be perceived that the on-going CTF campaign might have had a negative impact on terrorist organisations (by constraining their financial activities) whereby forcing them to act covertly. However, due to the limited level of implementation and positive outcomes, the current CTF regime has not reached its potential or a level of establishing a significant impact on terrorist organisations in Turkey.

There are two possible explanations for this trend. Firstly, CTF measures may be effective enough to create an impact on terrorist organisations; however, owing to Turkey's insufficient CTF implementation, there has not been the desired effect on terrorist organisations. The second alternative is that even though the CTF system in Turkey was implemented competently, the CTF measures and applications are not suitable for dealing with the financial aspects of the unique terrorist threats in Turkey. Although the exact reasons for this situation are difficult to determine with certainty, it can be noted with certainty that there

351 Interview with a Senior Level CTF Practitioner from a Law Enforcement Agency No: LE9.
352 Interview with a Senior Level CTF Practitioner from a Law Enforcement Agency No: LE2.
353 Interview with a Senior Level CTF Practitioner from a Law Enforcement Agency No: LE9.

has been no or very limited impact on the financial capacity of terrorist organisations targeting Turkey.

5.7.2 *The success level of the CTF system in Turkey*

After examining the level of impact of CTF applications on terrorist organisations and their activities, in this section the overall success of the main CTF system in Turkey and its applications both on the domestic and the international aspects of the terrorist financing problem will be analysed as the last part of our analysis. Similar to the previous section, opinions and conclusions of CTF practitioners and experts are mixed. It can be noted that each opinion has valid points and arguments. Every interviewee responded to the question of whether the existing CTF system is successful according to their own interpretation or definition of success. According to a scholar, being successful in terms of counterterrorism or CTF is defined as Turkey's capability to limit and control the violence and threats caused by terrorists, to a degree that citizens would feel themselves safe and perceive the risk of terrorist threat at an acceptable and agreeable level in order to continue their daily lives.[354] Therefore, it might be asserted that the level of the state's control and management of terrorist threats indicates the level of success against terrorism and CTF *vis-à-vis* to what extent citizens feel themselves safe and secure.

Another scholar argued that due to the difficulty states face in identifying legitimate sources of terrorists in comparison to the illegitimate financial sources, terrorist organisations are inclined to raise funds via legitimate methods and resources. In this case, it is suggested that the level of interdicted legal financial activities and sources of terrorist organisations can indicate the real success of the CTF efforts carried out by states.[355] Therefore, according to this interpretation, if a country is successful in addressing legal activities of terrorist financing, then it may be claimed that they are successful in their CTF efforts.

Another alternative approach suggested by a CTF practitioner is that in order to assess whether a CTF system is effective and successful against terrorist financing, it is important to look at how much property belonging to terrorists has been confiscated or forfeited by applying the CTF system.[356] In other words, the amount of confiscation and asset freezing can be used as indicators showing the success level of the CTF efforts.

According to FATF, the purpose of AML/CTF efforts is to protect the financial system against any kind of exploitation. In this regard for an effective and successful AML/CTF system the "high-level objective" is defined as "[f]inancial

354 Interview with a Scholar who is anExpert on International Law – Professor at a University No: AC7.

355 Interview with a Scholar who is an Expert on International Relations – Professor at a University No: AC3.

356 Interview with a Senior Level CTF Expert from the Turkish FIU-MASAK No: FIU1.

systems and the broader economy are protected from the threats of money laundering and the financing of terrorism and proliferation, thereby strengthening financial sector integrity and contributing to safety and security" (FATF, 2016a).

Correspondingly, the success of the CTF system can be determined by achieving the ultimate objective. In this case, the ultimate aim of the CTF system is defined as the elimination of terrorism or at least the control and disruption of terrorist organisations and their hostile acts within a determined level. According to most of the practitioners, Turkey's CTF system is not successful in dealing with financing of terrorism. In this regard, the experts and the practitioners evaluate that Turkey's efforts and applications in terms of countering financing of terrorism have not been effectively implemented, and the current CTF system is not successful.

According to a senior judge, Turkey's CTF activities and efforts are not successful in terms of legal processes and implementation of the CTF provisions.[357] A scholar noted that there are not many successful outcomes by implementing CTF methods. In brief, Turkey's CTF system is accepted as not successful by the practitioners and scholars.[358]

While some experts claimed that Turkey's efforts against terrorist financing are not successful and effective, others noted that they cannot say clearly whether the CTF system is successful or not due to a lack of CTF implementation and official statistics which can be used to assess the level of success. One scholar indicated that:

> In order to determine whether these measures are successful from first hand, we need to look at some specific periods when terrorist organisations were affected. I do not remember such specific periods. For example, I do not remember instances when [terrorists] money was cut off, and consequently they quit their activities.[359]

A CTF practitioners argued that effectiveness can be measured by the outcome; however, Turkey's current system is not successful due to a lack of CTF implementation. If a terrorist organisation can continue its activities and survive, then it shows that the current CTF applications are not successful.[360] According to a senior level director from MASAK – FIU, the results of the CTF are the only evidence of success:

> Actually, the result is obvious, is it very successful? We should follow the outcomes for this, how we can follow them, we can look at the solid outcomes,

357 Interview with a Senior Level Judge from the Department of Justice No: JD1.

358 Interviews with Scholars No: AC5, AC7, AC8, and CTF Practitioners No: LEC0, LE4, LE6, LE11 and CO1.

359 Interview with a Scholar who is an Expert on International Relations – Professor at a University No: AC3.

360 Interview with a Middle Level CTF Practitioner from a Law Enforcement Agency No: LE4.

> how much money was seized, how the money was tracked and who was reached, and how terrorist organisation was affected from our actions, did they panic?[361]

As another FIU expert noted that even though Turkey has been dealing with terrorism since the 1970s and has been very successful with its armed struggle, the statistical figures show that the number and amount of confiscated assets are very limited. Thus, the same expert reached the conclusion that Turkey could not combat the financing of terrorism competently.[362] The number of investigations and court files and the amount of assets forfeited are extremely limited, and this shows the ineffectiveness of the CTF regime. Regarding this, another expert opined that, "I cannot say that there is a serious success. In order to say this, however we, also, do not have the relevant data in terms of application of CTF measures such as how much asset seized, confiscated".[363] As previously mentioned, there is no accurate statistical data on efforts on terrorist financing; without reliable data, it seems impossible to claim that CTF is successful in Turkey. It is also worth noting that interpreting success by utilising the amount of confiscated and/or frozen money, as Eckert and Biersteker (2010) note, can be misleading for a consistent analysis.

The scope and number of the CTF operations are very small in Turkey.[364] Dealing with terrorist financing requires broad and complex operations, which need to consider virtually all aspects of the financial activities of terrorists and their networks, not only focus on prevention of smuggling and criminal sources. When the media outlets' reports on CTF efforts are examined, it can be seen that rather than legitimate financial sources of terrorism, the majority of the news is dominated by curbing the criminal financing activities of terrorists such drug trafficking, cigarette smuggling and other types of smuggling and trafficking. This situation may indicate that criminal activities are targeted in terms of combating financing of terrorism rather than other fundraising or legitimate business activities that feed terrorists. It should be noted that even though these operations are reported in the news as disrupting terrorists' financial activities, in the content of these news reports, the explicit links to and evidence of terrorist organisations or specific individuals are not included. Furthermore, the lack of operations on legitimate sources of terrorists may indicate that CTF efforts are not successful against these types of sources of terrorist financing.

While Turkey's current CTF system and its applications are not successful enough to prevent or disrupt terrorist organisations and their attacks, some practitioners view success in terms of the level of international compliance and international integration, increasing awareness of terrorist financing and conducting

361 Interview with a (former) Senior Level Director from MASAK – FIU No: FIU2.
362 Interview with a Senior Level CTF Expert from the Turkish FIU – MASAK No: FIU1.
363 Interview with a Senior Level CTF Expert from the Turkish FIU – MASAK No: FIU4.
364 Interview with a Senior Level CTF Practitioner from the Department of Justice No: JD2.

the CTF campaign without violating human rights and respecting the rule of law. It is argued that Turkey's efforts, participation and fulfilment of the requirements of the CTF regime at the international level should be evaluated as an indicator of Turkey's success on the CTF front. At the same time, it is accepted that while Turkey's devotion to compliance and being part of international CTF agreements and efforts can be accepted as a success story for the state, Turkey has inherent problems regarding practising CTF domestically against its unique set of security threats.[365]

On a positive note, it is suggested that CTF awareness among both public and private sectors is increasing because of the recent CTF related efforts and legal instruments in Turkey. Therefore, it is claimed that Turkey's will for fighting against terrorist financing is growing in comparison to the past. Following decades of military responses to terrorism, in the minds of both government officials and public at large, a new perception seems to have started, which demonstrates that there are other ways of countering terrorism beside mere armed struggle.[366]

It can be said that although Turkey's compliance efforts at the international level are important and perhaps are a direct result of economic, diplomatic and reputational concerns, it is suggested that these efforts at international compliance are genuine signs of the willingness for integration in and solidarity with the international community. Nevertheless, the level of compliance with international legal instruments alone cannot be the benchmark for CTF success. Similarly, the increasing awareness of the financing of terrorism demonstrates the positive improvement of the CTF system; however, assessing it as an element of success might not be possible. Respecting human rights and the rule of law are positive aspects regarding how to conduct CTF efforts, yet these do not demonstrate the success level of the CTF system either. All in all, these indicators demonstrate that Turkey is working on improving its CTF system in order to conduct an effective CTF regime, and it has not reached a level whereby one can produce convincing evidence to suggest that it has done enough.

During the interviews, it was asked what the possible reasons were for the ineffectiveness of the CTF system in domestic and international domains. In this regard, various reasons such as the role of the unrecorded economy, the political and bureaucratic will, the level of implementation, coordination-cooperation, specialisation on CTF and international support for the existing success level of Turkey's CTF system were stated.

One of the main factors identified during the interviews affecting the CTF success was the volume of unrecorded economy in Turkey. It can be said that there is a correlation between the size of the informal economy and the terrorist financing and money laundering. In countries where the low level of transparency

365 Interviews with Senior Level CTF Practitioners from Law Enforcement Agencies No: LE2 and LE9

366 *Ibid.*

provided by an unrecorded informal economy in which financial transactions cannot be easily monitored, there is a suitable eco-system for both terrorists' and criminals' financial activities. In order to conduct a successful CTF struggle, Turkey should control and record the economic activity in the country better and more accurately.

The CTF perception and the determined will of the political elite and the bureaucracy in terms of conducting strict CTF efforts are significant factors affecting the success level of CTF in Turkey. Political elites need to be aware of the necessity of CTF, and more importantly, they should see this activity as a significant priority. Although there is a clear tendency towards addressing Turkey's international CTF requirements, the same cannot be claimed for the domestic application of CTF due to a lack of political will.

Turkey's general counter-terrorism strategy has not been designed comprehensively by taking into account financial, ideological, human resources and other dimensions of terrorism. Armed struggle in the form of military response has been the dominant feature in response to terrorism so far. Turkey should have a well-designed comprehensive counter-terrorism strategy which includes sub-financial strategies in order to prevent the financial aspects of terrorism. These should not be confined to CTF measures but include also investment in and financial incentives for local areas where terrorists thrive as a result of the absence of these services.

The outcomes of CTF applications such as the amount of frozen or confiscated assets, numbers of convicted members and conducted CTF operations are very limited compared to the volume of the Turkish economy and the number of financial transactions therein. Moreover, the current implementation of the CTF system in Turkey has not produced satisfactory results in terms of success stories. One of the reasons is that the legal provisions of CTF cannot be applied competently. Discovery and analysis of the links between legal financial resources and illegal organisations with solid evidence are real challenges for law enforcement agencies who lack financial expertise. In addition, inclusion of the private sector and civilians as part of CTF efforts in order to undertake successful CTF (without enough support and direction) is not sufficient. Thus, public-private partnerships need to be forged to improve information and communication flows between the public and private sectors.

In this part of the analysis, the possible impacts of CTF applications on terrorist organisations and the overall success of the CTF system in Turkey were examined. Terrorist organisations do not seem to be affected and continue their operations and terrorist attacks, increasing their violence. Currently there is hardly any clue as to whether and how much financial hardship has been experienced by terrorist organisations. This might be due to the inadequacy of Turkey's CTF system or the inappropriateness of the selected CTF measures for that purpose. With the current available data, it is difficult to determine this. However, our empirical evidence via the narrative collected at our interviews confirms these findings.

5.8 Conclusion

In this chapter, the Turkish CTF regime has been examined in detail. In the first part, the effectiveness and efficacy of the CTF system in Turkey and its applications were examined from different perspectives. One of the significant observations during the interviews was that most of the speakers gave their answers using or citing the financial activities of PKK. It is understandable that PKK has been perceived as one of the most important terrorist threats for Turkey for nearly 40 years; however, there are other terrorist organisations continuing their activities against Turkey or operating on Turkish soil to harm other states. It can be argued that this singular and dominant consideration of PKK as the focal threat provides clues regarding the PKK oriented understanding of and responses to terrorist financing in Turkey, which exclude other terrorist organisations and prospective ones for the future.

The development and the level of countering terrorist financing have been examined from a chronological perspective starting from the 1980s. It is seen that countering terrorist financing was not an instrument or a part of Turkey's counterterrorism strategy, although Turkey has been sustaining counter terrorist campaigns against different terrorist groups since the 1970s. It is argued that security-based counter-terrorism approaches such as using military forces in terms of counter-terrorism purposes and leaving the responsibility to the military is one of the possible reasons for not having a systematic counter terrorist financing strategy. In addition, the lack of legal, administrative and operational capacity and expertise in Turkey during that time is suggested as another possible reason why Turkey did not utilise CTF methods in its counter-terrorism efforts. Finally, it was found that applying a systematic CTF is a new tool for Turkey as most of the other countries established their CTF regimes in 2001 or 2002 shortly after the 9/11 attacks. Turkey enacted its first CTF legislation in 2013.

In the next part, the level of adequacy of the administrative and legal structure of the CTF system established after the 2000s was examined. Regarding the legal base, as far as the legal provisions are concerned, the CTF regime in Turkey is perceived by the majority of the interviewees as adequate and complete apart from a couple of minor issues. It can be stated that the role of the international actors, especially the UN, FATF and the US, has been instrumental in establishing Turkey's CTF system. Rather than fulfilling its own requirements in terms of addressing specific terrorist threats against Turkey, it is observed that Turkey primarily accepted this transformation in order to comply with the international responsibilities determined in the aftermath of 9/11. It can be argued that the potential economic costs and reputational concerns were the main incentives for Turkey to enact its new CTF legislation. In addition to the legal system, it can be said that Turkey has the fundamental institutions for conducting CTF operations in terms of curbing financial activities of terrorists. There are problems regarding the bureaucratic positioning of FIU among other institutions which need to be addressed. Turkey has, as it is evaluated, the required legal and institutional structures for CTF on both the domestic and international levels.

The second part of the analysis was focused on the level of CTF implementation. In other words, we considered to what extent the existing legal and administrative structures are applied to the terrorist financing cases in practice. In addition to the general evaluation of CTF implementation, the adequacy of CTF capacity, training, technological capabilities and coordination and cooperation capacities were scrutinised. It can be argued that implementation is not at the desired level. Although Turkey has vast financial and human resources, the level of expertise and the competency of practitioners and responsible institutions are generally problematic. It can be argued that for Turkey to reach the optimum implementation level needs time. From an organisational perspective, as Turkey's case demonstrates, for countries which adopt CTF as a new instrument, it is not a simple and quick process to implement these provisions in practice effectively. The cultural, political and institutional peculiarities and capacity are equally as important as sound legal provisions.

Another factor affecting the implementation is that CTF has its own inherent difficulties, such as addressing legitimate financial sources. This aspect has been given scant attention in Turkey.

Even though CTF training is not at the expected level, it should be noted that there are serious efforts to improve Turkey's CTF related awareness and expertise. In terms of technological dimension, it can be said that Turkey acquired newly released CTF software and other related tools, and the level of competency of the users of these tools is satisfactory. However, the coordination and cooperation between different institutions is not at the desired level, and this situation has a negative influence on the effectiveness of the implementation. Although Turkey signed and became part of bilateral and multilateral international agreements, at the international level coordination and cooperation efforts addressing Turkey's primary security problems are not at the expected level due to the fact that Turkey is not successful in convincing other actors to support Turkey's CTF efforts. However, on the other hand, there is a problem regarding the sincerity of foreign counterparts' taking action against terrorist organisations targeting Turkey rather than providing these terrorists safe havens and significant amounts of financial and logistical support. Overall, for the implementation part, it can be argued that the current level of effectiveness of the CTF implementation is not satisfactory, because there are very limited implementation and outcomes, such as the total value of confiscated or frozen terrorist assets.

As the last part of our analysis, the impact level of CTF implementation on the terrorist organisations and the general assessment of the whole CTF system are examined by answering whether the CTF system functions successfully. Due to a lack of or very limited implementation and limited results, it is observed that the existing applications of the CTF system in Turkey might not have had any explicit impact on the terrorist organisations targeting Turkey. It is a fact that these organisations have been continuing their struggle without showing any sign of weakness or any financial restraint due to the CTF efforts undertaken by Turkey. This situation has two possible explanations. The first explanation might be that the measures and methods introduced recently are not effective against terrorist financing and using them does not produce any constraints on terrorist organisations in contrast to the unconfirmed expectations. The second possible explanation might be that low and inadequate levels of implementation of CTF in Turkey could not create the expected impact on the terrorist organisations. In other words, either the deficiency of the CTF measures and applications or the deficiency of the states might be the reason for the lack of impact on the terrorist organisations.

Lastly, the overall success level of the CTF system in Turkey was assessed as unsuccessful and inadequate. Even though some of the interviewees assessed success in terms of international compliance, integration efforts and increasing awareness, there is clearly no CTF implementation which has influenced behavioural changes in terrorist organisations in terms of financial, operational and organisational matters or in mitigating, limiting or diminishing their threats to Turkey. These are the ultimate benchmarks for the efficacy and effectiveness of any CTF regime. In light of the shortcomings identified by both CTF practitioners and academia, Turkey continues to improve its CTF efforts and record in good faith.

6 Conclusions

6.1 General end remarks

Among many different security challenges faced by states, terrorism has been one of the most significant problems shaping both domestic and international security policies and practices all around the globe. Notably after the horrendous terrorist attacks of 9/11, addressing the monetary aspect of terrorism has begun to be a regular feature of virtually all counter-terrorism regimes around the world. In this endeavour, states and international organisations have been taking serious steps to build a robust financial and regulatory regime that deals with the financial activities of terrorists, although there were primordial examples in the past. After the famous Rose Garden speech of the US president in 2002, a financial war against terrorists was initiated by the US leadership. Since that date both domestic and international efforts and resources have been directed towards disrupting, interdicting and punishing financial activities of designated terrorist groups, individuals and affiliated persons and entities all around the world.

Although there is ample literature which attempts to answer different dimensions of terrorist financing and counter these activities (Price, 2013), there has been very limited research on the effectiveness and the success of current CTF applications. Furthermore, it is difficult to find analysis of the efficacy of the established international CTF regime which drives many countries' national CTF framework and CTF practices which are often implemented without testing and at a huge cost. Therefore, understanding whether and to what extent the current international CTF regime and the national CTF measures are compatible and complementary is a critically important question to pose. This monograph has done that.

As Passas (2006), Wittig (2009) and other scholars argue, these counter terrorist financing efforts and regimes haven been deemed suitable and effective ways for countering terrorism in the light of limited or no available empirical data from different jurisdictions. Correspondingly, these counter-terrorism efforts have been dominated and designed by a handful of states which have subsequently shaped and/or coerced how the international community forms, adopts and implements them. One of the main aims of this book, therefore, is to determine the effectiveness of Turkey's counter terrorist financing which was put in place following pressures by certain states and international organisations.

It is important to re-state the rationale as to why Turkey was selected as the focus of this monograph. Firstly, Turkey has been subjected to nearly all types of different terrorism waves since the 1970s. Secondly, compliance with the new international CTF regime (under the guardianship of FATF) and incorporating it into the legal system has been a unique and troublesome process for Turkey. The examination of these challenges provides good lessons. Lastly, given its geographically unique position as a bridge between the Middle East and the Western world, Turkey stands out as a region where international terrorist organisations such as PKK, Al Qaeda and ISIS are operating and raising funds. While Turkey has terrorism problems on its soil, it is also a transit country for terrorist organisations and their financing activities which aim to reach Europe and further afield. Thus, Turkey is and should be an essential part of regional (e.g. the EU, NATO) and international CTF mechanisms. Furthermore, Turkey has been conducting a serious counter-terrorism campaign against several terrorist organisations for decades, mainly by deploying the military tools at its disposal. This strategy has not managed to eradicate the terrorist threats therein. In these circumstances, examining Turkey's case could yield convenient insights for comprehending the transformation of its counter-terrorism and CTF compliance process (in line with international CTF standards) and reveal the extent of the impact of applying CTF measures on terrorist organisations in a national context. Moreover, this monograph contributes to the understanding of the limits and capabilities of CTF measures on countering terrorism threats.

This monograph answers the questions regarding the level of the success, efficacy and effectiveness of the CTF regime in Turkey by empirical research (via interviews) and by adding the data acquired from the official reports, the Turkish Grand National Assembly's meeting minutes, other documents and secondary literature. In doing so, we reveal numerous indicators for determining whether there is an effective and successful CTF system in Turkey and, last but not the least, what kinds of challenges and obstacles Turkey has encountered since the inception of its CTF practice. In order to reach conclusive and comprehensive analysis and results, we further inquired if the new CTF regime in Turkey is fit for its purpose at both domestic and international levels. With this aim in mind, the nature, size and dimensions of terrorist financing activities and related literature are examined. Secondly, the genesis of counter terrorist financing at the national and international levels is also analysed critically. Thirdly, as a case study, Turkey's CTF system is analysed in detail so as to understand the quality of pre-2013 CTF efforts, in light of the perceptions and opinions among CTF practitioners and experts. Lastly, the effectiveness of the current CTF regime operating in Turkey is scrutinised from legal, administrative, application, impact and success perspectives.

The synthesis of the key findings of this study is provided below. In addition, a number of suggestions for reform and development of the CTF regime in Turkey are put forward. Finally, we identify areas for future research.

6.2 Synthesis of findings

Firstly, having focused on the level of effectiveness and the success of CTF practices in Turkey, we sought to answer whether the Turkish CTF regime and its provisions address Turkey's unique set of terrorist threats and the financing problems therein. In order to understand the level of effectiveness of the CTF system in Turkey, it is important to understand the eclectic dimensions of terrorist financing, related applications and theoretical approaches in this field. For this purpose, in Chapter 2 of this monograph, various types and features of terrorist financing were examined. As a result of this examination, a broader understanding of the nature of terrorist financing and how terrorists raise, transfer and store funds was established. One of the criticisms that was posited revolves around the lack of a systematic theoretical CTF framework. We have found that most of the analyses made on the topic of financing of terrorism are not underpinned by a theoretical framework and thus mostly depend on untested assumptions and anecdotes for supporting and establishing policy decisions.

After examining different fundraising and asset transfer methods employed by terrorist organisations in Turkey, we found that there are a virtually unlimited number of methods and avenues available for terrorists, their sympathisers or affiliated entities for supporting and providing financial income for their maintenance and operations. Terrorists can raise funds from both legal and illegal as well as formal and informal financial channels and activities. Moreover, the availability of various value transfer systems allows terrorist organisations to funnel the money to the end users easily without being detected by law enforcement agencies and private sector enablers such as banks.

This part of our analysis also demonstrates that defence mechanisms built for monitoring, detecting, preventing and punishing proceeds of crime and money laundering are used for CTF purposes. While this approach may yield certain results if terrorist organisations are funnelling the proceeds of their crimes and laundering these for terrorist purposes, it is difficult to reconcile the appropriateness of this AML approach for legitimate sources of terrorist finance.

In addition to the inherent and acute problems pertaining to definitions of terrorism, terrorist financing across different jurisdictions, the sources and the methods for raising, transferring and storing terrorist financing are equally diverse. The combination of these poses a great challenge for those tasked with counter terrorism across borders. After demonstrating the flexibility and adaptation capacity of terrorists, it is important to look at the CTF measures which are designed to deal with terrorist financing activities. In other words, are these national and international level CTF systems really addressing the challenges mentioned above?

In the next part of the monograph, the birth and transformation of the Turkish CTF system and its national interactions within the current national factors and against international efforts and counter terrorist financing systems are analysed. In this framework, besides the initiatives from the US, international CTF regimes and standards such as the UNSC Resolutions, the FATF Recommendations and the EU legal instruments are analysed. The role of the US in establishing a new collective CTF perception is acknowledged, and it is noted that the US has managed to export its narrow CTF perception and applications to the international and national actors by using hard and soft coercive powers via the United Nations and FATF.

It is discovered that the US oriented approach to CTF does not always address the terrorist threats or issues which are faced by other countries such as Turkey. Subsequently, these CTF standards are adopted in a piecemeal fashion and with a cost-effectiveness rationale. As a general tendency, it can be observed that many countries around the world, including Turkey, have chosen to adhere to the minimum legal requirements and instigated superficial implementation of these CTF measures. In other words, this monograph concludes that there is monopolisation of both the predetermined threat of terrorism and predetermined counter terrorist financing responses for addressing such threats with no due regard to the actual challenges countries face in their unique security and political environments. This trend dents the quality, integrity and ultimately the effectiveness of international CTF efforts.

Following this conclusion, we turn to the question of whether the current practices of listing or designating terrorist organisations, terrorists or affiliated individuals or entities on suspicious transaction reports are effective or not. Although there are various positions regarding the usefulness and the effectiveness of these CTF applications, the general consensus is that they are not as effective as was expected. As argued in this monograph, one of the significant reasons for the negative results might be the enforcement of a 'one for all' CTF approach, which has been globalised by the efforts and shaped by the requirements of the US and which cannot meet the necessities of other countries and regions which have different terrorism threats and social, cultural, political and economic realities. In this context, the CTF system in Turkey is analysed in order to assess its efficacy and effectiveness. For this analysis, the main data was collected through 35 interviews conducted with 37 CTF practitioners from different law enforcement, judicial and academic backgrounds in Turkey.

A critical finding which emerged through our research was where the financial war against terrorism was placed in Turkey's counterterrorism strategy in the past. This monograph demonstrates that although there were signs that Turkey was aware of the financial activities of terrorist organisations well before 9/11 and pressures from the international community to enact specific CTF laws, there were not any systematically conducted CTF operations or strategy against the financial activities of terrorists. Rather, it is possible to conclude that there were limited efforts against individuals who were abetting and assisting terrorists without conducting a thorough and holistic CTF strategy against terrorist organisations in Turkey. Our analysis also reveals that the main driver for the CTF efforts in Turkey is the desire to achieve short-term goals for publicity and punish individuals who provide support to the terrorists, rather than discovering terrorists' support and logistical networks or disrupting these complex activities. We conclude it is not possible to assert that Turkey has had a systematic CTF practice, although there were a few examples and lessons available on the use of systematic financial operations against terrorists which have been conducted in different parts of the world, such as those instigated by the UK against the IRA and by Germany against Baader Meinhof since the 1970s.

The monograph also raises a fundamental question: given Turkey's intensive counter-terrorism experience, why has it not addressed the financial aspects of terrorism before? According to our interviewees and the accounts from books, the first and most important reason for this trend is the application of a narrow and military oriented security approach for countering terrorism instead of implementing a comprehensive counterterrorism strategy, which would have included the political, economic and sociological aspects of the phenomenon. In other words, the responsibility for combating terrorism had been merely left on the shoulders of security forces, especially the military. Despite this military oriented approach to counter-terrorism, we found that the legal system of the past era could have been fit for conducting a CTF campaign, yet the state departments responsible for national security chose to concentrate their efforts on applying military and police operations, rather than focusing in tandem on financing of terrorism.

In Chapter 5, we elaborated further on the fact that the leaders of the security forces, who were experts on armed conflicts but not on reading financial figures or tracking financial activities of terrorists, could not foresee the potential role of a CTF campaign against terrorist organisations. In contrast, countries such as the US and the UK have had a significant amount of experience in using financial tools or sanctions against criminals, terrorists or other states in the past; consequently, they could apply this knowledge with little alteration to new situations. However, this was not the case for Turkey and its institutions. Furthermore, we found that the selection of the right institution and its status and powers in the general law enforcement bureaucracy are critical issues when it comes to coordination of CTF tasks and operations and the success of these endeavours.

Another reason for Turkey's myopic approach to counter-terrorism was the concerns of the Cold War period. Due to the dual polarisation of the world (West versus East or capitalism versus communism), most state executives were able to evaluate active threats and decide what counter actions to employ. Thus, in the height of the Cold War in the 1970 and 1980s, Turkey saw terrorism as a state sponsored issue (which might be accurate for that period). However, after the Cold War, it seems that Turkey's perception did not change, and the financial activities of terrorist organisations were seen as tough and big issues which could be dealt with only by diplomatic means or military intervention/coercion between states. To a certain degree this idea reflected the terrorist threats of that time; however, the generalisation of this approach for encapsulating all kinds of terrorist support activities resulted in the ignorance or neglect of terrorists' financing methods undertaken in Turkey and abroad. In the post–Cold War period, the symbiotic relationship between terrorist organisations and their state sponsors changed, whereby terrorist organisations started to become more independent and stand on their own feet. This had consequences for Turkey as is seen in the case of PKK; however, Turkey could not adapt swiftly to this pragmatic shift and prevent terrorists from building their financial networks.

We have also discovered that Turkey has decided to deploy a CTF campaign by piecemeal application of the FATF standards, yet the level of institutional knowledge and experience and the legislative and institutional frameworks fell short of the standards necessary to support and realise such efforts. Rather than building a CTF system which is tailored towards and able to respond to the unique security priorities and needs of Turkey, applying traditional security-based methods was preferred as an easy and guaranteed way to achieve short-term gains.

In order to determine the level of effectiveness of the CTF system in Turkey, the existing system was analysed under three main themes:

a) the effectiveness level of legal and institutional structures;
b) the effectiveness level of CTF implementation/practice; and
c) the level of impact and end results of the CTF system.

Even though the Turkish CTF legal base on CTF is quite new and the concept of CTF is rather novel to CTF agencies, the legal provisions are relatively robust and provide a comprehensive domain for conducting a legitimate CTF campaign. In other words, the CTF provisions in books offer legitimate conditions and legal bases for CTF operations and enforcement. This positive feature of the CTF regime in Turkey is a direct result of its agreement to adopt international CTF standards. However, Turkey's willingness to implement some of the CTF standards was not an organic development or a natural aspiration for addressing the terrorism threats in Turkey. Rather, international pressures especially by the FATF (the threat of suspending Turkey's membership in FATF) and the pressure by the US Treasury and the EU were the key driving forces behind of this transformation. Apart from a degree of consciousness about its international responsibilities, Turkey was compelled to accept these changes because of potential economic sanctions and damage to its reputation. After all, Western perceptions regarding terrorist threats and financing of terrorism are different than those held by Turkey. For Turkey, elimination of the immediate security threats, mainly PKK terrorism, are the priority. For the US and the EU, 'religiously motivated terrorism' (sustained by Al Qaeda, the Islamic State or Al Shabaab) is the main threat. Due to this perception gap and the international pressure, the current CTF regime in Turkey mainly targets the internationally accepted threats without giving due consideration to domestic and more pressing threats such as PKK, DHKP-C and Hizbullah. The monograph thus demonstrates that the international CTF regime is not fit for meeting the interests and the priorities of differing countries. This rift is one of the significant reasons for a country not to internalise or support this framework. Turkey's case is important as it shows that despite having years of counter-terrorism experience and an ample amount of resources to redesign its CTF strategy against local threats, most of its efforts have focused on accomplishing international CTF requirements.

Regarding the institutional structure, we found that Turkey has the required CTF institutions (e.g. LEAs and FIU), and the CTF organisations do not have any problems regarding personnel numbers or other resources and tools.[1] However, in terms of the bureaucratic structure and designation of authority and responsibilities, the situation is less than ideal. As a key component of the CTF regime, the FIU should be effective, empowered and proactive in the bureaucratic system. The Turkish FIU, MASAK, has none of these attributes.

Besides the problems regarding the suitability and usefulness of the overall CTF regime, the institutions and staff who are responsible for undertaking CTF tasks are not competent or well trained on this subject. These findings are supported by the CTF practitioners who were interviewed. It is clear that being compliant with the international CTF provisions does not ensure positive CTF outcomes and end results in terms of their implementation.

Our study has found that specialisation on CTF is one of the key weaknesses in terms of CTF capability, which depends on the level of training and knowledge exchange. Specialisation in CTF requires not only well-trained experts in financial reporting and financial crimes and forensic accounting, but also well-informed analytical skills on terrorist organisations, the legal framework and criminal justice processes of foreign countries, international law, intelligence gathering, analysis of financial investigation and information exchange. It has transpired that existing staff recruited in the CTF institutions in Turkey, including the FIU, mainly come from the same or similar backgrounds and do not understand or appreciate other disciplines and approaches. Consequently, it becomes almost impossible to create synergies which can complement the CTF responses towards complex and diverse terrorist financing structures. While the FIU auditors are not experts on terrorism or conducting criminal investigations, law enforcement officers and prosecutors do not know how to interpret financial data. This gap is a significant factor which obstructs an effective CTF implementation. This monograph has found that in principle, there is no resistance to establishment of such a multidisciplinary environment in which different experts can share their ideas and co-create and operate an effective CTF regime. Therefore, it can be concluded that the role and the level of CTF training and recruitment at both the institutional and individual levels emerge as the most important key components for an effective CTF system.

Although literature on terrorist financing accommodates and supports various ideas regarding the adoption of AML for CTF purposes, in the case of Turkey, it is not possible to say, especially in the banking sector, that the AML system works

1 According to the MASAK Annual Activity Report, the number of personnel employed at the MASAK was 232 by the year 2015 (Financial Crimes Investigation Board, 2016, p. 14). In comparison to other FIU's personnel numbers, MASAK's number is slightly lower than the others but comparable when looked in light of its population, economy, etc. For instance, US FIU FinCEN employed approximately 340 personnel in 2013 (FinCEN, 2013); Australian FIU AUSTRAC employs 276 personnel (AUSTRAC, 2015) and Canadian FIU FINTRACK has more than 300 employees (FINTRAC, 2016).

well against detecting terrorists finance. As some interviewees argued, the financial sector has limited information, yet their responsibilities are heavy, and the consequences of non-compliance are serious. Consequently, the financial sector naturally chooses the option of not taking any risks and applies all the requirements in terms of checking lists or applying reporting mechanisms and therefore reports nearly everything without much elaboration and/or critique. However, this course of action creates an unnecessary workload and information pollution for financial analysis units. This monograph demonstrates that the lack of mutual information sharing between private and public sectors emerges as a key obstacle to an effective CTF in Turkey.

Similarly, blacklists or designation lists do not effectively work in practice due to the fact that most of these lists have the basic names of terrorist organisations but nothing specific regarding their operatives. As Turkey is not a source country for such suspected and actual terrorist on these lists, using these lists for preventing terrorist finance is not suitable in Turkey.

Another problematic area we identified is the cooperation and coordination efforts between CTF agencies. In the Turkish CTF system, there is no designated institution which can coordinate the CTF efforts in harmony with domestic and international actors. This monograph illustrates that the current CTF regime which hosts separate and independent agencies (who follow narrowly defined institutional priorities, informed by their limited understanding of complex issues around CTF) not only makes it hard to achieve an effective coordination and cooperation, but also hinders the effectiveness of on-going CTF efforts. We suggest that the Turkish CTF system needs to be re-designed in an interagency style approach in which all the different skills, expertise and multidisciplinary dimensions can be honed into CTF tasks. The current CTF regime with its separately positioned and disparately operating agencies does not work.

Besides the importance of coordination and cooperation in the national CTF environment, international coordination and cooperation are equally important. This monograph has shown that having strong diplomatic relations with other states is critical for creating a shared awareness, solidarity and commitment on CTF efforts.

Our examination has revealed that, despite explicit obligation under international law to criminalise and deter terrorist financing, (e.g. the UNSC Resolution 1373 (2001) clearly states that states are obligated to take necessary actions in order to prevent financial activities of terrorist organisations), it is possible to observe that some of the advanced legal systems of the world continue to ignore financial activities of terrorist organisations which are prohibited and designated as such by their governments, as long they do not pose a direct threat to their security. The supportive or permissive attitudes of some of the EU member states towards financial and publicity activities of PKK and its affiliated organisations (such as PYD/YPG or DHKP/C) in their territories are given as clear examples of this trend.

In addition, this monograph has demonstrated that the level of international coordination and cooperation is mainly informed by the interests of individual states rather than designation lists which are compiled at the UN. Without sincerity and solidarity in countering international terrorism, any CTF initiative is doomed to fail. Even if a state or a number of states apply the most effective CTF measures or solutions, these would not work if terrorists are able to find an alternative safe haven or new method for meeting their financial requirements.

After examining the implementation level of the CTF system in Turkey, we tried to assess the end results of this regime. Firstly, there is no shift or change of behaviour of the terrorist organisations or their financial assets. Naturally, a minimum expectation from any CTF regime would be a level of reduction in the financial abilities and assets of terrorist organisations. With no official or unofficial data available on the number of frozen assets or the number of convictions for terrorist finance offences, it has not been possible to conduct case studies to explore and identify granular details of CTF investigations, prosecution techniques and methods. Subsequently, our analysis is confined to responses from our interviewees and our observation and understanding of the CTF environment based on secondary sources of information. All of these indicate that the CTF system in Turkey is not functioning well, and it has not mitigated the current security risks and threats. In the interest of fairness, the positive efforts and developments in Turkey should not be underestimated. Turkey is working on improving its CTF system, but reaching a robust CTF system will take some time.

6.3 Suggestions for practitioners and further studies

The CTF system in Turkey focuses on the prevention of terrorist financing, yet it has not been possible to cut off financial sources of terrorist organisations completely or even with little effect. While continuing its CTF activities by targeting on-going terrorist financing activities, improvements on intelligence gathering should not be omitted. The quality of intelligence has a direct impact on the quality of evidence which is needed for criminal investigation and prosecution.

This monograph has discovered that the majority of mutual assistance request and/or initiatives for joint CTF operations are declined or curtailed because of poor intelligence and evidence provided to authorities. Especially in the case of terrorist organisations with transnational and well-established financial systems, such as PKK, the CTF measures targeting a singular offence or activity in a single jurisdiction alone would have limited effect. Consequently, an intelligence based and comprehensive CTF strategy towards such terrorist organisations would be more appropriate to reveal their networks, links and locations and to foil future attacks.

Turkey desperately needs a central CTF coordination unit with statutory powers to lead and authorise national and international CTF operations. In tandem with this central unit, it is clear that the existing law enforcement agencies need specialised CTF and economic crime units which can operate along with the regular counter-terrorism units. At the national level the main coordination unit should be established as an interagency model which will be comprised of members such as terrorism experts, criminal investigators, financial analysts, intelligence experts, national/international legal advisors and financial auditors from different public and private sectors including academics. The independence and empowerment of this new unit are critically important for an effective CTF system. Currently, Turkey does not have such an organ which creates gaps in information exchange between state departments, as well as the public and private sectors and security agencies.

At the international level, Turkey needs to concentrate on lobbying and PR activities and use international law and its tools in a way that will support its CTF priorities and efforts. In addition, CTF liaison units can be established, on a reciprocal basis, in countries terrorist organisations use as safe havens.

To Turkey, the UNSC Resolution 1373 (2001) looks like a symbolic gesture rather than a binding legal instrument which has an effect on state behaviour. This monograph has provided examples of designated terrorist organisations operating in the open with impunity in Western democracies even though such terrorist organisations are designated not only by the UN but also by national legal instruments. Controversially, FATF does not check the requirements of UNSC Resolutions pertaining to CTF or if and how they are implemented by states. The FATF should take a broader assessment and show the same coercive approach towards these countries on applying the requirements of UNSC Resolutions as it does for its 40+ Recommendations. For example, according to the EU, PKK is a terrorist organisation. Normally, financial or recruitment and publicity activities of PKK should be prohibited and prevented in the EU. But it is clear that such measures do not exist.

This monograph has argued that understanding and addressing the root causes of any terrorism movement are as important as dealing with their symptoms. However, within the confines of this monograph, we have not been able to examine the influence and role of society on the financial activities of terrorists in detail and how states can address and incorporate these in their CTF strategies. This is an area for future multidisciplinary research whereby questions such as why people are assisting terrorist activities and if and what benefits people get by supporting terrorism need to be posed. It should be conceived that CTF research needs analysis of the ethnographic, social, cultural, economic and political dimensions of terrorism. Understanding the anthropological aspect of this issue would complement legal literature and could give important insights for developing more effective counter-strategies.

Another suggestion for future research is the emerging dimensions of terrorist financing online. Although terrorists have been using cyberspace for publicity, recruitment, radicalisation, glorification and fundraising activities, with the use blockchain technology, the sophistication and autonomy of their financial transactions might increase. In this regard, understanding how international and national efforts should be designed for countering terrorist activities is important. For example, there are no internationally agreed standards as to how cryptocurrencies (which operate on the back of a blockchain technology) should be regulated. This gap leaves many opportunities for criminal and terrorist use of these digital assets.

If there is one important lesson that should be taken from this monograph, it would be this: the CTF struggle against a terrorist organisation should be conducted as early as possible, before a terrorist organisation reaches that robust level of self-sufficiency and sustainability. The case of Turkey illustrates that PKK has already reached that sophisticated organisational structure and capability with its rich resources and adaptable financing activities. It seems that at best, this terrorist organisation's financial activities could be utilised for intelligence purposes rather than interdicting its funds.

Appendices

Appendix A

Interview questions

CTF PERCEPTIONS
What do you understand by CTF? What is your role in CTF? Worldwide, how do you define a successful and effective CTF system? What should be the characteristics of this kind of CTF system?
CTF SYSTEM IN TURKEY
How new is the Turkish CTF system? Would you agree that Turkey's main CTF strategy now is Asset Freezing? What are the aims of Turkish CTF strategy?
ADMINISTRATIVE AND LEGISLATIVE EFFECTIVENESS
What do you think about the provision of legal, administrative and institutional structures for countering terrorist financing in Turkey? Do you agree that FATF's requirements have played a role? Given the latest legislation and related regulations, might there be further opportunities to develop policies?
IMPLEMENTATION EFFECTIVENESS OF CTF MEASURES IN TURKEY
What do you think about the applicability of the measures and efforts within the scope of countering financing of terrorism, and the existing problems regarding the same? What do you think about the capacity of the responsible institutions for countering terrorist financing? What do you think about the CTF staff's level of awareness and training in terms of countering financing of terrorism? What do you think about the proficiency of the training provided? How do you assess the level of deployment of the technological skills and means in order to prevent financing of terrorism? What do you think about the sufficiency of the staff who can use these tools competently? What do you think about the level of cooperation and coordination between responsible institutions? Can this be improved? Can we learn from other institutions in terms of capacity, coordination and cooperation?

(*Continued*)

Appendix A (Continued)

How do you evaluate Turkey's international level CTF efforts in terms of its terrorism threat? What are your ideas on the level of international support and assistance of other states and organisations to prevent financial activities of terrorist organisations operating in Turkey? What kind of problems does exist? What are the reasons for these problems?
THE CTF IMPACT ON TERRORIST ORGANISATIONS
What do you think about the impact of the CTF efforts, applied by Turkey, on terrorist organisations? How do you evaluate the success of the current CTF applications in overall counter-terrorism framework? If it is successful, then how do you explain this success? If it is not successful, then what are the reasons behind this situation?
RECOMMENDATIONS
Do you have any recommendations in terms of improving the success and the effectiveness of the CTF system in Turkey?

Appendix B

List of interviewees

No	*Code*	*Position*	*Institution/Expertise*
1	LEC0	Civilian Staff	Law Enforcement Agency
2	LE1	Senior Level Officer	Law Enforcement Agency
3	LE2	Senior Level Officer	Law Enforcement Agency
4	LE3	Senior Level Officer	Law Enforcement Agency
5	LE4	Middle Level Officer	Law Enforcement Agency
6	LE5	Senior Level Officer	Law Enforcement Agency
7	LE6	Middle Level Officer	Law Enforcement Agency
8	LE7	Senior Level Officer	Law Enforcement Agency
9	LE8	Middle Level Officer	Law Enforcement Agency
10	LE9	Senior Level Officer	Law Enforcement Agency
11	LE10	Senior Level Officer	Law Enforcement Agency
12	LE11	Middle Level Officer	Law Enforcement Agency
13	LE12	Senior Level Officer	Law Enforcement Agency
14	FIU1	Senior Level Expert	MASAK
15	FIU2	Senior Level Director	MASAK
16	FIU3	Senior Level Director	MASAK
17	FIU4	Senior Level Expert	MASAK
18	FIU5	Senior Level Director	MASAK
19	JD1	Senior Level Judge	Department of Justice
20	JD2	Senior Level Judge	Department of Justice
21	JD3	Senior Level Judge	Department of Justice
22	CO1	Senior Level Expert	Directorate General of Customs Enforcement
23	CO2	Senior Level Director	Directorate General of Customs Enforcement
24	GS1	Middle Level Officer	Turkish Armed Forces
25	EU1	Expert	Delegation of the European Union to Turkey
26	EU2	Expert	Delegation of the European Union to Turkey
27	EU3	Expert	Delegation of the European Union to Turkey
28	MFA1	Senior Level Director	Ministry of Foreign Affairs
29	BS1	Senior Level Director	Banking Sector
30	AC1	Scholar	International Law
31	AC2	Scholar	Terrorism/Counterterrorism

(*Continued*)

Appendix B (Continued)

No	*Code*	*Position*	*Institution/Expertise*
32	AC3	Scholar	International relations, security studies and terrorism
33	AC4	Scholar	Security studies
34	AC5	Scholar	Terrorism/Counterterrorism
35	AC6	Scholar	Terrorism/Counterterrorism
36	AC7	Scholar	International Law
37	AC8	Scholar	Security and Intelligence

Bibliography

Acharya, A. (2009). Small Amounts for Big Bangs? Rethinking Responses to "Low Cost" Terrorism. *Journal of Money Laundering Control, 12*(3), 285–298.

Adalet Bakanlığı [Ministry of Justice]. (2016). *Adli Sicil ve İstatistik Genel Müdürlüğü.* Retrieved 27.11.2018, from www.adlisicil.adalet.gov.tr/ac-cik.html.

Adams, J. (1986). *The Financing of Terror: Behind the PLO, IRA, Red Brigades, and M-19 Stand the Paymasters: How the Groups that are Terrorizing the World Get the Money to Do It.* New York: Simon and Schuster.

Akın, E. (2009). *Terör ve Terörün Finansmanı Suçu [Terror and Financing of Terror Crimes]* (Vol. 478). Ankara: Adalet Yayınevi.

Aktan, G. S., & Köknar, A. M. (2002). Turkey. In Y. Alexander (Ed.), *Combating Terrorism: Strategies of Ten Countries* (Fourth ed., pp. 260–298). Ann Arbor: University of Michigan Press.

Alexander, D. C. (2004). *Business Confronts Terrorism: Risks and Responses.* Madison: University of Wisconsin Press.

Altunyaldız, Z. (2013). *Gümrüklerde Nakit Kontrolleri* [Cash Controls at the Customs]. Ankara: T. C. Gümrük ve Ticaret Bakanlığı.

Amicelle, A., & Favarel-Garrigues, G. (2012). Financial Surveillance. *Journal of Cultural Economy, 5*(1), 105–124.

Amoroso, D. (2016). Armed Opposition Groups' (and Foreign Fighters') Abidance by International Human Rights Law: The Issue of Compliance of Syria and Iraq. In A. de Guttry, F. Capone, & C. Paulussen (Eds.), *Foreign Fighters under International Law and Beyond* (pp. 205–229). The Hague: Springer Asser Press.

Ankara Chief Public Prosecutor's Office. (2017). The indictment No. 2017/1258. Retrieved 27.11.2018, from www.ankara.adalet.gov.tr/sayfalar/duyuru/iddianameler/2016-103566/2016-103566-kisim_1.pdf.

Anti-Drug Abuse Act, Pub. L. No. 100–690, 102 Stat. 4181 (1988).

Anti-Terrorism Law [Terörle Mücadele Kanunu], Official Gazzette [Resmi Gazete], Pub. L. No. 20843, 3713 Stat. (1991).

Antiterrorism and Effective Death Penalty Act, 735 Stat. (1996).

Asbarez. (2010). *US Pressuring warned Turkish Banks to Cut Ties with Iran.* Retrieved 31.10.2018, from http://asbarez.com/84960/us-pressuring-turkish-banks-to-cut-ties-with-iranian-counterparts/.

Aufhauser, D. D. (2003). *Written Testimony of David D. Aufhauser, General Council Department of the Treasury, Before the Senate Judiciary Committee Subcommittee on Terrorism, Technology and Homeland Security.* Retrieved 27.11.2018, from www.treasury.gov/press-center/press-releases/Documents/js5071.pdf.

AUSTRAC. (2015). *AUSTRAC Annual Report 2014–2015*. Retrieved 24.10.2018, from www.austrac.gov.au/sites/default/files/austrac-ar-14-15-web.pdf.

Aydınonat, N. E. (2012). What Does the FATF Ask Turkey to Do? *Evaluation Note*, 1–7. TEPAV. Retrieved 27.11.2018, from www.tepav.org.tr/upload/files/1353327705-7.What_does_the_FATF_Ask_Turkey_to_Do.pdf.

Aydoğan, M. (2016). *PKK-affiliate PYD Opens Office in Paris as France Extends State of Emergency*. Retrieved 27.11.2018, from www.dailysabah.com/politics/2016/05/24/pkk-affiliate-pyd-opens-office-in-paris-as-france-extends-state-of-emergency.

Aykın, H., & Sözmen, H. K. (2009). *Terörün Finansmanı [Financing of Terror]* (Second ed., Vol. 12). Ankara: Mali Suçları Araştırma Kurulu Başkanlığı (MASAK).

Bacık, G., & Coşkun, B. B. (2011). The PKK Problem: Explaining Turkey's Failure to Develop a Political Solution. [Article]. *Studies in Conflict & Terrorism*, *34*(3), 248–265. doi: 10.1080/1057610x.2011.545938.

Baldwin, F. N. (2004). The Financing of Terror in the Age of the Internet: Wilful Blindness, Greed or a Political Statement? *Journal of Money Laundering Control*, *8*(Part 2), 127–158.

Bank Secrecy Act, Pub. L. No. 91–508, 84 Stat. 1114. (1970).

Bantekas, I. (2003). The International Law of Terrorist Financing. [Article]. *American Journal of International Law*, *97*(2), 315–333. doi: 10.2307/3100109.

Barrett, R. (2012). Preventing the Financing of Terrorism. *Case Western Reserve Journal of International Law*, *44*(3), 719–736.

Başıbüyük, O., Karakuş, O., & Akdoğan, H. (2007). Fundamentalism as a Universal Mindset-Case Study of Religious Fundamentalism: Turkish Hizbullah. In S. Özeren, I. D. Güneş, & D. M. Al-Badayneh (Eds.), *Understanding Terrorism: Analysis of Sociological and Psychological Aspects* (pp. 42–50). Amsterdam: IOS Press.

Basile, M. (2004). Going to the Source: Why Al Qaeda's Financial Network Is Likely to Withstand the Current War on Terrorist Financing. *Studies in Conflict and Terrorism*, *27*(Part 3), 169–186.

BBC NEWS. (1999). *Rebels Funded by Greek Churches*. Retrieved 27.11.2018, from http://news.bbc.co.uk/2/hi/europe/286512.stm.

BBC News. (2014). *Gaza Flotilla Raid: No Israel Charges Over Mavi Marmara*. Retrieved 27.11.2018, from www.bbc.co.uk/news/world-middle-east-29934002.

BBC World. (2013). *Kurdish PKK Co-founder Sakine Cansiz Shot Dead in Paris*. Retrieved 27.11.2018, from www.bbc.com/news/world-europe-20968375.

Bell, R. E. (2003). The Confiscation, Forfeiture and Disruption of Terrorist Finances. *Journal of Money Laundering Control*, *7*(Part 2), 105–125.

Bensted, G. (2012). Hi Terrorist Financing and the Internet: Dot Com Danger. *Information & Communications Technology Law*, *21*(3), 237–256.

Biersteker, T. J. (2009). Targeted Sanctions and Individual Human Rights. *International Journal*, *65*(1), 99–118.

Biersteker, T. J., & Eckert, S. E. (2008a). Conclusion: Taking Stock of Efforts to Counter the Financing of Terrorism and Recommendations for the Way Forward. In T. J. Biersteker & S. E. Eckert (Eds.), *Countering the Financing of Terrorism* (First ed., pp. 289–304). London; New York: Routledge.

Biersteker, T. J., & Eckert, S. E. (2008b). Introduction: The Challenge of Terrorist Financing. In T. J. Biersteker & S. E. Eckert (Eds.), *Countering the Financing of Terrorism* (First ed., pp. 1–17). London; New York: Routledge.

Biersteker, T. J., Eckert, S. E., & Romaniuk, P. (2008). International Initiatives to Combat the Financing of Terrorism. In T. J. Biersteker & S. E. Eckert (Eds.), *Countering the Financing of Terrorism* (First ed., pp. 234–260). London; New York: Routledge.

Bila, F. (2007). *Komutanlar Cephesi* (Fourth ed.). İstanbul: Detay Yayıncılık.

Bond, D. (2017). *Four Expert Views on the UK's Fight Against Terrorism. The Financial Times.* Retrieved 27.11.2018, from www.ft.com/content/839c1fac-e70c-11e7-97e2-916d4fbac0da.

Bozdağ, B. (2015). *Genelge: Suçtan Kaynaklanan Malvarlığı Değerlerinin Aklanmasının ve Terörizmin Finansmanının Önlenmesi.* Ankara: Adalet Bakanlığı.

Breen-Smyth, M. (2014). Theorising The "Suspect Community": Counterterrorism, Security Practices and The Public Imagination. *Critical Studies on Terrorism, 7*(2), 223–240. doi: 10.1080/17539153.2013.867714.

Bryman, A. (2015). *Social Research Methods* (Fifth ed.). Oxford: Oxford University Press.

Brzoska, M. (2011). The Role of Effectiveness and Efficiency in the European Union's Counterterrorism Policy: The Case of Terrorist Financing. Economics of Security Working Paper, 51.Berlin: Economics of Security.

Builta, A. J., & Heller, N. (2011). Reflections on 10 Years of Counterterrorism Analysis. *Studies in Intelligence, 55*(3). Retrieved 21.03.2018, from www.cia.gov/library/center-for-the-study-of-intelligence/csi-publications/csi-studies/studies/vol.-55-no.-3/pdfs/Builta-Heller-CTBestPractices-Eversion-7-Oct-2011.pdf.

Bureau for International Narcotics and Law Enforcement Affairs. (2014). *International Narcotics Control Strategy Report Money Laundering and Financial Crimes* (Vol. II). Washington, DC: Department of State.

Bureau of Counterterrorism. (2015). *Country Reports on Terrorism 2014* (Vol. 2014). Washington, DC: Bureau of Counterterrorism.

Bures, O. (2010). EU's Fight Against Terrorist Finances: Internal Shortcomings and Unsuitable External Models. *Terrorism and Political Violence, 22*(3), 419–438.

Bures, O. (2011). *EU Counterterrorism Policy a Paper Tiger?* (First ed.). Farnham; Burlington, VT: Ashgate.

Bures, O. (2012). Private Actors in the Fight Against Terrorist Financing: Efficiency versus Effectiveness. [Article]. *Studies in Conflict & Terrorism, 35*(10), 712–732. doi: 10.1080/1057610x.2012.712032.

Burke, J. (2003). *Al-Qaeda: The True Story of Radical Islam.* London: IB Tauris.

Burke, J. (2004). *The Murder that Shattered Holland's Liberal Dream.* London: The Guardian. Retrieved 23.08.2018, from www.theguardian.com/world/2004/nov/07/terrorism.religion.

Bush, G. W. (2001a). *Executive Order 13224.* Retrieved 27.11.2018, from www.state.gov/j/ct/rls/other/des/122570.htm.

Bush, G. W. (2001b). *President Freezes Terrorists' Assets.* Retrieved 27.11.2018, from http://georgewbush-whitehouse.archives.gov/news/releases/2001/09/20010924-4.html.

Byman, D. (1998). The Logic of Ethnic Terrorism. *Studies in Conflict & Terrorism, 21*(2), 149–169.

Byman, D. (2005). *Deadly Connections: States that Sponsor Terrorism.* Cambridge: Cambridge University Press.

Çağlar, A. (2006). Religion-Based Terrorism in Turkey. In R. W. Orttung & A. Makarychev (Eds.), *National Counter-Terrorism Strategies* (pp. 145–154). Amsterdam: IOS Press.

Çağlar, A. (2008). Left-Wing Terrorism in Turkey. In A. Erdemir & N. Ç. Kaya (Eds.), *Social Dynamics of Global Terrorism and Prevention Policies, NATO Science for Peace and Security Series* (First ed., Vol. 38, pp. 97–104). Washington, DC: IOS Press.

Çakirozer, U. (2010). ABD'den Ankara'ya Kara Liste Uyarisi. *Cumhuriyet*, p. 8.

Çakmak, H., & Altunok, T. (Eds.). (2009). *Financing of Terrorism and Its Economy (Terörizmin Finansmanı ve Ekonomisi)* (First ed., pp. 171–215). Ankara: Barış Platin Kitapevi.

Çakmak, H., & Çapar, G. (2009). Global Efforts of the United Nations and G-8 Against Financing of Terrorism (Terörizmin Finansmanına Karşı Küresel Mücadelede Birleşmiş Milletler ve G-8'in Faaliyetleri). In H. Çakmak & T. Altunok (Eds.), *Financing of Terrorism and Its Economy (Terörizmin Finansmanı ve Ekonomisi)* (First ed., pp. 171–215). Ankara: Barış Platin Kitapevi.

Center for Strategic Research. (2007). *Armenian Claims and Historical Facts Questions and Answers*. Retrieved 27.11.2018, from www.mfa.gov.tr/data/DISPOLITIKA/ErmeniIddialari/Ermeni_ingilizce_Soru_CevapKitapcigi.pdf.

Cerrah, İ. (2008). Countering Terrorism in a Democratic Society: The Turkish Case. In K. N. Çabuk & A. Erdemir (Eds.), *Social Dynamics of Global Terrorism and Prevention Policies* (First ed., pp. 139–145). Amsterdam: IOS Press.

Chepesiuk, R. (2003). *The Bullet or the Bribe: Taking Down Colombia's Cali Drug Cartel*. London: Greenwood Publishing Group.

Cline, L. E. (2004). From Öcalan to Al Qaida: The Continuing Terrorist Threat in Turkey. *Studies in Conflict & Terrorism, 27*(4), 321–335.

Clunan, A. L. (2006). The Fight against Terrorist Financing. *Political Science Quarterly, 121*(4), 569–596.

COE. (2005). *Council of Europe Convention on Laundering, Search, Seizure and Confiscation of the Proceeds from Crime and on the Financing of Terrorism (CETS no. 198)*. Retrieved 27.11.2018, from http://conventions.coe.int/Treaty/en/Treaties/Html/198.htm.

COE. (2015). COUNCIL DECISION (CFSP) 2015/2430. In O. J. o. t. E. Union (Ed.), *2015/2430* (Vol. L334, pp. 18–21). Brussels: Council of Europe.

Cohen, D. (2014). *The Islamic State and Terrorist Financing. Under Secretary for Terrorism and Financial Intelligence, Department of the Treasury, Testimony before the House Committee on Financial Services*. Retrieved 13.03.2018, from http://financialservices.house.gov/uploadedfiles/hhrg-113-ba00-wstate-dcohen-20141113.pdf.

Cohen, D. (2014a). *Confronting New Threats in Terrorist Financing. Remarks of Under Secretary for Terrorism and Financial Intelligence David Cohen before the Center for a New American Security on March 4, 2014*. Retrieved 16.02.2018, www.treasury.gov/press-center/press-releases/Pages/jl2308.aspx.

Council on Foreign Relations. (2011). *The Global Regime for Terrorism. Issue Brief, 31 August 2011*. Retrieved 27.11.2018, from www.cfr.org/report/global-regime-terrorism.

Crelinsten, R. D. (2009). *Counterterrorism* (First ed.). Cambridge: Polity Press.

Crenshaw, M. (1987). Theories of Terrorism: Instrumental and Organizational Approaches. *The Journal of Strategic Studies, 10*(4), 13–31.

Criminal Code Act (Australia), Section 3, Part 5.3, Division 102, Subdivision B, 102.6. (1995). Retrieved 27.11.2018, from www.austlii.edu.au/au/legis/cth/consol_act/cca1995115/sch1.html.

Criminal Code [Canada], R.S.C., 1985, c. C-46 (2017). Retrieved 27.11.2018, from http://laws-lois.justice.gc.ca/PDF/C-46.pdf.

Criss, N. B. (1995). The Nature of PKK Terrorism in Turkey. *Studies in Conflict and Terrorism, 18*(1), 17.

Criss, N. B., & Çetiner, Y. T. (2000). Terrorism and the Issue of International Cooperation. *The Journal of Conflict Studies, 20*(1). Retrieved 21.3.2018, from https://journals.lib.unb.ca/index.php/jcs/article/view/4337/4976.

Croissant, A., & Barlow, D. (2007). Following the Money Trail: Terrorist Financing and Government Responses in Southeast Asia. *Studies in Conflict and Terrorism, 30*(2), 131–156.

Cronin, A. K. (2009). *How Terrorism Ends: Understanding the Decline and Demise of Terrorist Campaigns.* Princeton, NJ: Princeton University Press.

Cuellar, M. (2003). The Tenuous Relationship between the Fight Against Money Laundering and the Disruption Criminal Finance. [Review]. *Journal of Criminal Law & Criminology, 93*(2–3), 311–465.

Dağlar, A. (2015). *Yurda Istenilen Miktarda Nakit Girisi Artik Serbest.* Retrieved 27.11.2018, from www.hurriyet.com.tr/yurda-istenilen-miktarda-nakit-girisi-artik-serbest-28882410.

Danish Supreme Court. (2014). *Supremecourt – ROJ TV Disqualification. Human Rights Decisions.* Retrieved 27.11.2018, from www.supremecourt.dk/supremecourt/nyheder/Afgorelser/Pages/ROJTV%E2%80%93Disqualification.aspx.

Danziger, Y. (2012). Changes in Methods of Freezing Funds of Terrorist Organisations Since 9/11: A Comparative Analysis. *Journal of Money Laundering Control, 15*(2), 210–236.

de Goede, M. (2003). Hawala Discourses and the War on Terrorist Finance. [Article]. *Environment and Planning D-Society & Space, 21*(5), 513–532. doi: 10.1068/d310t.

de Goede, M. (2008). Risk Preemption and Exception in the War on Terrorist Financing. In L. Amoore & M. de Goede (Eds.), *Risk and the War on Terror* (First ed., pp. 97–112). London; New York: Routledge.

de Goede, M. (2012). *Speculative Security: The Politics of Pursuing Terrorist Monies* (First ed.). Minneapolis: University of Minnesota Press.

Devlet İstihbarat Hizmetleri ve Milli İstihbarat Teşkilatı Kanunu, 2937, Official Gazette (1983).

Dishman, C. (2001). Terrorism, Crime, and Transformation. *Studies in Conflict & Terrorism, 24*(1), 43–58. doi: 10.1080/10576100118878.

Dishman, C. (2005). The Leaderless Nexus: When Crime and Terror Converge. *Studies in Conflict and Terrorism, 28*(3), 237–252.

Donohue, L. K. (2006). Anti-Terrorist Finance in the United Kingdom and United States. *Michigan Journal of International Law, 27*(2), 303–436.

Donohue, L. K. (2008). *The Cost of Counterterrorism: Power, Politics, and Liberty.* Cambridge; New York: Cambridge University Press.

Dow, R., & Turksen, U. (2017). Independence and Protection of Auditors in the EU Anti-money Laundering Framework. In Ryder et al., (Eds.), *The Financial Crisis and White Collar Crime – Legislative and Policy Responses* (pp. 211–242). Oxon: Routledge.

Durna, T., & Hançerli, S. (2007). Implementing Democratic Policing in the PKK Terrorism Torn Areas of Turkey. In O. Nikbay & S. Hançerli (Eds.), *Understanding and Responding to the Terrorism Phenomenon A Multi-Dimensional Perspective.* NATO Security through Science Series E, Human and Societal Dynamics (First ed., Vol. 21, pp. 326–338). Amsterdam; Oxford: IOS Press.

Eccarius-Kelly, V. (2012). Surreptitious Lifelines: A Structural Analysis of the FARC and the PKK. *Terrorism and Political Violence, 24*(2), 235–258.

Eckert, S. E. (2008). The US Regulatory Approach to Terrorist Financing. In T. J. Biersteker & S. E. Eckert (Eds.), *Countering the Financing of Terrorism* (pp. 209, 233). London; New York: Routledge.

Eckert, S. E., & Biersteker, T. J. (2010). (Mis)Measuring Success in the Countering the Financing of Terrorism. In P. Andreas & K. M. Greenhill (Eds.), *Sex, Drugs, and Body Counts: The Politics of Numbers in Global Crime and Conflict* (First ed., pp. 247–263). New York: Cornell University Press.

Egmont. (2014a). *About | The Egmont Group*. Retrieved 15.07.2018, from https://egmontgroup.org/en/content/about.

Egmont. (2014b). *The Egmont Documents*. Retrieved 16.06.2018, from https://egmontgroup.org/en/document-library.

Egmont. (2018). *Financial Intelligence Units (FIUs)*. Retrieved 18.06.2018, from https://egmontgroup.org/en/content/financial-intelligence-units-fius.

Emniyet Genel Müdürlüğü [Turkish National Police] (Producer). (2012). *Kaçakçılık-Kamu Spotu* [Smuggling Public Service Announcement]. Retrieved 27.11.2018, from http://trt1.web.tv/video/emniyet-genel-mudurlugu-kacakcilikkamu-spotu__00ljzpop7wu.

EU Action Plan on Combating Terrorism. (2011). 17594/1/11 REV 1Â, Council of European Union 54.

EU Commission. (1998). *1998 Regular Progress Report for Turkey*. Retrieved 01.06.2018, from www.ab.gov.tr/files/AB_Iliskileri/Tur_En_Realitons/Progress/Turkey_Progress_Report_1998.pdf.

EU Commission. (2009). *Turkey 2009 Progress Report, COM (2009) 533*. Retrieved 01.10.2018, from https://ec.europa.eu/neighbourhood-enlargement/sites/near/files/pdf/key_documents/2009/tr_rapport_2009_en.pdf.

EU Commission. (2013). *A European Terrorist Finance Tracking System (EU TFTS). COM (2013) 842 Final*. Brussels: European Commission. Retrieved 10.05.2015, from https://eur-lex.europa.eu/resource.html?uri=cellar:a0a8fa0b-7867-11e3-b889-01aa75ed71a1.0001.01/DOC_1&format=PDF.

EU Commission. (2013). *Joint Report from the Commission and the U.S. Treasury Department Regarding the Value of TFTP Provided Data Pursuant to Article 6 (6) of the Agreement between the European Union and the United States of America on the Processing and Transfer of Financial Messaging Data from the European Union to the United States for the Purposes of the Terrorist Finance Tracking Program. COM (2013) 843 Final*. Brussels: European Commission. Retrieved 15.05.2015, from https://ec.europa.eu/home-affairs/sites/homeaffairs/files/what-is-new/news/news/docs/20131127_tftp_annex_en.pdf.

EU Commission. (2016a). *Third Report on Progress by Turkey in Fulfilling the Requirements of Its Visa Liberalisation Road Map Report from the Commission to the European Parliament and the Council*. Brussels: European Commission.

EU Commission. (2017). *Report from the Commission to the European Parliament and the Council on the Joint Review of the Implementation of the Agreement between the European Union and the United States of America on the Processing and Transfer of Passenger Name Records to the United States Department of Homeland Security COM (2017) 29 Final*. Retrieved 13.04.2018, from https://ec.europa.eu/home-affairs/sites/homeaffairs/files/e-library/documents/policies/crisis-and-terrorism/19012017_pnr_report_en.pdf.

EU Commission. (2018). *Directive (EU) 2018/843 of the European Parliament and of the Council. Document 32018L084.* Retrieved 25.08.2018, from https://eur-lex.europa.eu/legal-content/EN/TXT/?uri=CELEX%3A32018L0843.

EU Commission. (2018a). *Guidance Note – Questions and Answers: Adoption of Update of the Blocking Statute (2018/C 277 I/03).* Retrieved 15.09.2018, from https://eur-lex.europa.eu/legal-content/EN/TXT/?toc=OJ%3AC%3A2018%3A277I%3ATOC&uri=uriserv%3AOJ.CI.2018.277.01.0004.01.ENG.

EUR-Lex. (2018). *Directive (EU) 2018/843 of the European Parliament and of the Council of 30 May 2018 Amending Directive (EU) 2015/849 on the Prevention of the Use of the Financial System for the Purposes of Money Laundering or Terrorist Financing, and Amending Directives 2009/138/EC and 2013/36/EU.* Retrieved 16.06.2018, from https://eur-lex.europa.eu/legal-content/EN/TXT/?uri=celex:32018L0843.

EUROJUST. (2017). *Terrorism Convictions Monitor. Issue 28, 2/L/2017.* Retrieved 27.11.2018, from www.eurojust.europa.eu/doclibrary/Eurojust-framework/TCMs/TCM%20Issue%2028%20-%20May%202017/2017-05_TCM-28_EN.pdf.

European Union. (2015). *DIRECTIVE (EU) 2015/849 OF THE EUROPEAN PARLIAMENT AND OF THE COUNCIL of 20 May 2015 on the Prevention of the Use of the Financial System for the Purposes of Money Laundering or Terrorist Financing, Amending Regulation (EU) No 648/2012 of the European Parliament and of the Council, and Repealing Directive 2005/60/EC of the European Parliament and of the Council and Commission Directive 2006/70/EC.* Retrieved 27.11.2018, from http://eur-lex.europa.eu/legal-content/EN/TXT/PDF/?uri=OJ:JOL_2015_141_R_0003&from=ES.

Europol. (2009). *The European Union Terrorism Situation and Trend Report (TE-SAT) 2009.* The Hague: European Police Office. Retrieved 27.11.2018, from www.europol.europa.eu/activities-services/main-reports/te-sat-2009-eu-terrorism-situation-trend-report.

Europol. (2010). *The European Union Terrorism Situation and Trend Report (TE-SAT) 2010.* The Hague: European Police Office. Retrieved 27.11.2018, from www.europol.europa.eu/activities-services/main-reports/te-sat-2010-eu-terrorism-situation-trend-report.

Europol. (2011). *The European Union Terrorism Situation and Trend Report (TE-SAT) 2011.* The Hague: European Police Office. Retrieved 27.11.2018, from www.europol.europa.eu/activities-services/main-reports/te-sat-2011-eu-terrorism-situation-and-trend-report.

Europol. (2012). *The European Union Terrorism Situation and Trend Report (TE-SAT) 2012.* The Hague: European Police Office. Retrieved 27.11.2018, from www.europol.europa.eu/activities-services/main-reports/te-sat-2012-eu-terrorism-situation-and-trend-report.

Europol. (2013). *The European Union Terrorism Situation and Trend Report (TE-SAT) 2013.* The Hague: European Police Office. Retrieved 27.11.2018, from www.europol.europa.eu/activities-services/main-reports/te-sat-2013-eu-terrorism-situation-and-trend-report.

Europol. (2014). *The European Union Terrorism Situation and Trend Report (TE-SAT) 2014.* The Hague: European Police Office. Retrieved 27.11.2018, from www.europol.europa.eu/activities-services/main-reports/te-sat-2014-eu-terrorism-situation-and-trend-report.

Europol. (2015). *The European Union Terrorism Situation and Trend Report (TE-SAT) 2015.* The Hague: European Police Office. Retrieved 27.11.2018, from www.europol.europa.eu/activities-services/main-reports/european-union-terrorism-situation-and-trend-report-2015.

Europol. (2018). *European Union Terrorism Situation and Trend Report 2018.* Retrieved 18.09.2018, from www.europol.europa.eu/activities-services/main-reports/european-union-terrorism-situation-and-trend-report-2018-tesat-2018.

Europol & European Monitoring Centre for Drugs and Drug Addiction. (2016). *EU Drug Markets Report In-Depth Analysis* (Vol. 2016). Luxemburg: European Union.

FATF. (2007). *Third Mutual Evaluation Report Anti-Money Laundering and Combating the Financing of Terrorism.* Paris: FATF Secretariat.

FATF. (2010a). *Improving Global AML/CFT Compliance: Update On-going Process.* Retrieved 27.11.2018, from www.fatf-gafi.org/countries/d-i/greece/documents/improvingglobalamlcftcomplianceupdateon-goingprocess-february2010.html.

FATF. (2010b). *Improving Global AML/CFT Compliance: Update On-going Process – June 2010.* Retrieved 27.11.2018, from www.fatf-gafi.org/countries/d-i/greece/documents/improvingglobalamlcftcomplianceupdateon-goingprocess-june2010.html.

FATF. (2010c). *Improving Global AML/CFT Compliance: Update On-going Process – October 2010.* Retrieved 27.11.2018, from www.fatf-gafi.org/countries/d-i/greece/documents/improvingglobalamlcftcomplianceupdateon-goingprocess-october2010.html.

FATF. (2011a). *FATF Public Statement – 24 June 2011.* Retrieved 27.11.2018, from www.fatf-gafi.org/countries/s-t/turkey/documents/fatfpublicstatement-24june2011.html.

FATF. (2011b). *FATF Public Statement – 28 October 2011.* Retrieved 27.11.2018, from www.fatf-gafi.org/countries/s-t/turkey/documents/fatfpublicstatement-28october2011.html.

FATF. (2011c). *Improving Global AML/CFT Compliance: On-going Process – 25 February 2011.* Retrieved 27.11.2018, from www.fatf-gafi.org/countries/d-i/greece/documents/improvingglobalamlcftcomplianceon-goingprocess-25february2011.html.

FATF. (2012a). *FATF Public Statement – 19 October 2012.* Retrieved 27.11.2018, from www.fatf-gafi.org/countries/s-t/turkey/documents/fatfpublicstatement-19october2012.html.

FATF. (2012b). *FATF Public Statement – 22 June 2012.* Retrieved 27.11.2018, from www.fatf-gafi.org/countries/s-t/turkey/documents/fatfpublicstatement-22june2012.html.

FATF. (2012c). *Outcomes of the Plenary Meeting of the FATF, Paris, 17–19 October 2012.* Retrieved 27.11.2018, from www.fatf-gafi.org/countries/a-c/argentina/documents/outcomesoftheplenarymeetingofthefatfparis17-19october2012.html.

FATF. (2013). *FATF Public Statement – 22 February 2013.* Retrieved 27.11.2018, from www.fatf-gafi.org/countries/s-t/turkey/documents/fatfpublicstatement-22february2013.html.

FATF. (2014a). *15th Follow-Up Report – Mutual Evaluation of Turkey* (Vol. October 2014). Paris: Financial Action Task Force.

FATF. (2014b). *Countries – Financial Action Task Force (FATF).* Retrieved 27.11.2018, from www.fatf-gafi.org/countries/.

FATF. (2014c). *Improving Global AML/CFT Compliance: On-going Process – 24 October 2014*. Retrieved 27.11.2018, from www.fatf-gafi.org/countries/a-c/argentina/documents/fatf-compliance-oct-2014.html.

FATF. (2014d). *International Standards on Combating Money Laundering and the Financing of Terrorism & Proliferation – The FATF Recommendations*. Retrieved 27.11.2018, from www.fatf-gafi.org/topics/fatfrecommendations/documents/internationalstandardsoncombatingmoneylaunderingandthefinancingofterrorism proliferation-thefatfrecommendations.html.

FATF. (2014e). *IX Special Recommendations*. Retrieved 27.11.2018, from www.fatf-gafi.org/topics/fatfrecommendations/documents/ixspecialrecommendations.html.

FATF. (2016a). *An Effective System to Combat Money Laundering and Terrorist Financing*. Retrieved 27.11.2018, from www.fatf-gafi.org/publications/mutualevaluations/documents/effectiveness.html.

FATF. (2016b). *Anti-Money Laundering and Counter-Terrorist Financing Measures-United States Mutual Evaluation Report*. Retrieved 30.06.2017, from www.fatf-gafi.org/media/fatf/documents/reports/mer4/MER-United-States-2016.pdf.

FBI. (2018). *Oklahoma City Bombing*. Retrieved 27.05.2018, from www.fbi.gov/history/famous-cases/oklahoma-city-bombing.

Fighel, J. (2003). *Great East Islamic Raiders Front (IBDA-C) – A Profile*. Herzliya: International Institute for Counter-Terrorism. Retrieved 14.07.2017, from www.ict.org.il/Article.aspx?ID=892#gsc.tab=0.

Financial Crimes Investigation Board. (2011a). *MASAK Activity Report 2010* (Vol. 2010). Ankara: Financial Crimes Investigation Board [MASAK].

Financial Crimes Investigation Board. (2011b). *Organization Chart*. Retrieved 27.11.2018, from www.masak.gov.tr/userfiles/file/sema(1).png.

Financial Crimes Investigation Board. (2011c). *Activity Reports*. Retrieved 27.11.2018, from www.masak.gov.tr/en/content/activity-report/151.

Financial Crimes Investigation Board. (2014). *MASAK Activity Report 2013* (Vol. 2013). Ankara: Financial Crimes Investigation Board [MASAK].

Financial Crimes Investigation Board. (2015). *MASAK Activity Report 2014* (Vol. 2014). Ankara: Financial Crimes Investigation Board [MASAK].

Financial Crimes Investigation Board. (2016). *MASAK Activity Report 2015* (Vol. 2015). Ankara: Financial Crimes Investigation Report [MASAK].

Financial Crimes Investigation Board (MASAK). (2016). *PRESENTATION*. Retrieved 27.11.2018, from www.masak.gov.tr/en/content/presentation/146.

FinCEN. (2005). *10th Anniversary 1995–2005 The Egmont Group of Financial Intelligence Units Exceeds the 100-member Mark During Its Annual Meeting Hosted by the Financial Crimes Enforcement Network*. Washington, DC: FinCEN.

FinCEN. (2013). *Remarks of Jennifer Shasky Calvery, Director, Financial Crimes Enforcement Network at Global Gaming Expo*. Retrieved 27.11.2018, from www.fincen.gov/news/speeches/remarks-jennifer-shasky-calvery-director-financial-crimes-enforcement-network-6.

FINTRAC. (2016). *Join FINTRAC in the Fight against Terrorist Financing and Money Laundering*. Retrieved 03.03.2017, from www.fintrac-canafe.gc.ca/emplo/1-eng.asp.

France 24. (2016). *Suspect in Murders of Kurdish Activists Dies in Paris Hospital*. Retrieved 27.11.2018, from www.france24.com/en/20161217-france-kurdish-assassination-suspect-dies-paris-hospital.

Freeman, M. (2011). The Sources of Terrorist Financing: Theory and Typology. *Studies in Conflict and Terrorism*, *34*(6), 461–475.

Freeman, M. (2012). Thinking Critically about Terrorist Financing. In M. Freeman (Ed.), *Financing Terrorism: Case Studies* (First ed., pp. 237–243). Farnham; Burlington, VT: Ashgate.

Ganguly, M. (2001). *A Banking System Built for Terrorism. Time 5 October.* Retrieved 10.09.2018, from http://content.time.com/time/world/article/0,8599,178227,00.html.

Ganor, G. (2002). Defining Terrorism: Is One Man's Terrorist Another Man's Freedom Fighter? *Police Practice and Research*, *3*(4), 287–304. doi: 10.1080/1561426022000032060.

Gardella, A. (2004). The Fight against the Financing of Terrorism between Judicial and Regulatory Cooperation. In A. Bianchi (Ed.), *Enforcing International Law Norms against Terrorism* (First ed., Vol. 4, pp. 415–453). Oxford; Portland, OR: Hart Publishing.

Geiger, H. (2007). The Fight against Money Laundering: An Economic Analysis of a Cost-Benefit Paradoxon. *Journal of Money Laundering Control*, *10*(1), 91–105.

Geltzer, J. A. (2011). Taking Hand-Outs or Going It Alone: Nationalization versus Privatization in the Funding of Islamist Terrorist Groups. *Studies in Conflict and Terrorism*, *34*(2), 144–170.

General Prosecution Office of the Supreme Court of Appeal. (2018). *July 15: The Fetullahist Terrorist Organization (FETO) Behind the July 15 Coup Attempt in The Republic of Turkey.* Retrieved 23.09.2018, from www.yargitaycb.gov.tr/documents/15temmuzbrosurEN.pdf.

Gergin, N., Balcı, F., & Eldivan, I. S. (2009). Turkey's Counter Terrorism Policies Against The PKK: The "Fish" or the "Water"? In S. Ekici & D. A. McEntire (Eds.), *Building Terrorism Resistant Communities: Together Against Terrorism NATO Science for Peace and Security-E Human and Societal Dynamics* (First ed., pp. 264–283). Amsterdam; Washington, DC: IOS Press.

Gergin, N., Duru, H., & Çetin, H. C. (2014). Profile and Life Span of the PKK Guerrillas. *Studies in Conflict & Terrorism*. doi: 10.1080/1057610X.2014.981989.

Glazer, M. P., & Glazer, P. M. (1989). *The Whistleblowers*. New York: Basic Books.

Göktepe, F., & Erçıktı, S. (2007). Comparative Analysis of the Role of Intelligence in Counterterrorism in Turkey and in the United States. In O. Nikbay & S. Hançerli (Eds.), *Understanding and Responding to the Terrorism Phenomenon: A Multi-Dimensional Perspective E, Human and Societal Dynamics Vol. 21 NATO Security through Science Series* (First ed., pp. 378–393). Amsterdam; Oxford: IOS Press.

Goldman, Z. K., Maruyama, E., Rosenberg, E., Saravalle, E., & Solomon-Strauss, J. (2017). *Terrorist Use of Virtual Currencies*. Washington, DC: Center for New American Security. Retrieved 30.07.2018, from www.lawandsecurity.org/wp-content/uploads/2017/05/CLSCNASReport-TerroristFinancing-Final.pdf.

Gordon, R. (2012). Terrorism Financing Indicators for Financial Institutions in the United States. *Case Western Reserve Journal of International Law*, *44*(577), 765.

Gottselig, G., & Underwood, S. (2004). *Financial Intelligence Units: An Overview*. Washington, DC: International Monetary Fund/World Bank.

Greenberg, M. R., Wechsler, W. F., & Wolosky, L. S. (2002). *Terrorist Financing*. New York: Council on Foreign Relations. Retrieved 27.11.2018, from www.cfr.org/content/publications/attachments/Terrorist_Financing_TF.pdf.

Gunter, M. (2014). *Out of Nowhere: The Kurds of Syria in Peace and War*. London: Hurst.

Gupta, D. K. (2005). Exploring Roots of Terrorism. In T. Bjørgo (Ed.), *Root Causes of Terrorism: Myths, Reality and Ways Forward*. London: Routledge.

Gürses, E. (2008). Ideological Basis and Tactics of Organized Ethnic Terrorism: The Cases of IRA, ETA, and PKK. In A. Erdemir & N. Ç. Kaya (Eds.), *Social Dynamics of Global Terrorism and Prevention Policies NATO Science for Peace and Security Series E* (Human and Societal Dynamics Vol. 38, pp. 75–95). Washington, DC: IOS Press.

Gurule, J. (2009). The Demise of the U.N. Economic Sanctions Regime to Deprive Terrorists of Funding. *Case Western Reserve Journal of International Law, 41*(1), 19–63.

Güven, E. (2004). *DGM'de Yargi Krizi*. Retrieved 27.11.2018, from http://arsiv.ntvmsnbc.com/news/272102.asp.

Hafeez, M. (2009). Ethnic Conflict in Sri Lanka. *Ethnic and Racial Studies, 9*, 264–269.

Heng, Y.-K., & McDonagh, K. (2009). *Risk, Global Governance and Security: The Other War on Terror*. London; New York: Routledge.

High Council of Judges and Prosecutors. (2016). *Decision of the General Assembly of High Council of Judges and Prosecutors*. Retrieved 25.07.2018, from www.judiciaryofturkey.gov.tr/pdfler/hsyk_karar440.PDF.

Hinnen, T. M. (2004). The Cyber-front in the War on Terrorism: Curbing Terrorist Use of the Internet. *The Columbia Science and Technology Law Review, 5*(5), 1–42.

HM Government. (2006). *Countering International Terrorism: The United Kingdom's Strategy*. London: HM Government, July.

HM Treasury. (2007). *The Financial Challenge to Crime and Terrorism*. London: Home Office, Serious and Organized Crime Agency and Foreign and Commonwealth Office, HM Treasury, February.

Hoffman, B. (2006). *Inside Terrorism*. New York: Columbia University Press.

Horgan, J., & Taylor, M. (1997). The Provisional Irish Republican Army: Command and Functional Structure. *Terrorism and Political Violence, 9*(3), 1–32. doi: 10.1080/09546559708427413.

Horgan, J., & Taylor, M. (1999). Playing the 'Green Card' – Financing the Provisional IRA: Part 1. [Article]. *Terrorism and Political Violence, 11*(2), 1–38. doi: 10.1080/09546559908427502.

Horgan, J., & Taylor, M. (2003). Playing the 'Green Card' – Financing the Provisional IRA: Part 2. [Article]. *Terrorism and Political Violence, 15*(2), 1–60. doi: 10.1080/09546550312331293027.

House of Lords Select Committee on Economic Affairs. (2007). *The Impact of Economic Sanctions* (Vol. 1). London: House of Lords.

Housing and Community Development Act, Pub. L. No. 102–550, 106 Stat. 3672 (1992).

Human Rights Watch. (2014). *Turkey: Spy Agency Law Opens Door to Abuse*. Retrieved 27.11.2018, from www.hrw.org/news/2014/04/29/turkey-spy-agency-law-opens-door-abuse.

Hurriyet Daily News. (2014a). *Danish Court Frees 10 over PKK Funding Charges*. Retrieved 27.11.2018, from www.hurriyetdailynews.com/danish-court-frees-10-over-pkk-funding-charges.aspx?pageID=238&nID=73413&NewsCatID=351.

Hurriyet Daily News. (2014b). *Turkish FM Says 600 Turkish Nationals Joined Jihadists, More Than 100 Killed*. Retrieved 27.11.2018, from www.hurriyetdailynews.com/turkish-fm-says-600-turkish-nationals-joined-jihadists-more-than-100-killed.aspx?pageID=238&nID=74813&NewsCatID=359.

Hurriyet Daily News. (2015). *YPG Not a Terrorist Organization for US, Spokesman Says*. Retrieved 27.11.2018, from www.hurriyetdailynews.com/ypg-not-a-terrorist-organization-for-us-spokesman-says.aspx?PageID=238&NID=88832&NewsCatID=359.

Hutchinson, S., & O'Malley, P. (2007). A Crime-Terror Nexus? Thinking on Some of the Links between Terrorism and Criminality. *Studies in Conflict and Terrorism*, *30*(12), 1095–1107.

IEP. (2014). *Global Terrorism Index 2014 – Measuring and Understanding the Impact of Terrorism* (First ed.). Sydney: Institute for Economics & Peace.

İl İdaresi Kanunu [Provincial Administration Law], 5442 (1949).

International Emergency Economic Powers Act, 50 USC § 1702, 35 Stat. (1977).

International Monetary Fund. (2012). *Turkey: Financial System Stability Assessment*. Washington, DC: International Monetary Fund.

International Monetary Fund. (2018). *Anti-Money Laundering/Combating the Financing of Terrorism – Topics*. Retrieved 02.06.2018, from www.imf.org/external/np/leg/amlcft/eng/aml1.htm.

Irwin, A. S. M., Choo, K. K. R., & Liu, L. (2012a). An Analysis of Money Laundering and Terrorism Financing Typologies. *Journal of Money Laundering Control*, *15*(1), 85–111.

Irwin, A. S. M., Choo, K. K. R., & Liu, L. (2012b). Modelling of Money Laundering and Terrorism Financing Typologies. *Journal of Money Laundering Control*, *15*(3), 316–335.

Jacobson, M. (2010). Terrorist Financing and the Internet. *Studies in Conflict & Terrorism*, *33*(4), 353–363. doi: 10.1080/10576101003587184.

Joosse, P. (2007). Leaderless Resistance and Ideological Inclusion: The Case of the Earth Liberation Front. *Terrorism and Political Violence*, *19*(3), 351–368. doi: 10.1080/09546550701424042.

Joseph, Z. (1990). The Application of RICO to International Terrorism. *Fordham Law Review*, *58*(5), 1071–1084.

Kamu Düzeni ve Güvenliği Müsteşarlığının Teşkilat ve Görevleri Hakkında Kanun [The Law on Organisation and Tasks of Undersecretariat of Public Order and Security]. (2010).

Kamu Düzeni ve Güvenliği Müsteşarlığı [Undersecretariat of Public Order and Security]. (2013).

Karmon, E. (1998). Islamic Terrorist Activities in Turkey in the 1990s. *Terrorism and Political Violence*, *10*(4), 101–121. doi: 10.1080/09546559808427484.

Kartalis, A. (2017). The 4th AML Directive. *European Institute of Management & Finance*. Retrieved 30.06.2017, from http://eimf.eu/the-4th-aml-directive/.

Keatinge, T. (2014). Turkey's Dirty Money-Why Ankara Is Still on the FATF's Gray List. *Foreign Affairs*. Foreign Affairs website: doi. Retrieved from www.foreignaffairs.com/articles/turkey/2014-02-25/turkeys-dirty-money.

Kiser, S. (2005). *Financing Terror: An Analysis and Simulation to Affect Al Qaeda's Financial Infrastructures*. Santa Monica, CA: RAND Company.

Kochan, N. (2005). *The Washing Machine*. Mason, OH: Thomson.

Koh, J. M. (2006). *Suppressing Terrorist Financing and Money Laundering* (First ed.). New York: Springer.

Krahenmann, S. (2016). The Obligations under International Law of the Foreign Fighters' State of Nationality or Habitual Residence, State of Transit and State of

Destination. In A. de Guttry, F. Capone, & C. Paulussen (Eds.), *Foreign Fighters under International Law and Beyond* (First ed., pp. 229–258). The Hague: Springer Asser Press.

Krais, J. (2018). *EU: 5th EU Anti-Money Laundering Directive Published (Global Compliance News, 16 July 2018)*. Retrieved 20.10.2018, from https://globalcompliancenews.com/eu-5th-anti-money-laundering-directive-published-20180716/.

Kundakçı, H. (2005). *Güneydoğu'da Unutulmayanlar* (Fifth ed.). İstanbul: Alfa Yayınları.

Law on Prevention of Laundering Proceeds of Crime, 5549, Official Gazette [Resmi Gazete] – 26323. (2006).

Law on the Prevention of Financing of Terrorism, 6415, Official Gazette [Resmi Gazete] – 28561. (2013).

Legislationonline. (2004). *Turkish Criminal Code*. Retrieved 27.11.2018, from http://legislationline.org/documents/action/popup/id/6872/preview.

Lemieux, F., & Prates, F. (2011). Entrepreneurial Terrorism: Financial Strategies, Business Opportunities, and Ethical Issues. *Police Practice and Research, 12*(5), 368–382.

Levey, S. (2004). *Testimony of Stuart A. Levey, Under Secretary Terrorism and Financial Intelligence U.S. Department of the Treasury Before the Senate Committee on Banking and Urban Affairs*. Retrieved 27.11.2018, from www.treasury.gov/press-center/press-releases/Pages/js1965.aspx.

Levi, M. (2010). Combating the Financing of Terrorism. [Article]. *British Journal of Criminology, 50*(4), 650–669. doi: 10.1093/bjc/azq025.

Levitt, M. (2003). Stemming the Flow of Terrorist Financing: Practical and Conceptual Challenges. *Fletcher Forum of World Affairs, 27*(Part 1), 59–70.

Levitt, M., & Jacobson, M. (2008). The U.S. Campaign to Squeeze Terrorists' Financing. *Journal of International Affairs – Columbia University, 62*(1), 67–86.

Lewis, J. A. (2005). The Internet and Terrorism. *In Proceedings of the ASIL Annual Meeting* (Vol. 99, pp. 112–115). Cambridge: Cambridge University Press.

LexisNexis, Uncover the True Cost of Anti-Money Laundering & KYC Compliance – A LexisNexis Risk Solutions Report Study on Financial Institutions across Six Markets in Asia. (2016). Retrieved 21.03.2018, from www.lexisnexis.com/risk/intl/en/resources/research/true-cost-of-aml-compliance-apac-survey-report.pdf.

Lichtblau, E., & Risen, J. (2006). Bank Data Is Sifted by U.S. in Secret to Block Terror. *The New York Times*. Retrieved 27.11.2018, from www.nytimes.com/2006/06/23/washington/23intel.html?pagewanted=all&_r=0.

Malkin, L., & Elizur, Y. (2002). Terrorism's Money Trail. *World Policy Journal, 19*(1), 60.

Mango, A. (2005). *Turkey and the War on Terror: 'For Forty Years We Fought Alone'*. Oxon: Routledge.

Marcus, A. (2007). *Blood and Belief: The PKK and the Kurdish Fight for Independence*. New York: New York University Press.

MASAK. (2014). *Legal Framework of CFT*. Retrieved 27.11.2018, from www.masak.gov.tr/en/content/relevant-legislation/1334.

Matthews, B., & Ross, L. (2010). *Research Methods* (First ed.). Edinburgh: Pearson Education Limited.

Maxwell, N., & Artingstall, D. (2017). *The Role of Information-Sharing Partnerships in the Disruption of Crime. RUSI Occasional Paper*. London: Royal United Services Institute for Defence and Security Studies. Retrieved 27.11.2018, from https://rusi.org/sites/default/files/201710_rusi_the_role_of_fisps_in_the_disruption_of_crime_maxwwell_artingstall_web_4.2.pdf.

McCulloch, J., & Pickering, S. (2005). Suppressing the Financing of Terrorism. *British Journal of Criminology*, *45*(4), 470–486.

Mert, A. O. (2016). *15 July Coup Attempt and the Parallel State Structure. Publications of the Presidency of the Republic of Turkey Department of Corporate Communications* (Second ed.). Retrieved 21.05.2018, from http://15.07.gov.tr/assets/files/doc/15-july-coup-attempt.pdf.

MGK Genel Sekreterliği [Secretariat General of National Security Council]. (2010). *27 Ekim 2010 Tarihli Toplanti.* Retrieved 27.11.2018, from www.mgk.gov.tr/index.php/27-ekim-2010-tarihli-toplanti.

MGK Genel Sekreterliği [Secretariat General of National Security Council]. (2013). *Calismalar [Researches].* Retrieved 27.11.2018, from www.mgk.gov.tr/index.php/calismalar.

Ministry of Finance. (2008). *Regulation on Program of Compliance with Obligations of Anti-Money Laundering and Combating the Financing of Terrorism.* Retrieved 06.05.2018, from www.masak.gov.tr/userfiles/file/RoC_amended_11_june_2014.pdf.

Ministry of Foreign Affairs. (2007). *Press Release Regarding Legal Case about MED TV No: 127.* Retrieved 27.11.2018, from www.mfa.gov.tr/_p_no_127_ – 8-september-2007_-press-release-regarding-legal-case-about-med-tv-_unofficial-translation_-__p_.en.mfa.

Ministry of Foreign Affairs. (2014). *Press Release Regarding the Decision of Supreme Court of Denmark on ROJ TV and Its Parent Company Mesopotamia Broadcast No: 66.* Retrieved 27.11.2018, from www.mfa.gov.tr/no_-66_-27-february-2014_-press-release-regarding-the-decision-of-the-supreme-court-of-denmark-on-roj-tv-and-its-parent-compan.en.mfa.

Ministry of Foreign Affairs. (2016). *PKK.* Retrieved 27.11.2018, from www.mfa.gov.tr/pkk.en.mfa.

MI5. (2018). *Threat Levels.* Retrieved 30.06.2018, from www.mi5.gov.uk/threat-levels.

Money Laundering and Financial Crimes Strategy Act (1998). Pub. L. 105–310, 112 Stat. 2941.

Myres, G. (2012). Investing in the Market of Violence: Toward a Micro-Theory of Terrorist Financing. [Article]. *Studies in Conflict & Terrorism*, *35*(10), 693–711. doi: 10.1080/1057610X.2012.712031.

Narcotic Division. (1994). *General Evaluation of Illicit Drug Trafficking* (Vol. 1993). Ankara: General Directorate of the National Police – Department of Anti-Smuggling, Intelligence and Operation.

National Consortium for the Study of Terrorism and Responses to Terrorism (START). (2013). *Global Terrorism Database (GTD). (201302010003).* Retrieved 27.11.2018, from www.start.umd.edu/gtd/search/IncidentSummary.aspx?gtdid=201302010003.

National Consortium for the Study of Terrorism and Responses to Terrorism (START). (2018). *Global Terrorism Database.* Retrieved 09.05.2018, from www.start.umd.edu/gtd/search/Results.aspx?chart=target&casualties_type=&casualties_max=&perpetrator=449.

National Intelligence Agency [MIT]. (2016). *Intelligence Production.* Retrieved 25.04.2016, from www.mit.gov.tr/eng/isth-olusum.html.

NATO. (2016). *NATO's Military Concept for Defence against Terrorism, International Military Staff, 19 August 2016.* Retrieved 27.11.2018, from www.nato.int/cps/ic/natohq/topics_69482.htm.

NATO. (2017). *Countering Terrorism*. Retrieved 22.08.2018, from www.nato.int/cps/ua/natohq/topics_77646.htm.

Navias, M. S. (2002). Finance Warfare as a Response to International Terrorism. *The Political Quarterly*, *73*(1), 57–79.

Navias, M. S. (2007). Global Terror and International Finance in the Immediate Aftermath of 9/11. In C. Ankersen & M. O'Leary (Eds.), *Understanding Global Terror* (First ed., pp. 171–194). Cambridge: Polity Press.

Norton Rose Fulbright. (2017). *Turkish Parliament Passes New Law to Encourage Repatriation of Funds (Varlık-Barışı)*. Retrieved 03.06.2018, from www.nortonrosefulbright.com/knowledge/publications/149872/turkish-parliament-passes-new-law-to-encourage-repatriation-of-funds-varlik-barisi.

O'Donoghue, T. (2007). *Planning Your Qualitative Research Project: An Introduction to Interpretivist Research in Education*. London: Routledge.

OECD. (2013). *Bribery and Corruption Awareness Handbook for Tax Examiners and Tax Auditors*. Paris: OECD Publishing.

O'Neill, M. (2012). *The Evolving EU Counter-terrorism Legal Framework*. London: Routledge.

Orhan, M. (2010). Al-Qaeda: Analysis of the Emergence, Radicalism, and Violence of a Jihadist Action Group in Turkey. *Turkish Studies*, *11*(2), 143–161. doi: 10.1080/14683849.2010.483846.

Oudraat, C. d. J. (2004). *The United Nations and the Campaign Against Terrorism* (Vol. 1, pp. 29–37). Disarmament Forum.

Oudraat, C. d. J. (2007). Economic Sanctions and International Peace and Security. In C. A. Crocker, F. O. Hampson, & P. R. Aall (Eds.), *Leashing the Dogs of War: Conflict Management in a Divided World* (pp. 335–354). Washington, DC: United States Institute of Peace Press.

Özalp, G. (2016). *AP ile Gerilim Tırmanıyor*. Retrieved 27.11.2018, from www.amerikaninsesi.com/a/ap-ile-gerilim-tirmaniyor/3325785.html.

Özcan, N. A. (2009). PKK Terrorism in Turkey. In J. Ker-Lindsay & A. Cameron (Eds.), *Combating International Terrorism-Turkey's Added Value* (pp. 9–12). London: Royal Services United Services Institute (RUSI), Stephen Austin & Sons Ltd.

Özeren, S. (2008). The Turkish Counter-Terrorism Experience. In Centre of Excellence Defence Against Terrorism (Ed.), *Organizational and Psychological Aspects of Terrorism, Nato Science for Peace and Security Series* (First ed., pp. 155–164). Washington, DC: IOS Press.

Özeren, S., Sever, M., & Başıbüyük, O. (Eds.). (2011). *Counter Terrorism Experiences of SECI Member Countries* (First ed.). Ankara: Başak Matbaacılık ve Tan. Hiz. Ltd. Şti.

Özeren, S., & Van De Voorde, C. (2006). Turkish Hizballah: A Case Study of Radical Terrorism. *International Journal of Comparative and Applied Criminal Justice*, *30*(1), 75–93. doi: 10.1080/01924036.2006.9678747.

Özgenç, İ. (2013). *Suç Örgütleri [Criminal Organisations]* (Sixth ed.). Ankara: Seçkin.

Parker, M., & Taylor, M. (2010). Financial Intelligence: A Price Worth Paying? *Studies in Conflict and Terrorism*, *33*(11), 949–959.

Passas, N. (2005). *Informal Value Transfer Systems and Criminal Activities*. The Hague: WODC.

Passas, N. (2006a). Fighting Terror with Error: The Counter-productive Regulation of Informal Value Transfers. *Crime Law and Social Change*, *45*(4–5), 315–336.

Passas, N. (2006b). Setting Global CFT Standards: A Critique and Suggestions. *Journal of Money Laundering Control*, *9*(3), 281–292. doi: 10.1108/13685200610681805.

Passas, N. (2007). Terrorism Financing Mechanisms and Policy Dilemmas. In J. K. Giraldo & H. A. Trinkunas (Eds.), *Terrorism Financing and State Responses* (First ed., pp. 21–38). Stanford: Stanford University Press.

Passas, N., & Jones, K. (2006). Commodities and Terrorist Financing: Focus on Diamonds. *European Journal on Criminal Policy and Research*, *12*(1), 1–33.

Picarelli, J. T. (2012). Osama Bin Corleone? Vito the Jackal? Framing Threat Convergence through an Examination of Transnational Organized Crime and International Terrorism. *Terrorism and Political Violence*, *24*(2), 180–198.

Picarelli, J. T., & Shelley, L. I. (2007). Organized Crime and Terrorism. In J. K. Giraldo & H. A. Trinkunas (Eds.), *Terrorism Financing and State Responses*. Stanford: Stanford University Press.

PKK Merkez Komitesi [PKK Central Committee]. (1978). *PKK Kuruluş Bildirgesi [PKK Foundation Manifesto]*. Retrieved 27.11.2018, from www.serxwebun.org/index.php?sys=naverok&id=45.

Presidential Decree No: 1. (2018). *Cumhurbaşkanlığı Teşkilatı Hakkında Cumhurbaşkanlığı Kararnamesi [Presidential Decree on Presidential Organisation], Official Gazette [Resmi Gazete]-30474*. Retrieved 25.10.2018, from www.resmigazete.gov.tr/eskiler/2018/07/20180710-1.pdf.

Presidential Decree No: 17. (2018). *Bazi Cumhurbaşkanlığı Kararnamelerinde Değişiklik Yapılması Hakkında Cumhurbaşkanlığı Kararnamesi [Presidential Decree on Amending Some Presidential Decrees], Official Gazette [Resmi Gazete] – 30534*. Retrieved 19.10.2018, from www.resmigazete.gov.tr/eskiler/2018/09/20180913-6.pdf.

Price, E. (2013). Literature on the Financing of Terrorism. *Perspectives on Terrorism*, *7*(4), 112–130. Retrieved 17.08.2018, from www.jstor.org/stable/26296986.

Punch, K. F. (2013). *Introduction to Social Research: Quantitative and Qualitative Approaches* (Third ed.). London: Sage.

Ranstrop, M. (2007). *Mapping Terrorism Research – State of the Art, Gaps and Future Directions*. Oxon: Routledge.

Raphaeli, N. (2003). Financing of Terrorism: Sources, Methods, and Channels. *Terrorism and Political Violence*, *15*(4), 59–82.

Rapoport, D. C. (2004). The Four Waves of Modern Terrorism. In A. K. Cronin & J. M. Ludes (Eds.), *Attacking Terrorism: Elements of A Grand Strategy* (First ed., pp. 46–73). Washington, DC: Georgetown University Press.

Republic of Turkey Office of the Prime Minister Directorate General of Press and Information. (2016). *PYD is 'PKK's Syrian Affiliate', US Document Reveals*. Retrieved 27.11.2018, from www.byegm.gov.tr/english/agenda/pyd-is-pkks-syrian-affiliate-us-document-reveals/91222.

Resolution 1267. (1999). *The United Nations Security Council*. Retrieved 27.11.2018, from https://undocs.org/S/RES/1267(1999).

Resolution 1269. (1999). *The United Nations Security Council*. Retrieved 27.11.2018, from https://undocs.org/S/RES/1269(1999).

Resolution 1333. (2000). *The United Nations Security Council*. Retrieved 27.11.2018, from https://undocs.org/S/RES/1333(2000).

Resolution 1363. (2001). *The United Nations Security Council*. Retrieved 27.11.2018, from https://undocs.org/S/RES/1363(2001).

Resolution 1373. (2001). *The United Nations Security Council.* Retrieved 27.11.2018, from https://undocs.org/S/RES/1373(2001).

Resolution 1390. (2002). *The United Nations Security Council.* Retrieved 27.11.2018, from https://undocs.org/S/RES/1390(2002).

Resolution 1452. (2002). *The United Nations Security Council.* Retrieved 25.05.2018, from https://undocs.org/S/RES/1452(2002).

Resolution 1455. (2003). *The United Nations Security Council.* Retrieved 25.05.2018, from https://undocs.org/S/RES/1455(2003).

Resolution 1456. (2003). *The United Nations Security Council.* Retrieved 27.11.2018, from https://undocs.org/S/RES/1456(2003).

Resolution 1526. (2004). *The United Nations Security Council.* Retrieved 25.05.2018, from https://undocs.org/S/RES/1526(2004).

Resolution 1535. (2004). *The United Nations Security Council.* Retrieved 27.11.2018, from https://undocs.org/S/RES/1535(2004).

Resolution 1566. (2004). *The United Nations Security Council.* Retrieved 27.11.2018, from https://undocs.org/S/RES/1566(2004).

Resolution 1617. (2005). *The United Nations Security Council.* Retrieved 25.05.2018, from https://undocs.org/S/RES/1617(2005).

Resolution 1624. (2005). *The United Nations Security Council.* Retrieved 25.05.2018, from https://undocs.org/S/RES/1624(2005).

Resolution 1699. (2006). *The United Nations Security Council.* Retrieved 25.05.2018, from https://undocs.org/S/RES/1699(2006).

Resolution 1730. (2006). *The United Nations Security Council.* Retrieved 27.11.2018, from https://undocs.org/S/RES/1730(2006).

Resolution 1735. (2006). *The United Nations Security Council.* Retrieved 25.05.2018, from https://undocs.org/S/RES/1735(2006).

Resolution 1822. (2008). *The United Nations Security Council.* Retrieved 27.11.2018, from https://undocs.org/S/RES/1822(2008).

Resolution 1904. (2009). *The United Nations Security Council.* Retrieved 12.10.2014, from https://undocs.org/S/RES/1904(2009).

Resolution 1988. (2011). *The United Nations Security Council.* Retrieved 25.05.2018, from https://undocs.org/S/RES/1988(2011).

Resolution 1989. (2011). *The United Nations Security Council.* Retrieved 12.10.2014, from https://undocs.org/S/RES/1989(2011).

Resolution 2083. (2012). *The United Nations Security Council.* Retrieved 12.10.2014, from https://undocs.org/S/RES/2083(2012).

Resolution 2133. (2014). *The United Nations Security Council.* Retrieved 25.05.2018, from https://undocs.org/S/RES/2133(2014).

Resolution 2161. (2014). *The United Nations Security Council.* Retrieved 25.05.2018, from https://undocs.org/S/RES/2161(2014).

Resolution 2170. (2014). *The United Nations Security Council.* Retrieved 25.05.2018, from https://undocs.org/S/RES/2170(2014).

Resolution 2178. (2014). *The United Nations Security Council.* Retrieved 25.05.2018, from https://undocs.org/S/RES/2178(2014).

Resolution 2195. (2014). *The United Nations Security Council.* Retrieved 25.05.2018, from https://undocs.org/S/RES/2195(2014).

Resolution 2199. (2015). *The United Nations Security Council.* Retrieved 25.05.2018, from https://undocs.org/S/RES/2199(2015).

Resolution 2214. (2015). *The United Nations Security Council.* Retrieved 25.05.2018, from https://undocs.org/S/RES/2214(2015).

Resolution 2249. (2015). *The United Nations Security Council.* Retrieved 25.05.2018, from https://undocs.org/S/RES/2249(2015).

Resolution 2253. (2015). *The United Nations Security Council.* Retrieved 25.05.2018, from https://undocs.org/S/RES/2253(2015).

Resolution 2309. (2016). *The United Nations Security Council.* Retrieved 25.05.2018, from https://undocs.org/S/RES/2309(2016).

Resolution 2322. (2016). *The United Nations Security Council.* Retrieved 25.05.2018, from https://undocs.org/S/RES/2322(2016).

Resolution 2331. (2016). *The United Nations Security Council.* Retrieved 25.05.2018, from https://undocs.org/S/RES/2331(2016).

Resolution 2341. (2017). *The United Nations Security Council.* Retrieved 25.05.2018, from https://undocs.org/S/RES/2341(2017).

Resolution 2347. (2017). *The United Nations Security Council.* Retrieved 25.05.2018, from https://undocs.org/S/RES/2347(2017).

Resolution 2354. (2017). *The United Nations Security Council.* Retrieved 25.05.2018, from https://undocs.org/S/RES/2354(2017).

Resolution 2368. (2017). *The United Nations Security Council.* Retrieved 25.05.2018, from http://undocs.org/S/RES/2368(2017) 2354 (2017).

Reuter, P., & Truman, E. M. (2004). *Chasing Dirty Money.* Washington, DC: Institute for International Economics.

Reuters. (2013). *Female Kurdish Activists Including Former Guerrilla Shot in Paris.* Retrieved 27.11.2018, from www.reuters.com/article/france-kurds/female-kurdish-activists-including-former-guerrilla-shot-in-paris-idINDEE90909O20130110.

Ridley, N. (2011). Legal and Intelligence Difficulties in Combating Financing of Terrorism. In A. Duyan & M. Kibaroglu (Eds.), *Defence Against Terrorism* (First ed., pp. 49–54). Amsterdam; Washington, DC: IOS Press.

Ridley, N., & Alexander, D. C. (2011). Combating Terrorist Financing in the First Decade of the Twenty-first Century. *Journal of Money Laundering Control, 15*(1), 38–57.

Roberge, I. (2007). Misguided Policies in the War on Terror? The Case for Disentangling Terrorist Financing from Money Laundering. *Politics, 27*(3), 196–203.

Rodoplu, U., Arnold, J., & Ersoy, G. (2003). Terrorism in Turkey. *Prehospital and Disaster Medicine, 18*(02), 152–160.

Romaniuk, P. (2014). The State of the Art on the Financing of Terrorism. *The RUSI Journal, 159*(2), 6–17.

Rosenthal, J. (2008). For-profit Terrorism: The Rise of Armed Entrepreneurs. *Studies in Conflict and Terrorism, 31*(6), 481–498.

Roth, J., Greenburg, D., & Wille, S. (2004). *National Commission on Terrorist Attacks upon the United States: Monograph on Terrorist Financing, Staff Report to the Commission.* Retrieved 27.11.2018, from www.9-11commission.gov/staff_statements/911_TerrFin_Monograph.pdf.

Roth, M. P., & Sever, M. (2007). The Kurdish Workers Party (PKK) as Criminal Syndicate: Funding Terrorism through Organized Crime, a Case Study. *Studies in Conflict and Terrorism, 30*(10), 901–920.

Rudaw, (2015). *PKK'nin kaynakları ve para trafiği [The PKK's funding sources and their traffic].* Retrieved 20.05.2015, from http://www.rudaw.net/turkish/interview/13082015.

Rudner, M. (2006). Using Financial Intelligence against the Funding of Terrorism. *International Journal of Intelligence and Counterintelligence, 19*(1), 32–58.

Rudner, M. (2010). Hizbullah Terrorism Finance: Fund-Raising and Money-Laundering. *Studies in Conflict and Terrorism, 33*(8), 700–715.

Ruehsen, M. (2012). Partiya Karkeren Kurdistan (PKK). In M. Freeman (Ed.), *Financing Terrorism: Case Studies* (First ed., pp. 63, 74). Farnham; Burlington, VT: Ashgate.

Ryder, N. (2015). *The Financial War on Terror: A Review of Counter-terrorist Financing Strategies Since 2001*. London: Routledge.

Ryder, N. (2018). Out with the old and . . . in with the old? A critical review of the Financial War on Terrorism on the Islamic State of Iraq and Levant. *Studies in Conflict & Terrorism, 41*(2), 79–95.

Ryder, N., & Turksen, U. (2009). Islamophobia or an Important Weapon? An Analysis of the US Financial War on Terrorism. *Journal of Banking Regulation, 10*(4), 307–320.

Ryder, N., & Turksen, U. (2013). Banks in Defense of the Homeland: Nexus of Ethics and Suspicious Activity Reporting. *Contemporary Issues in Law (Special Issue on Law, Ethics and Counter-Terrorism), 12*(4), 1–43.

Saygun, E. (2008). *Closing Remarks*. Paper presented at the Global Terrorism and International Cooperation, Ankara.

Sayıştay Başkanlığı [Turkish Court of Accounts]. (2013). *Sayıştay Denetim Raporları [Supreme Court of Accounts Auditing Reports]*. Retrieved 18.04.2016, from www.sayistay.gov.tr/tr/?p=2&CategoryId=103.

Schott, P. A. (2006). *Reference Guide to Anti-money Laundering and Combating the Financing of Terrorism*. Washington, DC: World Bank. Retrieved 11.12.2017, from http://documents.worldbank.org/curated/en/558401468134391014/pdf/350520Referenc1Money01OFFICIAL0USE1.pdf.

Shapiro, J. N. (2007). Terrorist Organizations' Vulnerabilities and Inefficiencies. In J. K. Giraldo & H. A. Trinkunas (Eds.), *Terrorism Financing and State Responses* (First ed., pp. 56–71). Stanford: Stanford University Press.

Shapiro, J. N., & Siegel, D. A. (2007). Underfunding in Terrorist Organizations. *International Studies Quarterly, 51*(2), 405–429.

Shelley, L. I. (2014). *Dirty Entanglements: Corruption, Crime, and Terrorism*. Cambridge: Cambridge University Press.

Shetterly, D. (2005). Starving the Terrorists of Funding: How the United States Treasury Is Fighting the War on Terror. *Regent University Law Review, 18*, 327–348.

Shields, P. (2005). When the 'Information Revolution' and the US Security State Collide: Money Laundering and the Proliferation of Surveillance. *New Media & Society, 7*(4), 483–512.

Silke, A. (1998). In Defense of the Realm: Financing Loyalist Terrorism in Northern Ireland – Part One: Extortion and Blackmail. *Studies in Conflict and Terrorism, 21*(4), 331–362.

Silke, A. (2000). Drink, Drugs, and Rock 'n' Roll: Financing Loyalist Terrorism in Northern Ireland – Part Two, *Studies in Conflict and Terrorism, 23*(Part 2), 107–128.

Silke, A. (2004). An Introduction to Terrorism Research. In A. Silke (Ed.), *Research on Terrorism: Trends, Achievements and Failures* (First ed.). London: Routledge.

Simpson, G. R. (2006). *Treasury Tracks Financial Data in Secret Program: Since 9/11, U.S. Has Used Subpoenas to Access Records from Fund-Transfer System*. Retrieved 27.11.2018, from www.wsj.com/articles/SB115101988281688182.

Smith, P. J. (2007). Terrorism Finance: Global Responses to the Terrorism Money Trail. In J. J. F. Forest (Ed.), *Countering Terrorism and Insurgency in the 21st*

Century: International Perspectives (Vol. 2, pp. 142–162). Westport, CT: Praeger Security International.

Sonyel, S. R. (1987). *The Ottoman Armenians: Victims of Great Power Diplomacy.* London: K. Rustem.

Soylu, R. (2016). *Archives, Testimonies Confirm PYD/YPG's Organic Link with PKK Terror Organization.* Retrieved 27.11.2018, from www.dailysabah.com/war-on-terror/2016/02/20/archives-testimonies-confirm-pydypgs-organic-link-with-pkk-terror-organization.

Sözen, A. (2006). Terrorism and the Politics of Anti-Terrorism in Turkey. In A. S. Makarychev & R. W. Orttung (Eds.), *National Counter-Terrorism Strategies Legal, Institutional, and Public Policy Dimensions in the US, UK, France, Turkey and Russia, NATO Security through Science Series* (Vol. 14, pp. 131–144). Amsterdam: IOS Press.

Sözer, M. A., & Sever, M. (2011). Violent Extremism in Terrorist Organizations. In I. Bal, S. Özeren, & M. A. Sözer (Eds.), *Multi-Faceted Approach to Radicalization in Terrorist Organizations* (Vol. 87, pp. 22–31). Amsterdam: IOS Press.

Spiegel. (2013). *Murdered Kurdish Activists Had Ties to Germany.* Retrieved 27.11.2018, from www.spiegel.de/international/world/kurdish-activists-murdered-in-paris-had-german-ties-a-877352.html.

Sproat, P. A. (2010). Counter-terrorist Finance in the UK: A Quantitative and Qualitative Commentary Based on Open-source Materials. *Journal of Money Laundering Control, 13*(4), 315–335.

Srividhya, S., & Shelly, S. (2012). Whistle Blowing Protection – A Watch Dog for the Organisation. *International Journal of Social Science & Interdisciplinary Research,* 1(10). Retrieved from http://indianresearchjournals.com/pdf/IJSSIR/2012/October/17.pdf.

Statista. (2018). *At the Present Time How Worried, if at All, Are You Personally about a Terrorist Attack Happening in Britain?* Retrieved 03.04.2018, from www.statista.com/statistics/488048/worry-about-terror-attacks-in-britain-uk/.

Suskind, R. (2006). *One Percent Doctrine: Deep Inside America's Pursuit of Its Enemies Since 9/11.* New York: Simon and Schuster.

Takáts, E. (2007). *A Theory of "Crying Wolf": The Economics of Money Laundering Enforcement.* Washington, DC: International Monetary Fund, Western Hemisphere Department.

Taştekin, F. (2016). *Syrian Kurds Expand Diplomatic Network in Europe.* Retrieved 27.11.2018, from www.al-monitor.com/pulse/originals/2016/04/turkey-syria-rojava-kurds-expand-diplomatic-network-europe.html.

T.C. İçişleri Bakanlığı [Republic of Turkey Ministry of Interior]. (2011). *Türkiye Mülki İdare Bölümleri Envanteri.* Retrieved 27.11.2018, from www.e-icisleri.gov.tr/Anasayfa/MulkiIdariBolumleri.aspx.

T.C. İçişleri Bakanlığı. (2015). *Terörle Mücadele Kapsamına Giren Suçların Faillerinin Yakalanmasına Yardımcı Olanlara Verilecek Ödül Hakkında Yönetmelik.* Retrieved 05.03.2016, from http://www.resmigazete.gov.tr/eskiler/2015/08/20150831-1.htm.

Templeton, T. (2002). *9/11 in Numbers, The Guardian, 18 August 2002.* Retrieved 21.03.2018, from www.theguardian.com/world/2002/aug/18/usa.terrorism.

Terörizmin Finansmanının Önlenmesi Hakkında Kanun Tasarısı ile İçişleri Komisyonu ve Adalet Komisyonu Raporları, Türkiye Büyük Millet Meclisi, 62 Sess. (2013).

Terrorism Act [United Kingdom]. Chapter 11, Section 22. (2000). Retrieved 27.11.2018, from www.legislation.gov.uk/ukpga/2000/11/pdfs/ukpga_20000011_en.pdf.

Terrorism Analysis Branch. (1984). *The Armenian Secret Army for the Liberation of Armenia: A Continuing International Threat – A Research Paper.* Central Intelligence Agency Directorate of Intelligence. Retrieved from www.foia.cia.gov/sites/default/files/document_conversions/89801/DOC_0005462031.pdf.

The Court of Justice of the European Union. (2018). Retrieved 12.08.2018, from https://curia.europa.eu/jcms/jcms/j_6/en/.

The EU General Data Protection Regulation Portal. (2018). Retrieved 12.08.2018, from www.eugdpr.org.

The European Court of Human Rights. (2018). Retrieved 12.08.2018, from www.echr.coe.int/Pages/home.aspx?p=home.

The Fight against Terrorist Financing. (2004). Brussels: Council of the European Union.

The Guardian. (2013). *Kurdish Activists Shot Dead in Paris.* Retrieved 27.11.2018, from www.theguardian.com/world/2013/jan/10/kurdish-activists-shot-dead-paris.

The International Convention for the Suppression of the Financing of Terrorism. (1999). Retrieved 27.11.2018, from www.un.org/law/cod/finterr.htm.

The Meir Amit Intelligence and Terrorism Information Centre. (2008). *The War on Financing Terrorism.* Retrieved 27.11.2018, from www.terrorism-info.org.il/en/article/18443.

The National Counterterrorism Center. (2014). *Counterterrorism Calendar 2014-Domestic Terrorism in Turkey.* Retrieved 27.11.2018, from www.nctc.gov/site/groups/turkey.html.

The 9/11 Commission Report, National Commission on Terrorist Attacks upon the United States., Kean, T. H., et al. (2004). *The 9/11 Commission Report: Final Report of the National Commission on Terrorist Attacks upon the United States* (Official government ed.). Washington, DC: U.S Government Publishing Office. Retrieved 21.03.2018, from www.9-11commission.gov/report/911Report.pdf.

Thomas, T. L. (2003). Al Qaeda and the Internet: The Danger of "Cyberplanning". *Parameters, 33*(1), 112.

Thomas Jr, J. E. (2009). Narco-terrorism: Could the Legislative and Prosecutorial Responses Threaten our Civil Liberties? *Washington & Lee Law Review, 66,* 1881.

Tibbetts, P. S. (2002). *Terrorist Use of the Internet and Related Information Technologies.* Fort Leavenworth, KS: United States Army Command and General Staff College. (AY 01–02).

Tofangsaz, H. (2012). A New Approach to the Criminalization of Terrorist Financing and Its Compatibility with Sharia Law. *Journal of Money Laundering Control, 15*(4), 396–406.

Trafton, J. L. (2007). Fighting Al Qaeda: Understanding the Organizational, Ideological and Financial Aspects of a Global Network of Terror. In J. J. F. Forest (Ed.), *Countering Terrorism and Insurgency in the 21st Century: International Perspectives* (Vol. 2, pp. 479–495). Westport, CT: Praeger Security International.

Tupman, W. A. (2009). Ten Myths about Terrorist Financing. *Journal of Money Laundering Control, 12*(2), 189–205.

Tupman, W. A. (2014). Top 5 Terrorist Groups 2013 (Modelled on Forbes Top 5 List of Business Groups). *ECPR Standing Group on Organised Crime Newsletter, 11*(3), 6–7. Retrieved from http://sgocnet.org/sgoc-newsletter-sept-2014-volume-11-number-3/.

Turkish Court of Accounts. (2018). Home Page. Retrieved 23.07.2018, from www.sayistay.gov.tr/en/.

Turkish Criminal Code [Türk Ceza Kanunu], 765, Official Gazette [Resmi Gazete] – 320. (1926).

Turkish Criminal Code (TCC) [Türk Ceza Kanunu], 5237, Official Gazette [Resmi Gazete] –25611. (2004).

Turkish Criminal Procedure Code, 5271, Official Gazzette [Resmi Gazete] – 25673. (2004).

Turkish National Police Academy. (2017). *A New Generation of Terrorism: An Analysis of FETÖ.* Report No: 14, Turkish National Police Academy Press, Ankara. Retrieved 13.09.2018, from www.pa.edu.tr/Upload/editor/files/A%20NEW%20 GENERATION%20OF%20TERRORISM.pdf.

Turksen, U. (2010). *Protection Seekers, States and the New Security Agenda.* Izmir: Altin Nokta.

Turksen, U., et al. (2011). Anti-money Laundering Law of Turkey and the EU: An Example of Convergence? *Journal of Money Laundering Control, 14*(3).

Turksen, U. (2017). *The Financial Crisis and White Collar Crime – Legislative and Policy Responses: A Critical Assessment.* Oxon: Routledge.

Turksen, U. (2018). Independence and Protection of Auditors in the EU AML Framework. In K. Ligeti & S. Tosza (Eds.), *White Collar Crime: A Comparative Perspective.* London: Hart Publishing.

Türkiye Büyük Millet Meclisi İnsan Haklarını İnceleme Komisyonu. (2013). *Terör ve Şiddet Olayları Kapsamında Yaşam Hakkı.* Ankara: TBMM İnsan Haklarını İnceleme Komisyonu.

Türkiye Büyük Millet Meclisi Tutanak Dergisi, 62 Sess. (2013a).

Türkiye Büyük Millet Meclisi Tutanak Dergisi, 63 Sess. (2013b).

Türkiye Cumhuriyeti Anayasası (Constitution of the Republic of Turkey), 2709 Stat. (1982).

Uçarmak, S. (2015). *Gümrüklerde Nakit Kontrolleri.* Ankara: T.C. Gümrük ve Ticaret Bakanlığı.

Unger, B., & Van der Linde, D. (Eds.). (2015). *Research Handbook on Money Laundering.* Cheltenham: Edward Elgar Publishing.

UN Monitoring Team. (2005). *Second Report of the Analytical Support and Sanctions Monitoring Team Appointed Pursuant to Resolution 1526 (2004) Concerning Al-Qaida and the Taliban and Associated Individuals and Entities.* New York: UN Security Council.

UN Treaty Collections. (2017). *International Convention for the Suppression of the Financing of Terrorism.* Retrieved 27.11.2018, from https://treaties.un.org/Pages/ViewDetails.aspx?src=IND&mtdsg_no=XVIII-11&chapter=18&lang=en.

United Nations. (2004). *Report of the Secretary-General's High-Level Panel on Threats, Challenges and Change: A More Secure World – Our Shared Responsibility.* New York: United Nations Department of Public Information.

United Nations. (2016). *Global Survey of the Implementation of Security Council Resolution 1373 (2001) by Member States.* Retrieved 21.03.2018, from www.un.org/sc/ctc/news/document/global-survey-of-the-implementation-of-security-council-resolution-1373-2001-by-member-states-2016/.

United Nations. (2016a). *United Nations Treaty Collection.* Retrieved 27.11.2018, from https://treaties.un.org/pages/ViewDetails.aspx?src=TREATY&mtdsg_no=XVIII-11&chapter=18.

United Nations General Assembly. (1998). *Ad Hoc Committee on the Elaboration of a Convention against Transnational Organised Crime: Proposals and Contributions Received from Governments*. Vienna: United Nations.

United Nations General Assembly. (1999). *Third Committee: Summary Record of the 18th Meeting Official Records* (Vol. 44th Session). New York: United Nations.

United Nations General Assembly. (2000a). *Report of the Ad Hoc Committee on the Elaboration of a Convention against Transnational Organised Crime on Its Tenth Session, Held in Vienna from 17 to 28 July 2000*. Vienna: United Nations.

United Nations General Assembly. (2000b). *Third Committee: Summary Record of the 12th Meeting Official Records* (Vol. 44th Session). New York: United Nations.

UNODC. (2004). *United Nations Convention against Transnational Organised Crime and the Protocols Thereto* (Vol. General Assembly Resolution 55/25). Vienna: UNODC.

UNODC. (2010). *World Drug Report*. Retrieved from www.unodc.org/documents/data-and-analysis/tocta/5.Heroin.pdf.

UNODC. (2015). *Drug Money: The Illicit Proceeds of Opiates Trafficked on the Balkan Route* (Vol. 2015). Vienna: UNODC Research.

UNSC Subsidiary Organs. (2018). *Security Council Committee Pursuant to Resolutions 1267 (1999) 1989 (2011) and 2253 (2015) Concerning Isil (Da'esh), Al-Qaida and Associated Individuals, Groups, Undertakings and Entities*. Retrieved 10.10.2018, from www.un.org/sc/suborg/en/sanctions/1267/aq_sanctions_list/procedures-for-delisting.

US Department of State. (2018). *Iran Sanctions*. Retrieved 18.09.2018, from www.state.gov/e/eb/tfs/spi/iran/index.htm.

US Department of Treasury. (2005). *Testimony of Stuart Levey, Under Secretary Office of Terrorism and Financial Intelligence, before the Senate Committee on Banking, Housing, and Urban Affairs*. Retrieved 27.11.2018, from www.investigativeproject.org/documents/testimony/238.pdf.

US Department of Treasury. (2012). *Treasury Sanctions Supporters of the Kurdistan Workers Party (PKK) Tied to Drug Trafficking in Europe*. Retrieved 27.11.2018, from www.treasury.gov/press-center/press-releases/Pages/tg1406.aspx.

US Department of Treasury. (2017). *Designated Charities and Potential Fundraising Front Organizations for FTOs*. Retrieved 15.04.2018, from www.treasury.gov/resource-center/terrorist-illicit-finance/Pages/protecting-fto.aspx.

USA PATRIOT ACT, H.R.3162, Financial Crimes Enforcement Network, Pub. L. No. 107–56 (2001).

Uzun, C. D., Akgün, M. H., & Yücel, H. (2017). *İddianamelerde 15 Temmuz Darbe Girişimi ve FETÖ. SETA Yayinlari 87*. İstanbul: Turkuvaz Haberleşme ve Yayıncılık A.Ş. Retrieved 13.06.2018, from https://setav.org/assets/uploads/2017/07/Rapor87.pdf.

Vittori, J. (2009). All Struggles Must End: The Longevity of Terrorist Groups. *Contemporary Security Policy*, *30*(3), 444–466.

Vittori, J. (2011). *Terrorist Financing and Resourcing [electronic resource]*. Basingstoke: Palgrave Macmillan.

Vlcek, W. (2007). Surveillance to Combat Terrorist Financing in Europe: Whose Liberty, Whose Security? *European Security*, *16*(1), 99–119.

Ward, C. A. (2003). Building Capacity to Combat International Terrorism: The Role of the United Nations Security Council. *Journal of Conflict and Security Law*, *8*(2), 289–305.

Weimann, G. (2006). *Terror on the Internet: The New Arena, the New Challenges*. Washington, DC: United States Institute of Peace Press.

Weiner, T., & Johnston, D. C. (2001). *A NATION CHALLENGED: THE PAPER TRAIL; Roadblocks Cited in Efforts to Trace bin Laden's Money*. Retrieved 27.11.2018, from www.nytimes.com/2001/09/20/business/nation-challenged-paper-trail-roadblocks-cited-efforts-trace-bin-laden-s-money.html.

Weiss, M. A. (2009). Terrorist Financing: U.S. Agency Efforts and Inter-Agency Coordination. In L. S. MacLeod & O. C. Thomson (Eds.), *New terrorism issues* (pp. 27–75). New York: Nova Science Publishers.

Welch, D. A. (1992). The Organizational Process and Bureaucratic Politics Paradigms: Retrospect and Prospect. *International Security*, *17*(2), 112–146.

Wesseling, M. (2014). *Evaluation of EU Measures to Combat Terrorism Financing: In-Depth Analysis for the LIBE Committee*. Brussels: European Parliament Directorate General for Internal Policies Policy Department C: Citizens' Rights and Constitutional Affairs.

Wesseling, M., de Goede, M., & Amoore, L. (2012). Data Wars beyond Surveillance. *Journal of Cultural Economy*, *5*(1), 49–66.

Williams, P. (2001). Crime, Illicit Markets, and Money Laundering. In P. J. Simmons & C. d. J. Oudraat (Eds.), *Managing Global Issues: Lessons Learned* (pp. 106–150). Washington, DC: Carnegie Endowment for International Peace.

Williams, P. (2005). Warning Indicators, Terrorist Finances, and Terrorist Adaptation. *Strategic Insights*, *IV*(1).

Williams, P. (2008). Terrorist Financing and Organised Crime: Nexus, Appropriation, or Transformation? In T. J. Biersteker & S. E. Eckert (Eds.), *Countering the Financing of Terrorism* (pp. 126–149). London: Routledge.

Winer, J. M. (2008). Countering Terrorist Finance: A Work, Mostly in Progress. *ANNALS – American Academy of Political and Social Science: Terrorism: What the Next President Will Face*, *618*, 112–132.

Wittig, T. (2009). Terrorist Finance: Asking the Right Questions. *Politics*, *29*(1), 145–153.

Wittig, T. (2011). *Understanding Terrorist Finance*. Houndmills; Basingstoke Hampshire; New York: Palgrave Macmillan.

Wood, P. (1999). *Greece Dogged by Öcalan Affair*. Retrieved 27.11.2018, from http://news.bbc.co.uk/2/hi/europe/287232.stm.

World Justice Project. (2018). *The WJP Rule of Law Index 2017–2018 Report*. Retrieved 02.10.2018, from https://worldjusticeproject.org/sites/default/files/documents/WJP-ROLI-2018-June-Online-Edition_0.pdf.

XE. (2018). *XE Currency Charts: GBP to TRY*. Retrieved 12.06.2018, from www.xe.com/currencycharts/?from=GBP&to=TRY&view=10Y.

Yavuz, M. H., & Koç, R. (2016). The Turkish Coup Attempt: The Gülen Movement vs. the State. *Middle East Policy*, *XXIII*(4), Winter.

Yenidünya, A. C., & Değirmenci, O. (2008). Mukayeseli Hukuk ve Türk Hukukunda Terörün Finansmanı Suçu [The Offence of Financing of Terror in Comparative Law and Turkish Law]. In K. Bayraktar, Z. Donmezer, & H. Kizilarslan (Eds.), *Ord. Prof. Dr. Sulhi DÖNMEZER Armağanı [The Gift of Ord. Prof. Dr. Sulhi DÖNMEZER]*

(First ed., Vol. 2, pp. 1263–1294). Ankara: Türk Ceza Hukuku Dernegi Atatürk Araştırma Merkezi Başkanlığı.

Yıldırım, Z. (2012). *Hukuksal Açıdan Terörizmin Finansmanının Önlenmesi [The Prevention of Financing of Terrorism from the Legal Perspective]* (First ed., Vol. 1007). Ankara: Adalet Yayinevi.

Yıldırım, Z. (2013). *Türk Hukukunda Terörizmin Finansmanı Suçu ve Malvarlıklarını Dondurma [The Offence of Financing Terrorism and Asset Freezing in Turkish Law]* (First ed., Vol. 1227). Ankara: Adalet Yayinevi.

Yıldız, G. (2013). *Analysis*. Retrieved 27.11.2018, from www.bbc.com/news/world-europe-20968375.

Zagaris, B. (2004). The Merging of the Anti-money Laundering and Counter-terrorism Financial Enforcement Regimes after September 11, 2001. *Berkeley Journal of International Law*, *22*, 123.

Zarate, J. C. (2013). *Treasury's War* (First ed.). New York: PublicAffairs.

Zehorai, I. (2018). The Richest Terror Organizations: #6 – PKK – Kurdistan Workers' Party. *Forbes Israel*. Retrieved 03.01.2018, from http://e.forbes.co.il/6-pkk-kurdistan-workers-party/.

Zelinsky, A., & Shubik, M. (2009). Research Note: Terrorist Groups as Business Firms: A New Typological Framework. *Terrorism and Political Violence*, *21*(2), 327–336.

Index

For Product Safety Concerns and Information please contact our EU representative GPSR@taylorandfrancis.com Taylor & Francis Verlag GmbH, Kaufingerstraße 24, 80331 München, Germany